# GOD'S GLORY

# REVEALED IN CHRIST

# GOD'S GLORY

# REVEALED IN CHRIST

*Essays on Biblical Theology in Honor of*

THOMAS R. SCHREINER

DENNY BURK | JAMES M. HAMILTON JR. | BRIAN VICKERS

*editors*

ACADEMIC
NASHVILLE, TENNESSEE

# Dedication

*For Tom Schreiner*

# Contents

# Foreword: In Appreciation of Thomas R. Schreiner

*by R. Albert Mohler Jr.*

Where the Christian church is found faithful, faithful teachers are found. In the Old Testament, priests were honored for faithful instruction. In the New Testament, the most important office in the church is the teaching office. As Paul instructed Timothy, "what you have heard from me in the presence of many witnesses entrust to faithful men, who will be able to teach others also" (2 Timothy 2:2 ESV[1]).

Where Professor Tom Schreiner is found, faithful teaching is found. One of the greatest privileges of my life is to teach and serve among some of the leading Christian scholars of our day, and Tom Schreiner is in the highest rank among them. He is the very model of a Christian teacher and scholar.

Tom became a Christian at age seventeen, partly through the witness of the woman who would become his wife, Diane. He received a call to ministry soon thereafter, and he has been engaged in answering that call for his entire adult life. His educational ambitions took him to Western Oregon University for his undergraduate work, then on to Western Conservative Baptist Seminary for his master of divinity and master of theology. He would receive his doctor of philosophy from Fuller Theological Seminary. Like his education, Tom's first academic post was in the west, at Azusa Pacific University.

Later he would teach New Testament at Bethel Theological Seminary before joining the faculty of The Southern Baptist Theological Seminary in 1997, where he has now taught for more than twenty years.

---

[1] The ESV® Bible (The Holy Bible, English Standard Version®). ESV® Text Edition: 2016. Copyright © 2001 by Crossway, a publishing ministry of Good News Publishers. The ESV® text has been reproduced in cooperation with and by permission of Good News Publishers. Unauthorized reproduction of this publication is prohibited. All rights reserved.

At the same time, Tom has been deeply involved in the preaching ministry of the local church, serving as elder in three churches over the same span that took him to three academic postings. For most of those years, Tom's academic context was the theological seminary, explicitly committed to the teaching of preachers and pastors.

There is only one excuse for a preacher to teach in a theological seminary and to devote his life and energies to theological education. It all comes down to the fact that God invests unique gifts of intellect and scholarly vocation in some ministers of the gospel. God then grants these men the stewardship of scholarship in order that future generations of Christians will be more faithfully taught by their preachers. That calling has defined Tom Schreiner's life, and Tom defines that calling in our times.

The ideal of the Christian scholar reaches back to the apostles themselves and continues through towering figures such as Jerome and Augustine in the church's early centuries. Those two massive models of Christian scholarship have nourished the church for more than a millennium. Both were exegetes of Holy Scripture. Both were models of devotional dedication to the church. Both have exerted an influence that continues to this day.

The same is true of Martin Luther and John Calvin, the most significant among the Reformers of the sixteenth century. In *The Christian Scholar in the Age of the Reformation*, E. Harris Harbison would remark: "The truest way, then, to describe the meaning of the Reformation, is to say it originated in a scholar's insight, born equally of spiritual struggle and hard intellectual labor."[2]

Luther and Calvin loom large as we think of the Christian scholar in the service of the church. Both were master exegetes. One of Martin Luther's greatest achievements would be his translation of the New Testament into German. The expositional sermons and commentaries of both Calvin and Luther remain in print today, readily available in good English translations. Why? The answer can only be that the power of their scholarship and preaching continues to nourish the church five centuries after the start of the Reformation—in scholarship, teaching, and preaching.

Tom Schreiner is the living refutation of any claim that the highest level of Christian scholarship cannot be accomplished while deeply involved in the life and ministry of the local church. Tom has authored at least fifteen major books and dozens of academic articles, each a work of scholarship. His *New Testament Theology* and *Romans,* his commentary in the Baker Exegetical Commentary on the New Testament series, are representative of the gift of scholarship that Tom has given to the church.

---

[2]  E. Harris Harbison, *The Christian Scholar in the Age of the Reformation* (Scribner, 1956), 121.

Tom's scholarship is confessional. He teaches within a confessional school and he is clear about his personal convictions. Like Luther and Calvin, Tom Schreiner is committed to the theology of the Reformation. Of course, he would prefer to say that he is first committed to the theology of the New Testament, and rightly so. He is a Baptist, an evangelical, a Protestant, and a model of Reformed scholarship and teaching. He is not a controversialist, but he does not run from controversy when the issues at stake are important.

The respect of his academic peers was evident when he was elected to serve as president of the Evangelical Theological Society in 2014. His investment in other scholars is extensive. His doctoral students now serve throughout the world of theological education. He is, in effect, a teaching legend in his own time.

One of the highest compliments students pay to teachers is to talk about them—with respect and affection. Students talk about Tom Schreiner that way all the time. They leave his classroom and talk about the lecture and discussion. They pick up on his language and his verbal cues. They love his humor and his eagerness to teach. They know the personal respect for students that Tom brings to every classroom. They return that respect by their acknowledgement that when in Tom's classroom, they are in the presence of a master teacher.

I came to The Southern Baptist Theological Seminary as president in 1993—twenty-five years ago as I write this. I was assigned a monumental challenge. My charge was to return Southern Seminary to its confessional identity. My ambition was even more monumental. With all my heart, I wanted to build Southern Seminary into the most faithful theological seminary that could serve the church. I needed professors who would share that same challenge and stewardship and would see such a mission as a grand adventure. I needed scholars of the top rank, and I needed them quickly.

Early in that effort, I knew that my hope was for Tom Schreiner to teach at Southern Seminary. In 1997, that hope was realized. For that fact, I am more thankful than I know how to express. Tom and many colleagues came and joined in this great effort, which God has tremendously blessed.

As I grow older, my appreciation and love for these colleagues grows only stronger and richer. Over the decades, you get to know each other deeply. I have seen Tom as a husband, tenaciously loving his cherished wife Diane and showing that love in the aftermath of a horrible accident. I have seen Diane show her abiding and cheerful love for her husband. I am so thankful to see them now, both healthy and loving life as grandparents.

I have seen Tom as father, and I have seen his love for Daniel, Patrick, John, and Anna—and I have seen his pride in them, their spouses, their callings, and their children.

I have seen Tom as colleague, caring deeply for those with whom he shares this great calling.

I often think and speak of Augustine's argument that the Christian teacher must be driven by three loves—love of God, love of truth, and love of students. Tom Schreiner is a living example of those three loves. Thus, he is a living example of the Christian teacher and scholar at work. I am highly honored to write this foreword to a book that honors this teacher and that high calling.

> *"Keep a close watch on yourself and on the teaching.*
> *Persist in this, for by so doing you will save*
> *both yourself and your hearers."*
> 1 Timothy 4:16 (ESV)

# WHOLE BIBLE APPROACHES
# TO BIBLICAL THEOLOGY

*Chapter 1*

# A Progressive Dispensational Understanding of Scripture as a Whole

*by Bruce A. Ware*

## INTRODUCTION

One of the greatest delights of my life is my friendship with Tom Schreiner. We met during our years in seminary, both attending Western Seminary (Western Conservative Baptist Seminary, back then) in the mid- to late-seventies, in Portland, Oregon. Tom was an amazing student. I'm convinced that the worst day of the semester for him was the first day of classes when professors would pass out the course syllabi—worst, not because of the work that needed to be done, but because none of it was done yet! Tom is highly disciplined and he couldn't wait to get going on completing what had been assigned. It was common for him to complete the semester's assignments for all his classes several weeks before the term ended, giving him time to read other recommended materials. I also admired his devotion to the languages in seminary. He read Greek on a regular basis with the most difficult and demanding Greek professor on campus, and when he decided to stay on for a master of theology, he chose to write his thesis on the Old Testament prophet Zephaniah, thus requiring a greater mastery of Hebrew.

We became friends over our years at Western, but neither of us knew then how intertwined our lives would end up being. Following Western, we both decided independently to pursue our PhD studies at Fuller Seminary in Pasadena, California. Those years together were bonding since we were clearly more conservative than most at Fuller, and it prompted us to think about and discuss the many issues we were facing. Shortly thereafter, in God's kind providence, we taught together at Bethel Seminary in St. Paul, Minnesota, and then, after several years apart, we both felt God's call to teach at Southern Seminary, where we've been together again for over twenty years.

We are devoted friends, though we disagree on a number of issues on which we both have strong convictions. And it just so happens that one of those issues is the subject of this chapter. Shortly after his days at Western, Tom began moving away from the dispensationalism that we had been taught at Western to a more covenantal perspective, whereas I continued to embrace a fundamentally dispensational understanding, albeit with some significant adjustments from what we were taught. Tom finds closer affinities with new covenant theology and progressive covenantalism; I remain committed to some of the core ideas in dispensationalism while favoring the realignments made in progressive dispensationalism.

Just one more word of introduction before sketching some features of the progressive dispensational view I've embraced. It would be hard to overestimate the influence in my own thinking (particularly on this issue) of the theology of George Eldon Ladd. During my MDiv years at Western Seminary, Ladd was usually portrayed negatively as that harsh critic of dispensational premillennialism. While Ladd was applauded for his strong defense of premillennialism (historic), his criticism of dispensationalism tended to overshadow the positive features of his contribution, and we were discouraged, as students, from exploring Ladd's larger theological view. Following the completion of my MDiv, in the months prior to starting my ThM program (in the summer of 1978), I decided to read Ladd's *A Theology of the New Testament* for myself.[1] I cannot express adequately how monumental this book was to my developing theological understanding. I was awestruck by the insight God granted to Ladd, and in particular, I saw the beauty and importance of the already/not yet understanding of much of biblical prophecy and of eschatology, more broadly.

What became clear to me over that summer is that Ladd's inaugurated eschatology[2] can actually be thrust into the service of dispensationalism such that weaknesses and problems with the traditional dispensational model can be overcome while retaining the heart and core of dispensational distinctives and commitments. This realization stood contrary to what I had been taught, since in classic dispensationalism every aspect of the promises made to Israel

---

[1]  George Eldon Ladd, *A Theology of the New Testament* (Grand Rapids: Eerdmans, 1974).

[2]  The term "inaugurated eschatology" is sometimes used as a helpful descriptor of the already/not yet understanding that the fulfillment of some of Scripture's prophecies are at first inaugurated, i.e., fulfilled in part (already), and then only later, perhaps not until the new creation, are their fulfillments fully consummated, i.e., fulfilled in their completeness (not yet). For an insightful discussion of inaugurated eschatology, see Anthony A. Hoekema, "Inaugurated Eschatology," part 1 in *The Bible and the Future* (Grand Rapids: Eerdmans, 1979), 3–75.

in the Old Testament were seen to be fulfilled completely only after the church age, in the millennium and the eternal state. There just wasn't a place for the notion of the fulfillment of those promises in a partial way now in the church while we await the fullness later. I'll spell this out more fully shortly, but I think it important to acknowledge at the outset the formative role Ladd's New Testament theology had in the development of my "modified"[3] dispensational understanding.

In what follows, I would like to sketch briefly what, in my view, commends progressive dispensationalism as a compelling framework for understanding both the redemptive historical flow of biblical revelation and the Bible taken as a whole. As we'll see, the changes I've incorporated into my version of progressive dispensationalism find significant affinities with aspects of covenantalism, particularly progressive covenantalism, yet I continue to favor this modified version of dispensationalism I've developed and taught now for over thirty-five years. In the relatively short space of this chapter, I will focus attention on the hermeneutics of progressive dispensationalism. I'll discuss four hermeneutical observations which are central to the way in which progressive dispensationalism both interprets particular texts and sees how the whole Bible fits together. As these points are discussed, comment will be made regarding just where progressive dispensationalism stands in relation to classic dispensationalism, classic covenantalism, and progressive covenantalism.

## ASPECTS OF THE HERMENEUTICS OF PROGRESSIVE DISPENSATIONALISM

It is important to discuss briefly four hermeneutical observations which are essential to progressive dispensationalism. The first and second are shared by both traditional and progressive forms of dispensationalism (albeit with some modifications in the progressive dispensational view), but the third and fourth show departures from the strict, classic dispensational understanding.

---

[3] For years, I referred to my own view as merely "modified dispensationalism," indicating particularly the role that Ladd's inaugurated eschatology played in the changes I made to the traditional dispensational view. In time, the movement of progressive dispensationalism arose, led most directly by Craig Blaising and Darrell Bock. I resisted this name at first. "Progressive" had connotations of superiority over what preceded, it seemed to me. Then, it came clear to me that the word "progressive" was used to identify and embrace the concept of progressive revelation, which is at the heart of any dispensational approach. As I continued to read their proposal, I concluded that my own view was close enough to theirs to adopt also this name. For the most influential writings on progressive dispensationalism, see Craig A. Blaising and Darrell L. Bock, eds., *Dispensationalism, Israel and the Church: The Search for Definition* (Grand Rapids: Zondervan, 1992); Craig A. Blaising and Darrell L. Bock, *Progressive Dispensationalism* (Grand Rapids: Baker, 1993); Robert L. Saucy, *The Case for Progressive Dispensationalism: The Interface Between Dispensational and Non-Dispensational Theology* (Grand Rapids: Zondervan, 1993); and Michael J. Vlach, *Dispensationalism: Essential Beliefs and Common Myths*, 2nd ed. (Los Angeles: Theological Studies Press, 2017).

## *The Plain Sense of Scripture*

First, both traditional and progressive forms of dispensationalism have been committed to understanding the teaching of Scripture in its natural, normal, plain sense.[4] Since God has given his revelation in and through human language, we should seek to interpret that revelation according to its plain and natural meaning as derived from its grammatical/syntactical construction and its historical/cultural situatedness. This certainly is not all that needs to be said about correctly interpreting the Bible, but this is bedrock and essential to all correct interpretation. Whether what is written in Scripture is standard prose or poetry or figurative or apocalyptic, the goal is the same, viz., interpreters are responsible to endeavor to determine what the author has meant from what he has said.

Perhaps an example will help. The prophet Ezekiel speaks of a day of the future restoration of the people of Israel, writing, "My servant David will be king over them, and they will all have one shepherd; and they will walk in My ordinances and keep My statutes and observe them" (Ezek 37:24 NASB[5]). While there are metaphorical elements here, the plain and natural meaning of the passage is apparent. The reference to King David is shorthand for God's promise in 2 Samuel 7 of the coming son of David who would reign over his kingdom forever. David himself has long been dead, but the promise to David is alive and well, to be fulfilled in this future son of David. And this king will "shepherd" his people, not as a literal shepherd of literal sheep, but metaphorically this Shepherd/King will care for his people and lead them to pastures of satisfaction and security. Furthermore, God's people will, in this day, be marked by their faithfulness and obedience to their Shepherd/King. They will no longer stray in stubborn rebellion or negligence to God's statutes. They will be the obedient and faithful people of God as God has often promised they one day would be. And finally, those spoken of here are none other than the ethnic, cultural, and national (see 37:22) people of Israel. These descendants of Abraham,

---

[4] One sometimes sees the term "literal hermeneutic" used in dispensational literature to convey this same notion. I'm avoiding the term "literal hermeneutic" simply due to the misunderstanding that sometimes accompanies its use. For dispensationalists, "literal" (as in "literal hermeneutic") refers to what the author actually intended or meant by what he said, and this is also captured by talking about the natural, normal, plain sense of a particular text. At other times, however, "literal" may be used to stand in contrast to "figurative" or "metaphorical" types of speech. But this is not what is intended by the word "literal" when it is used as a general descriptor as in the term "literal hermeneutic." Dispensationalists have always understood there to be great numbers of figures of speech in the Bible, but the "literal" meaning of those figures of speech would be just that which the author intended to convey or meant to communicate through that figurative language. Even with this explanation, I still think it best to avoid the word "literal" as a general term describing the overall hermeneutic of dispensationalism, and instead reserve the word "literal" for those occasions when it stands in contrast with figurative or metaphorical uses of language.

[5] Scripture taken from the NEW AMERICAN STANDARD BIBLE®, Copyright © 1960,1962,1963, 1968,1971,1972,1973,1975,1977,1995 by The Lockman Foundation. Used by permission.

Isaac, and Jacob, those whom God has chosen from among all the nations of the world (Deut 7:6; 14:2), will be transformed into the obedient people of God.

So, whether the language of revelation includes literal, straightforward prose and declaration, or whether it contains metaphorical expressions and figures of speech, the interpreter is responsible to endeavor to understand what the author meant by what he said. The plain, natural, normal sense of the text—whether conveyed in literal or figurative language—should be sought.

### Progressive Revelation

Second, dispensationalists—both traditional and progressive—hold that particular biblical passages must be understood within the historical and revelatory framework in which that biblical revelation was given. Here, the notion of "progressive revelation" is central to all of dispensationalism—not merely the notion that God gave us his revelation in deposits of that revealed truth over protracted historical periods of time, but more importantly that when a new deposit of revelation was given, these newly given commandments, laws, promises, etc., would necessarily affect just how God would regulate the affairs of his people. Progressive revelation, then, conveys a progressive unfolding manner in which God relates to his people, in terms of what he expects of them, what they are promised, and how exactly they shall live before him as his chosen people. As new revelation is given, while some aspects of previous requirements and promises continue and while others come to an end,[6] inevitably there are new aspects of God's promises to his people and new expectations and laws that they now are to embrace. These periods of new revelation, marked then by new ways in which God administers the affairs of his people, are referred to as "dispensations." Just how many of these dispensations there are (e.g., seven in classic dispensationalism, which is disputed variously in progressive dispensationalism) is far less important than that there are clearly identifiable dispensations, marking the progression not only of God's revelation to his people, but marking their new understandings of who they are, what they are to do, and what God has promised to them.

The hermeneutical implications of observing that God's revelation is given progressively, and through his progressively given revelation God regulates the

---

[6] For example, when new revelation comes to Abraham (Genesis 12 ff.), the previous commandment to Adam not to eat of the tree of the knowledge of good and evil (Gen 2:16–17) has come to an end. While that commandment/prohibition was extremely important for the period of the revelation of God to Adam, it did not pertain to anyone else following the fall into sin and God's sending the couple from the garden of Eden. On the other hand, the promise made to Noah (Gen 9:1–17) that God would never again destroy the whole earth through a flood continues. When new revelation is given, then, some aspects of previous revelation end while others continue, all while new revelation is given with its own distinctive features.

affairs of his people in ways appropriate to the distinctives of the dispensational period in which they live, are quite significant. Perhaps the most important implication that marks dispensationalists from traditional covenant theology is the simple observation that promises made to Israel under the old covenant actually relate to ethnic, national Israel, and hence, those promises must be fulfilled with the people to whom they were given, i.e., ethnic, national Israel. As you can see, the first and second hermeneutical observations thus far given are both relevant here. Since the plain and normal meaning of these promises involves what God pledges he will do to and for ethnic, national Israel (first hermeneutical observation, above), and since those promises relate to a time when God was dealing with his chosen people Israel, who were chosen from among the nations of the world and stood in contrast to the other nations of the world (the second hermeneutical observation considered here), the fulfillment of these promises, then, would require God's reestablishing the nation of Israel as his own, with Messiah reigning as their king, in the land of promise given to them, all to fulfill the plain sense of what God promised to the very people who were the people of God when the promise was given, viz., to ethnic, national Israel.

Consider again a text we looked at earlier, now with a bit larger context. The prophet Ezekiel writes,

> Say to them, 'Thus says the Lord God, "Behold, I will take the sons of Israel from among the nations where they have gone, and I will gather them from every side and bring them into their own land; and I will make them one nation in the land, on the mountains of Israel; and one king will be king for all of them; and they will no longer be two nations and no longer be divided into two kingdoms. They will no longer defile themselves with their idols, or with their detestable things, or with any of their transgressions; but I will deliver them from all their dwelling places in which they have sinned, and will cleanse them. And they will be My people, and I will be their God. My servant David will be king over them, and they will all have one shepherd; and they will walk in My ordinances and keep My statutes and observe them. They will live on the land that I gave to Jacob My servant, in which your fathers lived; and they will live on it, they, and their sons and their sons' sons, forever; and David My servant will be their prince forever. I will make a covenant of peace with them; it will be an everlasting covenant with them. And I will place them and multiply them, and will set My sanctuary in their midst forever. My dwelling place also will be with them; and I will be their God, and they will be My people. And the nations will know that I am the Lord who sanctifies Israel, when My sanctuary is in their midst forever.' (Ezek 37:21–28 NASB).

As one considers the plain, natural meaning of this text, and when one considers the subjects to whom these magnificent and glorious promises were given, the conclusion is clear. God has pledged himself to ethnic, national Israel, that he will restore them as a nation, that he will reestablish them in their land, that the coming Son of David will reign as king over them, that they will be remade to be the righteous and obedient people of God, and that all this will be done as a testimony to the nations of the world that God is indeed Yahweh, the covenant God of Israel, who has been faithful to fulfill the promises he has made to save, restore, and transform his chosen people, Israel. Amen!

And of course, if one wonders whether the scope of these promises might have been fulfilled with ethnic, national Israel during the period of the Old Covenant itself, the answer is a resounding no. Even with the return from exile, and with the rebuilding of the temple and wall in the post-exilic period, and the revival that took place under Ezra, these promises stand far short of being fulfilled. Yes, they are in their land, but Israel requires military, material, and financial support from a pagan nation to survive. And yes, they have fine leaders in Zerubbabel or Nehemiah, yet neither of these was the anticipated Son of David who was promised to reign over them as king. And yes, they returned to the law in repentance and faith (Ezra 8–10), yet this lasted only briefly and they turned again to their idolatry and flagrant disobedience (see Neh 13:23–28 and Mal 3:8–15). So, when will the fulfillment of these promises take place? They did not happen during the time of the Old Covenant itself. And now we have a time when Israel is cut off (Matt 21:42–43; Rom 11:17, 19–21, 25) and the gospel is spreading from Jerusalem to all of the Gentile nations of the world (Matt 28:19–20; Acts 1:8). There must be a time yet future in which these promises to ethnic, national Israel are fulfilled. In a very significant sense, then, the dispensational view is grounded on the promises of God made to Israel, as understood by employing these first two hermeneutical observations.

### Human and Divine Authorship

Third, while progressive dispensationalism is committed to discerning the plain and natural meaning of texts of Scripture (first hermeneutical observation, above), this is sometimes complicated by the fact that all of Scripture is dually authored. Our doctrine of inspiration assures us that whereas all of Scripture is genuinely written by human authors who convey the meanings they intend through the language and expressions they choose, Scripture is simultaneously directed by the Spirit of God (2 Pet 1:20–21) such that all that the human authors write likewise accords exactly and fully with what God wanted written. Hence, the singular intended meaning of a text may best be thought of as complex, not simple; as thick, not thin. Given that God does not violate the integrity of the human authorship of Scripture as the Spirit moves them to write what they do, it cannot be the case that the meaning intended by the human author and the meaning intended by the divine author would conflict. But rather, it may well be the case, and arguably sometimes is, that the intended meaning of the human author, while affirmed and included in the meaning of the divine author, is likewise surpassed in fullness by what the divine author intends.[7]

The new covenant of Jer 31:31–34 provides a case in point. Clearly the intended meaning of the human author (Jeremiah) was to convey that "the house of Israel" and "the house of Judah" (31:31 NASB) would be the recipients of God's promised new covenant. And no doubt this is likewise the intended meaning of the divine author. Indeed, there will come a day when ethnic Jews, the people of Israel, will be brought into the fullness of God's restorative work through their Messiah and they will all "know the Lord" (cf. Rom 11:26). But we know from references to the new covenant in the New Testament that Gentile believers in Christ are likewise brought into the reality of new covenant transformation (e.g., Hebrews 8–10). When one considers what Jeremiah said in the new covenant promise of Jer 31:31–34, there simply is no hint that this promised future covenant would apply to any beyond the house of Israel and the house of Judah. The intended meaning of the human author, it would seem, is restricted to Israel. Yet, notice that Jeremiah does not say that *only* Israel will be included. So, while the human author spoke of the new covenant as being made with Israel, the divine author intended this *and more*! God may do more than his promise explicitly states, but he cannot (because he will not) do less or other. So, the intended meaning of the human author is restricted (applying it to Israel alone), while the divine author intends to apply the new covenant to Israel *and* to Gentiles who will become circumcised of heart through faith in Christ (Rom 2:28–29), even though only the fulfillment with Israel is explicitly announced in Jeremiah's text.

This notion of a "thick" understanding of some of the promises of God, in which a larger divine intention may be present that surpasses (while including and never conflicting with) the explicit promise as stated in the Old Testament, is one of the places where progressive dispensationalism has embraced a needed corrective to a strict traditional dispensational hermeneutic. Readers may be aware that in the mid-twentieth century, leading dispensationalists argued that there had to be two new covenants. After all, since the new covenant of Jer 31:31–34 was made "with the house of Israel and with the house of Judah"

---

[7] Graham A. Cole, *The God who Became Human: A Biblical Theology of the Incarnation* (Downers Grove, IL: InterVarsity Press, 2013), 89, helpfully comments in regard to a number of Old Testament prophecies, that "such Old Testament texts take on a legitimate depth of significance that may not have been apparent to the original writer."

in the Old Testament, then it simply could not apply to the New Testament multi-ethnic, multi-national church. Therefore, the new covenant announced by Jesus (Luke 22:20), repeated by Paul (1 Cor 11:25; 2 Cor 3:6), and referenced in Hebrews (8:8; 9:15; 12:24) must refer, instead, to a different "new covenant."[8] The strict separation between Israel and the church required that only Israel be in view in the new covenant expressed by Jeremiah. But given that 1) there is no indication whatsoever in the New Testament that the new covenant there is different from the new covenant of Jeremiah 31, and 2) Jeremiah 31 is quoted by Hebrews as being fulfilled both with saved Jews and Gentiles who comprise the church,[9] there is no sustainable case for two new covenants.[10]

Progressive dispensationalism, then, holds that while the explicit promise of the new covenant is given to Israel, God has intended, and deemed it good and gracious, to include also Gentiles who come to him through faith in Christ. Yet, this does not preclude the promise being fulfilled with Israel, for indeed the day will come when "all Israel will be saved" (Rom 11:26) and so enter fully into the reality and experience of the new covenant through their faith in Christ. While the intention of the human author in Jeremiah 31 focused only on God's promise to enact the new covenant with his people, the Jews, God's intention all along had been to do just this, and more! We (Gentiles who believe in Christ) get in as well, and this was God's intention from the outset, fulfilling in an unanticipated way what he long ago had promised in the covenant made with Abraham—"in you [Abraham] all the families of the earth will be blessed" (Gen 12:3).[11]

### Inaugurated Eschatology

Fourth, the progressive dispensational view gladly embraces the inaugurated eschatology of George Eldon Ladd, and as articulated and held by so many evangelicals in our day.[12] Although the "already and not yet" is nowhere

---

[8] See, for example, Lewis Sperry Chafer, *Systematic Theology* (Dallas: Dallas Seminary Press, 1947), 4:325, 7:98–99; and Charles C. Ryrie, *The Basis of the Premillennial Faith* (New York: Loizeaux Brothers, 1953), 105–125.

[9] See esp. Heb 12:23–24 where the new covenant is said to include both the "church of the firstborn" along with "the spirits of the righteous made perfect" indicating both saved Old Testament Jews and New Testament members of the church are recipients of new covenant promises.

[10] For further discussion on why the two-new-covenant theory fails, see Homer A. Kent Jr., "The New Covenant and the Church," *Grace Theological Journal*, Vol 6 (1985): 297–98.

[11] For further discussion of the important place of the new covenant in a broader progressive dispensational understanding, see Bruce A. Ware, "The New Covenant and the People(s) of God," in Blaising and Bock, eds., *Dispensationalism, Israel, and the Church*, 68–97.

[12] See the fascinating discussion in Carl F. H. Henry, *The Uneasy Conscience of Modern Fundamentalism* (Grand Rapids: Eerdmans, 1947); and the intriguing development of the significance of the broad embrace of inaugurated eschatology as discussed by Russell D. Moore, *The Kingdom of Christ: The New Evangelical Perspective* (Wheaton: Crossway Books, 2004).

explicitly taught in Scripture, its validity and verification comes in how it illumines so many biblical prophecies. One of my favorite examples comes from Jesus's quotation of Isa 61:1–2 in Luke 4:18–19. Whereas Jesus stops quoting from the Isaiah passage with the words, "to proclaim the favorable year of the Lord" (Luke 4:19 NASB), and then announces, "Today this Scripture has been fulfilled in your hearing" (Luke 4:21 NASB), the text of Isa 61:2a reads, "To proclaim the favorable year of the Lord and the day of vengeance of our God" (NASB). Clearly, the Son was sent in his first coming not to bring the vengeance of God on the earth but to bring salvation, as John tells us in his Gospel, "For God did not send the Son into the world to judge the world, but that the world might be saved through Him" (John 3:17 NASB). Therefore, the only way rightly to understand the fulfillment of the Messianic promise of Isa 61:1–3 is that the Spirit-anointed Messiah would come first securing God's gracious favor in salvation from sin, and then this same Messiah will come again executing the vengeance of God upon continuing sinful rebels. Although two comings of Christ are not explicitly taught in the Old Testament, the fulfillment of this and several other prophecies requires just this. The "favorable year of the Lord" is now; the "day of the vengeance of our God" is not yet.

What relevance does this hermeneutical observation have for progressive dispensationalism? Just this: Because much Old Testament prophetic teaching should best be seen as fulfilled in an already/not yet fashion, this provides a framework that fits within a modified dispensational model for understanding how some of the promises made to Israel might be fulfilled now, in the church, in a preliminary and partial manner, while the fulness of those promises await their complete fulfillment, not only with the church but with the people of Israel as well. Therefore, the strict *continuity* of traditional covenantalism (all the promises of Israel are fulfilled in the New Testament church which is the new Israel) and the strict *discontinuity* of traditional dispensationalism (none of the promises to Israel are fulfilled in the church but all await a future fulfillment with a restored Israel) are not our only options.[13] Instead, we can see how the New Testament church may be the recipient of the blessings of promises made to Israel, through faith in Christ, and yet New Testament believers enter into them now in only partial ways. But also, there will come a day when the "not yet" aspects of those promises will be fulfilled in their completeness, and this will involve not only the church entering into the fulness of those blessings, but the final realization of these promises will be fulfilled with the very people to whom those promises were explicitly made, viz., with ethnic, national Israel.

---

[13] On issues of continuity and discontinuity, one of the most helpful volumes is John S. Feinberg, ed., *Continuity and Discontinuity: Perspectives on the Relationship Between the Old and New Testaments* (Wheaton: Crossway Books, 1988).

A very important New Testament passage here is Eph 2:11–16:

> Therefore remember that formerly you, the Gentiles in the flesh, who are called "Uncircumcision" by the so-called "Circumcision," which is performed in the flesh by human hands—remember that you were at that time separate from Christ, excluded from the commonwealth of Israel, and strangers to the covenants of promise, having no hope and without God in the world. But now in Christ Jesus you who formerly were far off have been brought near by the blood of Christ. For He Himself is our peace, who made both groups into one and broke down the barrier of the dividing wall, by abolishing in His flesh the enmity, which is the Law of commandments contained in ordinances, so that in Himself He might make the two into one new man, thus establishing peace, and might reconcile them both in one body to God through the cross, by it having put to death the enmity. (NASB)

Notice that Paul indicates that Israel (the physically circumcised) had a tremendous advantage over the Gentiles (the physically uncircumcised).[14] Israel exclusively was given God's covenant promises such that their hope was grounded in what God had specifically and directly given to them that he had not given to the other nations of the world. Although their salvation likewise would be by grace alone, in Christ alone, at least they had the promise of God granted specifically to them that they would be the recipients of all that would be required to make them, in the end, God's forgiven and transformed people. But what about all the rest of the inhabitants of the world (i.e., the Gentiles)? Their condition was extremely dire, in contrast. Since they were not part of the commonwealth of Israel, they were not among those who had been given these covenant promises of a future and certain salvation. As a result, they had absolutely no hope and faced both a present and a future in which they would live every day in despair, without God.

And then comes the glorious shift of Eph 2:13 (which parallels somewhat the earlier "But God" shift of Eph 2:4). Paul writes of these Gentiles, "But now in Christ Jesus you who formerly were far off have been brought near by the blood of Christ" (Eph 2:13). And here is the point we are to make. Although Gentiles were not given the promise of the Davidic covenant, or the promise of the new covenant—these were given exclusively to the people of Israel—nevertheless, God has devised a means by which these otherwise hopeless Gentiles who were far off might enter into the reality of these covenants of salvation, hope, and restoration. How? Through faith in Christ, the promised Messiah, Son of David, and the mediator of the new covenant. Through Christ, Gentiles

---

[14] See also Rom 3:1–2; 9:4–5, for other expressions of the advantage Israel had in being made God's people and given God's covenant promises.

would be granted access to the benefits of those covenants that were not theirs, that were not made with them. But in Christ they now become sharers fully in everything that those covenants have promised such that they, with believing Jews, both experience equally (cf. Gal 3:28) the fullness of what is theirs in Christ.

But seeing that Gentiles are granted, by God's grace and through their faith in Christ, incorporation into the covenants of promise made with Israel, are we then to conclude that God will not fulfill the promises of his covenants also with those to whom he directly and specifically made these covenants? Absolutely not! Surely this is what stands behind Paul's discussion in Romans 9–11, that God will be faithful to his promise to Israel, and that we may be assured that the day is coming when "all Israel will be saved" (Rom 11:26). As we saw before, God may do more than his explicit promise stated, but he cannot do less or other. The salvation of the Jews will occur displaying, among other things, the glory of the faithfulness of God to his Word. He will not fail to keep every promise he has made, and this requires the future salvation of the Jewish people.

The contribution of inaugurated eschatology to this progressive dispensational hermeneutic, then, is vital. On the one hand, it provides a way of accounting for the present fulfillment of the promise of the new covenant, in this age, with the church, and yet we all realize that this fulfillment is both preliminary (it's just the beginning) and partial (there's much more to come, in the end). The fulfillment at present is inaugurated but not yet consummated. On the other hand, it also accounts for the future completion of the fulfillment when we in the church are made fully like Christ and enter into the endless joy of those who "know the Lord." But it will also mean the fulfillment of these promises with Israel herself who alone was the recipient of these covenant promises when they were made. Everything God promised Israel will be fulfilled with Israel. They too will know the Lord. They too will be made like Christ. They too will receive full forgiveness and Spirit-empowered transformation through faith in Christ. The truthfulness and faithfulness of God assures that this will take place.

And in addition, one more dimension of the fulfillment of these promises with Israel should be included. They will, as Ezekiel 37 asserts, be reconstituted as the nation of Israel, in their land, obediently following the Lord, with Messiah reigning over them as King. Even though the day will come when the reign of the Greater David (Jesus) will encompass all of the earth, still—even in the new creation—the center of this reign is the capital of Israel, Jerusalem. And since God promised to put on display among all the nations of the world that he has reconstituted his people again as one nation (Ezek 37:21–22, 28), surely he will do just what he has promised. Since the new creation will be a place where all the nations of the world enter and bring their glory with them (Rev 21:24, 26), it is not difficult to see that Israel likewise will be a nation among the nations present. She, too, will bring her glory into the new Jerusalem, and in her case, this glory is especially brilliant. She will display, among all the rest of the nations of the world, that Yahweh, the God of Israel and Savior of his people, has been true to his promises. There she is. The redeemed of the Lord, the chosen covenant people of God, those through whom Messiah has come to bring salvation and the covenant blessings of Israel to the nations. Though believing Jews and Gentiles are one in Christ and share equally in all the riches of what Christ has merited for them, yet she will display a distinctive glory by which the faithfulness of God, and the truth of his word, will shine forth for all to see.

### Concluding Remarks

These four hermeneutical observations are what drive the progressive dispensational view I have adopted, and they provide for me compelling reason to accept and commend this model. Much could be added (indeed, needs to be added) to give a more complete and satisfying explanation. For example, one may wonder about the place of typology here. Briefly, I would simply say that biblically grounded typological linkages in Scripture fit well with a progressive dispensational understanding, in that the divine author intends at times to reveal through some person, or event, or institution that the type prefigures what God has ordained to occur in greater measure later, in the anti-type. Still, this all fits nicely within the four hermeneutical points stated, providing greater depth and richness to the progressive revelation God has given us. Others might wonder how a redemptive-historical understanding of Scripture fits with progressive dispensationalism. Again here, I believe it fits beautifully with its emphasis on the progression and development of God's redemptive purposes that run through the biblical narrative. But I believe that the redemptive-historical approach, on its own, lacks what the notion of progressive revelation adds, viz., that God purposes to establish particular requirements, and give particular promises, and regulate the affairs of his people in particular ways, in various periods (dispensations) of that revelatory history. So, a redemptive-historical approach is compatible with a full understanding of progressive revelation, but both are needed, I believe, to give a fuller picture of what God is doing in the progressive unfolding of his truth to his people. Yet others might wonder how progressive covenantalism and progressive dispensationalism compare and contrast. It seems to me that there is much in common between these two systems, even though (as their names indicate), each is birthed from its own mother—covenant theology and dispensationalism, respectively. Yet, both have "come to the middle" in many respects and see both areas of continuity and discontinuity in the relationship between Israel and the church. Yet, it does seem to me that progressive covenantalism is inclined to think of the church as largely the "new Israel" in ways that diminish the ongoing reality of the rejected nation of Israel in the present age, which will be saved and restored in the end, owing to the promise of God to them. Also, the progressive dispensational view has a larger place for what the salvation of Israel means—not only their salvation from sin and entrance into the new covenant, but also their restoration as a nation, in fulfillment of what God promised them, to the greater glory of his name.

In the end, the progressive dispensational view seeks to honor the revelation God has given, endeavoring to understand what God has declared he will do, and to believe that since God has said this, it must be true and his promises will be fulfilled. It is a wonder for us all that God has chosen a people for his name, through whom he has brought salvation to the world. Even where we struggle to see clearly all the details, may we never forget the glory of this good news, and may our hope always be in the character of God who speaks truthfully and never fails to do what he has promised.

*Chapter 2*

# New Covenant Theology and Biblical Theology

*by D. A. Carson*

When the editors invited me to contribute to this Festschrift by writing the chapter on new covenant theology as an approach to biblical theology, I confessed to a certain reluctance. This reluctance did not spring from any hesitation about honoring Tom Schreiner. It is a matter of no small wonder that he has been able to maintain his teaching load and pastoral responsibilities while writing excellent commentaries and other theological works; it is a privilege to honor him in this way.

No, my initial hesitation sprang from my growing suspicion that not a few of the labels we use to refer to the work we do and the camps to which we belong are problematic. It's not that these labels have no utility; they do. Nevertheless, they function in our discussions in ways that are sometimes unclear and even unnecessarily divisive. I assumed I was asked to write the chapter on new covenant theology because many perceive me to be a new covenant theologian, a partisan of that camp—though those who know me better recognize that I am reluctant to describe myself in those terms. As a result of these reflections, I had the impertinence to ask the editors if they could bear with me if I wrote a slightly different sort of essay. Although I shall try to say some pertinent things about new covenant theology, I want to engage in slightly broader reflection on some of the relevant theological labels we casually deploy, and end with some pastoral reflections, mirroring, however inadequately, the ease with which Tom Schreiner himself moves back and forth between technical discussion and pastoral care.

I shall proceed by raising three questions, and then by offering a few synthetic conclusions.

## WHAT IS BIBLICAL THEOLOGY?

If we are to evaluate a variety of "approaches" to biblical theology, we need to share some common understanding of what biblical theology is. We may usefully begin with the helpful analysis of Klink and Lockett.[1] After a brief introduction that surveys the "spectrum" of biblical theology, Klink and Lockett outline five current "types" and attach at least one scholar to each type as a kind of representative exemplar. First, to "biblical theology as historical description," Klink and Lockett attach the name of James Barr. This first type is the heir of and successor to the history-of-religions school that flourished at the end of the nineteenth and the beginning of the twentieth centuries. This school sought to understand the biblical documents as reflecting the religion(s) of particular groups at different times and places, to be studied by scholars with a deep commitment to objectivity combined with philosophical naturalism, and an equally deep suspicion of the dogmatics of pastor-theologians. This biblical theology was essentially a descriptive and historical enterprise, an enterprise deeply suspicious of attempts at synthesis, or of any thesis that argues (or, horrors, presupposes) one Mind behind the biblical text, a text which in some ways conveys *theological* truth.[2]

The second type of biblical theology surveyed by Klink and Lockett is biblical theology as history of redemption, and to this they attach my name. Here the focus is on reading Scripture as an historically developing collection of documents,[3] which of course presupposes that, however diverse those documents are, there is finally one Mind behind the whole, and his purposes and plan constitute a cohesive whole that can be discerned, indeed that is best discerned, by being viewed through the lens of the historically developing revelation that God has given. In some ways, then, biblical theology is a bridge discipline between exegesis and systematic theology. Biblical theology tends to stand a little closer to the text than does systematic theology because it

---

[1]  Edward W. Klink III and Darian R. Lockett, *Understanding Biblical Theology: A Comparison of Theory and Practice* (Grand Rapids: Zondervan, 2012).

[2]  Barr's first book, *The Semantics of Biblical Language* (Oxford University Press, 1961), was in large measure a convincing linguistic attack on the biblical theology that dominated the field at the time, with its inelegant and reductionistic dependence on word studies that were unjustifiably extrapolated into theological concepts. Barr's last book, *The Concept of Biblical Theology: An Old Testament Perspective* (Minneapolis: Fortress, 1999), is not only a sustained defense of his approach, but an equally sustained attack on alternatives, especially those of the synthetic sort. See the penetrating review article by Robert Yarbrough, "James Barr and the Future of Revelation in History in New Testament Theology," *Bulletin for Biblical Research* 14 (2004): 105–26. For a more recent handling of Scripture along similar lines (though it does not probe the meaning of "biblical theology" per se), see Dale B. Martin, *Biblical Truths: The Meaning of Scripture in the Twenty-First Century* (New Haven: Yale University Press, 2017).

[3]  Cf. D. A. Carson, "Current Issues in Biblical Theology: A New Testament Perspective," *Bulletin for Biblical Research* 5 (1995): 17–41 (esp. 27); Carson, "Systematic and Biblical Theology," *New Dictionary of Biblical Theology*, 89–104 (esp. 94).

is committed to using the categories in each of the biblical texts themselves, while systematic theology develops categories that link different texts together, and on the whole is more sensitive than biblical theology to formulations that engage contemporary culture. Though it is a matter of degree rather than an absolute distinction, systematic theology tends to be ordered topically, while biblical theology focuses more attention on the temporal development of the themes it treats. Klink and Lockett are sympathetic to this second type of biblical theology but wonder if Carson has erected too much discontinuity between biblical theology and systematic theology, while at the same time failing to recognize how treacherous and sometimes ambiguous an historically conscious exegesis can be.

The third type of biblical theology surveyed by Klink and Lockett is biblical theology "as worldview-story," best exemplified by N. T. Wright. Here there is less concern to unpack the sequence of the historical development and greater interest in discerning the "story shape" that connects the Old Testament narrative and the New Testament narrative; there is somewhat less focus on tracing individual biblical themes across the canon, or on outlining the theological contribution of each biblical book and corpus, and more focus on describing "the worldview story that stands behind Jesus, Paul, and the NT."[4] Wright argues that his understanding of "story" properly links history and theology together. "To be truly Christian, [theology] must show that it includes the story which the Bible tells, and the substories within it. Without this, it lapses into a mere *ad hoc* use of the Bible, finding bits and pieces to fit into a scheme derived from elsewhere."[5] This "story" so shapes Paul and other New Testament writers that they operate with a "worldview" that sometimes functions at a precognitive or presuppositional level. Wright wants to avoid sharp-edged polarities and the philosophical naturalism of the first type of biblical theology, and what he perceives as the bittiness of the second type. Epistemologically, he defends "critical realism," distancing himself from the naiveté of historical positivism, insisting that there is something to be known and understood (hence "realism") that shapes the categories of the New Testament authors. For Wright, biblical theology is properly normative but most of it, in his understanding, is narrative or, more precisely, his reconstructed worldview-story. And the end of his story, the "fifth act" (in his well-known Shakespearean analogy) plays itself out against the background of the previous acts and the actors of the New Testament era and beyond. Klink and Lockett assign high marks to Wright for cleverly linking history and theology in narrative, but join with others in thinking that Wright's version of biblical theology rigidly rests

---

[4] Klink and Lockett, *Understanding Biblical Theology*, 111.
[5] N. T. Wright, *The New Testament and the People of God* (London: SPCK, 1992), 138.

on history—more precisely, on his own reconstruction of history, which constitutes a "methodological naturalism"[6] where the price paid is Wright's easy
self-distancing from some of the church's traditional stances, on grounds that
are not so much exegetically constrained as dictated by the hegemonic control
of his massive reconstruction.

For a fourth type, Klink and Lockett treat biblical theology "as canonical
approach," and tie this to Brevard Childs. Like the third type, this fourth tries
to bring together history and theology, using the horizon of the canon as the
"foundational axis."[7] However complex the underlying history, the canon lights
the path taken by many traditions to reach a stable point, and we participate
in this tradition as we follow its traces. The terminology associated with this
fourth type is confusing: Childs never owns "canon criticism" as a valid label
for his own work, while James Sanders does—but Sanders deploys the canon
to track the trajectory of the traditions in a way that makes the trajectory more
important and potentially more normative than the traditions themselves.
Regardless of the diversity of positions defended by the canonical approach,
the common element is the elevation of the canon to a controlling position. In
the hands of Childs, the purpose of biblical theology of this type is to uncover
the theology of the Bible in its canonical form. "The literal sense of the text is
the plain sense witnessed to by the community of faith. It makes no claim of
being the original sense, or even being the best. Rather, the literal sense of the
canonical Scriptures offers a critical theological norm for the community of
faith on how the tradition functions authoritatively for future generations of
the faithful."[8] Thus, rather than envisaging the two poles of biblical theology,
history and theology, as at odds with each other, or as moving linearly from history to theology, Childs sees the two in a dynamic tension shaped and reshaped
by the form the tradition takes in the developing canonical frame. Yet Childs
seems to use "canon" and "canonical" in diverse ways, making it sometimes unclear what he means. Moreover, because the "historical" component for Childs
is tied to the kind of naturalistic "history" that has dominated biblical scholarship for the last two hundred years, while "theology" for Childs is tied to what
comes from outside the text (from God himself?), there is an instability in
where Childs locates authority. And some argue that because Childs listens so

---

[6] The expression is that of C. Stephen Evans, "Methodological Naturalism in Historical Biblical
Scholarship," in *Jesus and the Resurrection of Israel: A Critical Assessment of N. T. Wright's* Jesus and the Victory
of God, ed. Carey C. Newman (Downers Grove, IL: InterVarsity Press, 1999), 180–205; cf. Klink and
Lockett, 122.

[7] The expression is that of Klink and Lockett, *Understanding Biblical Theology,* 125.

[8] Brevard S. Childs, "The *Sensus Literalis* of Scripture: An Ancient and Modern Problem," in *Beiträge zur
Alttestamentlichen Theologie*, ed. Herbert Donner, Robert Hanhart, Rudolf Smend (Göttingen: Vandenhoeck
& Ruprecht, 1977), 80–93 (esp. 92).

sympathetically to the theology of the church, he sometimes subordinates his exegesis of Scripture to tradition that is not exegetically grounded.

The fifth and final kind of biblical theology treated by Klink and Lockett is biblical theology as theological construction, and this they find well exemplified in the work of Francis Watson. They conceive of this fifth type as "part of a movement that is concerned to retrieve the convictions and skills that allowed previous Christians to permit scriptural interpretation to shape and be shaped by Christian principles and practices . . . to recast the Bible from its status as an ancient historical text to contemporary Christian Scripture."[9] In short, they associate this approach with TIS, Theological Interpretation of Scripture, a movement Robert Morgan tags as "all theologically motivated interpretation,"[10] however varied the interpretive forms that fly under that banner. The task of this fifth type of biblical theology "*is to affirm the integrated nature of biblical theology as a theological, hermeneutical, and exegetical discipline with overriding theological concerns, incorporating biblical scholarship into the larger enterprise of Christian theology.*"[11] It encourages conversation, indeed hermeneutical exchange, between systematic theology and the exegesis of the ancient texts, and is the work of the confessing church, not just the academy. Watson specifically wants "to dismantle the barriers that at present separate biblical scholarship from Christian theology."[12] Faithful interpretation of Scripture, however grounded in the past, continues its work as ongoing divine communication, and thus distinguishes itself from forms of biblical theology that focus on historical criticism or on the discrete moments of the past when the text was written. In other words, this is what it means to interpret the Bible *as Scripture*, and only in this way is our interpretation truly theological. The influence of Barth is transparent. This "redefined" biblical theology "is open-ended in its theological orientation and is sensitive to theological 'issues' and theological 'concerns' within the contemporary context."[13] As for the relationship between the Old Testament and the New, Watson dismisses a linear development which, he says, destroys the distinctiveness of both Testaments; rather, he develops a complex pattern that he labels a two-Testaments reading of the Christian tradition. The assessment of this fifth type of biblical theology proffered by Klink and Lockett is very largely positive, though they acknowledge multiplying redefinitions and Watson's multi-layered interactions with biblical theology and Theological Interpretation of Scripture have the effect of making

---

[9] Klink and Lockett, 157.

[10] "Can Critical Study of Scripture Provide a Doctrinal Norm?" *Journal of Religion* 76 (1996): 212.

[11] Klink and Lockett, 159 (emphasis theirs).

[12] Francis Watson, *Text and Truth: Redefining Biblical Theology* (Grand Rapids: Eerdmans, 1997), vii.

[13] Klink and Lockett, 178.

the discussion complex and sometimes unclear: Watson has "inadvertently added more clutter in the path."[14]

So what are we talking about when we speak of new covenant theology as an approach to biblical theology? What is the biblical theology of which we are speaking? First, all must recognize that biblical theology is an historically late and invented category. It is not an expression used in Scripture, such that by careful scrutiny of its use in the primary documents we might make a case for such and such a meaning. As far as I am aware, it was not used before the beginning of the seventeenth century—but that doesn't mean that Christians thought that all earlier theology was *un*biblical. In its first usage in a title, *Teutsche Biblische Theologie* (1604), the work captured by the expression was apparently[15] a slim volume of proof texts in support of Lutheran systematic theology. No one uses "biblical theology" with that meaning today. To locate the expression when it starts to carry many of its contemporary overtones, most scholars cite the inaugural address of J. P. Gabler at the University of Altdorf in 1787: "An Oration on the Proper Distinction between Biblical and Dogmatic Theology and the Specific Objectives of Each." Gabler was fed up with the many theological debates that stemmed, in his view, from the dogmatic constructions foisted on the subject by ecclesiastical bodies. What he advocated was a refocus on the study of the Bible itself—on *biblical* theology as opposed to systematic theology. He thought that if theologians studied the Bible together, i.e., focusing on such biblical theology, they could gain much greater consensus as to what the Bible actually says. At the end of a period of time, it might be possible to return to systematic theology, building on this renovated foundation. The common insistence today that what Gabler wanted was to treat biblical theology as an historical (as opposed to theological) topic[16] is somewhat anachronistic, reflecting later perceptions as to where the distinctive nature of biblical theology lies. But my point at this juncture is that on any reading of the evidence, the definition of biblical theology keeps shifting. Each suggestion cannot be evaluated against a neoplatonic ideal; we are making things up as we go along, trying to establish different responsible ways of interpreting the Bible, and then labeling them and defending them.

Second, some of the categories used in the preceding discussion turn out to be rather slippery—and none more so than "history." In the first type of approach to biblical theology, the history-of-religions approach, history is what takes place in space-time *on naturalistic assumptions*. It is explicitly *not* theology, for theology dares to talk about God, his nature, his self-disclosure, his attributes, even his speech. This first approach may of course *in one sense*

---

[14] Klink and Lockett, 182.

[15] "Apparently" because the volume is no longer extant.

[16] E.g., Klink and Lockett, 14–15.

talk about theology, but it is theology-as-people-think-and-talk-about-God (under naturalistic analysis), not theology-as-discourse-about-God-himself. The assumption of philosophical naturalism in the treatment of "history" is still alive and well in the world of biblical scholarship. For instance, here is Dale Martin: "Moreover, real historians do not include the actions of god in their histories."[17] By contrast, in the second approach to biblical theology, the redemptive history or salvation-historical approach, while we are talking about what takes place in space-time history, we are talking about what *God* is doing and saying in history, as well as about what people believe about this God. It is history because what it describes actually happens, and we are given warrant for saying that God does it, or because it is identified with the reliable report of such actions. What God is doing certainly includes all "natural" phenomena (he sends the rain, he feeds the lions, he stills the raging sea) but it also includes what we call supernatural phenomena (the burning bush, Jesus's resurrection from the dead). Under such an outlook, it is incoherent to pit history against theology; God discloses himself not only in words and personal encounters, but in history, whether that history is "natural" or "supernatural." Under the third approach, the worldview story, many proponents operate under the assumption that the biblical "story" is in fact history (as I've just described it), even if their focus lies rather more strongly on the worldview narrative features than on its historical reliability. Others care not at all for claims of history in the story and focus all their attention on the impact of the worldview formation of the narrative (e.g., some proponents of the so-called Yale school, most powerfully advanced by George Lindbeck). My point is that unless distinctions as to how "history" is being used are carefully observed, studies that propose to compare the various approaches to biblical theology will almost inevitably become skewed.

Third, most of these approaches to biblical theology are not entirely distinct. The first two, as we have just seen, are radically distinct when it comes to their respective understanding of history. But all of the approaches focus a great deal of energy on the relationships between the Old Testament and the New Testament, and on the relationship between history and theology. The third approach doesn't talk as much about salvation history as the second, but it engages in it quite a lot; the fourth approach, canonical theology, drills down into how earlier texts are used by later texts, but although the foci are sometimes different, the same drilling down into the relationship between earlier and later texts occupies (say) Tom Wright in the third approach or me in the second.

---

[17] Martin, *Biblical Truths*, 26.

The failure to think through these two points—the slipperiness of categories like "history," and the ways in which these various approaches to biblical theology commonly overlap, even when their emphases differ—seems to be what has led to one of the most bizarre analyses in recent discussion of these matters. I am referring to Darian Lockett's essay, "Limitations of a Purely Salvation-Historical Approach to Biblical Theology."[18] Lockett relies on the criticism of Hans Frei, Karl Barth, and especially of Brevard Childs. To respond to Lockett in detail would treble the length of this essay, so I must limit myself to a handful of observations. (1) Lockett repeatedly casts salvation-historical readings of biblical texts over against theological readings of the same texts.[19] But this disjunction is possible only if the "history" component is heavily tinged with naturalism, which is precisely what I and other proponents of biblical theology have taken some pains to renounce. How could any thoughtful believer operate under such assumptions? The God of the Bible is simultaneously the One who inhabits eternity, and the Lord of history, as Isaiah 40–45 and many psalms make clear. (2) Lockett states, "While the insights of a redemptive-historical biblical theology are important, even necessary, when *taken as the exclusive methodology for biblical theology* it risks flattening the relationship between the two Testaments and missing Scripture's theological subject matter" [emphasis added].[20] But: (a) Lockett keeps asserting that my approach to biblical theology is nothing but a redemptive-historical grid, "the exclusive methodology for biblical theology." But that is not true. I have repeatedly argued that in my understanding of biblical theology, the distinctive element is that it takes into account the time axis, whereas systematic theology, for all its many strengths, makes much less of that axis. Thus, passages like Romans 4, Galatians 3, and Romans 7 cannot faithfully be understood unless one perceives how much of the author's argument depends on sequence, on chronological order. Thus, those passages constitute *one* of the bits of evidence that legitimate my approach to biblical theology. Once one is sensitive to the temporal dimensions of God's revelation in Scripture, it is also possible to study, say, the theology of Ezekiel, or Lukan theology, in their respective genres and historical time slots, examining carefully how it fits into, partakes of, and contributes to canonical theology and systematic theology. Thus it is not surprising that some of the volumes in New Studies in Biblical Theology trace a theme right through

---

[18] Darian Lockett, "Limitations of a Purely Salvation-Historical Approach to Biblical Theology," *Horizons in Biblical Theology* 39, no. 2 (2017): 211–31.

[19] Lockett, 230. E.g., he says, "John Behr argues that we should no longer discuss Irenaeus in terms of salvation history for no other reason than the fact that Irenaeus understood history in profoundly theological terms."

[20] Lockett, 213.

the canon,[21] while others focus on the theological emphases of one particular book.[22] And it is also possible to refer to the Bible's large-scale story line that takes us to Jesus and the Gospels.[23] It is quite striking that in all his critique, Lockett says nothing about the important place of predictive prophecy and fulfillment, or of typological fulfillment, even though both these phenomena are plentifully attested in the biblical texts, *and depend on the passage of time.* (b) More seriously, Lockett jumps from his critique of reliance on "exclusive methodology for biblical theology" to "flattening the relationship between the two Testaments and missing Scripture's theological subject matter." But nowhere do I argue that the *only* legitimate method of reading holy Scripture is biblical theology as I have understood biblical theology. Biblical theology has no right to dismiss the legitimacy of systematic theology and its (largely) atemporal approaches to reading Scripture. (3) Again, Lockett approvingly cites Childs to the effect that the "New Testament bears witness to realities outside itself. . . . To recognize that the Bible offers a faith-construal is not that we are saved, not by the biblical text, but by the life, death, and resurrection of Jesus Christ who entered into the world of time and space"[24]—cited in such a way as to imply that defenders of the second approach to biblical theology want to remain locked into the text without perceiving that we are saved not by the text but by that of which the text speaks. I do not know how many times I have made the same point myself, so it is difficult to see how the argument is a refutation of the second approach to biblical theology, unless Lockett has seriously misunderstood his interlocutors. (4) Lockett rightly wants to reserve a place for figural readings of earlier texts, but wrongly casts such interests over against redemptive-historical readings. I fail to see how figural readings cannot be integrated with both biblical theology and systematic theology. In both cases, there must of course be warrant for such readings—but that is to venture upon a slightly different subject. It is difficult not to perceive that Lockett's critique has expended more than a little energy demolishing a straw man.

Fourth, the fifth approach to biblical theology held up and briefly evaluated by Klink and Lockett is what they call theological construction. A quick review of their survey (above) reminds us that they have thrown into its definition

---

[21] E.g., G. K. Beale, *The Temple and the Church's Mission: A Biblical Theology of the Dwelling Place of God*, New Studies in Biblical Theology 17 (Downers Grove, IL: InterVarsity Press 2004).

[22] J. Gary Millar, *Now Choose Life: Theology and Ethics in Deuteronomy*, New Studies in Biblical Theology 6 (Grand Rapids: Eerdmans, 1999).

[23] This may be done in a simple survey, such as found in the brief book by Nick Roark and Robert Cline, *Biblical Theology: How the Church Faithfully Teaches the Gospel* (Wheaton: Crossway, 2018). And, of course, it is possible to present a correspondingly simplified summary of the Bible's teaching using largely atemporal systematic categories.

[24] Lockett, "Limitations," 229–30, citing Brevard S. Childs, *New Testament as Canon: An Introduction* (Philadelphia: Fortress, 1984), 545.

everything but the kitchen sink: the task of this type of biblical theology "*is to affirm the integrated nature of biblical theology as a theological, hermeneutical, and exegetical discipline with overriding theological concerns, incorporating biblical scholarship into the larger enterprise of Christian theology.*"[25] Several things may usefully be said. (1) This fifth definition of biblical theology integrates theological, hermeneutical, and exegetical disciplines, with particular emphasis on "theological concerns," and incorporates "biblical scholarship into the larger enterprise of Christian theology." Is there anything it does *not* include? This approach to so-called biblical theology makes it impossible to distinguish biblical theology from, say, historical theology, or systematic theology, or biblical-exegetical scholarship, except to say that it is bigger than all of these and embraces all of them. In other words, this fifth approach uses "biblical theology" in a way it has never been used since the expression was first coined. It has engaged in a definitional heist and taken over all the terrain, damning all other options as too narrow. Fair enough: its proponents should feel free to adopt any definition they choose. (2) But then they should recognize that when those who adopt other definitions of biblical theology engage in interpreting, expounding, and integrating the Bible using the full panoply of approaches that have come down to us, they are doing roughly the same thing as the defenders of the fifth option, but not calling it biblical theology: they reserve "biblical theology" for some part of the task, as we've seen, but not for the whole. The proponents of this fifth approach to biblical theology are not deploying a superior method; they are merely attaching the biblical theology label to all that they do. (3) In this they are mirroring what is going on in the TIS movement (Theological Interpretation of Scripture movement), as we have seen. That is the connection that Klink and Lockett explicitly make: as far as I can see, their fifth approach to biblical theology is indistinguishable from TIS. TIS claims to be hegemonic: it engages in exegesis, historical criticism, historical theology, systematic theology, remembering that its work is for the church, learning from the patristic fathers in particular, well engaged with contemporary biblical scholarship, deeply interested in spirituality, rejecting all reductionisms, and so forth, and above all TIS makes it clear that the focus is theological (it's about God) and not historical (for most, this is code for not about God). Do all that and call it biblical theology. Or TIS. But that is why it is simultaneously difficult to criticize TIS, and irresponsible not to. On the one hand, who wants to criticize theology, exegesis, spiritual vitality, integration, and so forth? And on the other hand, the categories and the proponents are so diverse that some of the work being done in the name of TIS (or of biblical theology) is frankly

---

[25] See n.26.

*not* faithful to Scripture and *not* helpful,[26] so that flying under this banner is not particularly elucidating. The best parts of TIS have been pursued by some scholars for centuries; what is most innovative in TIS deserves some suspicion and hesitation. (4) In particular, the two-Testaments reading of Scripture anticipated by Childs and strongly defended by Watson, over against any linear development from the First Testament to the Second Testament, does not adequately take into account the numerous times in which New Testament writers correct readings of the Old Testament that fail to point to the coming of the Messiah and the dawning of the new covenant (e.g., John 5:39–40). This is not to say that the two Testaments are connected by nothing more than linearity, but one suspects that at least some proponents are so eager to distance themselves from any form of supersessionism that they are abandoning some of the unambiguous ways in which the Old Testament is declared to pave the way toward the Christ of the New Testament.

## WHAT IS AN APPROACH TO BIBLICAL THEOLOGY?

This question must be asked because the mandate I have been assigned is to discuss new covenant theology's *approach* to biblical theology. What might this mean? When Klink and Lockett lay out five different *approaches* to biblical theology, what they seem to be discussing is different ways of defining biblical theology. In other words, how might we understand what biblical theology is if methodologically we begin with something akin to history-of-religions studies, or with redemptive history, or with worldview construction, and so forth? That's why the evaluations offered by Klink and Lockett are essentially evaluations of these methods/approaches themselves—their adequacy, their faithfulness to Scripture, their coherence, and so forth—since these methods/approaches will determine what we understand biblical theology to be.

But in this volume, unlike the volume by Klink and Lockett, we are being asked to evaluate various theological *systems* as "approaches" to biblical theology—in my case, to evaluate new covenant theology as an "approach" to biblical theology. But neither new covenant theology nor dispensationalism nor covenant theology nor any of the other options is regularly treated as something that controls biblical theology, i.e., as something that defines what biblical theology *is*. The order of priority has now been reversed. Each theological system is begging for evaluation against the platonic (or at least some theoretical) ideal of biblical theology. The problem, of course, is that there is no agreed platonic ideal of biblical theology. By biblical theology, do we have in mind, say, the worldview story of Tom Wright, or the theological construction of Frances

---

[26] See D. A. Carson, "Theological Interpretation of Scripture: Yes, But . . . ," in *Theological Commentary: Evangelical Perspectives*, ed. R. Michael Allen (Edinburgh: T&T Clark, 2011), 187–207.

Watson, or the understanding of salvation history of Robert Yarbrough?[27] Transparently, the evaluations of the different theologies would prove rather different if they were made to line up against such diverse understandings of biblical theology.

So to keep the variables to a manageable minimum, I shall for the rest of my assignment adopt the definition of biblical theology that I have been implicitly defending so far in this paper.

## WHAT IS NEW COVENANT THEOLOGY?

Here I shall take four steps.

First, I must set the terrain. Probably the easiest way to flesh out what is meant by new covenant is to locate it within the matrix of its nearest cousins. We might usefully ask how the new covenant is understood in several strands of evangelical theology before asking, by comparison, what is unique or at least characteristic of new covenant theology.

Classic Reformed theology holds there is a single covenant of grace that is administered differently in the time of law over against the time of the gospel. The old and the new covenants are different with respect to their intrinsic efficaciousness but share the same redemptive intention. The Baptist variation, as measured by the Second London Baptist Confession of 1689, is similar, for it too envisages one redemptive covenant that is progressively disclosed, but it lays a little more emphasis on the newness of the new covenant. The progressive covenantalism of Peter Gentry and Steve Wellum[28] holds to one redemptive purpose but insists that the new covenant supersedes all antecedent covenants, and thus new covenant believers are not under the law covenant as a covenant: Christ is the *telos* of the law—not only its goal but its culmination. Similarly, the progressive dispensationalism espoused by, say, Craig Blaising and Darrell Bock[29] holds that the new covenant replaces the Sinai covenant, while serving as the fulfillment of the Abrahamic covenant.

These descriptions are so simplified that distinctive features in each system have not yet been identified. For example, so far as understanding the relationship of the new covenant to the Sinai code is concerned, there is not much difference between progressive covenantalism and progressive dispensationalism. In reality, the latter demands that place be made for a role for empirical Israel at the end of the age; the former does not. As for new covenant theology, it too

---

[27] Robert W. Yarbrough, *The Salvation Historical Fallacy? Reassessing the History of New Testament Theology* (Leidendorp: Deo, 2004).

[28] See esp. Peter J. Gentry and Stephen J. Wellum, *Kingdom through Covenant: A Biblical Theological Understanding of the Covenant* (Wheaton: Crossway, 2012).

[29] Craig A. Blaising and Darrell L. Bock, *Progressive Dispensationalism: An Up-to-Date Handbook of Contemporary Dispensational Thought* (Grand Rapids: Baker, 1993).

thinks of the new covenant as fulfilling the Abrahamic covenant and replacing the Mosaic covenant, serving as the one covenant that binds Christians today.[30]

Second, one gains greater definition of these varied positions when one pauses to assess how law is understood in them. Classic Reformed covenantalism depends not a little on the traditional threefold analysis of law: moral, civil, and ceremonial law. The civil law has disappeared because the locus of the people of God is no longer a nation; the ceremonial law has been superseded by Christ and his sacrifice. That leaves the moral law, which is eternal. That structure helps to anchor the covenant theologian's view that one covenant of grace runs right through Scripture. Doubtless the best recent defense of the eternal tripartite view of law is that of Philip S. Ross.[31] Ross is so careful with his sources that he faithfully draws attention to the remarkable reality: there are many texts, both biblical and extrabiblical, that make distinctions in law of one kind or another, but a threefold division that serves as the rationale for ordering lines of continuity between the old covenant and the new does not clearly appear in the historical record until Aquinas; Calvin appears to have picked it up from him.[32] In other words, despite his best efforts to anchor the tripartite division of the law in Scripture and the early church, his own careful marshaling of the evidence shows it is a medieval development. What is characteristic of most defenders of new covenant theology is that in their insistence that the new covenant fulfills the old covenant, they reject lines of argument that preserve the structure of a single covenant of redemption, and thus they remain suspicious of the tripartite division of the law as being without adequate biblical defense. The least charitable of them accuse their opponents of a kind of crypto-Judaism. Theologians of the mold of classic covenant theology sometimes return the favor by charging the defenders of new covenant theology with antinomianism.

Third, although it would go well beyond the demands of this essay to attempt even a superficial mediation of this theological dispute, and although this is certainly not the place to canvass the hundreds of relevant texts and the scores of theological arguments that have been advanced on both sides, nevertheless this must be said. Not a few defenders of new covenant theology have come over to this position from the classic Reformed camp, and thus almost inevitably feel obliged to defend their move, which tempts them to look for

---

[30] Doubtless the defining book on new covenant theology is by Tom Wells and Fred G. Zaspel, *New Covenant Theology: Description, Definition, Defense* (Frederick: New Covenant Media, 2002).

[31] Philip S. Ross, *From the Finger of God: The Biblical and Theological Basis for the Threefold Division of the Law* (Fearn: Mentor, 2010).

[32] See D. A. Carson, "The Tripartite Division of the Law: A Review of Philip Ross, *From the Finger of God*," in *From Creation to New Creation: Biblical Theology and Exegesis*, ed. Daniel M. Gurtner and Benjamin L. Gladd (Peabody: Hendrickson, 2013), 223–36.

differences rather than to seek out common ground. Absolute lines are sometimes drawn, where complementary differences in emphasis may be wiser.

For example, the new covenant theology position on the tripartite division of the law is often taken, both by its defenders and by its opponents, as writing off the very notion of moral law. Small wonder that many Christians get nervous. Strictly speaking, however, all that is required by the new covenant theologian is a rejection, not of moral law, but of the argument that the tripartite division is an *a priori* category that defines the lines of continuity and discontinuity between the covenants. In reality, it is easy to construct an argument in which the tripartite division remains heuristically useful, as an *a posteriori* category that emerges out of the observation that some stances keep recurring under every covenantal structure—and after the fact (i.e., *a posteriori*), it is easy enough to discern most of them. After all, the Paul who says, "One person considers one day more sacred than another; another considers every day alike. Each of them should be fully convinced in their own mind" (Rom 14:5 NIV) could not possibly have said, "One person considers adultery to be sinful; another considers every sexual act to be acceptable. Each of them should be fully convinced in their own mind." For after all, while there are some discontinuities between the demands of the old covenant and the demands of the new, there are also some continuities, and all sides recognize at least most of them. The issue is not whether there are continuities (for of course there are) that might usefully be labeled moral law, but whether that category is the *a priori* given, or the *a posteriori* result of the distinctions. On the one hand, Paul can insist he is not under the law (*sc.* covenant), while insisting he is "not under the law" but *ennomos Christou* (1 Cor 9:19–23 NIV[33])—which again raises the question of the points of continuity between being under the constraint of the Mosaic law and being under the constraint of Christ's law. Suddenly the respective charges of Judaizing and of antinomianism seem rather to miss the point. With a little effort, one might even make place for the traditional third use of the law.

Or again, while several centuries of Reformed expositors have used Galatians 3 in an atemporal fashion to justify the thesis that in the individual life the law must do its work and bring condemnation before faith in Christ rightly applies, a more sensitive reading of the chapter shows that Paul is less interested in this chapter in detailing the psychological profile of individual conversion than in unpacking the place of the law covenant between the Abrahamic promise and the fulfillment in the gospel. Nevertheless, before defenders of new covenant theology mount their chargers and ride off in victory,

---

[33] THE HOLY BIBLE, NEW INTERNATIONAL VERSION®, NIV® Copyright © 1973, 1978, 1984, 2011 by Biblica, Inc.® Used by permission. All rights reserved worldwide.

isn't it worth at least asking why, on Paul's argument, God devotes so many centuries to teaching his people that they are sinners and cannot please God on their own? In other words, even after rightly detecting the salvation-historical framework of Paul's argument in Galatians 3, is there not a place for pondering its pastoral application?

Or again, could we not prevail on some of our more traditional Reformed theological friends to undertake a careful study of every use of the word "new" in the New Testament, with the possibility of spurring some reflection as to whether one or two things might be learned from the defenders of new covenant theology after all?

In short, there are several different voices in the new covenant theology camp, and some are seeking to establish bridges to other theological syntheses, rather than emphasizing new covenant theology's distinctions in such an antithetical way that there are only winners and losers.

Fourth, if, then, having tried to think my way through what is meant by "new covenant theology," "approach," and "biblical theology," I am now asked to assess new covenant theology's approach to biblical theology, I would say that its focus on the Bible's developing story line, its grasp of old and new, its perennial interest in trajectories (typologies?), its wrestling with (predictive) prophecy and fulfillment, and much more of the same, nestle rather nicely into the contribution a salvation-historical understanding of biblical theology makes to the global undertaking of massive theological synthesis and pastoral reflection.

## CONCLUDING REFLECTIONS

One of the striking features of contemporary biblical and theological scholarship is the panting hunt for new tools and new methods. Doubtless some of this is fueled by the need to discover "new" areas of research for doctoral dissertations. Each is held forth as the golden key that will open up the Bible and transform theological studies. Implicit in this brief study of new covenant theology's approach to biblical theology, however, is an invitation to go beyond squabbling over the contributions (and definitions!) of various tools and syntheses, to glimpse the large vistas of theological exploration still open to us.

*Chapter 3*

# Covenant Theology

*by Shawn D. Wright*

Covenant theology is a holistic system of biblical interpretation built upon key transitional texts in Scripture such as God's covenant with Adam in Genesis 1–3, the Lord's calling of Abraham and covenanting with him in Genesis 12–17, and the parallel Paul draws between the work of Adam and Christ and the effect of their actions on their representatives in Rom 5:12–21. Michael Horton suggests that covenant theology serves as a way to organize the major themes of the Bible into one coherent whole, "to say what Scripture says and to emphasize what Scripture emphasizes."[1] In other words, what unites the Bible is

> an architectonic structure, a matrix of beams and pillars that hold together the structure of biblical faith and practice. That particular architectural structure that we believe the Scriptures themselves to yield is the covenant. It is not simply the concept of the covenant, but the concrete existence of God's covenantal dealings in our history that provides the context within which we recognize the unity of Scripture amid its remarkable variety.[2]

Covenant theology is thus a hermeneutical approach, as J. I. Packer suggests, "a way of reading the whole Bible that is itself part of the overall interpretation of the Bible that it undergirds."[3]

---

[1] Michael Horton, *God of Promise: Introducing Covenant Theology* (Grand Rapids: Baker, 2006), 12.
[2] Horton, 13.
[3] J. I. Packer, "Introduction: On Covenant Theology," in Herman Witsius, *The Economy of the Covenants between God and Man,* vol. 1 (1822; Grand Rapids: Reformation Heritage, 2010), 27.

Covenantalism arose, and continues to find its *raison d'être*, out of a desire to protect Reformed theology from the inroads of any sort of synergism that inserts unaided human ability into the salvation equation. Covenant theology, in fact, is virtually synonymous with Calvinism. Charles Spurgeon expressed this belief when he declared, "I love men who love the covenant of grace, and base their divinity upon it; the doctrine of the covenants is the key of theology."[4] Horton agrees. He stresses that Calvinism cannot be reduced simply to "five points" or predestination or some similar doctrine. All these truths, rather, "testify to a far richer, deeper, and all-embracing faith in the God of the covenant. *Reformed* theology is synonymous with *covenant* theology."[5]

In this chapter I shall proceed in three steps. First, I shall summarize the main contours of covenant theology by examining the three major covenants it stresses.[6] Second, I will notice the monergistic purpose of covenant theology's polemic against all forms of synergism. Third, I shall observe that one can promote Calvinism's soteriology while also differing with covenant theology's system, especially its neglect of the newness of the new covenant.

## OVERVIEW OF COVENANT THEOLOGY

Eugene Osterhaven's definition—"Covenant theology sees the relation of God to mankind as a compact which God established as a reflection of the relationship existing between the three persons of the Holy Trinity"—shows us that covenantalism is arranged around both "compact" and "relationship."[7] In other words, the idea of "covenant" (as used in Scripture) implies that an arrangement has been forged between parties. Sometimes that covenantal arrangement or compact is unilaterally imposed whereas at other times two equals agree to it. The goal, however, is to establish a relationship between formerly estranged parties. Ligon Duncan highlights this relational component when he defines covenant theology as "the Gospel set in the context of God's eternal plan of communion with his people, and its historical outworking in the covenants of

---

[4] Charles Spurgeon, cited in Peter Golding, *Covenant Theology: The Key of Theology in Reformed Thought and Tradition* (Fearn, UK: Christian Focus, 2004), 9.

[5] Horton, *God of Promise*, 11; his italics.

[6] We will limit our attention in this chapter mainly to the English-speaking covenantal tradition associated with the Westminster Confession of Faith (1646). Vos claims that "The Westminster Confession is the first Reformed confession in which the doctrine of the covenant is not merely brought in from the side but is placed in the foreground and has been able to permeate at almost every point." Geerhardus Vos, "The Doctrine of the Covenant in Reformed Theology," in *Redemptive History and Biblical Interpretation: The Shorter Writings of Geerhardus Vos*, ed. Richard B. Gaffin Jr. (Phillipsburg: Presbyterian and Reformed, 1980), 239.

[7] M. E. Osterhaven, "Covenant Theology," in *Evangelical Dictionary of Theology*, ed. Walter A. Elwell (Grand Rapids: Baker, 1984), 279.

works and grace."[8] Covenant theology, then, is the gospel. In it God makes the arrangement whereby his elect will be saved by establishing a new and everlasting relationship. In order to rescue them, the Lord institutes three covenants, one eternal, and two in human history.

### *The Covenant of Redemption*

This covenant (also called the *pactum salutis*, the "eternal covenant," and the "intra-trinitarian covenant") describes the arrangement in which the persons of the divine Trinity agreed in eternity past how they would save God's elect. To fulfil this covenant, the Father assigned a task to the Son, the Son did the work, and the Father promised him the reward for his work. Charles Hodge explains, "When one person assigns a stipulated work to another person with a promise of a reward upon the condition of the performance of that work, there is a covenant. Nothing can be plainer than that all this is true in relation to the Father and the Son."[9] Reflecting this thinking, seventeenth-century Calvinistic Baptists remarked, "It pleased God, in His eternal purpose, to choose and ordain the Lord Jesus, His only begotten Son, *according to the covenant made between them both*, to be the Mediator between God and man."[10]

The Bible teaches the components of the covenant of redemption. The whole course of Jesus's ministry was done because he was "sent" by the Father; he obeyed his Father's will (John 17:4, 18; Gal 4:4; 1 John 4:9–10). Duncan offers expansive biblical support for this eternal covenant: "it is the Father who sends the Son (John 5:37; 6:44, 57; 8:16, 18; 12:49; 14:24). The Son was sent and serves as the only Mediator. The Father did not die for the sins of his people, nor did the Spirit; it was the Son alone who performed this task (John 14:6; Acts 4:12; 1 Tim 2:5). Further, it is the Spirit who is the comforter of the people of God." These varied tasks of the divine persons, he continues, "were embraced before time in the eternal purposes of God, in which the three persons of the Godhead, in one common purpose, chose to save sinners (1 Pet 1:20)."[11] The covenant of redemption, then, is a biblical formulation. It magnifies the God-centeredness of our salvation, according to Geerhardus Vos, for "it is God who issues the requirement of redemption as God the Father. Again, it is God who for the fulfilment of that requirement becomes the guarantor

---

[8] Ligon Duncan, "Recent Objections to Covenant Theology: A Description, Evaluation and Response," in *The Westminster Confession into the 21st Century: Essays in Remembrance of the 350th Anniversary of the Westminster Assembly*, ed. J. Ligon Duncan III (Fearn, UK: Mentor, 2009), 467.

[9] Charles Hodge, *Systematic Theology* (Grand Rapids: Eerdmans, 1986), 2:360.

[10] Second London Confession, 8.1; my italics.

[11] Duncan, "Recent Objections," 486. Hodge notes that to fulfil his role as the Mediator, the Son did three works assigned him by his Father. He became a man; he obeyed God's law; he bore the elects' sin. The Father, in turn, agreed to, for example, give the Son the Spirit to aid his work, send the Spirit to renew the hearts of the elect, and deliver the Son from death. Hodge, *Systematic Theology*, 3:361–62.

as God the Son. Once again, it is God to whom belongs the application of redemption as God the Holy Spirit."[12]

### *The Covenant of Works*

The first covenant enacted in human history was a conditional agreement between God and Adam. If Adam obeyed, he (and his posterity) would live. Tragically, he failed. The Westminster Confession spells out the condition and the promise given to Adam: "The first covenant made with man was a covenant of works, wherein life was promised to Adam; and in him to his posterity, upon condition of perfect and personal obedience" (7.2).[13] Louis Berkhof remarks that the arrangement reflected a "mutual relationship between God and man," which amounts to the same thing as calling it a "covenant." This arrangement, he proffers, is "variously known as the covenant of nature, the covenant of life, the Edenic covenant, and the covenant of works."[14]

Three biblical lines of argument defend viewing the Edenic experience as a covenant. First of all, God's interaction with Adam here included all the elements of a biblical covenant. Berkhof points out that "two parties are named, a condition is laid down, a promise of reward for obedience is clearly implied, and a penalty for transgression is threatened."[15] In the second place, Hos 6:7 says, "But like Adam they transgressed the covenant; there they dealt faithlessly with me" (ESV). Here Adam is said to have disobeyed the "covenant." Thomas Schreiner expresses the majority opinion when he claims, "Even though the word *covenant* is lacking [in Genesis 1–3], the elements of a covenant relationship are present, and Hos 6:7 supports the idea that the relationship with Adam and Eve was covenantal."[16]

Third, Paul draws a parallel between the roles of Adam and Christ in Rom 5:12–21 in which we notice, according to Hodge, that "as God entered into

---

[12] Vos, "Doctrine of the Covenant," 247.

[13] Robert Letham observes that the Westminster Confession of Faith was the "first major confessional document in which this covenant [of works] is expressly mentioned." Robert Letham, *The Westminster Assembly: Reading Its Theology in Historical Context* (Phillipsburg, NJ: P & R, 2009), 226. The Reformed tradition has struggled with how to relate the covenant of works and the Mosaic covenant given to Israel. See the various options in John V. Fesko, *The Theology of the Westminster Standards: Historical Context and Theological Insights* (Wheaton: Crossway, 2014), 145–58.

[14] Louis Berkhof, *Systematic Theology,* 4th ed. (1939; repr., Grand Rapids: Eerdmans, 1984), 211. Not all in the Reformed tradition have approved of calling this Edenic administration a "covenant of works." John Murray, notably, disapproved since the word "covenant" was not employed and since "the elements of grace entering into the administration are not properly provided for by the term 'works'" (John Murray, "The Adamic Administration," in *The Collected Writings of John Murray,* vol. 2: *Select Lectures in Systematic Theology* [Edinburgh: Banner of Truth, 1977], 49). See Fesko, *Theology of the Westminster Standards,* 126–27. Convincing rebuttals to Murray's concerns are offered by Duncan, "Recent Objections," 487–92.

[15] Berkhof, *Systematic Theology,* 213.

[16] Thomas R. Schreiner, *Covenant and God's Purpose for the World,* Short Studies in Biblical Theology (Wheaton: Crossway, 2017), 28; his italics.

covenant with Adam so He entered into covenant with Christ."[17] Adam was given a work to do, but he failed; Christ was given a work to do, and he succeeded. "For as by the one man's disobedience the many were made sinners, so by the one man's obedience the many will be made righteous" (Rom 5:19 ESV). As the Mediator of the covenant of grace, Jesus fulfills the role that Adam had in the covenant of works, as the Westminster Confession stresses.

> The Lord Jesus, by his perfect obedience, and sacrifice of himself, which he, through the eternal Spirit, once offered up unto God, hath fully satisfied the justice of his Father; and purchased, not only reconciliation, but an everlasting inheritance in the kingdom of heaven, for all those whom the Father hath given unto him (8.5).

Berkhof insists that Jesus "came to do what Adam failed to do and did it in virtue of a covenant agreement. And if this is so, and the covenant of grace is, as far as Christ is concerned, simply the carrying out of the original agreement, it follows that the latter must also have been of the nature of a covenant."[18] Adam broke the covenant of works, explaining the predicament of all humankind and our need for redemption. Christ our Mediator's fulfilling the covenant of works, on the other hand, serves as the foundation of the covenant of grace.

### *The Covenant of Grace*

> Man, by his fall, having made himself uncapable of life by that covenant [of works], the Lord was pleased to make a second, commonly called the covenant of grace; wherein He freely offereth unto sinners life and salvation by Jesus Christ; requiring of them faith in Him, that they may be saved, and promising to give unto all those that are ordained to eternal life His Holy Spirit, to make them willing, and able to believe (WCF 7.3).[19]

The covenant of grace is different from the covenant with Adam. J. V. Fesko observes that whereas the covenant of works "relies upon man and his own obedience," the covenant of grace "relies upon Christ and his obedience and is received by faith."[20] This covenant of grace was promised in God's pronouncement that he would crush Satan in Gen 3:15, was disclosed in the covenant enacted with Abraham (see Genesis 12, 15, and 17), was furthered by God's covenant with the nation of Israel (see, e.g., Exodus 20–23), and reached

---

[17] Hodge, *Systematic Theology*, 2:360.

[18] Berkhof, *Systematic Theology*, 214.

[19] The Reformed tradition has debated exactly with whom this covenant was made—with the elect, or with Christ their representative? See Chad Van Dixhoorn, *Confessing the Faith: A Reader's Guide to the Westminster Confession of Faith* (Edinburgh: Banner of Truth, 2014), 100n1.

[20] Fesko, *Theology of the Westminster Standards*, 162.

its apex in the new covenant brought about by the death and resurrection of Christ. After Adam's failure, God's orientation towards his people was one of grace, requiring of them faith. Due to Adam's sin and their sinful recalcitrance, God's people could not obey him. So Christ obeyed perfectly in the stead of his people.

Progressively, across biblical history, God revealed his covenant of grace to people in various administrations. Yet there is only one covenant of grace, as Letham contends: "The covenant is administered differently under the law and the gospel. . . . However, it is a distinction that relates to the administration of the covenant, not to its substance or intrinsic nature."[21] The two major biblical categories of the administration of the covenant of grace are law and gospel. The law's "promises, prophecies, sacrifices," and other practices "foresignif[ied] Christ to come." In their time they were sufficient, since they were aided by "the operation of the Spirit, to instruct and build up the elect in faith in the promised Messiah" to come (WCF, 7.5). With the coming of Christ, however, "the administration of the covenant has changed in accordance with this all-determining reality."[22] Under the administration of the gospel, the covenant of grace "is held forth in more fullness, evidence, and spiritual efficacy, to all nations, both Jews and Gentiles." Yet "there are not therefore two covenants of grace, differing in substance, but one and the same, under various dispensations" (WCF, 7.6). The covenant of grace, then, is the gospel. "We can have confidence in this covenant because in this gracious offer God gives his own Son," Chad Van Dixhoorn declares. "There is nothing abstract or fictitious in this gospel."[23] The covenant of grace guards God's gracious sovereignty in salvation.

### Covenant Theology as a Calvinistic Apology

Covenant theology is associated with Calvinism for at least three interrelated reasons. First, covenant theology insists upon unmerited divine grace as the basis of Christians' salvation against any synergism. Covenantalists recognize that "what the God who speaks the Scriptures tells us about in their pages is his own sustained sovereign action in creation, providence, and grace."[24] God's grace is the very heart of covenant theology. According to the Westminster

---

[21] Letham, *Westminster Assembly*, 233.

[22] Letham, 234.

[23] Van Dixhoorn, *Confessing the Faith*, 100. John Murray confirms for us that the "covenant of grace" is closely tied to a Calvinistic understanding of the gospel when he points out that the graciousness of this covenant is shown in the Mediator's merit being freely imputed to his people, the faith to believe in him is freely given them by the Spirit, and God receives all the glory in it. John Murray, "Covenant Theology," in *Collected Writings of John Murray, Vol. 4: Studies in Theology* (Edingburgh: Banner of Truth, 1983), 225–26.

[24] Packer, "Introduction," 28.

Confession, this act of divine grace is expressed in terms of covenant (7.1). Covenant theology thus protects the heart of God's gracious, sovereign salvation.

Charles Hodge defends Calvinism (variously called the "Augustinian scheme" of salvation, the "covenant of grace," and the "plan of salvation") against four deficient Protestant systems: Pelagianism, Arminianism (which teaches that "Salvation under the gospel is as truly by works as under the law; but the obedience required is not the perfect righteousness demanded of Adam, but such as fallen man, by the aid of the Spirit, is now able to perform"), Wesleyan Arminianism (which is "essentially the same" as Arminianism), and Lutheranism.[25] The "covenant of grace" is different, for it magnifies the loving, effective work of God to save his children. Hodge contends it "originated in the mysterious love of God for sinners who deserved only his wrath and curse"; it "promises salvation . . . as an unmerited gift"; and "its benefits are secured and applied . . . by the supernatural influence of the Holy Spirit, granted to [the elect] as an unmerited gift."[26] Vos thus lauds the "Reformed principle" of covenant theology. "All of man's work has to rest on an antecedent work of God" in a Christian's salvation.[27] The covenant of grace equals Calvinism's grace.

Second, and related to this, covenant theology emphasizes the unified work of the three persons of the Godhead in the salvation of the elect. In his classic defense of Calvinism, Packer applauds "the three great acts of the Holy Trinity for the recovering of lost mankind—election by the Father, redemption by the Son, calling by the Spirit—as directed towards the same persons, and as securing their salvation infallibly."[28] Fueled by texts like Eph 1:3–14 and its implicit covenant of redemption, covenant theology trumpets the gracious particularity of the Trinity. It maintains that "in our salvation by grace God stands revealed as Father, Son and Holy Spirit, executing in tripersonal unity a single cooperative enterprise of raising sinners from the gutter of spiritual destitution to share Christ's glory for ever."[29]

Third, God's grace is magnified in the key doctrine of justification by faith alone when placed in a covenantal context. As Calvinist theologians developed their understanding of justification in the seventeenth century against Catholic, Arminian, and Socinian opponents, they noted that the covenantal elements in the doctrine of justification avoided the works orientation in these three errors. As the second Adam, Jesus fulfilled the law in the place of his people, obeying

---

[25] Hodge, *Systematic Theology*, 2:355–56.

[26] Hodge, 2:357.

[27] Vos, "Doctrine of the Covenant," 242–43.

[28] James I. Packer, "'Saved by His Precious Blood': An Introduction to John Owen's *The Death of Death in the Death of Christ*," chap. 8 in *A Quest for Godliness: The Puritan Vision of the Christian Life* (Wheaton: Crossway, 1990), 128.

[29] Packer, "Introduction," 28.

the Father completely in their place. His active obedience was thus essential, and it was imputed to his people. Similarly, their disobedience was imputed to him as their representative, so that when he bore the wrath of God in their stead, his passive obedience was imputed to them. Imputation, therefore, was integral to the remission of sin in justification.[30] The Westminster Shorter Catechism's definition of justification encapsulates this: "Justification is an act of God's free grace in which he pardons all our sins and accepts us as righteous in his sight, only for the righteousness of Christ imputed to us and received by faith alone" (Q. 33).

So covenant theology supports Calvinism by highlighting the gracious, Trinitarian salvation accomplished by God for his people.

## BAPTISTS AND COVENANT THEOLOGY

As Calvinistic Baptists have engaged with covenant theology, the question they have asked is: Have covenantalists followed their own hermeneutical principal of saying what Scripture says and emphasizing what Scripture emphasizes?[31] The answer to that question is tied up with the new covenant promise in Jer 31:31–34 and its fulfilment in Heb 8:1–13. Does covenant theology consistently stress this new and better covenant (Heb 7:22; 8:6, 8, 13)?

Non-Baptist covenant theologians see the "newness" of the new covenant to be its clarity. Covenant administrations before it were more opaque. Murray, for example, claims, "Even the New Covenant is not so called because it is contrary to the first covenant but because there is a clearer and fuller manifestation of the gratuitous adoption which the Abrahamic covenant revealed and the Mosaic confirmed."[32] As such, they believe the makeup of the people of God—going back to the covenant sign of circumcision in Genesis 17 and New Testament indications that baptism parallels circumcision and God continues to accept children of believers into the covenant community (Matt 19:14; Acts 2:39; 10:47–48; 11:14; 16:15, 33–34; 1 Cor 1:16; Col 2:11–12)—is similar throughout the whole covenant of grace. As Hodge argues, "the plan of salvation has been the same from the beginning. . . . the people of God before Christ constituted a Church, and that the Church has been one and the same under all dispensations."[33] Thus, the people of God throughout the covenant of grace compose a *corpus permixtum*, a "mixed body."

Calvinistic Baptist responses to this notion fall into two camps. First, historically a large group has adopted the covenant theology of the 1689 Second

---

[30] A classic expression of this doctrine is John Owen, *The Doctrine of Justification by Faith*, in *The Works of John Owen*, vol. 5, *Faith and Its Evidences* (Edinburgh: Banner of Truth, 1965), 1–400.

[31] See Horton, *God of Promise*, 12.

[32] Murray, "Covenant Theology," 224.

[33] Hodge, *Systematic Theology*, 2:373.

London Confession, which broadly follows the contours of the Westminster Confession.[34] The heirs of this tradition continue to hold to the usefulness of the "covenant of grace" concept, as long as it has been carefully defined so as not to imply an incorrect notion of a "mixed" body composing the church. Samuel Waldron, for instance, insists that even though the language of "covenant of grace" is not used in Scripture, it refers to a biblical truth "that the way or scheme of salvation has been one and the same in all ages of the world."[35] Yet he avers that the goal and fulfilment of the covenant of grace is the new covenant: "the normative revelation for our understanding of the covenant of grace must remain the New Covenant."[36] Baptists must not concede the "covenant of grace" to non-Baptists:

> It is only because the paedo-baptist persists in defining the covenant of grace in terms of the preparatory and typical covenants of the Old Testament period that he thinks it will be of help to him in defending paedo-baptism. When we understand that the covenant of grace is fully and clearly revealed in the New Covenant, then it is impossible to think that infants are included in it.[37]

A second group, represented by Thomas Schreiner, more consistently emphasizes the redemptive-historical progress across the biblical canon and God's arrangement of distinct covenants to mark the people with whom he is covenanted along with the makeup of those people.[38] They consider the moniker "covenant of grace" unhelpful in that it imports potential misunderstanding without having biblical warrant to bound its polemical power to

---

[34] See *A Tabular Comparison of the 1646 Westminster Confession of Faith, the 1658 Savoy Declaration of Faith, the 1677/1689 London Baptist Confession of Faith and the 1742 Philadelphia Confession of Faith*, accessed April 20, 2018, http://www.proginosko.com/docs/wcf_sdfo_lbcf.html.

[35] Samuel E. Waldron, *A Modern Exposition of the 1689 Baptist Confession of Faith* (Durham, UK: Evangelical Press, 1989), 107–9.

[36] Waldron, *Modern Exposition*, 110.

[37] Waldron, 111. Also see Pascal Denault, *The Distinctiveness of Baptist Covenant Theology: A Comparison between Seventeenth-Century Particular Baptist and Paedobaptist Federalism*, rev. ed. (Birmingham, AL: Solid Ground Christian Books, 2013).

[38] I would like to take the opportunity to acknowledge the manner in which Tom has encouraged and helped me for over twenty years through his friendship, his modeling the Christian life before me, his constant engagement with Scripture, his humility, and his service together with me as an elder. I cannot put into words how important Tom has been to me, to my family, to my church, and to the school where I have the privilege to teach. Tom, thank you for loving the Lord and his word and for being a genuine model of what it looks like to know God and to walk with him by faith.

justify infant baptism.[39] These Baptists have labelled their position "progressive covenantalism."[40]

As noted above, the purpose behind the system of covenant theology is to defend Calvinistic soteriology. Yet Schreiner ably defends Calvinism.[41] For example, he holds to Calvinism's belief in effectual calling:

> The plight of humanity due to Adam's sin . . . is reversed only by the electing grace of God. . . . All people are in bondage to sin. They will never turn to God because they are so enslaved by sin that they will never desire to turn to him. How then can any be saved? The Scriptures teach that the effectual calling of God is what persuades those who are chosen to turn to him. God's grace effectively works in the heart of the elect so that they see the beauty and glory of Christ and put their faith in him (2 Cor 4:6). Because God's choice lies behind our salvation, we cannot boast before him that we were noble or wise enough to choose him. We can only boast in the Lord who chose us to be his own (1 Cor 1:29, 31).[42]

He also believes in so-called "double predestination," a doctrine John Calvin believed Scripture taught.[43] Commenting on the last phrase of 1 Pet 2:8–9 ("which is also what they were destined for"), Schreiner notes, "God has not only appointed that those who disobey the word would stumble and fall. He has also determined that they would disbelieve and stumble." This notion "that calamity also comes from God" is taught throughout the Old Testament. In fact, "even the cruelest and most vicious act in history—the execution of Jesus of Nazareth, was predestined by God (Acts 2:23; 4:27–28)."

---

[39] For a critique of covenant theology's defense of infant baptism from the progressive covenantalism perspective, see Stephen J. Wellum, "Baptism and the Relationship between the Covenants," in *Believer's Baptism: Sign of the New Covenant in Christ*, ed. Thomas R. Schreiner and Shawn D. Wright (Nashville: B&H, 2006), 97–161.

[40] See Peter J. Gentry and Stephen J. Wellum, *Kingdom through Covenant: A Biblical-Theological Understanding of the Covenants* (Wheaton: Crossway, 2012); Peter J. Gentry and Stephen J. Wellum, *God's Kingdom through God's Covenants: A Concise Biblical Theology* (Wheaton: Crossway, 2015). See Thomas R. Schreiner, "Good-bye and Hello: The Sabbath Command for New Covenant Believers," in *Progressive Covenantalism: Charting a Course between Dispensational and Covenant Theologies*, ed. Stephen J. Wellum and Brent E. Parker (Nashville: B&H Academic, 2016), 159–88.

[41] Note, e.g., *Still Sovereign: Contemporary Perspectives on Election, Foreknowledge, and Grace*, ed. Thomas R. Schreiner and Bruce A. Ware (Grand Rapids: Baker, 2000); "'Problematic Texts' for Definite Atonement in the Pastoral and General Epistles," in *From Heaven He Came and Sought Her: Definite Atonement in Historical, Biblical, Theological, and Pastoral Perspective*, ed. David Gibson and Jonathan Gibson (Wheaton: Crossway, 2013), 375–97.

[42] Thomas R. Schreiner, "Does Scripture Teach Prevenient Grace in the Wesleyan Sense?," in *The Grace of God, The Bondage of the Will*, vol. 2, *Historical and Theological Perspectives on Calvinism*, ed. Thomas R. Schreiner and Bruce A. Ware (Grand Rapids: Baker, 1995), 382.

[43] See, e.g., John Calvin, *Institutes of the Christian Religion*, Library of Christian Classics, 2 vols., ed. John T. McNeill, trans. Ford Lewis Battles (Philadelphia: Westminster, 1960), 2:926 (3.21.5).

Yet, as Schreiner goes on to show, at the same time people are also responsible, for we must "add immediately another element of the biblical worldview. Biblical writers never exempt human beings from responsibility, even though they believe God ordains all things (cf. Rom 9:14–23)."[44] He champions God's sovereignty while at the same time stressing human responsibility.

Additionally, Schreiner advocates the doctrine of justification by faith alone through the imputation of Christ's righteousness. His summary statement on the relationship of justification to imputation and faith is reminiscent of the historic Calvinistic position:

> All human beings either belong to Adam or to Christ as their covenant heads; they are either condemned in Adam or righteous in Christ. Just as the sin of Adam is imputed to human beings, so the righteousness of Christ is imputed to believers. . . . Jesus became sin for us, and we receive the righteousness of God since we are united to Jesus Christ. The believer's union with Christ points strongly to imputation, for our righteousness doesn't lie in ourselves but in Jesus Christ as the crucified and risen one. . . . Justification is by faith alone, because it is achieved by Christ alone, and it is ours only through union with Jesus Christ.[45]

## CONCLUSION

The heartbeat of covenant theology is its defense of Calvinism. I applaud its rebuttal of Arminianism. Yet the work of Schreiner indicates that one can be a committed Calvinist without holding to all the accoutrements of covenantalism, especially its ill-defined "covenant of grace." As Schreiner upholds, the covenant towards which all the other biblical covenants point is the new covenant promised in Jeremiah 31 and fulfilled in Christ's death. This covenant shows a sweeping change in the makeup of the covenant community, for

> In contrast to the old covenant, every member of the new covenant is regenerate. . . . What differentiates the old covenant from the new is that in the latter the members of the covenant are regenerated by God's Spirit. . . . Striking here is the comprehensiveness of what Jeremiah says [in Jer 31:34]. Certainly people need teaching even after becoming believers. Jeremiah's point, however, is that they don't need to be instructed or commanded to know the Lord as if they are unconverted, for by definition all those in the new covenant know the Lord. Notice that Jeremiah says that this is true from the least to the greatest. In other

---

[44] Thomas R. Schreiner, *1, 2 Peter, Jude*, The New American Commentary (Nasville: B&H, 2003), 113.
[45] Thomas R. Schreiner, *Faith Alone: The Doctrine of Justification* (Grand Rapids: Zondervan, 2015), 189–90.

words, there are no exceptions. Everyone in the new-covenant community is regenerate.[46]

Covenant theology is Reformed theology. Rightly understood, it is also Baptist.

---

[46] Schreiner, *Covenant*, 92–93.

*Chapter 4*

# Salvation History

*by Robert W. Yarbrough*

The term "salvation history" and its English-language equivalents (redemptive history, history of salvation, history of redemption) is not found in the Bible. But what it describes is ever present in the background, and frequently in the foreground, across the entirety of Scripture. The honoree of the essays in this volume, whom I am grateful to call a long-time friend, attests to this in his fine recent book titled *Covenant and God's Purpose for the World*.[1]

Preferring the synonym "redemptive history," Thomas Schreiner refers to it in at least six passages of his book. He affirms that salvation history . . .

1. "centers on the promise that God will bring redemption to the human race (Gen 3:15)."[2] *Salvation history is not merely past but promissory.*

2. refers to "an overarching view" of the grand reality that "God inaugurated history with creation and will consummate it with the new creation, and thus the old creation anticipates and points forward to the new creation."[3] *Salvation history is inclusive of the whole created order, bestows sequential coherence on that order, and terminates in a grand climactic age to come.*

3. has as one of its main outcomes "that human beings are restored to the purpose for which they were made when they are 'conformed to the image' of God's Son (Rom 8:29)."[4] Further, "only those who belong to the last Adam, Jesus Christ, are restored to the purpose for which God

---

[1] Thomas R. Schreiner, *Covenant and God's Purpose for the World* (Wheaton: Crossway, 2017).
[2] Schreiner, 13.
[3] Schreiner, 20.
[4] Schreiner, 25.

created human beings as sons and daughters of God."[5] *Salvation history is relevant to every human being ever created, with saving results only to those who belong to Jesus Christ (or, in Old Testament times, received by faith God's promise of a deliverance that came through Christ).*

4. carries forth the promises and terms of salvation history asserted in Eden (see reference to Gen 3:15 above) and that continue through Noah and beyond, as God's covenant with Noah "guarantees the continuance of the world until the great events of redemptive history are consummated."[6] *Salvation history is highlighted by "great events" which God works (like restoration after the fall, or the flood and then saving promise in its wake), resulting in either the salvation or judgment to which all persons are subject.*

5. encompasses all of the great covenants through which God brings salvation to the world—Schreiner highlights the creation covenant; the covenants with Noah, Abraham, Israel, and David; and the new covenant. But it also ramps up to "a new stage of redemptive history" in which Jesus is revealed, "the crucified, risen, and exalted Lord."[7] *Salvation history prepares the way for and culminates in the person and work of Jesus Christ and the church age currently unfolding until his return.*

6. is Christologically oriented. While all of the major elements of biblical history interlink and interlock in myriad and mysterious ways, Jesus Christ is "the key and center of redemptive history."[8] *Salvation history integrates—Christ is "the key"—and conveys the redemptive substance of Christ's ministry to a world doomed to hopelessness apart from his gracious, self-sacrificial mediation.*

This is just a sampling of how salvation history (or "redemptive history," if one prefers) is an integral feature in Schreiner's biblical understanding. This comes to the fore perhaps even more noticeably in his presentation of New Testament theology and then also his panoramic summary of the entirety of Scripture.[9] In these two works there are in excess of a hundred explicit references to "history of salvation," "salvation history," and "redemptive history."

Schreiner's wide-ranging and voluminous writings in the area of biblical theology confirm that "salvation history" is an important aspect of our understanding and communication of the Bible and its message. In what follows, I will (1) define salvation history, (2) illustrate salvation-historical perspectives from various passages of Scripture, (3) highlight selected salvation-historical

---

5  Schreiner, *Covenant and God's Purpose*, 25.
6  Schreiner, 36.
7  Schreiner, 83.
8  Schreiner, 86.
9  *New Testament Theology: Magnifying God in Christ* (Grand Rapids: Baker Academic, 2008); *The King in His Beauty: A Biblical Theology of the Old and New Testaments* (Grand Rapids: Baker Academic, 2013).

treatments of the New Testament, and (4) offer concluding observations regarding salvation history's importance within a whole-Bible approach to biblical theology.

## 1. WHAT IS SALVATION HISTORY?

Justo L. González has written: "Today many theologians rightly doubt [the] division of history in two—the history of the world and the history of salvation—and insist that God's work of salvation takes place through the entirety of human history, and that therefore that history is the proper field of action for Christians."[10] While there is no disputing that Christians can and should be involved in the field of historical study, his assertion contradicts a central tenet of many books of the Bible and an underlying supposition of them all: within the totality of the human enterprise, which when we regard it in narrative sequence we can call "history," God has been at work in particular ways to rescue humans from the judgment to which sin in Eden and since makes us subject. To requote and suggest an alternative to González, "God's work of salvation" does *not* take "place through the entirety of human history" in the same way at all times and places and among all peoples. Rather, in that history God has repeatedly asserted and inserted himself in distinctive ways to alter and steer human history to an end at his time and choosing, especially through particular events, persons, and peoples as described in Scripture.

Some of these people were already glimpsed above in Schreiner's treatment of covenants: Adam and Eve, Noah, Abraham, David, the people of Israel. This can be extended into the New Testament with central figures like Zachariah and Elizabeth and Mary; John the Baptist and Jesus; and those whom Jesus chose like the Twelve and later Paul. And the roster of biblically significant persons is not all individual: there is a strong corporate dimension, as God worked powerfully through Abraham and his descendants. Redemption came not just through persons but through the history and people of Israel, with input from other peoples like Moab (Ruth), the Hittites (Uriah), and Babylon (Cyrus the king). For that reason Jesus could say, "Salvation is from the Jews" (John 4:22). Salvation is actually from God, as Jesus well knew, but in this passage he is setting the Samaritan woman straight about the stream of history through which saving knowledge of God primarily comes. The Samaritan woman wants to locate it in her heritage and holy sites. Jesus gently, deftly, but firmly corrects her. It is through Abraham that "all the peoples on earth will be blessed" (Gen 12:3). Since Jesus's time, through the proclamation of the gospel, "if you belong to Christ, then you are Abraham's seed, heirs according to the promise" (Gal 3:29).

---

[10] *The Mestizo Augustine: A Theologian between Two Cultures* (Downers Grove, IL: IVP Academic, 2016), 170–71.

"Salvation history" refers to the historical process, attested throughout Scripture, through which God brought, is bringing, and will bring about the redemption of his people and the world, transforming the current state of things into the eternal order foretold by Old Testament prophets and Christ the Messiah himself.[11] Brian Rosner affirms two major convictions undergirding the salvation-historical outlook. First, "God has acted in human history,"[12] and indeed as the Bible describes, however challenging that may be to grasp, much less explain. Second, while not all the books in the Bible are "history" in form, genre, or even substance, they "all relate to an unfolding narrative" of events through which God has acted and spoken (714). Moreover, integral to this narrative is the enscripturation of what took place—the God who acted and spoke, by his Spirit, saw to transcription of divine deeds, discourse, and often human response (like many psalms) that we know as Holy Scripture. It is inspired by God (2 Pet 1:21; 2 Tim 3:16–17) who does not and cannot lie (Titus 1:2; Heb 6:18) and is therefore fully reliable and authoritative in its message rightly understood. There is, accordingly, an intimate connection between salvation history and the collection of documents that far and away tell us the most about it: the Bible.[13]

In a salvation-historical outlook, like in what P. E. Satterthwaite calls a "biblical-theological outlook," all of Scripture is seen to describe "the progressive unfolding of God's purposes of salvation for humanity."[14] This unfolding history, its effects in the course of time, and its future fulfillment in this age and the next[15] are seen as a single, interrelated narrative reflecting God's superintendence, whether direct or indirect, and saving work.

## 2. VISTAS OF SALVATION HISTORY IN SCRIPTURE

We glimpse salvation history in these well-known words: "Long ago God spoke to the fathers by the prophets at different times and in different ways. In these last days, he has spoken to us by his Son. God has appointed him heir of all things and made the universe through him" (Heb 1:1–2). Viewed in

---

[11] A similar definition, with slight alteration, is found in Robert Yarbrough, "Salvation History (*Heilsgeschichte*) and Paul: Comments on a Disputed but Essential Category," in Matthew Harmon and Jay Smith, eds., *Studies in the Pauline Epistles* (Grand Rapids: Zondervan, 2014), 181.

[12] See his essay "Salvation, History of," in Kevin J. Vanhoozer, ed., *Dictionary for Theological Interpretation of the Bible* (London: SPCK/Grand Rapids: Baker Academic, 2005), 714–17. Parenthetical numbers in this paragraph refer to this article.

[13] This point is brought out effectively in Andreas Köstenberger and Michael Kruger, *The Heresy of Orthodoxy* (Wheaton: Crossway, 2010), 4–5.

[14] "Biblical History," in T. Desmond Alexander and Brian S. Rosner, eds., *New Dictionary of Biblical Theology* (Leicester, UK: Inter-Varsity/Downers Grove, IL: InterVarsity Press, 2000), 43.

[15] As Rosner notes, drawing on Oscar Cullmann, "History, to be salvation history, must involve eschatology. Salvation history is heading somewhere, and the end is always in mind" ("Salvation, History of," in Vanhoozer, ed., *Dictionary for Theological Interpretation of the Bible*, 716).

the light of the whole epistle of Hebrews, these words point to a creator God, sovereign in salvation across the sweep of history from the primordial "long ago" to the writer's present ("these last days"). He has appointed an "heir of all things," toward whose manifest lordship all things in history flow, as they already subsist in him (cf. Col 1:17). God the Son is central within all world history, as attested by God's speech "to the fathers by the prophets" and in their wake "by his Son."

Similar dynamics are at work more expansively in Stephen's valiant defense and appeal (Acts 7). From God's glorious self-disclosure to Abraham (7:1), to the patriarchs (7:9), to the children of Israel in Egypt (7:17), to Moses (7:20–38) who "received living oracles to give to us" (7:38), God was bearing with his people in deed and word ("oracles" refers to Moses's writings) and through them bearing witness to the world. Stephen emphasizes the organic connection between (a) events from Abraham to David and Solomon and (b) the situation in his present hour by calling them "our ancestors" (7:44, 45) and by calling those who persecuted God's prophets the stiff-necked "ancestors" of his increasingly enraged audience (7:51–54). Stephen's speech presupposes salvation history, God's coherent, interrelated, comprehensive, and (through Jesus) personal saving plan and presence through the course of time.

Psalm 111 refers to God's great works which are "studied by all who delight in them" (v. 2). It speaks of corporate memory and ultimately Scripture: "He has caused his wondrous works to be remembered" (v. 4). It speaks of God's covenant, his people, and "the nations" that are their "inheritance" (vv. 5–6). "The works of his hands are truth and justice; all his instructions are trustworthy" (v. 7), and by these "holy and awe-inspiring" means God "has sent redemption to this people" (v. 9). Both God's saving work and his verbal self-disclosure unite the past of the psalmist and his readers in a saving heritage of which they are now part. This is salvation history.

The panoramic Psalm 106 (the final psalm in the Psalter's fourth book) lays out a salvation-historical depiction of Israel's past seen in negative light. Salvation history does not only soar heavenward; at times it appears to veer into the ditch: "Both we and our fathers have sinned; we have done wrong and have acted wickedly" (v. 6). Beginning with Egypt and the rebellion of certain "fathers" before Moses (v. 7), the writer chronicles the people's fickleness: "They soon forgot his works and would not wait for his counsel" (v. 13). But through all their probation (vv. 14–23) and disbelief (v. 24) and grumbling (v. 25), God determined they would not thwart his saving intention (vv. 26–27). Despite their disobedience (v. 34), idolatrous child sacrifice (vv. 36–39), and eventual captivity (vv. 40–43), God "heard their cry . . . took note of their distress, remembered his covenant with them, and relented according to the abundance of his faithful love" (vv. 44–45). The psalmist summarizes with a plea that the historical sweep he describes might come to its optimal culmination: "Save us, Lord our God, and gather us from the nations, so that we may give thanks to your holy name and rejoice in your praise" (v. 47). Joined inextricably to a heritage that was often disastrous in its waywardness before God, the psalmist nevertheless draws on the promises and faithfulness of God that are also part of that history to express hope.

In both Acts and Paul's letters, Paul assumes and articulates a salvation historical understanding. In Acts, this comes to the fore in the synagogue sermon at Pisidian Antioch (13:14–41). The same dynamic is visible, for example, in Romans, with Paul's appeals to Abraham (Romans 4), to the Second Adam in the wake of the first (Romans 5), and to God's faithfulness to his promises (Romans 9–11). In Acts 13, appealing to his listeners on the basis of their Abrahamic identity (v. 26), Paul preaches Christ, starting with the patriarchs and then moving to the times of Moses and Joshua and the judges (vv. 17–19). He continues to Samuel's era (vv. 20–21), the kings Saul and David (vv. 21–22), and David's offspring Jesus (v. 23) as proclaimed by John the Baptist (vv. 24–25). In all this Paul declares the fulfillment of God's promises "made to our ancestors" (v. 32) and effective "for us, their children" (v. 33) based on statements from the Psalms (v. 33, 35) and prophets like Isaiah (v. 34) and Habakkuk (v. 41). It is a divine underlying and overarching historical continuum, God's ongoing saving work and presence with his people and in the world generally, that characterizes and unites the sequence Paul describes.

Scholars frequently call attention to Scripture's salvation-historical unity in their study of individual sections of the Bible. Donald L. Berry has traced the "glory" motif in Scripture and especially Romans to show a key "link between the major movements of redemptive history, from creation to the fall to God's covenant with Abraham and the Mosaic covenant all the way through to the redemptive work of Christ and the future consummation of God's kingdom."[16] Roland Deines has recounted "The Recognition of God's Acts in History in the Gospel of Matthew" in a book chapter he subtitles "An Exercise in Salvation History."[17] Rosner sets forth a concise overview of salvation history in Scripture as a whole, from the Old Testament to the Gospels to Paul and finally Revelation.[18] At both the exegetical and the synthetic level, careful readers detect the strong presence of salvation historical events, claims, and testimony.

---

[16] *Glory in Romans and the Unified Purpose of God in Redemptive History* (Eugene, OR: Pickwick, 2016), 195.
[17] See Roland Deines, *Acts of God in History: Studies Towards Recovering a Theological Historiography*, (ed. Christoph Ochs and Peter Watts, WUNT 317 (Tübingen: Mohr Siebeck, 2016), 311–50.
[18] Rosner, "Salvation, History of," 714–16.

Commenting on a recent study of Acts' historical perspective,[19] Kenneth D. Litwak observes, "The key distinctive of Hebrew historiography was the conviction that the living God was working out his plan in human history."[20] The same outlook, with certain refinements and advances, is present in Acts.[21] Both the topic of salvation history as reflected in various biblical books, and the particularities of what that outlook asserts, are the subject of ongoing inquiry in biblical scholarship.

## 3. SALVATION HISTORY IN BIBLICAL THEOLOGY

Recognition that the Bible's saving message, like God's work in Christ itself, comes through history is ancient. New Testament writers discount fanciful, non-historical "myths"[22] and contrast them with historical truth claims relating to gospel events. In the second century, when Gnostics advanced an interpretation of Christ that was a- if not anti-historical, with salvation by esoteric knowledge largely independent of the historical details and framework found in Scripture,[23] Irenaeus (ca. AD 130–202) countered with stress on the Bible's historical events: "salvation history must be centered on the historical Jesus Christ, whose obedience unto death canceled the work of Adam."[24] "In Irenaeus' doctrine of recapitulation [cf. Eph 1:10], we discover a comprehensive perspective on the work of God throughout history."[25] What the Gnostics abandoned and sought to transcend, Irenaeus advanced as central to the true and universal apostolic faith: God's saving work in and through history as testified in the Old and New Testament Scriptures.

Medieval reading of the Bible favored interpretive strategies (often associated with Origen, Augustine, and allegorical exegesis) that read the Bible with an eye to figural more than historical meaning.[26] Scripture was seen more as a timeless self-disclosure of God than "history" in the Enlightenment sense of a dead and bygone era.[27] While there is much to be said for the fruitfulness of figural understanding, it is neither necessary nor advisable to juxtapose it with salvation history in adversarial fashion. If Jesus of Nazareth was not dead,

---

[19] Scott Shauf, *The Divine in Acts and in Ancient Historiography* (Minneapolis: Fortress, 2015).

[20] Kenneth D. Litwak, *Review of Biblical Literature*, accessed August 29, 2017, https://www.bookreviews. org/pdf/10360_11503.pdf, 2.

[21] Litwak, 3.

[22] See 1 Tim 1:4, 7; 2 Tim 4:4; Titus 1:14; 2 Pet 1:16.

[23] Bryan M. Litfin, *Getting to Know the Church Fathers* (Grand Rapids: Brazos, 2007), 87.

[24] Litfin, 91.

[25] Litfin, 91.

[26] See Ephraim Radner, *Time and the Word: Figural Reading of the Christian Scriptures* (Grand Rapids: Eerdmans, 2016).

[27] Note the insightful review of Radner (previous note) by Michael C. Legaspi, "Figure It In," *First Things* (June 2017), accessed August 29, 2017, https://www.firstthings.com/article/2017/06/figure-it-in.

buried, and raised as attested by eyewitnesses (1 Cor 15:1–8), Christian faith is invalid (15:14). The spiritual depends on the actual (just as saving apprehension of the actual depends on the spiritual—God's Spirit must open sinners' eyes to the saving force of the Bible's "historical" testimony). The actual is accessed through attention to the past as preserved in documents, artifacts, and the social heritage of communities across languages, communities, spaces, and times. God exists beyond time and history as we know them, but saving knowledge of God is conditioned and facilitated by his historical self-disclosure, in former times and now, as attested in Scripture.

With the Reformation era, understanding of Scripture took an *ad fontes* ("to the sources") turn. Roman Catholics (and eventually Protestants) like Luther and Calvin cited the Bible, in what they took to be its true meaning as determined by Hebrew and Greek exegesis, against church teaching when they felt this was necessary. The "protest" implied in "Protestant" stems in part from nascent salvation historical conviction. The Reformers' linguistic turn in search of a fresh theological basis was at the same time a historical turn. Calvin in particular advanced a biblical understanding that focused on the historical unfolding of God's covenants (much in line with Schreiner's *Covenant and God's Purpose for the World*; see beginning of this essay). In subsequent generations, just as the Renaissance fostered return to the study of Roman and Greek classics for wisdom in the wake of the medieval millennium, the Reformation inspired fresh attention to texts, languages, and cultures of biblical times in Lutheran, Reformed, and Anglican realms.[28]

While the Bible has been read with theological interests throughout the history of the church—there has always been "biblical theology" of various sorts—"biblical theology" in a technical sense is a child of developments since the late 1700s. The movement was university based, most prominent in Germany, and generally "critical" of confessional reading of the Bible. The "history" discovered by "historical-critical" scholars was a reconstruction purified of miracles, of direct divine intervention in history, of an inspired and authoritative canon of Scriptures, and of theological convictions like original sin, the incarnation, Christ's divinity, and other cardinal Christian truths. An iconic and iconoclastic example of a presentation of New Testament theology in this vein is the (only recently translated) book by F. C. Baur, *Lectures on New Testament Theology*.[29]

---

[28] For orientation see Richard A. Muller, *Post-Reformation Dogmatics*, 2 vols. (Grand Rapids: Baker, 1987–93); and relevant essays in Donald K. McKim, ed., *Dictionary of Major Biblical Interpreters* (Downers Grove, IL: IVP Academic/Nottingham, England: InterVarsity Press, 2007), especially R. A. Muller, "Biblical Interpretation in the Sixteenth and Seventeenth Centuries," 22–44.

[29] Ed. Peter C. Hodgson, trans. Robert F. Brown (Oxford: Oxford University Press, 2016). It was published in German in 1864.

It is against the backdrop of this rejection of salvation history that the German word *Heilsgeschichte* was coined by J. C. K. von Hofmann in 1842.[30] *Heil* referred to salvation. *Geschichte* means "history." The two words together were Hofmann's way of affirming the knowable, redemptive presence of the divine (revealing *Heil*, or redemption) in and through history (*Geschichte*) despite "historical-critical" readings like Baur's that plainly deconstructed the Bible's salvation historical claims.

The dominant movement in European and eventually North American universities was in the "historical-critical" direction. But in addition to Hofmann, scholars like Theodor Zahn (1838–1933) and Adolf Schlatter (1852–1938) read Scripture more in line with Hofmann's understanding.[31] In contrast to "historical-critical" New Testament theologies that read the New Testament in ways comporting with liberal theological views,[32] history of religion understanding,[33] or insights from philosophers like Heidegger[34] Zahn, and Schlatter—and in their wake others like Martin Albertz (1883–1956), Oscar Cullmann (1902–1999), Leonhard Goppelt (1911–1973),[35] and George E. Ladd (1911–1982)[36]—produced New Testament theologies (or in Cullmann's case near facsimiles) that found the Bible to be more than a "historical" corpse slain by "critical" ideology and convictions.

To paraphrase the thesis of Michael C. Legaspi's book titled *The Death of Scripture and the Rise of Biblical Studies*,[37] historical-critical reading of the Bible reduced it to an artifact no more capable of conveying saving truth than any other document from the past. Salvation, if there be any, is found in us and in our present existence. Salvation historical interpreters found in Scripture a past

---

[30] See A. J. Greig, "A Critical Note on the Origin of the Term Heilsgeschichte," *Expository Times* 87 (1976): 118–19.

[31] On Zahn and Schlatter see Andreas Köstenberger, "Theodor Zahn, Adolf Harnack, and Adolf Schlatter," in *Pillars in the History of Biblical Interpretation*, vol. 1, *Prevailing Methods before 1980,* ed. Stanley E. Porter and Sean A. Adams (Eugene, OR: Pickwick, 2016), 163–88. Zahn's New Testament theology is *Grundriss der Neutestamentlichen Theologie*, 2nd ed. (Leipzig: A. Deichertsche Verlagsbuchhandlung D. Werner Scholl, 1932). Schlatter's two-volume New Testament theology appeared first around 1910, was updated in the early 1920s, and was finally translated in the 1990s by Andreas Köstenberger in the two volumes *The History of the Christ* and *The Theology of the Apostles* (Grand Rapids: Baker, 1997–1998).

[32] A classic nineteenth-century example was H. J. Holtzmann, *Lehrbuch der Neutestamentlichen Theologie*, 2 vols. (Freiburg/Leipzig: Akademische Verlagsbuchhandlung von J. C. B. Mohr [Paul Siebeck], 1897).

[33] Typified by H. Weinel, *Biblische Theologie des Neuen Testaments. Die Religion Jesu und des Urchristentums,* 3rd ed. (Tübingen: J. C. B. Mohr [Paul Siebeck], 1921).

[34] See Rudolf Bultmann, *Theologie des Neuen Testaments,* 8th ed. (Tübingen: J. C. B. Mohr, 1980). The first edition was translated and appeared as *Theology of the New Testament,* 2 vols., trans. Kendrick Grobel (New York: Charles Scribner's Sons, 1951–1955).

[35] On Albertz, Cullmann, and Goppelt, see Robert Yarbrough, *The Salvation Historical Fallacy?* (Leiden: Deo, 2004).

[36] See *A Theology of the New Testament,* rev. ed. (Grand Rapids: Eerdmans, 1993).

[37] Oxford: Oxford University Press, 2010.

to be researched, questioned, and reconstructed, but also a theological presence intertwined with that history then and still perceptible in the present.

Recent New Testament theologies in addition to Schreiner's that affirm salvation history, without regarding it as the sole central theme of the New Testament, include those by Frank Thielman, the late I. Howard Marshall, and (more cautiously) Frank Matera.

Frank Thielman's New Testament theology refers to "salvation history" over two dozen times.[38] This emphasis is most evident in the chapter titled "Luke–Acts: The Place of Christians in the Progress of Salvation History."[39] Luke wrote of salvation history to stabilize his readers in the faith and help them attain a social identity that would enable them to persevere despite marginalization by larger and more dominant social entities: "By emphasizing God's saving purpose for Israel and the nations, Luke was able to show his readers that, although marginalized within Greco-Roman society, they occupied an important place in the only society that really mattered—the people of God."[40] Luke presents Jesus in such a way as to underscore "the continuity between Jesus and the inherited tradition in order to show the central place that Jesus occupied in the progress of salvation history."[41] Not only Luke's Gospel but also Acts[42] and all four Gospels "give special emphasis to Jesus's death as an atonement, an exaltation, and a necessary step in the inevitable progress of salvation history."[43]

Thielman also finds salvation history to be central in Paul's thought behind the letters to the Galatians,[44] to the Romans,[45] and to the Colossians.[46] In summarizing Paul's view of the unity of the church, Thielman finds that "Paul has his eye on two events in salvation history," the cross and judgment day.[47] Salvation history also factors into Thielman's reading of Hebrews.[48]

I. Howard Marshall's *New Testament Theology*[49] refers to "history" over seventy times but "salvation history" just eight times.[50] Yet the two emphases are not unrelated. "The framework of Paul's thinking is determined by this

---

[38] Frank Thielman, *Theology of the New Testament* (Grand Rapids: Zondervan, 2005).

[39] Thielman, 111–49.

[40] Thielman, 148.

[41] Thielman, 181. See also 184–85.

[42] Thielman, 205.

[43] Thielman, 206.

[44] Thielman, 266n16, 268.

[45] Thielman, 362, 363n75.

[46] Thielman, 380n18.

[47] Thielman, 451.

[48] Thielman, 600.

[49] I. Howard Marshall, *New Testament Theology: Many Witnesses, One Gospel* (Downers Grove, IL: InterVarsity Press, 2004).

[50] Marshall, 145, 172, 173, 174, 186, 220, 221, 719.

'salvation history,'"[51] by which Marshall understands a theological stress that is not just a story but based on real events. The gospel presentation to which Galatians points is not merely something proclaimed: "The gospel is the interpretation of what happened (Gal 3:1), but it is an interpretation in that it makes plain what happened, or rather, as we might say, 'what really happened.'"[52] Just as salvation history formed the framework of Paul's outlook, there is "an understanding of the progress of salvation history" informing the New Testament in general.[53]

In concluding his New Testament theology, Marshall observes that all of the New Testament writers work within the same Jewish [i.e., drawn from the Old Testament] framework of understanding the world as the creation of God and history as the narrative of the ongoing relationship of God with the people whom he has chosen out of the nations, initially the Jews but then the people, Jewish and Gentile, who have a spiritual relationship with him.[54]

Marshall speaks of the "checkered history of the covenant people" and "the promises that God would make a new start with his people."[55] He points to "a profound continuity between the acts of God in both Testaments."[56] While Marshall is not captivated by the expressions "salvation history," "redemptive history," or some other equivalent, his reading of the New Testament comports significantly with other scholars who stress salvation history by name.

Frank Matera writes in summarizing his entire New Testament theology: "The appearance of certain themes again and again . . . indicates that the authors of the New Testament were aware that they and those for whom they wrote were part of *a history in which God had acted on their behalf.*"[57] The italicized words (emphasis added) encapsulate the key claim of salvation historical understanding. Matera continues, "The recurrent themes of their writings and the events of this *history* provide the foundation for what can be called *'the master story'* of the New Testament."[58] Again, the italicized words (emphasis added) support the conviction that the New Testament's saving message is rooted in events and attesting writings that underlie, overarch, and bring unity to the variegated documents of both Testaments through the story they tell of real matters that happened. To the extent Scripture's claim is true that God's

---

[51] Marshall, *New Testament Theology*, 221.

[52] Marshall, 220.

[53] Marshall, 719.

[54] Marshall, 718.

[55] Marshall, 718–19.

[56] Marshall, 719.

[57] Frank Matera, *New Testament Theology: Exploring Diversity and Unity* (Louisville/London: Westminster John Knox, 2007), 427. See also, e.g., 56, which speaks of "Israel's redemptive history that continues in the life of a reestablished and repentant Israel, the church," and of "Luke's understanding of God's purpose in history."

[58] Matera, 427.

saving work then extends to a horizon that encompasses the perennial human now and future, salvation history is no less relevant to readers around the world in the twentieth-first century than it was to its first witnesses, beneficiaries, and opponents.

## 4. CONCLUDING QUESTION AND OBSERVATIONS

How important is salvation history within a whole-Bible approach to biblical theology? The answer to that question will depend on the convictions and aims of the biblical theologian. If that theologian doubts that the redemptive events recounted in Scripture happened, or that they bear the soteriological weight that biblical writers place on them, then the theologian will gravitate to some other emphasis or thematic center.

It has been shown that about one hundred years ago, salvation historical outlooks were being systematically eliminated from mainstream academic conviction in Germany.[59] This had analogies and effects in North America still observable today.[60] While some scholars may be willing to acknowledge that biblical writers affirmed salvation history, far fewer write from the standpoint of the truth of that history, and from the standpoint of the validity of that history for our own thinking and living. One expert notes, "In retrospect, Germanophone historians of the nineteenth and twentieth centuries suffered from a certain weakness inasmuch as they engaged all too little in explicit reflection on the premises they shared with regard to how history should be written."[61] In their train biblical theologians often did not so much explain the Bible's claims as explain them away.[62]

Today there are scholars (like Thomas Schreiner and other contributors to this volume) convinced of Christ's living Lordship and Scripture's truth, including historical truth as that relates to Scripture's theological assertions. "Biblical theologies" of either or both Testaments are again in order.[63] Elsewhere I have given nine ways that a salvation historical approach to Paul's writings is fruitful;[64] these would all apply equally to whole-Bible theological analysis and

---

[59] Michael Murrmann-Kahl, *Die entzauberte Heilsgeschichte: Der Historismus erobert die Theologie 1880–1920* (Gütersloh: Gütersloher Verlagshaus Gerd Mohn, 1992).

[60] See Legaspi, *The Death of Scripture and the Rise of Biblical Studies*.

[61] Michael Murrmann-Kahl, "Historiography. B. Modern Europe," in Dale Allison Jr. et al., eds., *Encyclopedia of the Bible and Its Reception* (Berlin/Boston: De Gruyter, 2015), 11:1149.

[62] For reflection on this problem and ruminations on better solutions, see Roland Deines, "God's Role in History as a Methodological Problem for Exegesis," in Deines, *Acts of God in History*, 1–26.

[63] See, e.g., G. K. Beale, *A New Testament Biblical Theology: The Unfolding of the Old Testament in the New* (Grand Rapids: Baker Academic, 2011).

[64] See Yarbrough, "Salvation History (*Heilsgeschichte*) and Paul," in Harmon and Smith, eds., *Studies in the Pauline Epistles*, 192–97: a salvation historical approach can (1) claim consistency with the world view and theological convictions of many biblical writers; (2) claim fidelity to Jesus's convictions about God's presence, work, and authority (including authority-through-Scripture) in the world; (3) interact openly with and

synthesis. It is entirely possible and necessary for "biblical theology" of various descriptions to be plied without making salvation history the central focus. It is, however, important that it not be ignored (like skeptics might), radically reinterpreted (like the Gnostics of old), or devalued (like even well-meaning pious readers might who stress "spiritual" or devotional meaning, or pragmatic "application," to the exclusion of the relevance of Scripture's own historical context and claims).

We might say that salvation history is the sap that nourishes the tree of today's studies on biblical theology. Whatever types of tree, whatever fruit they bear, if they are healthy and growing, they will benefit readers most by full appropriation of the richly flowing substance of salvation history.

---

draw freely from mainstream biblical scholarship; (4) interact openly with and draw freely from confessional Christian bodies (the church); (5) capitalize on the self-defeating tendencies of successive "critical" schools of thought; (6) offer models for positive linkage of Old Testament and New Testament generally lost to mainstream biblical scholarship; (7) move "conservative" interpreters beyond questions of historicity to issues of theology, ethics, ecclesiology, and other matters; (8) offer resources for Christian interpretation in the growing world church that needs to account for Western academic readings of Scripture (often hostile to historic Christianity) and also needs to feed the flock with the Word of God understood with the aid of sound scholarship; and (9) give reflective Christians a sense of heritage as sons and daughters of Abraham (Gal 3:7), heirs according to promise (Gal 3:29), members of the household of God (Eph 2:19; 1 Tim 3:15) and of the faith delivered once for all to the saints (Jude 3), in history and through history and for history.

*Chapter 5*

# Canonical Biblical Theology

*by James M. Hamilton Jr.*

The setting was a PhD seminar on 1 Peter, and the discussion had turned to 1 Pet 1:10–12. Leading the seminar, Dr. Thomas R. Schreiner commented that in the New Testament the apostles model correct interpretation of the Old. I had been steeped in the view that only the inspiration of the Holy Spirit validated the New Testament's interpretation of the Old,[1] the clear implication being that apart from the inspiration of the Spirit the New Testament's interpretation of the Old could never be regarded as either valid or normative. Because the New Testament's interpretation of the Old was not valid, it could not be normative: no one not inspired by the Holy Spirit should interpret the OT the way the NT authors do. This view seemed so pervasive and obvious to me that when Dr. Schreiner said, in an offhand way, that we should follow the example of the NT authors, I almost fell out of my chair. When he asked why I had reacted so violently, I replied that I had never heard anyone legitimate say such a thing. With characteristic humility, Tom replied, "Maybe I'm not legitimate!" He then told me to go read Beale's "Right Doctrine from the Wrong Text"[2] essay. Around that time, Schreiner himself was at work on his theology of Paul, which he graciously allowed me to read in prepublication form.[3]

---

[1] See, e.g., Richard N. Longenecker, *Biblical Exegesis in the Apostolic Period*, 2nd ed. (Grand Rapids: Eerdmans, 1999).

[2] G. K. Beale, "Did Jesus and His Followers Preach the Right Doctrine from the Wrong Texts? An Examination of the Presuppositions of Jesus's and the Apostles' Exegetical Method," in *The Right Doctrine from the Wrong Texts? Essays on the Use of the Old Testament in the New*, ed. G. K. Beale (Grand Rapids: Baker, 1994), 387–404.

[3] Thomas R. Schreiner, *Paul, Apostle of God's Glory in Christ: A Pauline Theology* (Downers Grove, IL: InterVarsity Press, 2001).

It was as though Dr. Schreiner had shown me the trailhead of an enchanted path through a tangled forest. At that formative moment he not only took me to the starting point but provided a faithful example in his own life and teaching, making progress through the thickets while shepherding others. As Dr. Schreiner was supervising me and others in the PhD program, churning out his own books and articles, he was also my pastor, boldly preaching God's word at Clifton Baptist Church. I was becoming acquainted with the nettles and brambles of scholarly discussions, the vagaries of the academic way through the forest with its overgrown vines and rotted out bridges, and many a Sunday I wondered how Dr. Schreiner would handle the biblical text from the pulpit in light of all the surrounding issues. The man took his stand behind the sacred desk, opened the light-giving book, and preached like a Christian, like one whose heart has been broken and mended by the gospel, like one whose eyes have glimpsed the glory, whose tongue has tasted living water. He took the faithful way, the way believers through the years have gone.[4]

Dr. Schreiner showed me the path's starting point: the idea that the New Testament has correctly interpreted the Old. He taught me skills necessary for moving through the forest, demonstrating through his own practice, walking with me, then sending me on my own supervised foray. Over the years we have continued to explore the mysterious wood together. We agree on almost everything. I am a grateful student who has learned much from a faithful master. Tom Schreiner was my teacher and pastor, training me at Southern Seminary, shepherding me at Clifton Baptist Church, inspiring me with his example of scholarly productivity in publication. In terms of my own vocation, no one has influenced me more, and I seek to follow in his footsteps as a teacher and pastor.

At some points, however, we disagree, if only in emphasis. These disagreements likely result from my lack of nuance and wisdom, but there are places where we would take a different fork or attempt to surmount some obstacle in different ways.

One such disagreement is the respective significance we would attach to the arrangement of the books of the Old Testament.[5] This question is obviously not a life or death issue. Whatever view someone takes on the order of the OT books, he can be saved by grace through faith in the creating and redeeming triune God who sent his Son to die on the cross to pay the penalty for sin, as prophesied, narrated, and expounded in the inerrant word of God. Moreover, where one comes down on this question has no bearing on who gets baptized or

---

[4] See the trenchant critique of post-enlightenment biblical scholarship in Craig A. Carter, *Interpreting Scripture with the Great Tradition: Recovering the Genius of Premodern Exegesis* (Grand Rapids: Baker, 2018).
[5] For a review of scholarly discussion of this topic, see Stephen Dempster, "An 'Extraordinary Fact': Torah and Temple and the Contours of the Hebrew Canon, Part 1," *Tyndale Bulletin* 48 (1997): 23–56, esp. 23–49.

how,[6] nor does it affect who can partake of the Lord's supper.[7] This discussion, then, is a dialogue among friends on the best approach to the interpretation of the Old Testament. The positions Dr. Schreiner and I have taken can be seen in our respective attempts at whole-Bible biblical theology. In *God's Glory in Salvation through Judgment: A Biblical Theology*,[8] I go book by book through the whole Bible, and in the Old Testament I follow the tripartite Law–Prophets–Writings arrangement of the OT books. In Schreiner's *The King and His Beauty: A Biblical Theology of the Old and New Testaments*,[9] he follows the order of the Old Testament books found in modern English translations.

In fact, it is with a statement Dr. Schreiner makes in *The King and His Beauty* that I want to dispute in this essay in his honor. Schreiner writes,

> [M]y goal in this book is to unpack the canonical writings in their final form. We are still faced with an important decision with regard to the OT. Should the canon be explored in terms of its Hebrew order or the Christian order? Some regard this issue to be of major importance, but its significance is exaggerated. In my judgment, the central themes of OT theology are not affected dramatically whether one follows the Hebrew order or the order used in English translations. I am assuming here that the ordinary reader of English who is not even aware of the Hebrew order is at no disadvantage in trying to understand the theology of the OT. Therefore, in this book I follow the English order.[10]

I have already agreed with several points Schreiner makes here: one need not know the Hebrew order to be saved, and big themes of the OT can be understood without reference to it. I want to contend, however, that the Law–Prophets–Writings order *should be taught to all Christians* because Jesus himself made statements that cannot be understood apart from knowledge of the Hebrew order. This fact makes the Hebrew order important even for ordinary Christians reading the Bible translated into their mother tongue. If we are to be about the Great Commission work of making disciples and teaching them everything Jesus commanded (Matt 28:18–20), those disciples will need the Hebrew order of the books to understand certain statements Jesus made. I further contend that the available evidence indicates that the final form of the OT canon *extends* to the order of the books.

---

[6] See Schreiner's contribution to this discussion in Thomas R. Schreiner and Shawn D. Wright, eds., *Believer's Baptism: Sign of the New Covenant in Christ*, NAC Studies in Bible and Theology (Nashville: B&H, 2006).

[7] Here again Schreiner has served us: Thomas R. Schreiner and Matthew R. Crawford, eds., *The Lord's Supper: Remembering and Proclaiming Christ Until He Comes* (Nashville: B&H, 2010).

[8] James M. Hamilton, *God's Glory in Salvation through Judgment: A Biblical Theology* (Wheaton: Crossway, 2010).

[9] Thomas R. Schreiner, *The King in His Beauty: A Biblical Theology of the Old and New Testaments* (Grand Rapids: Baker, 2013).

[10] Schreiner, xv–xvi.

In honor of Dr. Thomas R. Schreiner, therefore, and in deep gratitude for his influence and ongoing friendship, I am going to argue, as Tom Schreiner taught me, that the New Testament authors teach us how to interpret the Old, and that this includes their approach to the organization of the books of the Old Testament.

I have argued that biblical theology is best approached as an attempt to understand and embrace the interpretive perspective of the biblical authors,[11] and this essay focuses on one aspect of that interpretive perspective, which can be framed in the form of a question: what assumptions did Jesus and his Apostles make about the arrangement of the books of the Old Testament? We will begin by attempting to answer that question from the New Testament before seeking to show that the assumptions made by Jesus and his followers are firmly supported by the final form of the Old Testament itself.

This essay is titled "Canonical Biblical Theology" for two main reasons: first, because to approach the biblical canon seeking the intent of its authors *extends* not only to the arrangement of the psalms in the Psalter and the minor Prophets in the Twelve but also to the organization of the whole collection that comprises the final form of the Old Testament; second, because the impetus for approaching the books in Law-Prophets-Writings order arises from within the canon itself: from the words of Jesus in the New Testament.[12]

As a consequence of these realities, I contend that *all Christian printings of the Old Testament should put the books in the tripartite Hebrew order (Law–Prophets–Writings)* because of the following two facts, which it is my purpose here to demonstrate. First, the authors of the New Testament themselves both assume the Hebrew order of the books of the OT and take for granted that their audience will also know that order. And second, the final form of the OT itself appears to have been carefully arranged and put into this particular order.

## THE OLD TESTAMENT CANON OF THE NEW TESTAMENT CHURCH[13]

Luke presents Jesus saying, "everything written about me in the Law of Moses and the Prophets and the Psalms must be fulfilled" (Luke 24:44b

---

[11] James M. Hamilton, *What Is Biblical Theology?* (Wheaton: Crossway, 2014).

[12] See further James M. Hamilton, *With the Clouds of Heaven: The Book of Daniel in Biblical Theology*, New Studies in Biblical Theology (Downers Grove, IL: InterVarsity Press, 2014), 27–30.

[13] I am deeply indebted to Roger T. Beckwith, *The Old Testament Canon of the New Testament Church and Its Background in Early Judaism* (Grand Rapids: Eerdmans, 1985). For an unconvincing attempt to suggest that there was no fixed canon by the time of Jesus, see Lee Martin McDonald, *The Biblical Canon: Its Origin, Transmission, and Authority* (Peabody: Hendrickson, 2007), e.g., 223. McDonald includes in his book an essay that unsuccessfully attempts to undermine Beckwith's credibility: R. Timothy McLay, "The Use of the Septuagint in the New Testament," in McDonald, 224–40. Unable to otherwise overcome Beckwith's magisterial treatment, McLay resorts to name-calling, casting upon Beckwith the aspersion of having

ESV).[14] If Jesus is on record with a statement about how he views the organization of the books of the Old Testament, why would his followers organize the OT any other way?[15] I recognize that sincere followers of Jesus *have* organized the OT in different ways than their master did, but should not following Jesus—taking every thought captive to the knowledge of him (2 Cor 10:5)—extend to the mental conception of the ordering of the Old Testament materials?

When Jesus spoke the words cited above, and when Luke recorded them in his Gospel, available technology made it impossible to put the whole of the Old Testament on one scroll or in one codex.[16] The onionskin paper on which modern Bibles are printed had not been invented. Still, those who cared for such things had to organize the individual scrolls, both for storage and for a mental accounting of the material.[17]

Several observations can be made from the words of Jesus in Luke 24:44b. First, he employs the tripartite divisions of the Old Testament canon that would have been universally accepted at the time: we see it in the prologue of Sirach, at Qumran, in rabbinic writings, and in the New Testament.[18] Jesus took this order for granted in his teaching.

In the words of Luke 24:44, Jesus clearly means to refer to the whole of the Old Testament.[19] If people knew the Hebrew order of the books of the OT, they would immediately see this for themselves. As things currently stand, like many others, my own children have memorized a song that gives them the order of the OT books in English translations, and as a result they need an explanation of what Jesus says in Luke 24:44. *The ordering of the OT books*

---

presuppositions and depending upon the confessional stance of his readers (McDonald, 228). Does McLay himself not have presuppositions? Do not all authors? Who is a blank slate?

[14] Unless otherwise noted, all Scripture citations in this chapter are ESV. Note Roger T. Beckwith, "Formation of the Hebrew Bible," in *Mikra: Text, Translation, Reading & Interpretation of the Hebrew Bible in Ancient Judaism & Early Christianity*, ed. Martin Jan Mulder, Compendia Rerum Iudaicarum Ad Novum Testamentum (Peabody: Hendrickson, 2004), 658: "A tripartite division of Scripture, not unlike that of Josephus and Philo, is also attributed to Jesus in Luke 24:44."

[15] I refer here to an official organization of the OT books in canonical order as in the printing of a Bible, not to something like what E. Earle Ellis indicates was done with the early codices that included the OT in Greek translation and the NT. As he puts it in "The Old Testament Canon in the Early Church," in *Mikra*, Mulder, 678: "No two Septuagint codices contain the same apocrypha, and no uniform Septuagint 'Bible' was ever the subject of discussion in the patristic church. In view of these facts the Septuagint codices appear to have been originally intended more as service books than as a defined and normative canon of Scripture." Similarly Beckwith, *Old Testament Canon*, 195: "the Septuagint manuscripts appear simply to reflect the reading habits of the early church."

[16] See Larry W. Hurtado, *The Earliest Christian Artifacts: Manuscripts and Christian Origins* (Grand Rapids: Eerdmans, 2006).

[17] See Dempster, "An 'Extraordinary Fact,'" 44–45.

[18] See the prologue to Sirach, lines 8–10; 4QMMT, line 10 (4Q397, Frags. 14–21); *Baba Bathra* 14b; Luke 24:44.

[19] See esp. Beckwith, *Old Testament Canon*, 111–15.

*in English translations makes understanding Luke 24:44 more difficult for English readers.* Granted that an uninitiated reader might not immediately arrive at the conclusion that Jesus means to refer to the whole of the OT even if the OT books were in that order, at least the evidence would be there for that reader to use to arrive at the conclusion. Further, *the explanation of Luke 24:44 would be easier if the OT books were in the Hebrew order.* Instead of having to explain the different order, teachers could simply point out the order, and by ordering the books the way Jesus clearly thought of them, Bible publishers make the meaning of Luke 24:44 seem less foreign.

Not only did the Lord reference the tripartite order of the Old Testament in Luke 24:44, he also assumed it when he spoke of all the martyrs from Abel to Zechariah (Matt 23:35//Luke 11:51). Luke presents Jesus telling one insulted by his teaching that those opposed to him will fill up the measure of their sins "so that the blood of all the prophets, shed from the foundation of the world, may be charged against this generation, from the blood of Abel to the blood of Zechariah, who perished between the altar and the sanctuary" (Luke 11:50–51 ESV). Genesis 4 narrates Abel's murder and 2 Chronicles 24 that of Zechariah. Jesus referenced "the blood of all the prophets," so he seems to employ a merism, in which mention of the first and last martyrs summarizes them all. This only works, however, if the book that tells of the stoning of Zechariah is placed where it was in the imagination of the Lord Jesus: at the end of the OT canon.

On at least these two occasions, in order to understand what Jesus meant, readers of the Gospel narratives must be aware of the tripartite order of the Hebrew canon. Jesus stopped to explain that canon on neither occasion. He felt no need to elaborate *either* on the threefold summary of the whole of the Old Testament *or* on the way that Abel and Zechariah are the first and last martyrs when the books are approached in a certain order. In his own day, Jesus could do this because everyone in his audience would share his assumptions about the arrangement of the Old Testament books. It is also noteworthy that neither Luke nor Matthew added any explanatory comments.

Matthew and Luke obviously wanted their audiences to understand what Jesus said. Like their master, they assumed that there was no need to explain the tripartite division of the books of the Old Testament.

Unfortunately, modern English translations universally order the books of the Old Testament in a way that obscures the meaning of what Jesus said on these two occasions. The sooner Bible publishers begin to print copies of the Bible with the OT in the only order acknowledged by Jesus the better.[20]

---

[20] See the claims of Christopher Seitz, "Canon, Narrative, and the Old Testament's Literal Sense: A Response to John Goldingay, 'Canon and Old Testament Theology,'" *Tyndale Bulletin* 59 (2008): 28–29: "In actual fact, the only order that settles down in the history of the Old Testament's reception is the tripartite of

# THE ORDER OF THE OLD TESTAMENT ITSELF

To this point I have argued that Jesus assumed the tripartite, Law-Prophets-Writings, order of the books of the Old Testament. This order breaks down as follows: five books of Moses—the Torah; four Former Prophets and four Latter Prophets; and the Writings consisting of three groups of material—a set of three books, a set of five books, and a set of three books. The material is easy to remember when ordered this way: the books are enumerated as five, two sets of four, followed by a set of three-five-three:

**Five books of Torah:**   Genesis, Exodus, Leviticus, Numbers, Deuteronomy

**Four Former Prophets:**   Joshua, Judges, Samuel, Kings

**Four Latter Prophets:**   Isaiah, Jeremiah, Ezekiel, the Twelve[21]

**The Writings in 3/5/3:**

    **3:** Psalms, Proverbs, Job

    **5:** Ruth, Song of Songs, Ecclesiastes, Lamentations, Esther

    **3:** Daniel, Ezra–Nehemiah, Chronicles

Note that several books referred to as 1 and 2 are counted as one: Samuel, Kings, Ezra, Nehemiah, and Chronicles.

The five small scrolls are easily remembered by a chiasm[22] with the two books about weddings first and last, the best and worst songs second and second to last, and Ecclesiastes in the middle:

    Ruth

        Song of Songs

            Ecclesiastes

        Lamentations

    Esther

---

the Hebrew order (with some minor movement in the writings). . . . What we find when we look at lists from antiquity is that there simply is no such thing as 'a Greek order' (or 'a Latin order' based upon a Greek order). The so-called 'fourfold order', such as we find in modern printed Bibles, has no single or obvious exemplar in the history of the Bible's reception. . . . The convention of modern printed Bibles, with a fourfold order, is just that: a convention, and it has no known exemplar before the modern period."

[21] Beckwith, *Old Testament Canon*, 121–27, 154–62, 209, argues that the order in *Baba Bathra* 14b, placing Jeremiah first among the Latter Prophets, is the oldest. The great Masoretic Codices Aleppo and B19A, however, evidence the order listed here, indicating that the Talmudic order was not viewed as definitive. See further below on the order of the Writings.

[22] I first encountered this in Timothy J. Stone, *The Compilational History of the Megilloth: Canon, Contoured Intertextuality and Meaning in the Writings*, Forschungen Zum Alten Testament (Tübingen: Mohr Siebeck, 2013), 206–7. Stone further writes, "I am not arguing that the MT order is original. It *does* appear to be the oldest surviving order in the Hebrew tradition. *BB* 14b appears to have developed from the MT order" (Stone, 4), and against the suggestion that the MT order is a later liturgical development he demonstrates its antiquity (Stone, *passim*).

We now turn our attention to inductive evidence from the Old Testament itself. My appeal to this evidence does not explain how it came to exist, only that it points to the tripartite order as having been intended by the Old Testament canonicler.[23] To clarify, some scholars suggest that the kind of evidence to which I am about to draw attention shows that a final editor, a canonicler, has stitched the Old Testament together. That much the evidence may indeed establish, but the question is how intrusive this canonicler was. Did he introduce material into the Old Testament, adding link words in key locations, perhaps even writing key verses? Or did he notice key terms that were already present and strategically arrange the material in light of existing statements, meaning to draw more attention to the statements by means of his arrangement of them.[24]

Either way, for the believing community to recognize the work of this proposed canonicler *as Scripture*, for them to embrace it as God's authoritative word to be memorized, meditated upon, obeyed, and passed on to coming generations, that believing community must have recognized the canonicler as one who had the authority to present God's word to them. In other words, *the reception of the Old Testament canon makes it likely that the believing community viewed the person or group of persons who put the books of the Old Testament into canonical form as prophets inspired by the Holy Spirit.*[25] This alone accounts for the canonical Old Testament's universal acceptance among all the various groups of Jews in the ancient world, from Philo to Josephus to the Essenes at

---

[23] For the term "canonicler," see John H. Sailhamer, *Introduction to Old Testament Theology: A Canonical Approach* (Grand Rapids: Zondervan, 1995), 240. I will refer to a "canonicler," but the canon could have been finalized either by an individual prophet or a team of prophets. David Noel Freedman writes, "We attribute the conception and execution to the Scribe Ezra and Governor Nehemiah, who may have worked partly in tandem, but also in sequence, with Ezra responsible chiefly for the conception and Nehemiah for the execution and completion of the project," in "The Symmetry of the Hebrew Bible," *Studia Theologica* 46 (1992): 105. As he was likely a contemporary of Ezra and Nehemiah, Micah could have been involved in the great work as well.

[24] Stone, *Compilational History of the Megilloth*, 23, writes concerning this question: "The redaction critic accounts for the intertextual connections by attributing them to the work of redactors; others claim compilers merely arranged the books to exploit or highlight pre-existing intertextual connections." I agree with the "others" Stone mentions.

[25] Compare the statements in 1 Macc 4:46; 9:27; and 14:41 that there was no prophet on the scene, nor does the author of 1 Maccabees claim to have arisen to fill the void. Similarly, the prologue to Sirach acknowledges that it does not belong with the "the Law and the Prophets and the others that followed them" but comments on that authoritative material, and in 2 Bar 85:1–3 "the prophets have fallen asleep." The point here is that these ancient authors *recognized* the distinction between Spirit-inspired prophecy and their own writings. For the view that "we can see that Hellenistic Judaism had a relatively well defined canon of 'Holy Scripture' already in the second century BC," see Robert Hanhart, "Introduction: Problems in the History of the LXX Text from Its Beginnings to Origen," in Martin Hengel, *The Septuagint as Christian Scripture*, trans. Mark E. Biddle (Grand Rapids: Baker, 2002), 1–17 (quote from 2). See further James M. Hamilton, "Still Sola Scriptura: An Evangelical View of Scripture," in *The Sacred Text: Excavating the Texts, Exploring the Interpretations, and Engaging the Theologies of the Christian Scriptures*, ed. Michael Bird and Michael W. Pahl (Piscataway: Gorgias, 2010), 224–28.

Qumran to the Pharisees to Jesus and his followers. The universal recognition that God spoke by his Spirit in a book separated it from the "sectarian compositions" accepted only in the circles that produced them.[26]

The link words and connections at seams we will consider here comprise the kind of evidence that has convinced many that the twelve so-called minor Prophets have been strategically arranged to form "The Book of the Twelve."[27] Similarly, this kind of evidence has convinced many that the 150 canonical psalms have been artfully ordered so that the Psalter has an impressionistic movement of thought, a sort of storyline that unfolds across the linked-up message, whereby the whole communicates more than the parts considered in isolation.[28]

What scholars have seen in the Twelve and the Psalter can likewise be discerned in the whole of the Old Testament canon: namely, that the parts and units have been purposefully organized so that the message of the whole communicates more than could be gleaned from the parts in isolation.[29] If the books of the Old Testament have indeed been strategically arranged, then to put the books in a different order is to conceal the macromessage intended by the canonicler.

I do not have chapter and verse for the claim that the canonicler was inspired by the Holy Spirit, but I suggest that the same argument used to recognize individual books of the Bible as inspired by the Holy Spirit applies to the final form of the Old Testament canon. That is, because the people of God *recognized* a book as the word of God and received it as authoritative, and because *the New Testament endorsed these books as Scripture*, we believe that in

---

[26] Here I adapt an argument made by Beckwith about the universal acceptance of the book of Daniel in *Old Testament Canon*, 357–58; for "The Witness of the OT to Its Own Canonicity," see Hamilton, "Evangelical View of Scripture," 220–23.

[27] See, e.g., Christopher R. Seitz, *The Goodly Fellowship of the Prophets: The Achievement of Association in Canon Formation* (Grand Rapids: Baker, 2009); James D. Nogalski and Marvin A. Sweeney, eds., *Reading and Hearing the Book of the Twelve* (Atlanta: Society of Biblical Literature, 2000); and Paul R. House, *The Unity of the Twelve*, Bible and Literature Series 27 (Sheffield, England: Almond Press, 1990).

[28] See Gordon J. Wenham, *Psalms as Torah: Reading Biblical Song Ethically* (Grand Rapids: Baker, 2012); Wenham, *The Psalter Reclaimed: Praying and Praising with the Psalms* (Wheaton: Crossway, 2013); along with Frank-Lothar Hossfeld and Erich Zenger, *Psalms 2: A Commentary on Psalms 51–100*, Hermeneia (Minneapolis: Fortress, 2005); and Frank-Lothar Hossfeld and Erich Zenger, *Psalms 3: A Commentary on Psalms 101–150*, Hermeneia (Minneapolis: Fortress, 2011).

[29] As argued in different ways by Stephen G. Dempster, *Dominion and Dynasty: A Biblical Theology of the Hebrew Bible*, New Studies in Biblical Theology (Downers Grove, IL: InterVarsity Press, 2003); David Noel Freedman, *The Unity of the Hebrew Bible* (Ann Arbor: University of Michigan Press, 1991); and John H. Sailhamer, *The Meaning of the Pentateuch: Revelation, Composition and Interpretation* (Downers Grove, IL: InterVarsity Press, 2009).

them God speaks.[30] Jesus himself endorsed the tripartite order of the books of the Old Testament (Luke 24:44).

We turn our attention to an inductive consideration of the evidence from key terms and phrases at the OT canon's seams.[31]

The Torah opens with world-making words. God speaks all creation into existence. The Bible is meant to be a mind-building book in the sense that its presentation intends to shape the way people think about God, the world, and life.[32] The Torah likewise closes with a focus on God's word, as Deut 34:10–12 looks back to the Lord's promise to raise up a prophet like Moses in Deut 18:15 and put his words in that prophet's mouth in 18:18.

The Torah thus starts with God speaking and finishes looking forward to God's promised spokesperson.

| Beginning of Torah | End of Torah |
|---|---|
| Genesis 1 | Deut 34:10–12 (18:15, 18) |
| God speaks creation into existence | God's promised spokesperson |

The beginning of the Former Prophets links up with the end of the Torah, stitching the two bodies of material together by means of the reference to the death of Moses in the first line of Joshua (Josh 1:1), which had just been narrated at the end of Deuteronomy (Deut 34:5–7). Yahweh tells Joshua that he will be with him just as he was with Moses (Josh 1:5), commands him to be strong in the language of Deuteronomy (Josh 1:6–7; Deut 31:6), and tells him that day and night meditation on Torah will *cause him success* (תשכיל, Josh 1:7, 8) and *give him prosperity* (תצליח, Josh 1:8). This statement at the beginning of the Former Prophets in Joshua links up with the beginning of Torah, where the serpent told the woman that disobedience to God's word would *cause her success* (להשכיל, Gen 3:6).

---

[30] For a concise summary of the argument, see Roger T. Beckwith, "The Canon of the Old Testament," in *The ESV Study Bible* (Wheaton: Crossway, 2008), 2577–579.

[31] In addition to my own study, I have been helped to see this evidence by Stephen Dempster "An 'Extraordinary Fact': Torah and Temple and the Contours of the Hebrew Canon: Part 2," *Tyndale Bulletin* 48 (1997): 191–218 ; John Sailhamer, "Creation, Genesis 1–11, and the Canon," *Bulletin for Biblical Research* 10 (2000): 89–106; and Sailhamer *Meaning of the Pentateuch*.

[32] David M. Carr, *Writing on the Tablet of the Heart: Origins of Scripture and Literature* (New York: Oxford University Press, 2005), 10, 157–58, writes, "the Old Testament is a countercurriculum to that of Hellenistic education. Texts that originally had been formed for a scribal curriculum came to serve a broader purpose in shaping the minds and hearts of Israelite males in general." He later explains, "This book . . . is proposing to understand most ancient literature as primarily instructional-enculturational literature. . . . Day after day, year after year, [they] would have ingested Israelite stories of creation, prophecies, psalms, and wisdom."

| Beginning of Torah | End of Torah | Beginning of Prophets |
|---|---|---|
| Gen 3:6 (שׂכל) | | Josh 1:7–8 (שׂכל) |
| | Deuteronomy 31, 34 | Josh 1:1–8 |
| | Whole Torah | Remember Torah, Josh 1:7–8 |

Dempster argues that this evidence betrays the work of an editorial hand.[33] If an editor created these connections, however, we would expect to find verbal links between the beginning and end of the Former Prophets, verbal links that, as far as I can tell, do not exist. If an editor were stitching things together, why wouldn't he run the Joshua 1 threads through the closing statements of 2 Kings 25? It seems more plausible to me, therefore, that the editor has not *generated* these verbal connections. Rather, the evidence suggests that he *noticed* connections and arranged the material to highlight them.[34] Where there were no connections—as there are not between Joshua 1 and 2 Kings 25—he did not create them, perhaps respecting sentiments like those stated in Deut 4:2, which warns against adding to or taking from the word (see also Deut 13:32).

| Beginning of Former Prophets | End of Former Prophets |
|---|---|
| *nothing* | *nothing* |

Similar comments can be made about the beginning of the Latter Prophets, where we find no verbal links between the beginning of Joshua, the end of 2 Kings, and the beginning of Isaiah. Some suggest an ordering that places Jeremiah first among the Latter Prophets, but even there we do not find link words as we have in other places.[35] The first chapters of Isaiah and Jeremiah do engage earlier Scripture, and plenty of it, and both Isaiah and Jeremiah present themselves as prophets like Moses (Deut 18:15, 18). The lack of link words, however, sounds like the dog that didn't bark. That is to say, I take the absence of link words to point to a light editorial hand, one that does not add to or take away from the texts as it arranges them in accordance with trajectories that have already been developing as the Scriptures were written and preserved through the centuries.

---

[33] Dempster, "An 'Extraordinary Fact,'" 192: "a deliberate editorial strategy," similarly 199, "a contextualising redaction," and see 205, where both phrases occur again.

[34] I have argued the same regarding the connections between the Twelve in *God's Glory in Salvation through Judgment*, 229–31.

[35] Dempster, *Dominion and Dynasty*, 159–60 writes, "Jeremiah 1 (vv. 4, 10, 16) has linguistic ties with 2 Kings 25 (vv. 6, 10, 11, 21); and the ending of Jeremiah (ch. 52) virtually repeats the last chapter of Kings. But the conceptual connections are more important..." The "linguistic ties" to which Dempster alludes pale in comparison to the links between Deuteronomy and Joshua, and the conceptual ties work as well for Isaiah as for Jeremiah. If a redactor was at work here, he did his work so subtly that it escapes notice.

| Beginning/End of Former Prophets | Beginning of Latter Prophets |
|:---:|:---:|
| *nothing* | *nothing* |

We do find a significant lexical connection between the beginning of the Former Prophets (Joshua) and the end of the Latter Prophets (Malachi). The phrase "Moses, my servant" (משה עבדי) occurs only three times in the whole of the Hebrew Bible, at Josh 1:2, 7, and Mal 4:4 (MT 3:22).[36] This connection ties together the opening and closing words of Prophets, Former and Latter, and the end of Malachi further urges people to remember the Torah of Moses (Mal 4:4 [MT 3:22]) even as it promises a new prophet Elijah (Mal 4:5 [MT 3:23]), which seems to point to fulfillment of the expectation for *the* prophet like Moses (Deut 18:15, 18; 34:10–12).

The end of Malachi not only links up with the beginning of Joshua, it also summons readers to the first two sections of the canonical collection. The command to remember the Torah of Moses obviously points people to his books (Mal 4:4 [MT 3:22]), and the reference to Elijah the prophet (Mal 4:5 [MT 3:23]) recalls a prominent figure narrated in the Former Prophets whose ministry was like that of those in the Latter Prophets, a ministry of applying the Torah of Moses, as prophets like Moses, to Israel's ongoing life (see also Zech 7:11–12).

| Beginning of Former Prophets | End of Latter Prophets |
|:---|:---|
| Josh 1:2, 7 | Mal 4:4 |
| Whole Torah and Prophets | Zech 7:11–12; Mal 4:4–5 |

The statements in Malachi 4:5 subtly refer to the Former and Latter Prophets. Here again if an editor were adding statements to existing texts, he could have made things much more explicit. More likely, it would seem, is a scenario that entails Malachi himself recognizing that he stands at or near the end of a long line of prophets, that his book contributes to a developing collection of material, and that he understands how that material has already begun to be arranged. Perhaps Malachi knew, or worked on a team with, Ezra and Nehemiah. Malachi could himself have led or been the last surviving member of such a team, canonicler(s) who put the Old Testament into its final form. In such a scenario, Malachi was inspired to write what his book contains, and he could have continued to experience the Spirit's guidance as he thought through, perhaps with Ezra and Nehemiah, the best way to arrange the whole of the Scriptural collection.

---

[36] A point brought to my attention by Dempster, "An 'Extraordinary Fact,'" 191.

We have seen connections between:

- the beginning and end of Torah (Genesis 1, Deuteronomy 34)

- the end of Torah and the beginning of the Former Prophets (Deuteronomy 34, Joshua 1)

- the beginning of Torah and the beginning of the Former Prophets (Genesis 3, Joshua 1)

- the beginning of the Former Prophets and the end of the Latter Prophets (Joshua 1, Malachi 4)

- the end of the Former Prophets and the Torah and Prophets (Malachi 4, Moses and Elijah)

We now turn to consider the Writings, where we find significant links between the opening statements of the Writings (Psalm 1) and the beginning of the Former Prophets (Joshua 1). Before proceeding, in view of the different orders of the books in the Writings, we should consider this matter briefly. Timothy Stone writes:

> if one records arrangements for the Writings up to and including the sixteenth century C.E., there are many orders. If, however, one considers only arrangements *earlier* than the twelfth century, then, based on available historical information, there are only two remaining orders in the Jewish tradition: the Talmudic, found in *Baba Batra* 14b (hereafter *BB* 14b), and the Masoretic (hereafter MT), in the Aleppo and Leningrad codices.[37]

Here are the two orders:

| BB 14b | Ruth | Ps | Job | Pro | Eccl | Song | Lam | Dan | Esth | Ez/ Ne | Chr |
|---|---|---|---|---|---|---|---|---|---|---|---|
| MT | Chr | Ps | Job | Pro | Ruth | Song | Eccl | Lam | Esth | Dan | Ez/ Ne |

The very obvious link words at the beginning of Psalms convince me that it should be listed first, with Chronicles last, and with Ruth grouped among the five small scrolls (the *Megilloth*). Placing Psalms first is not supported by either of these two ancient traditions, but Chronicles last and the grouping of the *Megilloth* both have ancient support. Neither the antiquity of the tripartite order, nor its endorsement by the Lord Jesus, is undermined by the slight variation in the order of the Latter Prophets and the Writings. There

---

[37] Timothy Stone, *The Compilational History of the Megilloth*, 4.

is a mainstream grouping that very consistently puts the books of the Old Testament in Law, Prophets, and Writings order.[38]

Psalm 1:2 describes the blessed man who meditates on Torah day and night, precisely what Joshua was urged to do in Josh 1:8. Psalm 1:3 speaks of how the blessed man "prospers" (יצלח), precisely what Joshua was promised in Josh 1:8 (תצליח).

Along with the links to the beginning of the Former Prophets, Psalm 1 has more subtle links to the end of the Latter Prophets. The wicked man will be like "chaff" (מץ) in Ps 1:4 and "stubble" (קש) in Mal 4:1 (MT 3:19). The way to avoid that fate is the same in both texts: meditation on the Torah in Ps 1:2; remembering the Torah in Mal 4:4 (MT 3:22). In both texts judgment comes: the wicked will not rise in Ps 1:5, and the day comes burning like an oven in Mal 4:1 (MT 3:19) resulting in utter destruction in 4:6 (MT 3:24).

| Beginning/End of Prophets | Beginning of Writings |
|---|---|
| Josh 1:8 | Ps 1:2–3 |
| Mal 4:1, 4, 6 | Ps 1:3, 5 |

We should note, too, that the emphasis on the Torah in Psalm 1 obviously points back to that section of the canon.

| Torah | Beginning of Writings |
|---|---|
| Torah | Ps 1 |

When Chronicles stands at the end of the Old Testament canon, its summarizing, synthesizing character stands out. The genealogies function like drop down menus, keying memories to the narratives that accompany many of the names in earlier Scripture. The very first name at the beginning of Chronicles, Adam, has obvious links with the beginning of Torah, where Adam was made in Genesis 1. Similarly, the end of Chronicles (2 Chronicles 36) retells events narrated at the end of the Former Prophets (2 Kings 25).

---

[38] Consider Beckwith's, *The Old Testament Canon of the New Testament Church*, 208, observation: "With such variety existing, it might seem that any order was possible, but this is in fact not so. Mathematically speaking, the eight books of the Prophets could be arranged not just in nine different orders but in 40,320, and the eleven books of the Hagiographa not just in seventy different orders but in 39,916,800! Clearly, all the possibilities were not in practice exhausted."

| Torah | Prophets | Writings |
|---|---|---|
| Genesis 1, Adam | | 1 Chronicles 1, Adam |
| | Exile, 2 Kings 25 | Exile, 2 Chronicles 36 |

Considered in this order, the Old Testament tells the story of the creation of the world and the early history of Israel in the Torah, a history that continues down to the exile in the Former Prophets. The Latter Prophets then come on the scene to comment on the Former Prophets from the perspective taught in Torah, and the Writings re-sing the whole song.

## CONCLUSION

Jesus endorsed the tripartite order of the Old Testament (Luke 24:44) and assumed it in his teaching (Luke 11:51). Because Jesus spoke of the Old Testament in these terms, this tripartite order should be considered the truly *Christian* ordering of the books. Any departure from the way Jesus thought about a matter does not deserve to be called Christian, as some are in the habit of doing when referring to the order of the books of the Old Testament in modern English translations. Not only is the tripartite order the one endorsed by Jesus, it is the one universally accepted in Judaism (with slight variations in the order of the Latter Prophets and the Writings).

When we examine the seams of the tripartite order, we find significant points of contact between the three sections, indicating perhaps that a canonicler or a team of prophets arranged the material to draw attention to the significance of God's word, the expectation of a future prophet like Moses, and the hope for a new David who would be a new Adam to bring about the longed-for new exodus and return from exile that God's people might inhabit the fulfillment of the land of promise in the new heaven and new earth.

I praise God for Thomas R. Schreiner, especially for the way that he taught me to see that we should imitate the interpretation of the Old Testament modeled for us in the New. I hope this attempt to apply his insight to the order of the books of the Old Testament has convinced him, and I look forward with gratitude to the ongoing discussion.

# MAJOR THEMES AND ISSUES
# IN BIBLICAL THEOLOGY

*Chapter 6*

# Sanctification for the Magnifying of God in Christ: How God Glorifies His Children for His Own Glory

*by John Piper*

Thomas Schreiner holds a unique place among contemporary biblical scholars. I am unaware of anyone in our day who has more consistently, extensively, or carefully shown that the supremacy of God in Christ is the "most important" reality in Scripture,[1] and that "the reason" for the entire history of redemption, including its ethical implications, is that God "be glorified in all things and by all people."[2] Or, as Schreiner puts it in his *New Testament Theology*, "God's purpose in all that he does is to bring honor to himself and to Jesus Christ. The NT is radically God-centered. We could say that the NT is about God magnifying himself in Christ through the Spirit."[3]

## THOMAS SCHREINER AND JONATHAN EDWARDS

Jonathan Edwards made this case philosophically and exegetically in *The End for Which God Created the World*: "All that is ever spoken of in Scripture as an

---

[1] Thomas Schreiner, *Paul: Apostle of God's Glory in Christ, a Pauline Theology* (Downers Grove, IL: InterVarsity Press, 2001), 15.
[2] Thomas Schreiner, *The King in His Beauty: A Biblical Theology of the Old and New Testaments* (Grand Rapids: Baker Academic, 2013), xiv.
[3] Thomas Schreiner, *New Testament Theology: Magnifying God in Christ* (Grand Rapids: Baker Academic, 2008), 13. Repeated in the condensed version of this book, *Magnifying God in Christ: A Summary of New Testament Theology* (Grand Rapids: Baker Academic, 2010), 16.

ultimate end of God's works, is included in that one phrase, *the glory of God*."[4]
At the end of his life, Edwards wanted to demonstrate this truth in a new kind
of book. He wrote to the College of New Jersey that one of the reasons he
hesitated to accept the call to be president was that

> I have had on my mind and heart ... a great work, which I call a *History of the
> Work of Redemption*, a body of divinity in an entire new method, being thrown
> into the form of a history; ... introducing all parts of divinity in that order which
> is most scriptural and most natural.[5]

Edwards died at the age of fifty-four and never completed the project.
Mercifully, God spared Tom Schreiner in his sixth decade to clarify "the reason" for the story of redemption while unfolding the story itself. "Scripture
unfolds *the story* of the kingdom, and God's glory is *the reason* for the story."[6]

### No Single Theme, One Ultimate Goal

Schreiner is keenly aware that "the centrality of God in Christ leads to abstraction if it is not closely related to the history of salvation." So he invites us to
"consider New Testament theology from a twofold perspective."

First, God's purpose in all that he does is to bring honor to himself and to
Jesus Christ. . . . (Second is the unfolding of how God achieves that purpose
in history.) No one can grasp the message of the New Testament if redemptive
history is slighted. . . . God's ultimate purpose is reflected in the fulfillment of
his plan. . . . God works out his saving plan so that he would be magnified in
Christ, so that his name would be honored.[7]

In unfolding the story of redemption, Schreiner does not argue that a
single "theme" or "center" can shed sufficient light on all of Scripture. "It is
common consensus that no one theme adequately captures the message of the
Scriptures."[8] He makes clear that the glory of God—the majesty of God in
Christ—is a uniting reality in Scripture *not* as "theme" or "center," but as the
*ultimate goal*, "the ultimate reason for the story." And since God plans his goals,
and reveals his plans, magnifying God in Christ also can be spoken of as the
"animating principle" of the inspired biblical writers.[9]

---

[4] Jonathan Edwards, *Concerning the End for Which God Created the World*, in Jonathan Edwards, *Ethical Writings*, ed. Paul Ramsey (New Haven, Yale University Press, 1989), 526.

[5] Jonathan Edwards, *A History of the Work of Redemption*, ed. John F. Wilson (New Haven: Yale University Press, 1989), 62–63.

[6] Schreiner, *The King in His Beauty*, xiii.

[7] Schreiner, *Magnifying God in Christ: A Summary of New Testament Theology* (Grand Rapids: Baker Academic, 2010), 16.

[8] Schreiner, *King in His Beauty*, xii.

[9] Schreiner, *Paul*, 37.

## Ultimate Aim of Romans and God

Schreiner's main scholarly attention has been devoted to the apostle Paul. He is the star witness in Schreiner's case that the ultimate purpose of history is that God "be glorified in all things and by all people." "Magnifying God in Christ was the animating principle of Paul's life and the foundational principle of his theology."[10] Schreiner even insists that the gospel itself, as Paul proclaims it, is not supreme. Only God is supreme.

Paul devoted the bulk of his life to preaching the gospel and planting churches, and he is filled with joy when his converts stay true to the gospel (1 Thessalonians 3) and deeply grieved when they abandon it (Gal 1:6–9). The gospel, however, is "the gospel of God" (Rom 1:1), indicating that the gospel cannot be prized over the God who makes it a reality. The gospel is nothing less than "the glory of Christ [who is the image of God]" (2 Cor 4:4).[11]

Indeed! It is "the gospel of the *glory* of the blessed God" (1 Tim 1:11 ESV[12]).

At the apex of Paul's inspired writings is his letter to the Romans. As with the totality of Scripture, Schreiner acknowledges that the book has "various purposes" but again asks, "Which purpose is ultimate?" His answer:

> Paul ultimately wrote Romans as a servant of God to honor his Lord. I have endeavored to show inductively in my exegesis of the letter that *God's glory is indeed ultimate*, and the credibility of my hypothesis stands or falls with my exegesis of the letter.[13]

## Ultimate Purpose in All Things

In fact, Paul seems to delight in repeatedly expressing the glory of God as the ultimate purpose of what he does. From predestination to incarnation to sanctification to consummation, the ultimate purpose is the same: that God in Christ be magnified as supremely glorious. For example (and these are only examples that use the term "glory" or "glorify"):

The purpose of election and predestination in Christ:

---

[10] Schreiner, *Paul,* 37.

[11] Schreiner, 22, 26.

[12] The ESV® Bible (The Holy Bible, English Standard Version®). ESV® Text Edition: 2016. Copyright © 2001 by Crossway, a publishing ministry of Good News Publishers. The ESV® text has been reproduced in cooperation with and by permission of Good News Publishers. Unauthorized reproduction of this publication is prohibited. All rights reserved. Emphasis added.

[13] Thomas Schreiner, *Romans* (Grand Rapids: Baker Books, 1998), 23 (emphasis added).

In love [God the Father] predestined us for adoption as sons through Jesus Christ, according to the purpose of his will, *to the praise of the glory of his grace.* (Eph 1:4–6 ESV)

The purpose of why Christ was incarnate as a Jew:

Christ became a servant to the circumcised . . . in order that the Gentiles might *glorify God for his mercy.* (Rom 15:8–9 ESV)

The purpose of Paul's apostolic ministry:

It is all for your sake, so that as grace extends to more and more people it may increase thanksgiving, *to the glory of God.* (2 Cor 4:15 ESV)

The purpose of why Christians welcome each other:

Welcome one another as Christ has welcomed you, *to the glory of God.* (Rom 15:7 ESV)

The purpose of Paul's collection for the poor:

He has been appointed by the churches to travel with us as we carry out this act of grace that is being ministered by us, *for the glory of the Lord himself.* (2 Cor 8:19 ESV)

The purpose of God's working all things according to his will:

He works all things according to the counsel of his will, so that we who were the first to hope in Christ might be *to the praise of his glory.* (Eph 1:11–12 ESV)

The purpose of being sealed by the Spirit:

You were sealed with the promised Holy Spirit, who is the guarantee of our inheritance until we acquire possession of it, *to the praise of his glory.* (Eph 1:13–14 ESV)

The purpose of being filled with the fruit of righteousness:

[I pray that you will be] filled with the fruit of righteousness that comes through Jesus Christ, *to the glory and praise of God.* (Phil 1:11 ESV)

The purpose of every tongue confessing Christ as Lord:

Every tongue [will] confess that Jesus Christ is Lord, *to the glory of God the Father*. (Phil 2:11 ESV)

The purpose of all promises being Yes in Christ:

All the promises of God find their Yes in him. That is why it is through him that *we utter our Amen to God for his glory*. (2 Cor 1:20 ESV)

The purpose of the second coming of Christ:

He comes on that day to be *glorified in his saints*, and to be marveled at among all who have believed, because our testimony to you was believed. (2 Thess 1:10 ESV)

### Overflow of Worshiping Hearts

Besides these explicit statements of purpose, Paul overflows with doxologies that express the ultimate aim of the worshiping heart—that all glory be ascribed to God.

- For from him and through him and to him are all things. To him be glory forever. Amen. (Rom 11:36 ESV)

- To the only wise God be glory forevermore through Jesus Christ! Amen. (Rom 16:27 ESV)

- To him be glory in the church and in Christ Jesus throughout all generations, forever and ever. Amen. (Eph 3:21 ESV)

- To our God and Father be glory forever and ever. Amen. (Phil 4:20 ESV)

- To him be the glory forever and ever. Amen. (2 Tim 4:18 ESV)

### Paul's God-centered Ethics

Descending from the macrovision of redemptive history and the consummation of all things, Schreiner shows that this God-centered vision of reality is essential to all Christian behavior. "The centrality of God and Christ in the warp and woof of life is woven into the fabric of Pauline ethics."[14] "Honoring God should be the goal of ethics"[15] because Paul exhorts us to "do everything in the name of the Lord Jesus" (Col 3:17) and "to eat and drink . . . or whatever

---

[14] Schreiner, *Paul*, 30.
[15] Schreiner, 28.

. . . to the glory of God" (1 Cor 10:31). In short, "Glorify God in your body" (1 Cor 6:20 ESV).

### My Aim

Here is where I would like to test Schreiner's thesis about Pauline ethics by probing into the relationship between God's glory and our sanctification. I am going to assume that sanctification is Paul's way of talking about "ethics." Therefore, my aim is to see how our sanctification relates to the glory of God in Paul. Is the goal of sanctification (ethics) "honoring God"? Or, as the title of this essay puts it, is sanctification for the magnifying of God in Christ? How does God glorify his children for his own glory?

### Our Destiny of Seeing the Glory of God

It is clear from the many texts cited above about God's aim to be glorified that the consummation of all things will include the sight of God's glory by the redeemed. If we are going to savor and speak and sing and celebrate his glory, we will have to see it—no longer "in a mirror dimly, but then face to face" (1 Cor 13:12 ESV).

This seeing will not be only a physical sight of material brightness, but a true spiritual sight with the "eyes of the heart" (Eph 1:18 ESV). God's glory is not only the brightness that is manifest in the world, but is primarily, and most essentially, the internal, spiritual beauty—the array of his essential, invisible, eternal perfections.

Jonathan Edwards concludes from a survey of many biblical texts that there is an "internal glory" and "external glory."

> As to internal glory. When the word is used to signify what is within, inherent or in the possession of the subject, it very commonly signifies excellency, or great valuableness, dignity, or worthiness of regard. . . . [As to the external glory.] The word "glory" is used in Scripture often to express the exhibition, emanation or communication of the internal glory. Hence it often signifies a visible exhibition of glory; as in an effulgence or shining brightness, by an emanation of beams of light.[16]

Since the resurrection of the redeemed will be a bodily resurrection—albeit a "spiritual body"—there will be both material and spiritual manifestations of the glory of God in the age to come. But the revelation of the internal beauty of

---

[16] Jonathan Edwards, *Ethical Writings*, ed. Paul Ramsey and John E. Smith, vol. 8, The Works of Jonathan Edwards (New Haven; London: Yale University Press, 1989), 513, 515–16.

God's manifold perfections is what will satisfy the redeemed heart most deeply. This is what the world cannot see ("seeing they do not see," Matt 13:13 ESV).

Paul portrays this double experience of God's glory at the coming of Christ as our calling, our joy, and our blessed hope.

- We exhorted each one of you and encouraged you and charged you to walk in a manner worthy of God, *who calls you into his own kingdom and glory*. (1 Thess 2:12 ESV)

- Through him we have also obtained access by faith into this grace in which we stand, and *we rejoice in hope of the glory of God*. (Rom 5:2 ESV)

- [We wait] for *our blessed hope, the appearing of the glory of our great God and Savior Jesus Christ*. (Titus 2:13 ESV)

And when he describes the final destruction of unbelievers, Paul focuses on the loss of this experience of God's glory: "They will suffer the punishment of eternal destruction, away from the presence of the Lord and *from the glory of his might*" (2 Thess 1:9 ESV).

### Beatific Vision, Beatific Transformation

But even more often than the hope of *seeing* God's glory, Paul describes the experience of *sharing* in that glory—an experience that begins in this life and is completed in the age to come. We are moving not only toward a beatific *vision*, but a beatific *transformation*. Romans 8 lays this out most fully. "If [we are] children, then heirs—heirs of God and fellow heirs with Christ, provided we suffer with him *in order that we may also be glorified with him*" (Rom 8:17 ESV). Union with Christ includes "being glorified with him."

The next verse (v. 18) could, perhaps, be only a reference to the sight of *God's* glory, not ours: "I consider that the sufferings of this present time are not worth comparing with *the glory that is to be revealed to us*" (Rom 8:18 ESV). But the very next verse says, "For the creation waits with eager longing for the *revealing of the sons of God*" (v. 19 ESV). And this is followed by our hope that "the creation itself will be set free from its bondage to corruption and obtain *the freedom of the glory of the children of God*" (Rom 8:20–21 ESV). So it is more likely that "the glory that is to be revealed to us" (v. 18) refers to the glory of a transformed universe, which arises *because* the children of God have been freed from all the painful and limiting effects of sin, and thus need a new world that accords with their glory. Thus, the incomparable glory that is revealed to us in verse 18 includes our own glorification.

### Glory of Risen Bodies

In that new world, the glory of our redeemed bodies is part of "the freedom of the glory of the children of God." We know this first because verse 23 says, "We ourselves, who have the firstfruits of the Spirit, groan inwardly as we wait eagerly for adoption as sons, *the redemption of our bodies*" (ESV). We also know it because Paul says in Phil 3:21, "The Lord Jesus Christ will transform our lowly body to be like his glorious body, by the power that enables him even to subject all things to himself" (ESV).

But the redemption of our bodies is not the primary glorification the saints will enjoy. To be sure, it will be a great joy to be free from physical pain and every deformity and disability. But even sweeter will be freedom from sinning. A new body will be wonderful, but a new heart and mind that never has another sinful thought or attitude or volition or emotion—that will be the greater glory.

### Glory of Moral Conformity to Christ

Thus Rom 8:29 promises, "Those whom he foreknew he also predestined *to be conformed to the image of his Son*" (ESV). This is more than getting a body like Jesus's glorious body. This is conformity to Christ's moral goodness and spiritual affections. We can see this in Eph 5:27 where Paul says that Christ will "present the church to himself in splendor (ἔνδοξον), without spot or wrinkle or any such thing, *that she might be holy and without blemish*" (ESV). The glorification of the bride includes her holiness—that is, her moral and spiritual likeness to Christ.

This is confirmed in the next verse of Romans 8. After saying that the foreknown are predestined for conformity to Christ, Paul says, "Those whom he predestined he also called, and those whom he called he also justified, and those whom he justified *he also glorified*" (v. 30 ESV). This glorification of the predestined would include their conformity to "the image of the Son" referred to in the preceding verse. How is this a confirmation that the conformity to the Son includes our moral and spiritual excellence?

### Present Sanctification Begins Glorification

The answer is found by asking: Why is "sanctification" missing from the golden chain of certainties in Rom 8:30? Why does it *not* say, "Those whom he predestined he also called, and those whom he called he also justified, and those whom he justified *he also sanctified, and those whom he sanctified* he also glorified"? My answer is that in Paul's mind, "he also glorified" is conceived as a divine act of beautification that *includes the present process of sanctification*. If that is true, then "being conformed to the image of the Son" in verse 29 (ESV) includes not only the physical likeness to Christ's glorified body, but also the moral and spiritual likeness to his soul.

That Paul does in fact conceive of glorification as beginning with the incremental transformation of the saints in this world is confirmed by 2 Cor 3:18 where he says that we are "being transformed into the same image [of the Lord] from one degree of glory to another" (ESV).[17] We have good reason, therefore, to see Paul's repeated promise of the glory of the saints as including both their physical, moral, and spiritual beauty:

- [He will] make known the riches of his glory for vessels of mercy, *which he has prepared beforehand for glory*. (Rom 9:23 ESV)

- We impart a secret and hidden wisdom of God, which *God decreed before the ages for our glory*. (1 Cor 2:7 ESV)

- This light momentary affliction is *preparing for us an eternal weight of glory* beyond all comparison. (2 Cor 4:17 ESV)

- When Christ who is your life appears, then *you also will appear with him in glory*. (Col 3:4 ESV)

- That the name of our Lord Jesus may be glorified in you, *and you in him*, according to the grace of our God and the Lord Jesus Christ. (2 Thess 1:12 ESV)

- To this he called you through our gospel, *so that you may obtain the glory of our Lord Jesus Christ*. (2 Thess 2:14 ESV)

### Our Glorification for the Sake of God's?

What, then, is the relationship between the glorification of God in Christ and the glorification of believers? If Schreiner and Edwards are right that "God's purpose in all that he does is to bring honor to himself and to Jesus Christ,"[18] that is, if the glory of God is "the ultimate reason for the story"[19] of redemption, then this would imply that the glorification of believers is designed by God to

---

[17] Numerous commentators point out that the grammatical possibility exists that "from glory to glory" (ἀπὸ δόξης εἰς δόξαν) could mean, not incremental process, but "from the divine glory beheld to the final glory experienced in the age to come," thus only implying *origin* and *goal*, not process. See the examples of this kind of interpretation in Murray J. Harris, *The Second Epistle to the Corinthians: A Commentary on the Greek Text*, New International Greek Testament Commentary (Grand Rapid: Eerdmans; Milton Keynes, UK: Paternoster Press, 2005), 317. Most commentators, however, reject this view and affirm that Paul means incremental glorification in this life leading to final glorification in the age to come. The main reason is that the present tense verbs (κατοπτριζόμενοι and μεταμορφούμεθα) most naturally point in this direction.

[18] Schreiner, *New Testament Theology*, 16.

[19] Schreiner, *The King in His Beauty*, xii. "God's glory is *the reason* for the story" (p. xiii.).

glorify himself. The end and process of the glorification of believers is planned and sustained by God "to honor himself and Jesus Christ." The remainder of this essay attempts to answer if and how that is the case. In answering "how," the most practical implications for life and ministry emerge.

Paul leaves us with little doubt that God glorifies his people for the sake of his own glorification. The ultimate end of our salvation resides in God, not us. In fact, part of what it means to be glorified is to have the kind of heart that is glad about that. Consider four passages in support of this, moving from the general to the specific.

### *Four Arguments That Our Glorification Is for God's Glory*

First, Paul concludes the magnificent overview of God's purposes in redemptive history in Romans 9–11 with these words: "'Who has given a gift to him that he might be repaid?' For from him and through him and to him are all things. To him be glory forever. Amen" (Rom 11:35–36 ESV). The point is that God's glory is exalted in the fact that "*to* him are all things." Not just *from* him and *through* him, but also "*to* him" are all things. The "all things" would include the divine work of glorifying his children. This too is "to him"—that is, ultimately for his honor and glory.

Second, in Eph 1:11–12 Paul refers to God as the one who "works all things according to the counsel of his will, so that we who were the first to hope in Christ might *be* to the praise of his glory [εἰς τὸ εἶναι ἡμᾶς εἰς ἔπαινον δόξης αὐτοῦ]" (ESV). Notice the logical purpose connection: God works all things *so that* we might *be*—exist—for his glory. That "being" would include our sanctified and glorified being. Thus God works "all things" so that our glorification—our glorified existence—would bring praise to the glory of God.

Third, in the very next verses of Ephesians (1:13–14 ESV), Paul says that believers were "sealed by the Holy Spirit of promise, the down payment of our inheritance unto the redemption of [God's] possession, *unto the praise of his glory*" (my translation). It seems from this that both the work of the Holy Spirit in sealing us, and the outcome of our final "redemption" (see Rom 8:23) have this ultimate goal: "the praise of his glory" (ESV). This final sealing and final redemption encompasses our glorification. Therefore, *our* glorification is for the glorification of *God*.

Fourth, in the prayer of Phil 1:9–11, Paul asks the Father that the Philippians might "be pure and blameless for the day of Christ, filled with the fruit of righteousness that comes through Jesus Christ, *to the glory and praise of God*" (ESV). Being "pure and blameless" at the day of Christ and being "full of the fruit of righteousness" is what glorification largely consists in. This glorious blamelessness and purity and righteousness is "to the glory and praise of God."

I conclude, therefore, that our glorification as believers is intended by God to be part of the entire history of redemption designed, as Schreiner writes, "to bring honor to himself and to Jesus Christ."

### The Question: How Does God Glorify Us for His Glory?

The question now becomes: *How* does God bring about our glorification in such a way that this goal—"to bring honor to himself and to Jesus Christ"—is accomplished? I will suggest four different ways this question can be answered.

### 1. Our Glory Is Derivative of God's Glory

Our glorification glorifies God in Christ, first, because our glory is derivative of his glory. It reflects his worth and beauty. It is not original to us, but comes from him, and therefore makes us images of an original, whose role is to image forth the original—and thus glorify him as the ultimate goal of all things.

Paul says in 2 Thess 2:13–14 that we are called to sanctification by the Spirit and belief in the truth "so that you may *obtain*[20] *the glory of our Lord Jesus Christ* [εἰς περιποίησιν δόξης τοῦ κυρίου ἡμῶν Ἰησοῦ Χριστοῦ]" (ESV). The glory that we will enter, and that will enter us, is not a glory that belongs to us by nature. We have it as a "possession" (περιποίησις) from Jesus Christ. It is *his* by nature. It is *ours* by conforming to him. That is what Rom 8:29 makes explicit: "Those whom he foreknew he also predestined to be *conformed to the image of his Son*" (ESV). He is the original. We are shaped into his likeness morally, spiritually, and physically (Phil 3:21).

In this life, the measure of newness that we enjoy is owing not to resources in us, but to a transformation into the image of Christ—specifically Christ's glory—through the "possession" of his glory. Thus Paul says in 2 Cor 3:18 that we "are being transformed into the same image from one degree of glory to another" (ESV).[21] The incremental glorification that we experience in this life glorifies

---

[20] Paul uses the word περιποίησις only here and 1 Thess 5:9 ("God has not destined us for wrath, but to obtain (περιποίησιν) salvation through our Lord Jesus Christ"). Henry Alford argues, rightly I think, that "the sense of περιποίησις is indicated by the parallel 1 Thess 5:9." The "salvation" the saints have as a "possession" is not only external to them, but effective in them. Thus also here in 2 Thess 2:14, Paul is referring to "your sharing in the glory which [Christ] *has*." He points to Rom 8:17, 29. Henry Alford, *Alford's Greek Testament: An Exegetical and Critical Commentary*, vol. 3 (Grand Rapids, MI: Guardian Press, 1976), 293.

[21] Some have argued that the "Lord" in 2 Cor 3:18 refers only to Yahweh: "We all, with unveiled face, beholding the glory of *the Lord (Yahweh)*, are being transformed into the same image from one degree of glory to another." For example, Scott Hafemann, *2 Corinthians: From Biblical Text to Contemporary Life*, The NIV Application Commentary (Grand Rapids: Zondervan, 2000), 160–62. His point is a valid one, in that Paul is at pains to show the experience of the Christian in the New Covenant is a fulfilment of Moses's experience of turning to the Yahweh unveiled in the tent of meeting (Exod 34:34). But the problem is that, as Paul

God in Christ because every measure of glory into which we grow is the glory of Christ, the image of God (2 Cor 4:4), that is, the "glory of God in the face of Christ" (2 Cor 4:6 ESV). We shine, if we shine at all, with a borrowed glory, and therefore the original—not the copy—is supremely honored.

The idea of "being transformed into the image" of Christ (2 Cor 3:18 ESV)—or God in Christ—is taken up by Paul, more or less, in at least three other metaphors of our incremental glorification in this life.

### Put on the New Self, Renewed and Created in God's Image

In Col 3:9–10 Paul writes, "You have put off the old self with its practices and have put on the new self, which is *being renewed in knowledge after the image of its creator*" (ESV). Similarly, in Eph 4:24, "[You were taught] to put on the new self, *created after the likeness of God in true righteousness and holiness*" (ESV). We are "being renewed" by another, not by resources resident in us. We are being "created" by another. We are not creating ourselves, as though the resources were in us. The work of renewal and the new creation is God's work, and he is modeling his work after his own likeness in Christ. Therefore, the beauty of this new self—the glory into which we are growing—is not native to us. It is God's. So when it is seen for what it is, it honors him and calls attention to his ultimate worth and beauty.

### Putting on Christ

Similar to the metaphor of putting on a new self is Paul's reference to putting on Christ himself. No doubt these are closely related in his mind, but the wording is different. In Gal 3:27 Paul says, "As many of you as were baptized into Christ have *put on Christ*" (ESV). And in Rom 13:14 he says, "*Put on the Lord Jesus Christ*, and make no provision for the flesh, to gratify its desires" (ESV). Paul had just said, "Let us cast off the works of darkness and *put on the armor of light*" (Rom 13:12 ESV). This suggests that putting on Christ means conforming to the moral glory of Christ—armor of *light*—which includes doing away with "works of *darkness*." In other words, the way Christ's presence and glory show themselves is in the visible moral transformation of believers. This change, when rightly understood, gives glory to Christ, because it is *his* glory that has been "put on."

---

unfolds this Christian experience in the following six verses, he refers to the glory that we behold in 2 Cor 3:18 as "the glory of Christ, who is the image of God" and "the glory of God in the face of Jesus Christ" (2 Cor 4:4, 6 ESV). So it seems better to say that the "Lord" whom we behold in 3:18 is "Yahweh in the face of Christ," or is "Christ, the image of Yahweh." Moreover, between these two verses (4 and 6) Paul explicitly says, "We proclaim Jesus Christ *as Lord*" (2 Cor 4:5 ESV).

*Christ Formed in You*

The third metaphor that picks up this idea of our present glorification as the incremental conformity to the image of Christ is found in Gal 4:19: "My little children, for whom I am again in the anguish of childbirth *until Christ is formed in you!*" (ESV). The metaphor is dramatically different here: Paul, as a mother in labor, and the birth as the coming forth of a people formed by the indwelling of Christ. The word "formed" (μορφωθῇ) links Paul's thought loosely with the *transformation* (μεταμορφούμεθα) in 2 Cor 3:18. In both texts the reality is that Christians are being (trans)formed into the image of Christ from one degree of glory to another. It is clear, then, that any measure of such formation in the image of Christ is owing to his intrinsic glory, not ours. He is glorified by our incremental glorification, because any glory we display was original with him.

In all these images of sanctification, Paul shows that the beginning of our glorification in this life is owing not to resources in us but to the glory of Christ applied to us as a "possession" (περιποίησις, 2 Thess 2:14). Our glory is not ours by nature but as a gracious gift worked in us. Therefore, our glorification, rightly understood, continually calls attention to the glory of God in Christ. Our glorification is for his glory.

## 2. Beholding God's Glory in Christ Is a Means of Our Glorification

The second way Paul shows that our glorification is ordained by God as a means of his own ultimate glorification is that an essential *means* of our glorification is beholding the glory of God in Christ. If we are made incrementally glorious with the glory of Christ *by means of looking upon Christ*,[22] then it is the glory of Christ that is magnified. Ours is reflective.

Paul describes this particular means of transformation only once in his writings, in 2 Cor 3:18: "we all, with unveiled face, beholding the glory of the Lord, are being transformed into the same image from one degree of glory to another. For this comes from the Lord who is the Spirit" (ESV). According to this verse, we *become* glorious by *beholding* glory.

Scholars have sought the explanatory background of this idea of *vision as a means of transformation* in Hellenistic religions and in the Jewish Wisdom of Solomon (7:25–26).[23] Margaret Thrall, however, after surveying the possible backgrounds concludes,

---

[22] See n. 20, p. 87 for my argument that "beholding the glory of the Lord" in 2 Cor 3:18 refers to Christ (the image of God) or, which is essentially the same, God (in the face of Christ).

[23] These and other possible backgrounds are surveyed by Margaret Thrall in an excursus, "*Mirror-vision and Transformation,*" in *A Critical and Exegetical Commentary on the Second Epistle of the Corinthians,* International Critical Commentary (London; New York: T&T Clark International, 2004), 290–95.

The pentateuchal background contains in itself all the necessary elements for the elucidation of the assertion in 2 Cor 3:18, in so far as this depends upon the material Paul had to hand from other than Christian sources: the vision of divine glory, the transformation of the visionary, and its non-eschatological setting. This is the best option.[24]

### Old-Testament Backdrop of Paul's Teaching

Thrall is surely correct, for we could hardly ask for a clearer instance of Old-Testament background for Paul's idea of being transformed by beholding glory. From 2 Cor 3:7–4:6, Paul is unfolding the superior glory of the new covenant over the Mosaic covenant. From the allusions he makes, we can tell that Paul was reading, at least, Exod 34:29–35.

> When Moses came down from Mount Sinai, with the two tablets of the testimony in his hand as he came down from the mountain, Moses did not know that the skin of his face shone because he had been talking with God. . . . And when Moses had finished speaking with them, he put a veil over his face. Whenever Moses went in before the Lord to speak with him, he would remove the veil, until he came out. And when he came out and told the people of Israel what he was commanded, the people of Israel would see the face of Moses, that the skin of Moses's face was shining. And Moses would put the veil over his face again, until he went in to speak with him. (ESV)

Paul adapts the Sinai situation to his own in two different ways. On the one hand, Paul compares the bulk of Jewish readers in his day to the people at Sinai who were kept from seeing the glory: "To this day, when they read the old covenant, that same veil remains unlifted" (2 Cor 3:14 ESV). But on the other hand, these same readers also are compared to Moses, who lifted the veil when he turned to the Lord in the tent of meeting. "When one turns to the Lord, the veil is removed" (3:16 ESV).

So Paul is showing us that there is an analogy between Moses's removing the veil and turning to Yahweh, and the Christian's turning to the Lord and "with unveiled face beholding the glory of the Lord" (v. 18 ESV). The result in both cases is that the beholder becomes glorious with the glory of the Lord.

Even though the immediate context of Exod 34:29–35 does not say that Moses beheld "the glory of God" but only that he spoke with him (34:34), the wider context makes plain that the speaking together included a seeing of God's glory. For example, just before Moses's transforming encounter with God on Sinai, he prayed, "Show me your glory" (Exod 33:18 ESV). And later,

---

[24] Thrall, *"Mirror-vision and Transformation,"* 295.

in Num 12:8, God says, "With [Moses] I *speak* mouth to mouth, clearly, and not in riddles, and he *beholds* the form of the Lord" (ESV).

### Veil Lifted for Believers

Paul's point, therefore, is that in the new covenant God has lifted the veil so that believers can see the glory of Yahweh in the face of Christ (2 Cor 4:6), or the glory of Christ who is the image of Yahweh (2 Cor 4:4). This is not essentially a seeing with the physical eyes. It is a seeing with the eyes of the heart (Eph 1:18). And the effect of this seeing is that we are "being transformed into the same image from one degree of glory to another."

Therefore, it is plain not only that the glory into which we are being changed is the glory of Christ, but also that this transformation happens *by means of* focusing our gaze on him. He is the origin and source of our glory not impersonally or mechanically—as if we might attain his glory with no knowledge of him or attention to him—but rather, only by a face-to-face beholding. In this way, he is made even more central in this transaction than if he were only the source of the glory without our knowing it. Thus, our glorification glorifies God because seeing God's glory in Christ is the necessary *means* of it.

### 3. Christ Himself Is the One Who Transforms Us into His Likeness

The third way Paul shows that our glorification is a means of God's ultimate glorification is by revealing that Christ himself is the one doing the transforming—Christ the Lord, who is the Spirit!

There are two agencies of transformation mentioned in 2 Cor 3:18. One is our beholding the glory of the Lord. The other is that "this comes from the Lord who is the Spirit" (ESV). Not all agree that καθάπερ ἀπὸ κυρίου πνεύματος at the end of verse 18 should be translated this way—identifying the Lord and the Spirit.

On the face of it, their case is good. They would rightly point out that the related thought in verse 17 is surely the key to how these words are to be taken. Verse 17 says, "Now the Lord is the Spirit, and where the Spirit of the Lord is, there is freedom" (ESV). This verse seems most likely to be Paul's comment on the reference to Moses's turning to the "Lord" in verse 16: "But when one turns to the Lord, the veil is removed" (ESV). In following this verse with "the Lord is the Spirit," Paul seems to say, "I am now connecting the Old Testament sight of Yahweh with the New Covenant work of the Spirit." When he says, "The Lord *is* the Spirit," the word "is" probably means "corresponds to."[25]

---

[25] See how Paul uses the word "is" in a similar way in 1 Cor 10:4 ("the Rock was Christ") and Gal 4:25 ("Hagar is Mount Sinai"). See also 1 Cor 11:24 ("This is my body") and Matt 13:38 ("The field is the world").

But having acknowledged that "the Lord is the Spirit" is not a direct affirmation of the identity of two members of the Trinity, nevertheless, we must come to terms with the next phrase: "the Spirit of the Lord." Verse 17b: "where *the Spirit of the Lord* is, there is freedom" (ESV). The phrase "the Spirit of the Lord" (τὸ πνεῦμα κυρίου) brings Yahweh and the Spirit into closest relationship. The Spirit is Yahweh's Spirit. This is more than a typological correspondence ("Yahweh corresponds to the Spirit").

### Two Agents of Transformation: Christ Seen, His Spirit Working

We ask, then, *Is Yahweh's Spirit, Christ's Spirit?* When verse 18 ends by saying our glorification comes "from the *Lord* who is the Spirit" (ἀπὸ κυρίου πνεύματος), two factors point to identifying the Spirit as the Spirit of Christ. One is that "the Lord" has already taken on the meaning of Yahweh as we see him *in Christ* (see above, especially n. 19); the other is that the unusual anarthrous and reversed word order, κυρίου πνεύματος (as opposed to the order in v. 17, τὸ πνεῦμα κυρίου) suggests that this is not a mere repetition of "the Spirit of the Lord." Rather it is a clarification that two agencies are at work in the glorification of the believers. "This comes from the Lord who is the Spirit" means, first, that our transformation from glory to glory is *from the Lord*, in the sense that we are beholding his glory as we change; and, second, it is *from the Spirit* who actually causes the spiritual and moral changes in us as we look to Christ.

And these two agencies of our transformation are united. It is "the Lord who is the Spirit." This is not the only place where Paul treats the Spirit as identified with Christ. For example, in Rom 8:9b–10a he says, "Anyone who does not have the *Spirit of Christ* does not belong to him. But if *Christ* is in you ..." (ESV).

Therefore, Paul teaches us here in 2 Cor 3:18 that Christ himself is not only the template of our glorification—the one we behold—but also the one who enters us and, by the Spirit, works the changes from one degree of glory to another. This would involve at least three actions.

First, the Lord, the Spirit, opens the eyes of our heart which are blind apart from this miracle of spiritual sight. "The god of this world has blinded the minds of the unbelievers, to keep them from seeing the light of the gospel of the glory of Christ, who is the image of God" (2 Cor 4:4 ESV). We cannot be transformed from glory to glory by seeing Christ if we remain blind to Christ. Therefore, when Paul says this seeing "comes from the Lord who is the Spirit," he implies that what the Lord does is enable us to see glory.

Before this miracle, we saw Christ, as Paul said, "according to the flesh" (2 Cor 5:16 ESV). He was a mere man—or worse, an imposter. He was not compellingly glorious in our eyes. We were like the "rulers of this age" whom Paul says did not see the glory of Jesus "for if they had, they would not have crucified the Lord of glory" (1 Cor 2:8 ESV). So the first action of the Spirit in the transaction of 2 Cor 3:18 is to open the eyes of the spiritually blind, who cannot see Christ as compellingly glorious.

Second, the action of the Spirit is also to present to the newly opened eyes the sight of the glory of Christ. No one will be changed from glory to glory if their eyes are opened and there is no Christ to see. The Christ we see by this miracle of spiritual sight is "the light of the *gospel* of the glory of Christ, who is the image of God" (2 Cor 4:4 ESV). We do not see a vision. We do not see a dream. We see the light of Christ's glory shining through the gospel, that is, through the story of Christ's death and resurrection and what it means. Therefore, when Paul says that this "comes from the Lord who is the Spirit" (ESV), I take him to mean that the Lord has done what needs to be done so that Christ is there to see when the eyes are opened. This would include both the great work of the cross itself as well as the providential acts to bring the gospel into our awareness.

Third, one more achievement is included in the words "this comes from the Lord who is the Spirit" (2 Cor 3:18 ESV). Why is it that seeing the glory of the Lord transforms us from glory to glory? How does that work? Whatever the answer to that is, Paul says, it "comes from the Lord" (ESV). This is so significant, and so full of practical implications, we will do well to treat it as a separate means (the fourth one) by which Paul shows that our glorification is a means of God's glorifications. But before we turn to that fourth and final point, I will sum up the third one we have just discussed.

I am assuming here on this third point that the one who works the wonder gets the glory. This principle is expressed in 1 Pet 4:11: "Whoever serves, [let it be] as one who serves by the strength that God supplies—in order that in everything God may be glorified through Jesus Christ" (ESV). In other words, the giver of power gets the glory. So it is in 2 Cor 3:18: the giver of the changes gets the glory for the transformation. When Paul says, "This [transformation] comes from the Lord who is the Spirit" (ESV), we are to infer that the Lord who makes our glorification work is the one who gets the glory. Or to use Tom Schreiner's words, "God works out his saving plan [including how his children are glorified] so that he would be magnified in Christ."[26]

### 4. God Is Glorified by the Way Beholding Produces Becoming

The fourth means by which God gets the glory for our present and final glorification is from the way seeing produces being—from the way beholding produces becoming. Why is it that seeing the glory of the Lord transforms us

---

[26] Thomas Schreiner, *Magnifying God in Christ: A Summary of New Testament Theology* (Grand Rapids, Michigan: Baker Academic, 2010), 16.

from glory to glory? How does that work? The fact that it does work, and that it "comes from the Lord," means that the Lord gets the glory. But that is not the point here. The point now is: How does the process actually work? How does beholding produce becoming? And does the very nature of the process itself—the process of our becoming glorious by seeing glory—glorify God?

I am sure there are depths of miraculous connections between beholding and becoming that I am not aware of. But there is one connection that seems plain in Paul's writings, and it goes a long way toward answering why beholding glory in Christ produces glory in us, and why that actual process glorifies the Lord of glory.

### Seeing Christ as Supremely Beautiful and Valuable

Clearly, when Paul refers to "beholding the glory of the Lord" in 2 Cor 3:18 (ESV), he is speaking of a beholding that is different from the way a natural man beholds Christ. Unbelievers, Paul says in 2 Cor 4:4, are blind to the glory of Christ. So they can study him and "behold" him (like the Pharisees did), but not see his glory. They might see him as a deluded fanatic, or a devious imposter, or an innocent peasant, or a moral teacher, or a merciful humanitarian. But they do not see him as the supremely glorious and worthy Son of God.

But when Paul refers to "beholding the glory of the Lord" in 2 Cor 3:18 (ESV), he refers to the kind of seeing that God makes possible in 2 Cor 4:6 ("He has shone in our hearts to give the light of the knowledge of the glory of God in the face of Jesus Christ" [ESV]). This beholding is a seeing of Christ for who and what he really is. He is the Messiah, the Son of God. And he is supremely beautiful and more valuable than anything in the world.

This means that "beholding the glory of the Lord" involves a change of heart—a change of desires and preferences—so that the Lord is not just seen as true, but also seen as precious, beautiful, valuable, desirable, satisfying—the greatest treasure one could ever want. If the eyes of our heart still see him as boring, inferior, unattractive, or unreal, we are not beholding the glory of the Lord, as Paul means it.

Once we realize that beholding the glory of the Lord means seeing him as beautiful, seeing him as valuable, seeing him as desirable and supremely satisfying—a treasure beyond all treasures—then we can see why it is that such a beholding of glory creates glory. For what is the glory of holiness, what is the glory of sanctification, if not a heart whose desires and preferences are so transformed that Christ is its supreme treasure?

### *Beholding as Beautiful Is the Transformation*

So my answer to why beholding glory creates glory is that the beholding which Paul intends involves the miracle of a heart transformation that sees and savors the glory of Christ as the supreme treasure of life. When Paul says, "Beholding the glory of the Lord we are being transformed from glory to glory" (ESV, τὴν δόξαν κυρίου κατοπτριζόμενοι τὴν αὐτὴν εἰκόνα μεταμορφούμεθα ἀπὸ δόξης εἰς δόξαν), he does not say that "being transformed from glory to glory" is *subsequent* to "beholding the glory." He does not say that we first behold glory and then, as a subsequent consequence, are transformed. In the way he express-es himself, it is possible that the very beholding of glory is the first experience of the transformation from glory to glory. That is, in fact, what I think is nec-essarily the case. Precisely the new capacity to behold the Lord as glorious—as supremely beautiful and valuable—is the essence of the transformation.

This implies that there is no temporal sequence between seeing the Lord as all-glorious and experiencing the beginnings of our transformation. They are simultaneous. Even if we ascribe to the glory of the Lord the awakening of our desire and preference for him above all others, that does not imply a temporal sequence (first see, then savor). No. Seeing Christ as preferable and the prefer-ring of Christ are simultaneous. The opening of the eye and the streaming in of light are simultaneous. The burning of a flame and the radiance of its heat and light are simultaneous. So I say again: our new capacity to behold the Lord as glorious—as supremely beautiful and valuable—is the beginning and essence of the transformation.

If this is correct, the way that beholding the glory of the Lord transforms us is by satisfying us with his beauty and worth. The revolution of the heart's pref-erences and desires makes Christ its supreme treasure, affecting all desires and preferences. The dying of the taste for the world and the awakening of the hun-ger for God is the essence of sanctification and the beginning of glorification.

We can confirm that we are on the right track here by noticing in Romans how Paul understands sin, and in Philippians how he understands contentment.

### *Confirmation from Paul's View of Sin*

In Rom 3:23 Paul says, "All have sinned and fall short of the glory of God" (ESV, ὑστεροῦνται τῆς δόξης τοῦ θεοῦ). Literally, "All have sinned and *lack* the glory of God." This "lacking the glory of God" is most naturally explained by Rom 1:22–23: "Claiming to be wise, they became fools, and *exchanged* the glory of the immortal God for images" (ESV). Lacking the glory of God is owing to exchanging the glory of God for what is not God.

From this, I infer that the essence of sin is preferring anything above the glory of God. Sin is, at root, the desire for anything more than God. Sin is the disposition to dethrone God from his position in the heart as supreme treasure.

What, then, would sanctification be? It would be the miracle of seeing the glory of the Lord as supremely valuable—more to be preferred, more to be desired than anything. Sin is overcome by seeing the glory of the Lord as more desirable than the promise of sin. Therefore, I think we are on the right track when we interpret the dynamics of transformation in 2 Cor 3:18 as owing to the heart's awakening to the supreme desirability of the glory of the Lord over all things.

### Confirmation from Paul's View of Contentment

A second confirmation is how Paul understands contentment in Philippians 3 and 4. Paul sees his contentment in Philippians 4 as a holy disposition protecting him from the sin of greed (just as the writer of Heb 13:5–6 does). In other words, Paul's contentment is key to his sanctification. He is thanking the Philippians for their financial support, and he senses that they might hear his gratitude as an evidence of the love of money. So he says, "Not that I am speaking of being in need, for I have learned in whatever situation I am to be content" (Phil 4:11). So his contentment is a protection against unduly desiring money and so sinning.

In the verse we just cited, Paul refers to "learning to be content" (ESV), and in verse 12 he says, "I have learned the secret" (ESV) of contentment in good times and hard times. What is this "secret"? How did he "learn" this? I think Paul would direct us back to Phil 3:7–8 for his answer. There he said, "Whatever gain I had, I counted as loss for the sake of Christ. Indeed, I count everything as loss because of the surpassing worth of knowing Christ Jesus my Lord" (ESV). In other words, the reason Paul can be content with little or much is that Christ is so satisfying to him that worldly losses and gains do not control his affections. His desires and preferences have been so transformed by the superior beauty and worth of Christ that nothing is more desirable to him than Christ.

So again, it appears that Paul's view of sanctification—how we are transformed from glory to glory—is that we are sanctified, transformed by beholding the glory of the Lord as supremely beautiful and valuable, more to be desired and preferred than anything else. This comes from beholding the glory of the Lord for what it really is—the greatest treasure in the universe.

### God Glorified in Our Being Satisfied in Him

This leaves one last question to answer: Does this dynamic of sanctification glorify the Lord? If so, how? My answer is that it does, and how it does is shown in Phil 1:20–23:

> It is my eager expectation and hope that I will not be at all ashamed, but that with full courage now as always Christ will be magnified in my body, whether by life or by death. For to me to live is Christ, and to die is gain. If I am to live in the flesh, that means fruitful labor for me. Yet which I shall choose I cannot tell. I am hard pressed between the two. My desire is to depart and be with Christ, for that is far better. (ESV)

The reason this text is relevant to our question is that it describes how Christ is "magnified" (v. 20). Paul says that he expects Christ to be magnified in his body "whether by life or by death" (ESV). Then he explains how that comes about in the next clause (v. 21) that begins with "for" (γὰρ): "For to me to live is Christ, and to die is gain" (ESV). Notice that "by life or by death" in verse 20 corresponds with "to live . . . and to die" in verse 21. Paul is explaining how it is that he expects his death to magnify Christ. His answer is "because to me to die is gain" (ESV).

The logic goes like this: "I expect Christ to be magnified in my death because I will experience death as gain." To make that logic work, we need to see why death would be gain for Paul. He answers that question in verse 23: "My desire is to depart and be with Christ, for that is far better" (ESV). The reason death will be gain for Paul is that it means being "with Christ," which is an experience of immediate joy unparalleled by anything in this world. So back in verse 21 the gain referred to his satisfaction of being with Christ after death.

Now we can restate the logic of verses 20 and 21 more fully: "I expect Christ to be magnified in my death because I will experience death as the door to an immediate joy that is greater than anything I could experience here, namely, the joy of being with Christ."

What does that Pauline logic tell us about how Christ is magnified? It tells us that *Christ is magnified in Paul when Paul is satisfied in Christ,* especially in a situation where most of the world would regard death as a reason not to be satisfied. From this I infer that the principle applies to all of life: if we gain our lives and yet find that Christ is more to us than all that life gives (Phil 3:8), or if we lose our lives and yet find that Christ is more satisfying than what was taken away (Phil 1:21–23), then in both cases Christ is wonderfully magnified. He is shown to be supremely beautiful and valuable.

## CONCLUSION

I began this essay by pointing out Tom Schreiner's unique place in biblical scholarship for the pervasive scope of his emphasis that "God's purpose in all that he does is to bring honor to himself and to Jesus Christ."[27] His point is not that there is one central "theme" in Scripture, but one ultimate goal. "It is common consensus that no one theme adequately captures the message of the Scriptures."[28] God's purpose to glorify himself is not the "theme" or "center" but rather "the ultimate reason for the story."[29]

I pointed to the basis of my agreement with this, and then narrowed the focus to Paul's view of ethics and sanctification. Schreiner says, "The centrality of God and Christ in the warp and woof of life is woven into the fabric of Pauline ethics."[30] "Honoring God should be the goal of ethics."[31] The question I have pursued is how, in Paul's understanding, the process of human transformation glorifies God. We saw first the general picture of God's design *that* he would be glorified by the way human beings are sanctified. Then we asked, more specifically, *how* God sanctifies (i.e., incrementally glorifies) us in such a way that this goal—"to bring honor to himself and to Jesus Christ"—is accomplished?

In the four answers given to that specific question, it became clear that our sanctification—the path of all Christian ethics—glorifies God not only because the Lord himself performs it, or because it happens as we behold the glory of the Lord, or because our own glory is derivative of God's. Even more fundamentally, our transformation glorifies God because the heart of holiness is a heart that sees the Lord as supremely beautiful, and supremely valuable, and is therefore satisfied in him as its greatest treasure in life and death. God is glorified by every deed that expresses the heart's satisfaction in God above all else.

Therefore, I rejoice to agree with Tom Schreiner's magnificent affirmations: "The centrality of God and Christ in the warp and woof of life is woven into the fabric of Pauline ethics."[32] "Honoring God should be the goal of ethics."[33] "Since God is the King and Lord, it is his purpose and design that he be glorified in all things and by all people."[34]

---

[27] Thomas Schreiner, *New Testament Theology: Magnifying God in Christ* (Grand Rapids: Baker Academic, 2008), 13. Repeated in the condensed version of this book, *Magnifying God in Christ: A Summary of New Testament Theology* (Grand Rapids: Baker Academic, 2010), 16.

[28] Schreiner, *King in His Beauty*, xii.

[29] Schreiner, xiii.

[30] Schreiner, *Paul*, 30.

[31] Schreiner, 28.

[32] Schreiner, 30.

[33] Schreiner, 28.

[34] Schreiner, *King in His Beauty*, 13–14.

*Chapter 7*

# The Newness of Paul's Gospel

*by Donald A. Hagner*

C hristianity, by its nature, is very Jewish. And it was certainly more Jewish in its early years than it became as the centuries passed. But do these facts justify the current trend among some scholars to regard early Christianity as a sect *within* Judaism? In particular, is Paul to be understood as in full continuity with Judaism—indeed, as remaining within Judaism?[1]

I am fully aware that the words "Judaism" and "Christianity" are anachronistic. It is of course clearly wrong to read the content of the fully developed Judaism and Christianity of later centuries into our first-century sources. It is also clear that there was much more variety within each of the two groups at the beginning than was the case in later centuries. At the same time, however, it seems impossible, given the evidence we have, to deny that there was an identifiable Judaism and an identifiable Christianity already in the first century. It is obvious from the NT that there were specific things believed by the Jews who followed Jesus and those who did not. Virtually all Jews held to a set of core beliefs such as monotheism, the election of Israel, the covenant and Torah, the Temple, and the promise of the land. And, on the other hand, from the NT itself it is clear that the earliest believers in Jesus already in the first century shared core Christian beliefs; for example, confession of Christ as Lord, his atoning death, belief in his resurrection from the dead, belief in the present dawning of a new age, and salvation by faith in Christ. That there was also some variety in the beliefs of the two groups is hardly to be denied. But at the same time, it is not difficult to see considerable stability in both groups,

---

[1] This essay is based largely on material from my book *How New is the New Testament?* (Grand Rapids: Baker, 2018), used here with the permission of the publisher.

easily sufficient enough to establish the identity of one over against the other. It therefore seems more appropriate to speak of varieties of, or within, Judaism than of "Judaisms" in the plural. So too of varieties of Christianity rather than "Christianities." There is enough of a common core within the actual varieties to justify speaking of singular entities within which some (limited) variety existed.

The frequently heard red herring that one cannot meaningfully speak of "Christianity" until the second century at the earliest because the actual word is not found until Ignatius is clearly a non sequitur. In addition to the obvious fact that *our* knowledge of the first use of a word is hardly proof that the word was not used earlier, it is perfectly possible for the reality to exist before the minting of the word. Already in the NT we have the word "Christian" (Acts 11:26; 26:28; 1 Pet 4:16) and the Pauline designation of being "in Christ" also functions as a clear identity marker. Therefore I do not think it is necessary, with the qualifications just noted, to avoid speaking of "Judaism" and "Christianity" in the first century.

Through most of the history of the church the emphasis has been on the discontinuity between Judaism and Christianity. But with the coming of the Enlightenment and the emancipation of the Jews, beginning in the late eighteenth century, the climate began to change. Here we encounter the beginnings of a *gradual movement from stress on discontinuity to stress on continuity.* For the first time it became possible for a more positive Jewish approach to Jesus. This new, open attitude, exhibited almost exclusively among Reform Jews, gave rise in the twentieth century to what would become known as "the Jewish reclamation of Jesus."[2]

Exactly because Jesus was so Jewish, it is not such a great surprise that Jews would be able to think of him as belonging within the fold. With "the homecoming of Jesus," it was thought no longer possible to understand Jesus as the founder of Christianity. It was Paul who now became regarded as mainly responsible for Christianity as we know it. All the more surprising then is the rise of a parallel movement: namely, the Jewish reclamation of Paul. The rediscovery of the Jewishness of Jesus has progressed to the rediscovery of the Jewishness of Paul. Here again, and startlingly, the pendulum has shifted from discontinuity to continuity. Given the hitherto common, seemingly self-evident, understanding of Paul as having in some sense broken with the law and Judaism—a view prevalent from Luther until recent times—the emphasis had always been on the discontinuity between Judaism and Paul's Christianity.[3]

---

[2] See my discussion in *The Jewish Reclamation of Jesus: An Analysis and Critique of Modern Jewish Study of Jesus* (Grand Rapids: Zondervan, 1984; repr., Eugene, OR: Wipf and Stock, 1997).
[3] See D. A. Hagner, "Paul's Quarrel with Judaism," in *Anti-Semitism and Early Christianity: Issues of Polemic and Faith*, 128–50. Hagner, "Paul as a Jewish Believer in Jesus—According to His Letters" in *Jewish Believers*

These developments stressing the full continuity of early Christianity and Judaism are consonant with the emerging view that Christianity from the beginning was and remained a sect within Judaism and that consequently there never was a parting of the ways between synagogue and church.[4] This extreme view is not shared by many, but an increasing number of scholars would place the parting no earlier than the fourth century.[5] In summary, it is clear that nowadays, for many scholars, both Jewish and Christian, the pendulum is swinging completely to the side of *full continuity between Judaism and Christianity*. This development accords not only with the relativistic spirit of our age, but especially with the concerns of post-Holocaust Jewish-Christian dialog.[6]

It is the thorough Jewishness of the NT, and of Paul too, that makes it possible to think of early Christianity as simply another sect of Judaism. Nevertheless, given the dominant reading of Paul vis-à-vis Judaism, it was rather surprising when the Jewish reclamation of Paul began.[7] There is currently a lively trend underway among a growing number of scholars to place *Paul* comfortably "*within Judaism*."[8] It is not only Jewish scholars who have

---

*in Jesus: The Early Centuries*, O. Skarsaune and R. Hvalvik, eds. (Peabody: Hendrickson, 2007) 1:96–120. See too Hagner, "Paul in Modern Jewish Thought," in *Pauline Studies. Essays Presented to Professor F. F. Bruce on his 70th Birthday*, ed D. A. Hagner and M. J. Harris (Exeter/Grand Rapids: Paternoster/Eerdmans, 1980) 143–65.

[4] See A. H. Becker and A. Y. Reed, eds., *The Ways That Never Parted: Jews and Christians in Late Antiquity and the Early Middle Ages* (Tübingen: Mohr Siebeck, 2003; repr., Minneapolis: Fortress, 2007). For a defense of a gradual parting of the ways, underway almost from the beginning, see D. A. Hagner, "Another Look at the 'Parting of the Ways'" in *Earliest Christian History: History, Literature and Theology. Essays from the Tyndale Fellowship in Honor of Martin Hengel*, WUNT 2.320, M. F. Bird and Jason Maston, eds. (Tübingen: Mohr Siebeck, 2012) 381–427.

[5] Much depends on how one defines the "parting(s)." If one thinks merely of the cessation of contact and discussion between Jews and Christians, then of course there may never have been a parting of the ways. But if one thinks of irreconcilable differences that made it impossible for a person to belong to both camps at the same time, then we must conceive of partings that began very early and continued at different speeds in different areas.

[6] The impact of Jewish-Christian dialog on the conclusions of NT scholarship is worth pondering. It has become increasingly difficult for Christian scholars to say anything negative about Judaism for fear of being labelled anti-Semitic.

[7] See Markus Barth, "St. Paul—A Good Jew," *HorBT* 1 (1979) 7–45, who mentions before him the Jewish scholars Joseph Klausner, Martin Buber, Leo Baeck, Hans-Joachim Schoeps, Michael Wyschogrod, and Schalom Ben-Chorin.

[8] The title of a recent representative volume is *Paul within Judaism: Restoring the First-Century Context to the Apostle*, Mark D. Nanos and Magnus Zetterholm, eds. (Minneapolis: Fortress, 2015); compare the earlier essay by Nanos, "Paul and Judaism: Why Not Paul's Judaism?" in *Paul Unbound: Other Perspectives on the Apostle*, Mark D. Given, ed. (Peabody: Hendrickson, 2010) 117–60. See too, K. Stendahl, *Paul among Jews and Gentiles and Other Essays* (Philadelphia: Fortress, 1976); W. S. Campbell, *Paul and the Creation of Christian Identity*. LNTS 322 (London: T&T Clark, 2006); Mark D. Nanos, *The Mystery of Romans: The Jewish Context of Paul's Letter* (Minneapolis: Fortress, 1996); *The Irony of Galatians: Paul's Letter in First-Century Context* (Minneapolis: Fortress, 2002); M. Zetterholm, *Approaches to Paul: A Student's Guide to Recent Scholarship* (Minneapolis: Fortress, 2009) 95–164; Kimberly Ambrose, *Jew Among Jews: Rehabilitating*

begun to read the NT in this way. Indeed, encouraged to an extent by Jewish-Christian dialogue, there are some for whom the goal seems to be the Jewish reclamation of the NT and early Christianity itself. This approach puts all stress on continuity and ignores or avoids speaking of discontinuities or new-ness; at least it empties them of any significance. These scholars have invented new vocabulary to describe what they believe they encounter in the NT, such as "NT Judaism," "Apostolic Judaism," and even "Christian Judaism." For them the NT represents a form of Judaism. The separation of Christians and Jews, the "parting of the ways," as we have noted, is now put as late as the fourth century, and even denied by some as happening at all.

The traditional reading of Paul has regularly put him in considerable ten-sion with, sometimes even in opposition to, Judaism. So it is no surprise that these revisionist scholars have focused their efforts on Paul, in pursuing an understanding of him they describe as being "beyond the new perspective," or as "a radical new perspective."[9] Essential to this new perspective or new para-digm is the denial of any "dichotomy" between Paul and Judaism.

A substantial recent treatment of the subject is to be found in Pamela Eisenbaum's book *Paul Was Not a Christian: The Original Message of a Misunderstood Apostle*.[10] Here we find practically all of the emphases made by the "Paul-within-Judaism" movement: there was no "Christianity" when the NT was written; believers in Jesus constituted a sect within Judaism; Paul con-tinued to obey Torah; Paul did not preach justification by faith; an import-ant key to understanding Paul's letters is that he wrote them not to Jews but to Gentiles; Paul's negative statements about the law therefore apply only to Gentiles; Paul was called rather than converted; and he rejected none of the fundamental tenets of Judaism.

These conclusions flow from the a priori starting point that Paul is to be understood as within Judaism, indeed as a good representative of Judaism. This exegesis of the Pauline texts is no less dominated by an a priori than is that of the "traditional" understanding of Paul within Christianity and as a repre-sentative of Christianity. Furthermore, as Magnus Zetterholm frankly admits, "the radical new perspective" is "neither neutral nor objective" and is affected

---

*Paul* (Eugene, OR: Wipe & Stock, 2015); *Paul the Jew: Rereading the Apostle as a Figure of Second Temple Judaism*, Gabriele Boccaccini and Carlos A. Segovia, eds. (Minneapolis: Fortress, 2016).

[9] They project an image of themselves as interested only in "scientific historiography" not "faith commit-ments." See Nanos and Zetterholm, *Paul within Judaism*, 4; and Magnus Zetterholm, *Approaches to Paul: A Student's Guide to Recent Scholarship* (Minneapolis: Fortress, 2009).

[10] Pamela Eisenbaum, *Paul Was Not a Christian: The Original Message of a Misunderstood Apostle* (New York: HarperOne, 2009). The title reminds one of the title of Amy-Jill Levine's book about Jesus: *The Misunderstood Jew: The Church and the Scandal of the Jewish Jesus* (San Francisco: HarperSanFrancisco, 2006). See too, the books by Daniel Boyarin, *A Radical Jew: Paul and the Politics of Identity* (Berkeley: University of California Press, 1994) and *The Jewish Gospels: The Story of the Jewish Christ* (New York: New Press, 2012).

by "ideological factors" such as "involvement in Jewish-Christian dialogue" and "a general consciousness about the connection between the traditional anti-Jewish theology of the church and the Holocaust, in some cases leading to a wish to contribute to the development of theological alternatives."[11]

The so-called "historical" readings of the Paul-within-Judaism scholars can often make sense of the Pauline texts only by means of a tortuous exegesis.[12] Quite remarkable is the fair-minded comment of Zetterholm: "It is, of course, fully possible that the theological interpretation of Paul that has developed over the centuries represents an accurate reconstruction of the historical Paul's thought world."[13] To my mind, the traditional understanding of Paul is indeed highly probable and makes by far the best sense of Paul. The understanding of Paul-within-Judaism can hardly account for the vast amount of *newness* in the Pauline letters.

The discussion of this subject has been seriously hindered by the frequent use of simplistic dichotomies on the part of those arguing for Paul-within-Judaism. Thus, Paul affirmed Judaism *or* Paul opposed Judaism; Paul was a Jew *or* Paul was a Christian; Paul affirmed Torah *or* he rejected Torah; Paul's views involve absolute continuity *or* discontinuity with Judaism and the OT. Historical reality, however, is usually more complicated, especially within a period of transitions.

The challenge is to make coherent sense of not just some of the Pauline texts—but *all* of them together, unless we are content with the conclusion that Paul was hopelessly confused and made numerous irreconcilable statements about important matters. The advocates of the Paul-within-Judaism perspective give insufficient consideration to the complexity of reality. They confront their readers with a kind of rigid either/or mentality that fails to allow tensions, nuances, and subtleties in Paul's affirmations. There is often a sense in which both sides of an either/or can be true and when it is necessary to conclude both/and. This is especially so in the present case, where we are dealing with the genealogical relationship of promise and fulfillment, the new flower growing out of the old seed.

It is of course occasionally possible to understand the same texts in different ways, which is one reason why starting assumptions are so important. Starting with the a priori convictions of the Paul-within-Judaism movement,

---

[11] Zetterholm, *Approaches to Paul*, 232.

[12] Eisenbaum frankly admits there are "a few stubborn passages," and that the meaning of some texts is debatable owing to exaggeration and rhetoric. Eisenbaum, *Paul Was Not a Christian*, 251.

[13] Nanos and Zetterholm, *Paul Within Judaism*, 42. The comment, however, simply reflects Zetterholm's post-modern hermeneutical conviction that there is no way of knowing Paul's intentions in the texts (see Zetterholm, *Approaches to Paul*, 237). Unfortunately, Zetterholm thinks that "the fundamental assumption" in the traditional understanding of Paul is "the vile character of ancient Judaism," and thus he finds it unacceptable. The traditional view of Paul, however, in no way requires such hostility towards Judaism.

certain texts can be taken as supporting their viewpoint. The question, however, is: Given the totality of the Pauline texts, which interpretations are the most plausible? The preponderance of relatively clear texts favours the traditional understanding of Paul and, indeed, makes the Paul-within-Judaism reading of the NT far less than convincing. So too the understanding of Christianity as a sect within Judaism.[14]

The new appreciation of Judaism as a religion of grace, and not a legalism wherein salvation is earned by works of righteousness,[15] is thought by some to support the idea of Christianity as a sect within Judaism.

Contrary to the Lutheran reading of Paul where the law is problematic, to say the least, serving primarily as a propaedeutic to the gospel (a *paidagōgos*, lit. "child-guide," a role of the law stressed by Paul in Gal 3:24), in the new perspective[16] the law retains a positive function of enabling the achievement of righteousness. What then does Paul polemicize against when he speaks negatively of the law and works of the law, as he so often does? "Works of the law" are understood by Dunn and others not as general observance of the law, but very specifically as referring to "Jewish badges of identity" (or "national righteousness") that mark out Jews from the Gentiles, namely circumcision, Sabbath observance, and *kashrut* (the dietary restrictions). Since Paul was called to preach the gospel to the Gentiles it is fully understandable that he would have been very much against "works of the law" in this sense, distinguishing the Jews, as the people of God, from the Gentiles. Given the understanding of Judaism as a "covenantal nomism," where, from the start, grace is an experienced reality, N. T. Wright's quip is appropriate: the issue for Paul is not grace but race.[17]

But an examination of the Pauline texts shows that Paul has a more fundamental problem with the law, one that applies equally to Jews and Gentiles.[18] It is well known that Paul makes both negative and positive statements about the law. Negatively he can write: "Now it is evident that no one is justified

---

[14] See further Donald A. Hagner, "Matthew: Apostate, Reformer, Revolutionary?" *NTS* 49 (2003) 193–209.

[15] The key work here is E. P. Sanders' *Paul and Palestinian Judaism* (Philadelphia: Fortress, 1977). This book was followed by his *Paul, the Law, and the Jewish People* (Philadelphia: Fortress, 1983). See now his *Paul: The Apostle's Life, Letters and Thought* (Minneapolis: Fortress, 2015).

[16] For definitive essays on the subject, see J. D. G. Dunn, *The New Perspective on Paul*, WUNT 185 (Tübingen: Mohr Siebeck, 2005). For a full critique of the new perspective, see S. Westerholm, *Perspectives Old and New on Paul: The "Lutheran" Paul and His Critics* (Grand Rapids: Eerdmans, 2004); and S. Kim, *Paul and the New Perspective: Second Thoughts on the Origin of Paul's Gospel* (Grand Rapids: Eerdmans, 2001). See too D. A. Hagner, "Paul and Judaism: Testing the New Perspective," in Peter Stuhlmacher, *Revisiting Paul's Doctrine of Justification* (Downers Grove, IL: IVP Academic, 2001) 75–105.

[17] Nicholas T. Wright, *The Climax of the Covenant: Christ and the Law in Pauline Theology* (Minneapolis: Fortress, 1991), 168.

[18] For helpful discussion, see Thomas R. Schreiner, *The Law and Its Fulfillment: A Pauline Theology of Law* (Grand Rapids: Baker, 1993); and Schreiner, *40 Questions about Christians and Biblical Law*, 35–152. See too my "Paul's Quarrel with Judaism," in *Anti-Semitism and Early Christianity: Issues of Polemic and Faith*, Craig A. Evans and Donald A. Hagner, eds. (Minneapolis: Fortress, 1993) 128–50.

before God by the law" (Gal 3:11 NRSV[19]). "For if a law had been given that could make alive, then righteousness would indeed come through the law" (Gal 3:21 NRSV). "For 'no human being will be justified in his sight' by deeds prescribed by the law, for through the law comes the knowledge of sin" (Rom 3:20 NRSV). "For we hold that a person is justified by faith apart from works prescribed by the law" (Rom 3:28 NRSV). "For Christ is the end[20] of the law so that there may be righteousness for everyone who believes" (Rom 10:4 NRSV). "You are not under law but under grace" (Rom 6:14–15 NRSV). "But now we are discharged from the law, dead to that which held us captive, so that we are slaves not under the old written code but in the new life of the Spirit" (Rom 7:6 NRSV). "Before faith came, we were imprisoned and guarded under the law until faith would be revealed. Therefore, the law was our disciplinarian until Christ came, so that we might be justified by faith. But now that faith has come, we are no longer subject to a disciplinarian" (Gal 3:23–25 NRSV).

It is evident that the issue here is not merely a sociological one, but also a soteriological one, and thus one of universal significance, that is, for both Jews and Gentiles. The law had only a temporary role to play in the pursuit of righteousness, and that role has come to an end with the coming of Christ. As in so much of what the NT has to say, a key turning point has now been reached in the history of salvation. We are in a new situation. Righteousness clearly remains the goal of God's people (e.g., Rom 8:4), who are God's people by grace, and *in that sense* Paul's gospel upholds the law. The radical difference in the new situation is the dynamic by which righteous living is now possible, namely the empowering of the Holy Spirit, which so characterizes the remarkable newness that arrives with the coming of the Christ. The Holy Spirit thus accomplishes in the Christian what the law could not.

This situation is true for both Jews and Gentiles. The conclusion of some that Paul's view of the law applies only to Gentile converts, not to the Jews, is unjustifiable. Neither the language nor the logic of these passages supports any such idea. Although Paul allows the specialness of Israel because of election, his argument (especially in Romans) applies to all of humanity, including the Jews. Therefore, it is necessary that the gospel be preached to Israel—indeed, first to them—as well as to the Gentiles.

But were there really any Jews in the first century, like those Paul seems to criticize, who were attempting to earn God's acceptance by their righteousness? It is admitted by more and more scholars that Ed Sanders overstated

---

[19] Scripture quotations marked NRSV are from the New Revised Standard Version Bible, copyright © 1989 the Division of Christian Education of the National Council of the Churches of Christ in the United States of America. Used by permission. All rights reserved.

[20] The word "end" [NRSV], *telos*, can also be translated "goal," but it is difficult here to rule out the notion of the law in some sense coming to an end.

his conclusion that the Jews universally recognized the foundation of their salvation as resting on covenant grace. There is a fair amount of evidence that some, even many, Jews thought of their salvation as being dependent upon their obedience to the law. Even Sanders had to take note of 4 Ezra, with its emphasis on works of the law, as an exception to the pattern of religion he presented from the literature of Second Temple Judaism.[21] The situation in the rabbinic sources is anything but clear and consistent. So, it is not difficult to find legalistic-sounding passages in the rabbinic literature. The argument of Sanders and others is that the grace of the covenant is the underlying assumption of such passages. What we appear to have in first-century Judaism is a classic instance of synergism, where grace and merit were held together in tension. In this paradoxical situation, we have an antinomy, famously articulated by Rabbi Akiba: "The world is judged by grace, and yet all is according to the amount of work" (*Aboth* 3.20).[22]

The balance between covenant grace and works of the law was lost in post-exilic Israel. The experience of the exile understandably drove the Jews to observance of the law with a renewed dedication and energy. The result appears to have been a *de facto* legalism that became dominant and all but obscured the reality of covenant grace. Under these circumstances, it should not be surprising to discover that many or even most Jews of Paul's day were *de facto* legalists, in contradiction of a proper understanding of covenant grace. Paul is not necessarily arguing against a straw man, as many scholars claim.

Although the contexts were decidedly different, Paul's argument against works-righteousness is similar to Luther's, who after all is dependent on Paul. Both writers are concerned with salvation, that is, how sinners can stand justified before God. For Paul, and Luther, all of humanity, both Gentiles and Jews, are under judgment as sinners. The law, Paul argues, followed by Luther, has no answer to this universal problem, neither for the Jews nor the Gentiles. The solution to humanity's common plight is found in one way only: by faith in Christ's atoning sacrifice on the cross.

The recent, remarkable stress on continuity between Judaism and Christianity raises the question of whether and to what degree the NT is to be regarded as new at all,[23] and to what extent, if any, this newness creates an appreciable discontinuity.

---

[21] "In IV Ezra, in short, we see an instance in which covenantal nomism has collapsed. All that is left is legalistic perfectionism." Sanders, *Paul and Palestinian Judaism*, 409. 2 Baruch, probably dependent on 4 Ezra, contains a similar perspective.

[22] After citing this text, Israel Abrahams adds, "the antinomy is the ultimate doctrine of Pharisaism." Israel Abrahams, *Studies in Pharisaism and the Gospels*, First Series (Cambridge: Cambridge University Press, 1917; repr., New York: KTAV, 1967), 146.

[23] I must here mention the recent book by my Fuller Seminary colleague, OT scholar John Goldingay, *Do We Need the New Testament? Letting the Old Testament Speak for Itself* (Downers Grove, IL: InterVarsity Press,

It is important to insist from the start that there is no doubt about the extensive and substantial continuity between Christianity and Judaism. This is not at all in question. There is hardly much need to document or review the vast discussion that supports this conclusion. I accept it as a given. Both Jesus and Paul are of course intensely Jewish, as indeed is the entire NT, and so too the earliest church and its theology. A church that is truly biblical, therefore, cannot affirm Marcionism. For the Christian the OT and the NT belong together. What happens in Jesus and the coming of the kingdom of God through him is part of the one great metanarrative of the Bible: the history of salvation.[24] Christianity is the goal and culmination of the story of Israel. In and through the church the story of Israel continues. So thought all the writers of the NT. Herein lies the *continuity*. The extensive discontinuity we encounter in the NT itself presupposes this continuity

We have therefore to deal with *both* old and new. This point is famously made by Jesus, according to Matthew: "Therefore every scribe who has been trained for the kingdom of heaven is like the master of a household who brings out of his treasure what is new and what is old" [*kaina kai palaia*, lit. "new things and old things"]. The unexpected order of new things mentioned before old things places an extra emphasis on the new. For this reason, the biblical word *fulfillment* is the perfect word to describe what we encounter in the NT. The concept of fulfillment reaches both ways, back to the promises of the past and forward to future (and present) realization of the promises. The word "fulfillment" captures *the unity of the realization together with its promise*, and it is thus no surprise that it becomes such an important word in the vocabulary and conceptuality, not only of Matthew, but of all the NT writers.

Christianity is not *other* than Judaism; it is the *fulfillment of Judaism*. The early church was at first entirely Jewish, and although it remained a sect within Judaism for a very short time, Christianity is to be understood as *fulfilled Judaism*, and could be described as a Judaism coming to its divinely intended goal in the full inclusion of the Gentiles in the people of God.

While all this is true, at the same time the extent of newness in the Gospels—and indeed the whole of the NT—is such that an unavoidable *discontinuity* with Judaism is caused. Fulfillment includes forward movement and thus also inevitably involves discontinuity. It is the eschatological/apocalyptic

---

2015). While I appreciate Goldingay's opposition to Marcionism and his desire to value the OT on its own terms, I think he underestimates the extent and importance of the newness of the NT. His answer to the question posed in his title would seem to be something like: yes, but just barely. Goldingay emphasizes continuity and downplays discontinuity between the testaments. There are some good things and some important correctives to gain from reading Goldingay's book, but the idea of the NT as little more than an extension of the teaching of the OT fails to appreciate the radical newness that so captivated the authors of the NT.

[24] See Tom Schreiner's masterful book *The King in His Beauty: A Biblical Theology of the Old and New Testaments* (Grand Rapids: Baker Academic, 2013).

character of what the Gospels announce in the coming of Jesus[25] that marks the pivotal turning point in salvation history. Roy Harrisville's conclusion remains valid:

> That which is concealed and only intimated here [in Matt 13:52] is that the new which Jesus embodies is not merely the chronologically new, but above all, the *eschatologically new.* The element of continuity between new and old is indeed present, but it is a continuity which must not be allowed to deprive the new of its uniqueness (its contrast with the old), its finality, and its dynamic, i.e., its eschatological character.[26]

The nature and extent of this newness makes it impossible to describe Christianity as merely a sect or a reform movement within Judaism.[27] As C. F. D. Moule said: "It is the positive note of fulfilment that, ironically, constitutes the real offence—the *skandalon.* Christianity is undoubtedly new wine."[28]

I am pleased to offer this essay in tribute to Tom Schreiner, one of my first doctoral students at Fuller Seminary. One could have hardly wished for a better student than Tom: highly motivated, hardworking, good spirited, prompt, highly gifted, and docile. From my experience of Tom as a doctoral student, it is no surprise to me that he has had such a highly distinguished career, both in the seminary classroom and through his prolific teaching and writing ministry. Tom has blessed very many through his clear and faithful exposition of the Scriptures. We congratulate you, Tom, for a life lived in the service of Christ and to the glory of God. And may God grant you many more fruitful and rewarding years!

---

[25] "Paradoxically, therefore, the greatest discontinuity is in the coming of Jesus. From one perspective he fulfilled the promises and hopes of the Old Testament, and yet from another he surpassed all expectations so that his coming inaugurated a new and final stage in the history of salvation." David L. Baker, *Two Testaments, One Bible: The Theological Relationship between the Old and New Testaments,* 3rd ed. (Downers Grove, IL: InterVarsity Press, 2010) 223–24.

[26] Roy A. Harrisville, *The Concept of Newness in the New Testament* (Minneapolis: Augsburg, 1960), 28, my italics. The concept of newness "with its attendant aspects of continuity, contrast, finality and the dynamic is central to the New Testament literature as a whole" (Harrisville, 108).

[27] Thus rightly, Morna D. Hooker, *Continuity and Discontinuity: Early Christianity in its Jewish Setting* (London: Epworth, 1986), 23.

[28] He adds, "What, in the light of the facts, are we really saying about those wineskins?" This quotation is from Charles Moule's "Introductory Essay" to the Festschrift written in honor of Morna Hooker, which is entirely dedicated to our subject, viz., "continuity and discontinuity between early Christianity and its Jewish parent." *Early Christian Thought in its Jewish Context,* John Barclay and John Sweet, eds. (Cambridge: Cambridge University Press, 1996), 6.

*Chapter 8*

# Spirit and Letter in Corinth[1]

*by Mark A. Seifrid*

As Paul makes clear in 2 Corinthians 3, the issue at stake in Corinth is finally hermeneutical. It is a question as to how the presence of Christ in the world and especially in the apostles is to be interpreted and understood. "You are seeking proof of Christ, who speaks in me, who is not weak but powerful among you—for he also was crucified out of weakness, but lives by the power of God" (2 Cor 13:3–4). Paul's description of the Corinthian agenda is instructive. Here, at the conclusion of Second Corinthians, it becomes clear that they understand themselves to be in the role of judges as to the legitimacy of those who claimed to be apostles.

According to Paul himself, they are to exercise that role, although not in the way or at the time that they suppose. As the "word of the cross" that the apostle bears in body and life, the gospel must perform its own interpretive work in them and on them in order for them to judge rightly. They themselves must be "interpreted," given and shown their true identity by the gospel, before they can rightly interpret and discern the world: "the spiritual person judges all things, and they themselves are judged by no one" (1 Cor 2:15). The hermeneutic that Paul presents here is unheard of. Normally we cannot crawl out of our own skin and rise above our own limited (and self-serving) perspectives. We cannot by our own methods, reflection, thought, and learning arrive at a final interpretation of all things—even if the false optimism of modernism still keeps this hope alive. We cannot gain the final perspective that will allow us to see all things as they are: "I've looked at clouds from both sides now, from up and down and still somehow, it's clouds illusions I recall, I really don't

---

[1] Unless otherwise noted, translations of biblical texts are the author's own.

know clouds at all" (Joni Mitchell).[2] We can't get there from here. Under the narcotic influence of dreams of power, and the idolization of the human being, the Corinthians suppose that they can. Throughout the Corinthian correspondence, Paul seeks to bring them back to the crucified Christ and thus back to themselves and to a realistic understanding of the world.[3] As a material hermeneutic that interprets all things, including us, from the work and word of the cross, the hermeneutic of the gospel is scandalous. It challenges not only the wisdom of rhetoric that the Corinthians adored but also the scientific optimism of modernism and the casual tolerance of clashing perspectives that characterizes our postmodern society.

The hermeneutical force of the gospel appears as the first and most prominent element of Paul's defense of his apostolic calling in Second Corinthians at 3:1–18. This relatively short passage remains a center of debate up to today, and no wonder, given the weighty issues at stake.

Although Paul's argument here marks the formal beginning of his self-defense in 2 Corinthians, it is really no "self-defense," as Paul himself makes clear to the Corinthians. Paul lets the gospel do its own talking and perform its own work. A self-defense on Paul's part would have amounted to an act of unbelief and a betrayal of the gospel. He is not a genius nor a charismatic rhetorician, as the Corinthians hoped they might obtain for themselves. He is an apostle, who in his whole person bears the message of another. As he has informed the Corinthians, he is not accountable to them, but to Christ (1 Cor 4:1–5). The Corinthians themselves, furthermore, are accountable to the crucified Christ who is present and speaks in the apostle. They shall have to give account of themselves to him (2 Cor 5:10). Up until now, they have imagined that they are the audience who has the right and duty to judge Christ's apostle, along with all the other apostolic candidates who have lined up before them. In refusing to defend himself, Paul informs them that the scene is radically different from the way in which they picture it. It is not they who are the audience nor is Paul the performer. It is God who is the audience. Paul is the prompter, who is there to teach them the lines for their own performance. It is God who is the judge as to whether they have learned their lines properly as the actors on the stage.[4]

In this chapter, Paul presents his gospel on the basis of Scripture. Like much of his use of Scripture, his use of the text is figural. That is to say, Paul

---

[2] Both Sides Now lyrics © Sony/ATV Music Publishing LLC, Crazy Crow Music / Siquomb Music Publishing.

[3] "Because we in Adam ascended to being like God, he has descended into our likeness, in order to bring us to the knowledge of ourselves . . . to make out of unhappy and proud gods, true human beings, namely, miserable mortals and sinners," Luther *WA* 5, 128,39–129,1.

[4] Søren Kierkegaard, *Purity of Heart is to Will One Thing*, trans. & introd. by D. V. Steere (New York: Harper and Row, 1948), 181.

finds within the stories of Israel the pattern of God's dealings with the world in judgment and salvation that have now come to fulfillment in Christ—a fulfillment that is greater than the promise. As he has earlier informed the Corinthians concerning the wilderness generation: "these things happened to them in a figural manner (τυπικῶς) and they have been written for our instruction, (we) upon whom the ends of the ages have come" (1 Cor 10:11; cf. 10:1–13). Just as he has done in 1 Corinthians 10, in 2 Corinthians 3 Paul holds up to the Corinthians the story of Scripture—in this case, Moses's administration of the Law to Israel (Exod 34:29–35)—as a "mirror" in which the Corinthians are to see God's dealings with them in Christ and thus to see themselves as well.[5]

Paul's introduction of the giving of the Law through Moses into his argument has created confusion among interpreters concerning Paul's opponents in Corinth. On the one hand, they bring a clearly Hellenistic perspective, as is especially clear in the high estimation of rhetoric and charismatic appearance that they share with the Corinthians (2 Cor 10:10–11). On the other hand, they claim to be thoroughly Jewish in language, heritage, and background (2 Cor 11:22).

Shouldn't we suppose that they advocated Judaizing in Corinth? Paul's contrast between his apostolic ministry and that of Moses has seemed to support this interpretation of the opponents and of the message of 2 Corinthians 3. The problem with this reading, however, is that the Corinthian correspondence provides no evidence that there was any problem of Judaizing within the church. In the only instance in which Paul deals with the question of circumcision in Corinth, he first urges Jewish believers not to remove the mark of their circumcision. Only then does he likewise tell his Gentile readers not to be concerned about being uncircumcised: neither circumcision nor uncircumcision is of any significance, only the keeping of the commandments of God (1 Cor 7:17–20). In a church in which Jews are considering becoming Greeks, there is little danger of Gentiles being compelled to become Jews. The ethical issues within the church with which Paul must deal point in the same direction: the man who has his father's wife, the open immorality coupled with the claim that "all things are permitted," and the issue of idolatry and eating meat sacrificed to idols all point to a highly Hellenized context, in which the adoption of Judaism as a necessary element of salvation could hardly have been imagined. According to Luke, the church had undergone a dramatic break with the synagogue (Acts 18:12–17). It is not likely that many within it had any desire to return there. Furthermore, in the passage before us, Paul does not speak in his usual terms of the Law, Jews, Gentiles, or circumcision or food

---

[5]  Paul, in fact, uses the very image of a mirror in 3:18 in description of our present vision of God.

laws. He instead uses the honorific term "sons of Israel" (3:7,13) and speaks of "the letter" (3:6), and makes no mention of Jewish practices, only the giving of the Law, or more precisely, Moses's administration of the letter. We have every reason to suppose that Paul is not addressing the question of Gentile circumcision and Law-keeping. Instead, as we have suggested, he finds within the Scriptures, and within the story of Israel in particular, the pattern of God's saving dealings that has come to its fulfillment in Christ. He appeals to the text of Exodus because he finds in Moses's administration of the Law and Israel's response figures that have come to fulfillment both in contrast and in correlation with the ministry of the gospel that has been entrusted to him.

There are three movements to Paul's argument in the chapter. In verses 1–3 he asserts that the Corinthians themselves are evidence of his apostolic calling. Through him, by the Spirit, Christ has "rewritten" them and made them new. Consequently, Paul requires no commendation for them or from them. He goes on to describe the basis of this confidence—surprisingly—in the figure of Moses's (second) administration of the Law (3:4–11; cf. Exod 34:29–35). He then describes the nature of his ministry, or more precisely, he describes his bold and open speech (παρρησία), by continuing to appeal to the story of Moses's (second) giving of the Law—now the contrasting pattern to his ministry of the Spirit (3:12–18).

Paul's opening rejection of any need for letters of commendation to or from the Corinthians is obviously a response to their desire or, perhaps, demand for such letters. His outright rejection of the need for commendation from the Corinthians is one of the most comforting aspects of his message in this letter for anyone who is called to Christian ministry, especially in a time in which job performance and skills are constantly subject to review and evaluation. The Christ who performs his work through the apostle performs his work through those who deliver the apostolic word as well. The work of the gospel is not subject to annual review. This is the very issue at stake in Corinth. Those who minister the gospel bear a gift that transcends human judgments. We do not quite face the Corinthian question, or at least not in the full force that Paul did. We dare not place ourselves above those whom we have been sent to serve. Not even Paul does so. He will not be lord over the faith of the Corinthians. In their faith they stand—they stand alongside him as equals in Christ (1:24). Furthermore, it is perfectly appropriate for a congregation or institution to hold accountable those whom they have called to serve to the outward and visible standards of performance that belong to the office of ministry, just as every other vocation has its own standards. Paul himself recognizes the validity of such standards with respect to his conduct.[6] And he pointedly calls attention

---

[6]  1 Cor 4:1–5; 2 Cor 4:1–2; 11:7–11.

to the way in which his opponents in Corinth treat the church abusively.[7] Paul leaves no room for an authoritarian pastor, who will not listen to the legitimate concerns of the congregation. The same applies to a lazy or negligent one. Nevertheless, Paul makes clear that there is a line set by the gospel that must not be crossed. The Corinthians had developed a taste for a more charismatic leadership and a finer rhetoric than Paul was willing or able to deliver. Nor were they willing to put up with his weak appearance and constant troubles. At this point, the Corinthians and Paul had their own "worship wars." And precisely at this point, Paul will not yield. Nor will he enter into comparisons in terms of influence and numbers (2 Cor 10:12–18). These limits of ministry are set by God for each one: he planted, Apollos watered, but it was God who gave the growth of the word among the Corinthians (1 Cor 3:6).[8] Admittedly, there are contexts of conflict in which the line between human responsibility and the authority of the gospel may be hard to discern. But especially within our cultural context, there is tremendous freedom—the kind of which Paul speaks later in 2 Corinthians 3—in reminding ourselves that the real work of the gospel—the impartation of life—is God's work and not our own, and that the limits and success of our ministry are set by God. We are called simply to be faithful stewards of the treasure entrusted to us.[9]

There is another element of the apostolic ministry of the gospel that appears within Paul's argument in vv. 1–3 that we should note. Paul does not merely appeal to the believing Corinthians as evidence of his apostolic calling. He interjects another significant element into his argument. The Corinthians are Paul's letter of commendation as they have been written within his heart. Indeed, this letter is "known and read by all human beings." All the world knows that Paul is Christ's apostle to the Corinthians. The love that Paul has for them, and yet more deeply, the way in which Christ himself has bound Paul and the Corinthians together in time and eternity, is open evidence of Paul's apostolic calling. The theme of the bond between the apostle and his church, as between a father and his children, appears already in 1 Corinthians, and recurs frequently in 2 Corinthians. It is essential to his ministry of the gospel. We shall return to this matter.

At the moment, we are interested in Paul's remarkable confidence in the power of the gospel to change human hearts, a power which Paul quite remarkably finds in the giving of the law itself. Paul introduces this contrast already in his opening assertion of his authority. The place that the Corinthians hold within his heart has its counterpart in the work of the Spirit in the hearts of the Corinthians. The Corinthians are a letter that Christ himself writes, through

---

[7]  2 Cor 11:20.

[8]  He speaks to the issue of comparisons directly in 2 Cor 10:11–18.

[9]  1 Cor 4:1–5; 2 Cor 4:1–15.

Paul, his agent (v. 3). They have been written, or we might say rewritten, not with ink on paper as the Corinthians have demanded of Paul, but "by the Spirit of the living God." Paul takes up the biblical contrast between Yahweh and the idols and applies it to the Corinthian demand for letters and their judgment based on outward appearance. He then suddenly shifts his metaphor in preparation for his scriptural exposition of apostolic ministry: the letter of Christ is written "not on tablets of stone, but on tablets of fleshly hearts."[10] The Corinthians are Christ's palimpsest. In writing upon their rebellious hearts, he has created them anew (compare 5:17).

Paul introduces this change in metaphors in order to describe the basis of his confidence as an apostle. He has been entrusted with the ministry of the new covenant, which as God's own work makes him sufficient for the task entrusted to him. He himself raises the issue of sufficiency for the ministry of the gospel in 2:16. As the apostle of Christ, led as a captive in a Roman triumph to his death, he serves as the "aroma of Christ" within the world. For some—those who believe—an "aroma of life bringing life" and for others an "aroma of death to death." The ministry of the gospel is nothing other than the imparting of eternal life. Where this word is rejected there remains nothing but judgment and death. Paul's rhetorical question, "Who is sufficient for these things?" is no mere response to the demands of the Corinthians. It is a declaration of the radically extrinsic nature of Christian ministry. The sufficiency of the apostle does not lie in himself, but in God, and in the ministry with which he has been entrusted (3:5).

At this point, Paul describes the basis and nature of his ministry in a remarkable appeal to Scripture. God has made him adequate as an agent of a new covenant, not of "the letter" (γράμμα) but of "the Spirit," for, as Paul explains, "the letter kills and/but (δε) the Spirit gives life."[11] In his description of his ministry as that of a "new covenant," Paul alludes to the promise of Jer 31:31–34. Here the Lord promises his rebellious people, who have not kept

---

[10] As is clear from the major English translations, Paul's final word is usually taken positively: "tablets of human hearts." But the term σάρκινος is to be taken negatively as a description of the human in rebellion, as Paul does in Rom 7:14 and 1 Cor 3:1. Moreover, the appeal to Ezek 36:26, which speaks of God giving Israel a "heart of flesh" so that they will love and obey him is misplaced. In that context, the "heart of flesh" is the result of God's saving work. In 2 Cor 3:3 the "fleshly hearts" are the rebellious human hearts upon which the Spirit performs its saving work. It is more likely that Paul alludes to Jer 17:1, which likewise speaks of Israel's hardened heart. He thereby reconfigures his muted appeal to Ezek 11:19 and 36:26. See M. Seifrid, *The Second Letter to the Corinthians*, (Pillar New Testament Commentary Grand Rapids: Eerdmans, 2014), 117–18.

[11] Paul's contrast of "the letter" with "the Spirit" has long been of interest to interpreters and continues to be so. We cannot here review the issues. A fresh history of interpretation would be of considerable benefit. Here I am taking the position, well-supported by the context, that the contrast is not between literal meaning and allegory, but between the law as outward demand and the Spirit as the gift of God's presence that recreates the human being. See Seifrid, *Second Corinthians*, 130–50.

the covenant given at Sinai, that he will "give his Law in their inward part" and "write it on their heart" (Jer 31:34). God promises to step on to the scene and work in his people's heart what the old covenant set before them as written code. In his description of the Corinthians as his commendation, Paul has already echoed the language of the Jeremianic promise (3:3), now he obviously alludes to it. The promise to Israel bears saving power for all the world.

The surprising element of Paul's argument here is that he finds a foreshadowing of the gift of the Spirit within the giving of the law. The connection that Paul draws here between "letter" and "Spirit," and thus between law and gospel, makes clear that he understands the two contrasting modes of divine revelation as constituting a unity—a coincidence of opposites though it is—within the divine purpose. He finds this paradoxical unity in the revelation of the divine glory associated with the giving of the law. He sees in this glory a promise which he unfolds in three movements in verses 7–11. "If the ministry of death came with such a brilliant, divine glory that the sons of Israel could not bear to look upon the face of Moses that was radiant with it, must not the ministry of the Spirit take place even more with glory?" (vv. 7–8). Paul's rewording of the ministry of the "letter" as a ministry of "death" makes it clear that he uses "letter" as a metonym for the law and that he understands the law as effecting death.

This death-effecting function of the law becomes clear in his following, parallel, elaboration in verses 9–10. Paul continues to appeal to the Exodus narrative concerning Moses's face: "If there was a glory to the ministry of condemnation, the ministry of righteousness shall abound *much more* in glory." The rhetorical question of verses 7–8 now is replaced by a direct assertion. Paul also defines "death" more closely: the ministry of the "letter" works *condemnation*. It pronounces the death sentence on Israel, and not merely on Israel, but on the entire world.[12] The ministry of the new covenant is one of "righteousness," the effective judgment of God that forgives, renews, and recreates the fallen human being. Most importantly, Paul elevates his claim. There is not only more glory to the apostolic ministry, but "much more" glory in it, no matter that this glory presently remains unseen. Indeed, the glory of this ministry is so great that it eclipses the glory of Moses's face so that it is no glory at all. Continuity and discontinuity coincide.

In his third and final description of the new covenant, Paul takes up the contrast that he has just voiced, shifting its location away from the ministry of Moses to Moses's face and thus implicitly from the divine revelation to the covenant that he administered. If there was a glory to that which is (now) done away, that which endures does so in glory (v. 11). This appeal to the glory of

---

[12] This claim appears elsewhere with Paul. See Rom 3:19–20; Gal 3:19–22.

Moses's face, now transcended by the glory of the apostolic ministry of the new covenant, is the basis of Paul's confidence. It is a glory that remains unseen, as the Corinthians were well aware.

Paul's assertion of the glory of the new covenant is his substitute for "boasting" and for the letters of commendation that the Corinthians apparently required of him. He thus speaks with great boldness and freedom (πολλῇ παρρησία). He does not cover his face as Moses did in the presence of "the sons of Israel."

Paul takes up the Exodus narrative again in vv. 2–18, now focusing on Moses's actions in contrast to his own conduct as an apostle of Christ. Moses placed a veil over his face, according to Paul, in order that the "sons of Israel might not look upon the goal of that which is done away" (v. 13). Paul enacts in speech what Moses enacted with his veil: he speaks in circumlocution concerning the divine glory of Moses's face. Moses's veil worked the hardening of the minds of the "sons of Israel." Indeed, says Paul, until today, the same veil lies upon their hearts—what Moses did comes upon Israel—upon the reading of the old covenant. It has not been revealed to them that "in Christ" the old covenant has been done away (v. 14).[13] Until today, whenever Moses is read, a veil lies upon their hearts (v. 15). Paul goes on in his following argument to speak (quite boldly) of "the god of this age" blinding the minds of unbelievers, so that they cannot see "the light of the Gospel of the glory of Christ, the image of God" (4:4). Moses's action in veiling his face from "the sons of Israel" was not only effective, but also serves a figural function. It presents the divine act of judgment that renders the world blind to his saving work. It is only from within God's saving work that we can see that life and righteousness arrive through death and condemnation—the death and condemnation of Christ's cross. We were blind, now in Christ we see. The Corinthians, who in their demand for letters, cannot at all perceive the glory of the apostolic ministry, are in danger of being in the same place as that of the sons of Israel, and thus that of blind unbelievers.

Paul's argument takes a turn at verse 16, just as Moses himself took a turn: "as often as he turned to the Lord, he removed the veil." Virtually all English translations interpret this verse as referring to the event of conversion: "as often as someone turns to the Lord, . . ." But since Paul understands Moses's veiling his face as an effective prophetic action, and since he continues to refer to the Exodus narrative here, it is more likely that he still refers in the first place to Moses, and merely suggests the event of conversion by his choice of the verb ἐπιστρέφειν. Just as Moses removed his veil, whenever he "turned" to go in to

---

[13] See Seifrid, *Second Corinthians*, 167–71.

the Lord, so "we all"—Paul includes the Corinthians—"with unveiled face" view the glory of the Lord in a mirror.

Before Paul speaks about our beholding the Lord's glory, he interjects a remarkable interpretive statement, drawn again from the Exodus narrative: "The Lord is the Spirit. And where the Spirit of the Lord is, there is freedom" (v. 17). Paul's puzzling predication is best understood as an interpretive statement: the Lord, whom Moses encountered in the tent of meeting, is none other than the Spirit, who is given through the new covenant administered by the apostle (cf. Exod 34:34). Just as Moses met the Lord in the tent of meeting, so the Spirit is to be found in a specific location, namely, in Christ and in the gospel that proclaims him: "And *where* the Spirit of the Lord is, *there* is freedom." The freedom with which Paul speaks of freedom is remarkable. He provides no definition, but simply allows it to be interpreted by allusion to the context of Exodus 34. It is no wonder that his statement has been regularly misinterpreted.[14] Yet Paul's freedom in speaking of freedom is a very expression of that freedom. It is the freedom from the death and condemnation worked by "the letter." And it is before all else a freedom from blindness and hardness of heart. The veil is removed. In Christ we meet God in the freedom of love and communication, a relationship that is given and established by the very Spirit of God given within our hearts. It is certainly not the case that God thereby merely talks to himself or comes to himself. It is instead the case that God comes to his fallen human creatures and speaks to them, communicates himself to them, from the innermost depths of his being to the innermost depths of their being:

> And we all, with unveiled face, beholding in a mirror the glory of the Lord, are transformed into the same image from glory to glory, just as from the Lord (whom Moses met), who is the Spirit. (v. 18)

This relationship of communication is effected by the proclamation of the gospel. That is Paul's point. That is why he needs no letters of commendation to or from the Corinthians. They are his letter. The visual imagery that Paul employs here must not be misunderstood. He is not speaking about a sort of glory that is visible or that we can discern directly in and of ourselves.[15] The glory of the apostolic ministry, which is nothing other than the in-breaking of the eschaton, is not apparent to the naked eye. The Corinthians certainly do not discern it in Paul. Nor do "the sons of Israel" recognize it as they hear Moses read in the synagogue. Nor do unbelievers, whose minds have been blinded by the "god of this world" (4:4). As is the case throughout this chapter, "seeing" is a figure for "perceiving with the heart." And what we perceive is the

---

[14] Here, too, a history of interpretation would be very interesting and useful.
[15] See Seifrid, *Second Corinthians*, 180–81.

message of the gospel: life and righteousness in the crucified Christ. We thus see with our ears. Paul brings to expression the indirect nature of our "seeing" with the figure of "beholding in a mirror" the glory of the Lord. This element of his statement is foreign to the Exodus narrative. He inserts it as a matter of eschatological reserve. The figure recalls the same reserve he articulates in 1 Cor 13:12, even if the terms differ: "For we see now by means of a mirror in a riddle, but then (we shall see) face to face." Paul is far bolder in 2 Corinthians 3, but he does not omit an eschatological reserve. The mirror through which we see is Christ, whom Paul proclaims. He is the image of God (4:4). In him we find the glory of God and we are transformed by that glory: "Arise, shine, for your light has come, and the glory of the Lord has risen upon you" (Isa 60:1).[16] This promise to Jerusalem is given in Christ to all believers. This is the confidence that Paul has in the ministry of the new covenant.

If the results of our preaching appear paltry to us, we must remind ourselves that the same was the case for Paul, especially in his relationship with the Corinthians. The church in Corinth was no megachurch. It is doubtful whether it consisted of more than 150 or so believers. And Paul was just about to lose his position of leadership within the church. They couldn't dismiss him from his call, because he had planted the church himself. But they certainly could ignore him and put someone else in his place. For his part, Paul, despite his expressions of confidence, was practically at his wits' end with the church. He had nearly been consumed emotionally, physically, and spiritually by its problems. He frames the entire body of the letter with his worry over them and relief at their fragile, yet positive response to him.[17] If Paul had measured the value of his life and his life's work by what stood before his eyes, he would have been "the most pitiful of all people" (1 Cor 15:19). These words were written in response to the Corinthian rejection of the resurrection. But they may still speak to us. Are not we as Christians, and especially as those called to Christian ministry, often tempted by a sort of pious paganism, one which substitutes visible success in ministry for trust and hope in God? The text from Ps 90:12, "so teach us to number our days, that we may present to you a heart of wisdom," may be readily abused in this way. We may not give ourselves to "eating, drinking, and being merry," but are we not tempted to put in their place the equivalent in labor "for the kingdom" and visible accomplishments in church life? I am not advocating laziness. But Paul is teaching us along with the Corinthians that the *real* results of ministry, the "gold, silver, and precious stones" that are to be built on Christ as the foundation (1 Cor 3:11–12), are the presently unseen realities of faith, hope, and love. And these realities are worked by the gospel alone.

---

[16] The expression concerning our transformation "from glory to glory" is not one of progress, but one of communication. See Seifrid, *Second Corinthians*, 186.

[17] See 2 Cor 2:12–13; 7:5–7. cf. 11:28–29.

# Chapter 9

# The Triune God of Hebrews

*by Barry Joslin*

In terms of my own academic career and ministry, no one has encouraged, mentored, and influenced me more than Tom Schreiner. His example as a scholar, friend, and family man has been a gift for which I regularly give thanks. Since the outset of my academic career, I have specialized in the book of Hebrews, and that specialization is due in no small part to Tom's influence. As my doctoral supervisor, he saw my love and curiosity for Hebrews, and encouraged me to make it a focus for my own research and writing. His own work on Hebrews has been a model of rigorous and yet humble scholarship that I desire to emulate in some small part. His is a legacy that has been minted not just in his many students, but also in their students. I am profoundly humbled to have the opportunity to contribute to a volume in honor of my teacher, mentor, colleague, and friend.

My aim in this essay is to examine what the book of Hebrews contributes to our trinitarian understanding of God. Is there a Trinity in Hebrews? Is it fair to the writer of Hebrews to speak in these terms when he does not? Or is such an exercise simply hoisting dogmatic categories onto the ancient text? If such questions can be answered satisfactorily, then perhaps we can draw helpful conclusions as to how the inspired writer understood the godhead.

I contend that the writer of Hebrews is indeed "Trinitarian," even though such nomenclature is anachronistic. His "trinitarianism" is not explicit but implicit. Hebrews precedes Nicea by 250+ years and Chalcedon by almost 400. Harold Attridge correctly states that there is no Chalcedonian-like confession of the Trinity in Hebrews.[1] This is, of course, true. But this is not to say that the writer of Hebrews is *not* "trinitarian," or that he contributes nothing to the church's understanding of this article of faith. Indeed, I will demonstrate that a robust trinitarian perspective is reflected in the pages of Hebrews. While other personalities in the book appear as models of faithfulness, only Father, Son, and Spirit are described in terms that are uniquely divine. [2]

## THE DEITY AS FATHER

Θεός appears sixty-eight times in sixty-three verses in the book of Hebrews. In every instance but one, the term refers to the Father. For example, the independent clause at the opening of the sermon reads, "God spoke in his Son" (1:1–2)[3]. In 1:9, it is "God, your God, has anointed you with the oil of gladness above your companions," referring to the Father blessing the Son. In 2:3–4 the words of the Lord (Jesus, the Son) are verified by God the Father's testimony by the miraculous works of the Spirit's power.[4] It is God the Father to whom we draw near through Christ the Son (7:19); Jesus the Son and High Priest saves forever all who draw near to God (the Father) through him (7:25). Jesus the Son, after completing his work on the cross, is resurrected and seated at the right hand of God the Father (12:2). The list is as lengthy as it is consistent: in Hebrews, θεός refers to the Father. The lone exception that proves the rule is Heb 1:8 (citing Psalm 45), in which θεὸς is used to refer to the Son. This Father creates, speaks, begets, is propitiated, sends (the Son), judges, is patient, covenants with humanity, gives grace, commands, builds, rests, calls,

---

[1]  Attridge insists that there is no such "Trinitarian speculation" in Hebrews. Harold Attridge, *The Epistle to the Hebrews*, Hermeneia (Philadelphia: Fortress, 1989), 250. Cf. James Moffatt, *A Critical and Exegetical Commentary on the Epistle to the Hebrews*, ICC (Edinburgh: T&T Clark, 1924; repr., 1952), 124. Otto Michel, *Der Brief an die Hebräer*, Kritisch-exegetischer Kommentar über das Neue Testament 13 (Göttingen: Vandenhoeck & Ruprecht, 1966), 314.

[2]  In recent years there has been a growing interest in the study of Hebrews and the Trinity. See Martin Emmrich, "*PNEUMA* in Hebrews: Prophet and Interpreter," *Westminster Theological Journal* 63 (2002): 55–71; José Rondón, "Trinitarian Solidarity with Mankind in the Book of Hebrews," *Faith and Mission* 21, no. 3 (2004): 46–64; Jonathan I. Griffiths, "Hebrews and the Trinity," in *The Essential Trinity: New Testament Foundations and Practical Relevance*, ed. Brandon D. Crowe and Carl R. Trueman, (Phillipsburg, NJ: P&R, 2017), 135–53; Nathan D. Holsteen, "The Trinity in the Book of Hebrews," *BibSac* 169 (2011): 334–46; C. Kavin Rowe, "The Trinity in the Letters of St. Paul and Hebrews," in Giles Emery and Matthew Levering, eds., *The Oxford Handbook of the Trinity* (Oxford: Oxford University Press, 2011), 41–54. The Griffiths essay is particularly helpful as he focuses on two main aspects, revelation and redemption.

[3]  Unless otherwise noted, biblical translations are the author's own.

[4]  This is an important text in that it refers to all three persons of the Trinity: The Lord (Son) speaks, God (the Father) bears witness by the works of the Spirit. It is the Father who bears witness, "συνεπιμαρτυροῦντος τοῦ θεοῦ σημείοις τε καὶ τέρασιν καὶ ποικίλαις δυνάμεσιν καὶ πνεύματος ἁγίου μερισμοῖς κατὰ τὴν αὐτοῦ θέλησιν" (Heb 2:4).

designates, blesses, is wrathful, promises, warns, lives, wills, takes up, is pleased, exists, provides, reigns, and receives sacrifices and praise.[5]

The priesthood of the old covenant obviously figures prominently into the argument of Hebrews. Attridge has argued that the priesthood itself bears witness to deity: "God is the indispensable horizon within which discussion of such a priest makes sense and the ultimate focal point of such a priest's action."[6] In the implicit narrative of Hebrews, there is a presupposed "theistic horizon" within which the actions of God in history are portrayed.[7] God is a being of revelation, who speaks and reveals himself in many portions and in many ways (1:1), who is said to "speak in a Son" in these "latter days" (1:2). Griffith avers, "The Son is himself God's revelatory Word, his speech in personal form."[8]

Further, the words that God has spoken are neither to be shunned nor ignored (2:1–4; 12:25–29), lest judgment be rendered. The importance of God's revelatory act can hardly be overemphasized for the writer of Hebrews. Such revelation, for Hebrews, is divine due to its having come from God the Father himself.[9] God as "Father" is presented with specificity in texts such as the exordium of 1:1–4, which informs the readers of the sermon that θεὸς *is* the divine Father. God (θεὸς) spoke through the prophets and now has spoken in the Son. Logically where there is Son, there is "Father," especially given the Jewish Christian context to which Hebrews was written. This is especially apparent when both θεὸς and υἱός occur in the same context.[10]

Further, when there is inheritance that is given to the eternal Son (cf 1:2, 4) whether it is "all things" or the divine name (1:4), the eternal Son inherits such from his eternal Father. This seems clear in the next verse, when θεὸς who speaks, addresses his "Son" (1:5). It is perhaps most clear that θεὸς is "Father" in a text such as Hebrews 12:7, "It is for discipline that you have to endure. God (θεὸς) is treating you as sons. For what son is there whom his father does not discipline?" Indeed, 12:4–11 rests on the author's point that θεὸς is the heavenly Father who loves and disciplines his legitimate children. Furthermore, there is a comparison between earthly fathers, and the heavenly

---

[5] See the following uses of θεὸς: 1:1, 6, 9 [2]; 2:4, 9, 13, 17; 3:4, 12; 4:4, 9, 10, 12, 14; 5:1, 4, 10, 12; 6:1, 3, 5, 6, 7, 10, 13, 17, 18; 7:1, 3, 19, 25, 8:10; 9:14 [2], 20, 24; 10:7, 12, 21, 29, 31, 36; 11:3, 4 [2], 5 [2], 6, 10, 16 [2], 19, 25, 40; 12:2, 7, 15, 22, 23, 28, 29; 13:4, 7, 15, 16, 20.

[6] Harold W. Attridge, "God in Hebrews," in *The Forgotten God: Perspectives in Biblical Theology*, ed. A. A. Das and F. J. Matera (Louisville: Westminster John Knox, 2002), 197.

[7] Attridge, 199.

[8] Griffiths, "Hebrews and the Trinity," 123.

[9] David Peterson, "God and Scripture in Hebrews," in *The Trustworthiness of God*, ed. Paul Helm and Carl R. Trueman (Grand Rapids: Eerdmans, 2002), 123ff.

[10] Each occurance of "Son of God" also implies the divine fatherhood of θεὸς (4:14; 6:6; 7:3; 10:29). In such passages, there seems to be a connection between the "Son" and his θεὸς as "Father."

θεὸς, the "father of spirits" who disciplines us for our good so that we may share his holiness" (12:9–10).

Further, it is God the Father whose will is done by the Son (10:5–10), who is seated in the heavens (1:3; 10:12; 1:4; 12:2), who eternally begets the Son (1:5; 5:5), receives the blood of the sacrificial Son offered through the eternal Spirit (10:14), receives the supplications and mediation of the Son (5:7; 7:25), and metes out judgment for those who trample underfoot the Son of God and insult the Spirit of grace (10:31). His divine will rules his righteous ones when they do not shrink back to destruction (10:37–39). Hebrews 11 teaches that he receives the sacrifice of Abel and takes up Enoch; is pleased by faith, and rewards those who seek him. He warns Noah and destroys the world by flood; he designs and builds the eternal city; he is not ashamed to be called the God of those who are of faith. In chapter 12, God the Father sovereignly disciplines his children unto holiness, without which they will not see him. He is the judge of all who speaks and shakes the earth and the heavens; he is an all-consuming fire (Heb 12:29; cf. Deut 4:24; 9:3).

## THE DEITY AS SON

Hebrews also identifies deity with the Son. The first line of evidence comes from the prologue. In contrast to the revelatory medium of the prophets of the previous era, God now speaks through his Son.[11] The finality and importance of God's revelation in the Son is heightened by the seven descriptors that follow; such descriptors argue for the Son's deity both individually and collectively. For instance, creation is an action performed by deity,[12] and for the writer to declare the Son's agency is to assert his deity. Against George Caird, John Webster argues that the preexistence of the Son is presupposed, yet preexistence does not rule out full humanity. By denying this, "Caird can, for example, make little sense of the Son's activity in creation and providence."[13] Rather, what is in view is an "eternal, inner-divine relation of θεός and υἱός."[14] God and God alone creates. This is a distinguishing feature of Greco-Roman Jewish monotheism, and is especially prevalent in the Christian Scriptures.

---

[11] Philip E. Hughes, *A Commentary on the Epistle to the Hebrews* (Grand Rapids: Eerdmans, 1977), 36n3.

[12] See Heb 2:10, 11:3. Whether or not one sees *creatio ex nihilo* in Hebrews, the fact of creation, however understood, is the action of God. See Col 1:16 and John 1:3 for similar thought.

[13] John Webster, "One Who is Son: Theological Reflection on the Exordium to the Epistle to the Hebrews," (plenary paper presented to the St. Andrews Conference on Hebrews and Christian Theology University of St. Andrews, Scotland, UK July 2006) 17. See G. B. Caird, "Son by Appointment," in W. Weinrich, ed., *The New Testament Age: Essays in Honor of Bo Reicke* (Macon, GA: Mercer University Press, 1984), 2:76.

[14] Webster, "One Who is Son," 19. Attridge may be correct when he avers that such an affirmation of a preexistence Christology has its background in the sapiential tradition, hearing a distinct echo of Proverbs 8 (Attridge, *Hebrews*, 40); Wis 9:9–11. For a similar idea in Hellenized Judaism, see Philo, *Special Legislation*, 1.81; 3.207; *Migration of Abraham* 6; *On the Cherubim*, 125–27; *On Flight*, 95.

Further, "sonship" in the prologue points to a unique relationship between the Father and the Son. He is not merely one of many sons (2:10), or one of a class of sons. There is a difference between "Son" (1:1–4) and "sons" (2:10–18; 12:4–14). Webster again is helpful on this point when he writes,

> "Son" is to have a particular nature which is neither common nor communicable, and to stand in a wholly unrepeatable relation to the Father. Later Christian tradition will come to conceptualise this by speaking of the Son as a hypostasis or mode of subsistence within the godhead, and of the Son's relation to the Father as one of filiation. Such terms . . . penetrate to and draw out the real force of the phrase here, which is to locate the being of the Son in God, and to reinforce his uniqueness.[15]

This becomes even more apparent when we are told that the Son shares the nature of God ("the exact representation of His nature"), and that the Son also upholds "all things by means of his powerful word." The whole exordium magnifies the excellence of the Son.[16] Given these seven descriptors of the Son, which exalt not just who he is, but also what he does, it seems apparent that the writer understands the Son to share the same essence with the deity. Both ontological and economic aspects are crucial, and without them, the homily itself loses its force.

A second line of evidence comes from the catena of texts in 1:5–13, especially 8–10.[17] Psalm 45:6–7 (LXX 44:7–8) and 102:25 (LXX 101:26) are striking since the speaker is God the Father speaking to/of the Son (πρὸς δὲ τὸν υἱόν). George Guthrie concludes, "It is clear that the author of Hebrews walks the path of other Jewish interpreters of the era in understanding the psalm [Psalm 45] as messianic, and thus, for him, Christological . . . and uses it to affirm Jesus as 'God'."[18] Yet in affirming the deity of the Son, Hebrews is careful not to equate the Father with the Son in every respect (1:9). What we see is an implicit trinitarian perspective "that affirms the Son as God but makes a distinction between him and the Father."[19]

A similar idea appears in verse 10, where the Son is κύριος in fulfillment of Ps 102:25 (LXX 101:26). These verses deepen the reader's understanding of

---

[15] Webster, "One Who is Son," 14.

[16] Ceslas Spicq, L'Épitre aux Hébreux (Paris: Gabalda, 1953), 2:1.

[17] See Herbert W. Bateman, Early Jewish Hermeneutics and Hebrews 1:5–13 (New York: Peter Lang, 1997); cf. G. Guthrie, "Hebrews," in Commentary on the New Testament Use of the Old Testament, ed. Beale and Carson (Grand Rapids: Baker, 2007), 925–44.

[18] Guthrie, "Hebrews," 939.

[19] Guthrie, 939. See also M. J. Harris, "The Translation and Significance of ho theos in Hebrews 1:8–9," Tyndale Bulletin 36:129–62; Harris, Jesus as God: The New Testament Use of Theos in Reference to Jesus (Grand Rapids: Baker, 1992), 205–27.

what was said of the Son as the agent of creation in 1:2, and center on his being Lord over creation. Verse 10 also supports the Son's preexistence, and 1:11–12 assert the Son's eternality (τὰ ἔτη σου οὐκ ἐκλείψουσιν). Taken together, Psalms 45 and 102 strengthen a previous point: the Son is coeternal with the Father and participates in the same divine activity as the Father.

A third piece of evidence is the Son's "speaking" Scripture. Beginning in 1:1–4, Hebrews places an emphasis on the revelatory act of God.[20] There is no other New Testament document so dense with OT quotations, yet the introductory formula is not what we find elsewhere such as in Matthew or Paul.[21] Instead, the OT is the living voice of God speaking to his audience, finding its locus of meaning in the person and work of the Son. It is in this sense that one sees continuity within discontinuity in the "speaking" of God across the testaments. For Hebrews, the one who speaks the living and active word is none other than God himself. Thus, while the writer of Hebrews does not deny the human element of revelation (1:1; 2:6; 4:7), the human element is merely the agent of divine speech.[22] One finds a clear pattern of usage in the forty-four occurrences of λέγω and sixteen of λαλέω[23] in Hebrews: the authoritative words are "spoken" by God and are thus authoritative in these "latter days," and are neither to be isolated from, nor in antithesis to, what the Father is saying in the Son. In Hebrews, to "speak" the OT Scripture is to be deity.[24] For this reason, such revelation is to be ignored only at great cost.

For Hebrews, Scripture is the revelation of God, and as an act of deity, the Son "speaks" Scripture twice (Heb 2:12–13; 10:5, 8). In 2:12, the Son proclaims the name of God via Ps 22:22 (LXX 21:23). In 2:13, the words of Isaiah 8:17–18 are put into the mouth of the Son. Both of these texts are laden with messianic themes and expectations,[25] and are fitting words "spoken" by the Son. The author of Hebrews says that the words of Scripture are authoritative and have their source in God.[26] In attributing Scripture to the Son, Hebrews affirms his deity.

In addition to the seven descriptors of the Son in the prologue, the application of the titles of "God" and "Lord" to the Son, and the Son's speaking divine

---

[20] Grammatically, the first independent clause of the sermon is, "God has spoken" (θεός . . . ἐλάλησεν).

[21] Hebrews never follows the patterns of Matthew or Paul (Peterson, "God and Scripture in Hebrews," 121).

[22] See notes on 2:6, 4:7, and 9:20.

[23] Though, λαλέω does not introduce OT passages except at 5:5, where it is used as a substantival participle, and 11:18. Other than these two occurrences, the introduction of an OT text is reserved for λέγω and its various forms.

[24] There are parallels in Philo (*On Drunkenness*, 61; *On Planting*, 90; see 1 Clement 15:2), and likely reflects a common practice where if something was generally known or presupposed, it did not have to be stated (Attridge, *Hebrews*, 70–71).

[25] See Guthrie, "Hebrews," 947–51.

[26] Hebrews "treats the words of human authors as the words of God" (Peterson, "God and Scripture in Hebrews," 121).

Scripture, there are other lines of argumentation for the Son's deity within the sermon that would reinforce this point (such as why Hebrews refers to him as Lord, Son, and Christ, and the description of the Son's exalted position to the right hand of God where he inherits the name). Taken together, all of these arguments suggest the deity of the Son in Hebrews.

## THE DEITY AS SPIRIT

A more challenging point concerns how the writer of Hebrews identifies the deity as spirit, a challenge extending to the earliest generations of Christianity. In the early days of the church, the deity of the Spirit was an unsettled matter for some time.[27] The challenge stems from the fact that there is less evidence concerning the Spirit as compared to the Father and the Son. Yet, is there sufficient evidence to affirm the deity of the Spirit in Hebrews? The following lines of evidence point to such a conclusion.

There are eight instances of the singular πνεῦμα in Hebrews.[28] One refers to the human spirit (4:12), six are clear references to the Holy Spirit (2:4; 3:7; 6:4; 9:8; 10:15; 10:29), and one is debated (9:14). Six times it is modified by the adjective ἅγιος, and once by αἰώνιος in 9:14, which I take as a reference to the Holy Spirit (see below).[29] Is the Spirit made holy, or is holiness intrinsic to the nature of the Spirit? This is not a new question and goes back to the early centuries of the Church in the patristic era, where the question of the Spirit's deity was addressed once the question of the Son's deity was established. Gregory of Nazianzus (ca. 329–390) drew attention to the fact that besides the title "unbegotten," all other titles applied to God in the Bible are also applied to the Spirit. Gregory emphasized the usage of the word "holy" when referring to the Spirit, and saw this as instructive in understanding the nature of the Spirit, given that the Spirit was not given this quality from someone or something external; it is intrinsic to who the Spirit is.[30] One might build on this particular argument by suggesting that if Hebrews 9:14 be understood as a reference to God's Spirit, then the modifier (αἰώνιος) further points to the divine nature of

---

[27] See Alister McGrath, *Christian Theology*, 6th ed. (Hoboken, NJ: John Wiley and Sons, 2016), 281–85.

[28] There are four uses of the plural, in which the reference is to angels (as "winds" or "ministering spirits," 1:7, 14), to the "Father of spirits" (12:9), and to the "spirits of the righteous" in the heavenly city (12:23).

[29] "Eternal spirit" or "Holy Spirit"? Most affirm πνεύματος αἰωνίου as the original reading. See Bruce M. Metzger, *A Textual Commentary on the Greek New Testament*, 2nd ed. (Stuttgart: United Bible Societies, 1994), 598–99. See Michel, *Der Brief*, 314; John J. McGrath, *Through the Eternal Spirit: An Historical Study of the Exegesis of Hebrews 9:13-14* (Rome: Pontificia Universitas Gregoriana, 1961), 90–103; Martin Emmrich, *Pneumatological Concepts in the Epistle to the Hebrews* (Lanham, MD: University Press of America, 2004), 4–5; Emmrich, "'Amtscharisma': Through the Eternal Spirit (Hebrews 9:14)," *Bulletin for Biblical Research* 12.1 (2002): 17–32; David Peterson, *Hebrews and Perfection*, Society for New Testament Studies Monograph Series 47 (Cambridge: Cambridge University Press, 2005), 138.

[30] A. McGrath, *Christian Theology*, 284. He writes that for Gregory, "The Spirit was to be considered as the one who sanctifies, rather than the one who requires to be sanctified."

the Spirit, that is, that for Hebrews, the Spirit is both holy (ἅγιος) and eternal (αἰώνιος) by nature.

Others, such as Didymus the Blind (ca. 313–98) and Basil of Caesarea (ca. 330–79) looked to what the Spirit *does* as evidence as to who he is. If the Spirit does what God does, such as the creation, renewal, and sanctification of God's creatures, then it follows that the Spirit also is divine. Function helps to clarify ontology.[31] This approach is particularly revealing when applied to Hebrews. What functions does the Spirit perform? In Hebrews, the functions of the Spirit are diverse, but when taken together a clear picture emerges; the Spirit is divine.

The first mention of the Spirit (2:4) occurs in a context of salvation and exhortation. While being mindful of the skepticism shown by Attridge and others[32] concerning the relevance of this verse to the present discussion, one can argue that there is a traditional teaching of the early church in this passage.[33] In contrast, Attridge sees no reference to the Spirit. He argues that what is actually in view is not a divine hypostasis, but rather, "an eschatological gift of God's power and life."[34]

Yet I would assert that in 2:3–4 one finds the Spirit to be involved in this "great salvation" spoken of by God in the Son.[35] This is greater revelation than what was mediated through angels to Moses on Sinai.[36] The Spirit's role is the distributor of "various gifts proceeding from the Holy Spirit."[37] The "signs, wonders, and various miracles" in verse 4 recall the Exodus as well as Pentecost, and many scholars point to Gal 3:5 as a possible parallel in Paul.[38]

---

[31] McGrath, 284. Concerning Didymus and Basil, McGrath concludes, "If the Holy Spirit performed functions which were specific to God, it must follow that the Holy Spirit shares in the divine nature." For Basil, there was a specific argument drawn from the sanctifying work of the Spirit, as something only deity does.

[32] Attridge, *Hebrews*, 67–68; see also the comments of Moffatt on 2:4 (*Hebrews*, 17–21).

[33] Paul Ellingworth, *The Epistle to the Hebrews*, New International Greek Testament Commentary (Grand Rapids: Eerdmans, 1993), 66–67. See also Spicq (*L'Épitre aux Hébreux*, 2:28), who is, according to Attridge, guilty of trinitarian speculation when he writes, "Cette notion si élevée de l'apostolat et aussi cette évocation de la Sainte Trinité à propos d'une exhortation morale sont spécifiquement pauliniennes."

[34] Attridge, *Hebrews*, 67–68; see Hans Windisch, *Der Hebräerbrief*, Handbuch zum Neuen Testament 14 (Tübingen: J. C. B. Mohr, 1931), 19. Contra William L. Lane, *Hebrews 1–8*, Word Biblical Commentary 47A (Nashville: Thomas Nelson, 1991), 1:40; Hughes, *Hebrews*, 81; Luke T. Johnson, *Hebrews*: A Commentary, New Testament Library (Louisville: Westminster John Knox, 2007), 89.

[35] Rondón ("Trinitarian Solidarity," 54) writes, ". . . the Trinitarian God in Heb 2:3–4 testifies through spoken words, through signs, wonders, and various miracles, and through gifts or distributions to validate the gospel and its salvific power." Similarly, Scot McKnight, "The Warning Passages of Hebrews: A Formal Analysis and Theological Conclusions," *Trinity Journal* 13 (1992): 39.

[36] Gal 3:19; *Jubilees* 1:24–27; see also Deut 33:2; Acts 7:53. Thus the comparison of Jesus to angels in 1:4–14.

[37] BDAG, *s.v.* "μερισμός," 633. πνεύματος should be understood grammatically as an objective genitive, and thus not referring to distributions of the actual Spirit himself. Ellingworth, *Hebrews*, 142.

[38] Thomas R. Schreiner, *Commentary on Hebrews*, Biblical Theology for Christian Proclamation (Nashville: B&H, 2015), 83–84; Alan C. Mitchell, *Hebrews*, Sacra Pagina Series 13 (Collegeville, MN: Liturgical Press, 2007), 62–63.

The point, then, is that the Holy Spirit has played a powerful role in salvation by confirming the divine word declared by God through the Son; the gifts from the Spirit confirmed the message they had heard. Therefore, the readers are warned against neglecting such a "Trinitarian" message.[39]

Second, the Spirit is also connected to the work of conversion in 6:4–5 and 10:29. Regardless of how one interprets the warning passages, it is clear that the Spirit plays a functional role. In 6:4 they have become partakers of the Spirit, which denotes full participation—nothing less than salvation.[40] This phrase points back to 2:4 (the first warning) where the Spirit's role in salvation has already been mentioned. The readers had seen and experienced the Spirit's power and work when they were first exposed to the word. In 10:29, the Spirit will be "outraged" should they proceed in their high-handed sin and return to Judaism.

It is helpful here to observe that in 10:29–31, both God and the Spirit are "outraged"[41] by such hubristic actions. The one who has partaken of the Spirit in 6:4 outrages the Spirit in 10:29 with his high-handed sin; this warrants the vengeance of God (10:27, 30–31). The context of the quote from Deuteronomy 32 makes it clear that God is angry at such sins committed, and thus will strike with divine vengeance.[42] Similar to 2:1–4, one sees in 10:26–31 the Son (τὸν υἱὸν τοῦ θεοῦ), the Father (τὸν εἰπόντα; θεοῦ ζῶντος), and the Spirit (τὸ πνεῦμα τῆς χάριτος). In 10:29–31 all three members of the Trinity are involved. The Son is trampled, the Spirit is outraged, and the Father repays with vengeance. The offense is trinitarian, and it is personal—against divine and eternal persons—and therefore the penalty is eternal retribution.[43]

Third, the deity of the Holy Spirit is on display in his role as revelator.[44] The Father speaks Scripture, as does the Son and the Spirit. In Hebrews 9:8–10 the Spirit makes known something that was previously hidden concerning the tabernacle (τοῦτο δηλοῦντος τοῦ πνεύματος τοῦ ἁγίου). The structure and regulations of the sanctuary have a profound meaning that is shown via the Spirit in the present (eschatological) time; the regulations have a symbolic significance now understood in the "time of reformation" (9:10). The construction of the tent itself has special meaning that has been previously hidden,

---

[39] Rondón, "Trinitarian Solidarity," 54.

[40] Schreiner, *Hebrews*, 184–85.

[41] Outrage, revile, insult, see EDNT, s.v. "ἐνυβρίζω." A derivative of this term is where we get the English term, "hubris," which points to the nature of such actions. See TDNT, "ὕβρις," 8:306.

[42] Guthrie, "Hebrews," 979–81. See also *2 Enoch 50:4*.

[43] Ellingworth notes that 10:29 "most vividly shows him as personal" (*Hebrews*, 143).

[44] On this point, see esp. Emmrich, "*PNEUMA* in Hebrews," 63ff. See also Barry Joslin, *Hebrews, Christ, and the Law: the Theology of the Mosaic Law in Hebrews 7:1–10:18*, Paternoster Biblical Monograph Series (Carlisle, England: Paternoster, 2008), 247–50.

and insight concerning the tabernacle is now available via the Spirit.[45] Michel notes that the entire arrangement has meaning—meaning that is assigned and taught by the Spirit.[46] For Hebrews, the Spirit reveals something significant about the old covenant ritual and tabernacle.[47]

The use of δηλόω in 9:8 is interesting, and is used only once more in Hebrews (12:27), and only seven times in the NT.[48] Attridge observes that the verb does not mean simply "to clarify" or "to point out."[49] Rather, what is in view is that there is a deeper meaning concerning the holy place, and that only in these latter days is this deeper meaning revealed, specifically by the Spirit. Here, δηλόω has the sense of "to interpret" or "to explain."[50] As such, the Spirit speaks "today" as the authoritative interpreter.[51] Emmrich concludes,

> In summary . . . the Spirit's interpretation of tabernacle-related texts indicates that the author of Hebrews saw the Holy Spirit as being engaged in leading the community into profound christological insights that were communicated ἐπ' ἐσχάτου τῶν ἡμερῶν τούτων ("in these last days," 1:2). Thus, the Spirit's revealing of interpretive secrets can be categorized as an . . . aspect of this intimate 'end-time dialogue.'[52]

For Hebrews, the Holy Spirit serves as an authoritative revelator-teacher to the community and interpreter of deeper truths buried even in the tabernacle's structure. This also points to the implicit Trinitarianism found in Hebrews.

---

[45] Hofius comments, "So lange dieses irdische Heilige im Unterschied zum Allerheiligsten hat, 'als die von Gott geordnete Kultusstätte Bestand und Geltung hat,' ist die himmlische Wohnung Gottes verschlossen" (Otfried Hofius, *Der Vorhang vor dem Thron Gottes* [Tübingen, Mohr, 1972], 62–63) and affirms Riggenbach's thoughts here too. See Eduard Riggenbach, *Die Brief and die Hebräer*, KNT 14 (Leipzig: Deichert, 1922), 249; and Michel (*Der Brief*, 306), who writes concerning 9:8a, "Dies Zugeständnis gibt aber nicht der Alte Bund von sich aus, sondern der Heilige Geist, der den Alten Bund recht zu verstehen lehrt."

[46] Michel writes, "In dieser ganzen Anordnung des Kultus und Priesterdienstes liegt eine Absicht und Kundgebung des Heiligen Geistes, der in Zeichen und Gleichnissen, und doch anders, als die Juden das Wort des Gesetzes verstehen, zu uns redet" (Michel, *Der Brief*, 306). He adds, "Der Heilige Geist ist also das lebendige Gotteswort, das auch durch das Wort des Gesetzes zu uns reden kann." See also Erich Grässer, *An die Hebräer (Hebr 7, 1–10, 18)*, Evangelisch-katholischer Kommentar zum Neuen Testament XVII/2 (Zurich: Bensiger, 1993), 2:132–33.

[47] Lane summarizes the meaning of the Spirit's disclosure when he states, "The Holy Spirit disclosed to the writer that, so long as the front compartment of the tabernacle enjoyed cultic status, access to the presence of God was not yet available to the congregation," (William L. Lane, *Hebrews 9–13*, Word Biblical Commentary 47B (Nashville: Thomas Nelson, 1991), 2:223).

[48] It is fairly common outside of the NT, however. See Rudolph Bultmann, "δηλόω," in *TDNT* 2:61–62. For other NT references to the Spirit as having a "revelatory capacity in the interpretation of Scripture" (Emmrich, "*PNEUMA* in Hebrews" 69), see 1 John 2:27; 1 Cor 2:15; Eph 1:17; cf. Philo, *On the Cherubim*, 27.

[49] Attridge, *Hebrews*, 240n120.

[50] Bultmann, sv. "δηλόω," in *TDNT* 2:62. See also BDAG, 222.2.

[51] Emmrich, "*PNEUMA* in Hebrews: 64.

[52] Emmrich, 71.

Fourth is the interpretation of "S/spirit" in 9:14, "How much more will the blood of Christ, who through the eternal Spirit offered himself without blemish to God, purify our conscience from dead works to serve the living God" (ESV). There is a textual problem here raising the question whether the writer intends to refer to the Holy Spirit, or to the eternal, heavenly nature of Christ's own spirit. This has been a question since early Christianity, yet internal and external evidence points to αἰωνίου being original.[53] Among others, Moffatt and Attridge deny any reference to the Holy Spirit and see this in spiritual/non-physical terms. Moffatt asserts, "(T)his sacrifice was offered in the realm or order of the inward spirit . . . in virtue of his spiritual nature . . . it is irrelevant to drag in the dogma of the trinity."[54] Attridge agrees, and asserts that, "Trinitarian speculation, advocated by patristic and some modern interpreters, is not involved."[55] Instead, he prefers to see the phrase "through the eternal spirit" as a reference to the spiritual nature of Christ's sacrifice as opposed to physical sacrifices (9:13). However, the contrast in vv. 13–14 is not merely physical versus spiritual. Rather, *both* the animals *and* Christ are physical sacrifices with spiritual realities. The real contrast here centers on old versus new, shadow versus form, promise versus fulfillment, and "insufficient" versus "superior."[56]

In contrast, there is no shortage of modern interpreters who see a reference to the Holy Spirit in 9:14.[57] In the explanation of the Christian Yom Kippur (9:11–14), all three (Father, Son, and Spirit) are working in tandem for the redemption of his people, especially in verse 14 where all three are mentioned together. There are good reasons for this interpretation. First, Frederick F. Bruce (see Lane) has observed an underlying framework of Isaiah's Suffering Servant in Hebrews 9,[58] who is introduced in Isaiah 42:1 as having the Spirit of YHWH on him. Second, Koester observes that prior to 9:14, all references to "spirit" in the singular (except 4:12 where the reference is clearly to the human

---

[53] "Eternal spirit" or "Holy Spirit"? Most rightly affirm πνεύματος αἰωνίου as the original reading. Note the {A} rating in Bruce Metzger, *A Textual Commentary on the Greek New Testament*, 2nd ed. (Stuttgart: United Bible Societies, 1994), 598–99. See Michel, *Der Brief*, 314; J. McGrath, *Through the Eternal Spirit*, 90–103; Emmrich, *Pneumatological Concepts* 4–5; Emmrich, "Amtscharisma," 17–32; Peterson, *Perfection*, 138.

[54] Moffatt, *Hebrews*, 124.

[55] Attridge, *Hebrews*, 250. For the history of interpretation, see J. McGrath, *Through the Eternal Spirit*.

[56] See Joslin, *Hebrews, Christ, and the Law*, 232–33.

[57] See Schreiner, *Hebrews*, 270; Peterson, *Perfection*, 138; Michel, *Der Brief*, 314; Ellingworth, *Hebrews*, 457; Craig Koester, *Hebrews*, Anchor Bible, vol. 36a (New York: Doubleday, 2001), 410–11; Lane, *Hebrews*, 2:240; F. F. Bruce, *The Epistle to the Hebrews* New International Commentary on the New Testament (Grand Rapids: Eerdmans, 1981), 217. Many modern translations take this view: NASB, ESV, NIV (1984, 2011), NRSV, NLT, NJB, REB, to name a few. See also the Latin Vulgate (*qui per Spiritum Sanctum*) which actually follows the (less likely) textual variant noted above in n.54.

[58] Bruce, *Hebrews*, 217; Lane, *Hebrews*, 2:240. See also Barry Joslin, "Christ Bore the Sins of Many: Substitution and the Atonement in Hebrews," *The Southern Baptist Journal of Theology* 11:2 (2007): 78, 88–91.

spirit) have been a reference to the Holy Spirit.[59] Third, referring to the Spirit as "eternal" is not out of step with the context of 9:14 where there seems to be a connection between the eternal Spirit, "eternal redemption" (9:12), and "eternal inheritance" (9:15). The evidence is persuasive, and πνεύματος αἰωνίου ought to be understood as a reference to the Holy Spirit. If this be granted, then two further points emerge about the Spirit: one that concerns the Spirit's ontology (that the Spirit is *eternal*[60]), and the second concerning the Spirit's function in the trinitarian economy (that the Spirit is connected to Christ's self-offering by having anointed him and empowered him for his unique ministry).

But perhaps the most persuasive point for the Spirit's deity in Hebrews is that the Holy Spirit speaks Scripture. This point could be definitive on its own given the writer's high view of the OT and the centrality of divine speech in Hebrews. It is God who has spoken and indeed who still speaks. Attridge states, "Hebrews finds particularly fruitful the notion that God has spoken and continues to speak in a vivid and compelling way . . . . [T]his homilist understands God to be doing what he himself aims to do: uttering a word that penetrates human hearts and minds."[61] To this he adds, "As a practitioner of sophisticated homiletic rhetoric, it is no surprise that Hebrews uses God's act of speech as a vehicle of theological insight."[62]

Hebrews is a dialogue between Father and Son, which we get to overhear.[63] This divine conversation begins at the outset of the sermon in 1:5. Yet, twice in Hebrews, it is the Holy Spirit who speaks the divine Word (3:7ff.; 10:15). In short, there is a third person in Hebrews who participates in this divine conversation.[64] The OT Scripture is the speech of the Father and Son, and yet there is a third speaker in the conversation who is sometimes overlooked.[65]

For the writer, God is the divine revelator—the one who speaks and whose word is to be heeded. It is precisely this point concerning divine speech that is essential for understanding how Hebrews views the Spirit. If the OT is spoken by God, and if the Spirit is said to speak Scripture,[66] then it follows that the Spirit is deity as well since he too takes part in this holy conversation. The Son also speaks Scripture (2:12–13; 10:5, 8). In short, the OT introductory formulas of Hebrews provide helpful insight into the author's theology

[59] Craig Koester, Hebrews, Anchor Bible, vol. 36a (New York: Doubleday, 2001), 410.

[60] Ellingworth, *Hebrews*, 457.

[61] Attridge, "God in Hebrews," 110.

[62] Attridge, 103.

[63] Such is an oft-used description of the "divine dialogue" of Hebrews. See, for instance, A. Katherine Grieb, "'Time Would Fail Me to Tell . . .' The Identity of Jesus Christ In Hebrews," in *Seeking the Identity of Jesus: a Pilgrimage*, Beverly Roberts Gaventa and Richard B. Hays, eds. (Grand Rapids: Eerdmans, 2008), 208.

[64] Griffiths, "Hebrews and the Trinity," 126–29.

[65] Attridge, *Hebrews*, 114 (on 3:7).

[66] Further, Ellingworth observes that nowhere else in the NT does the Holy Spirit appear in quotation formulas. See Ellingworth, *Hebrews*, 217, 512; Peterson, "God and Scripture in Hebrews," 121.

of God—a tri-unity of three persons who speak the divine word. This is the writer's theology.

The first text to consider is Hebrews 3:7, which introduces a citation from Psalm 95 (LXX 94:7b–11). The psalm includes direct speech with God as the speaker. Here God reiterates his wrath upon the Exodus generation for their rebellion and lack of faith. Yet in Hebrews it is the Spirit who speaks (καθὼς λέγει τὸ πνεῦμα τὸ ἅγιον). As Psalm 95 unfolds, it is presumably God (the Father) speaking. This does not mean that God equals the Spirit, as if affirming some kind of early modalism. Rather, it indicates that for the writer of Hebrews, both are deity since both speak the divine word. Both God and Spirit are the divine source of the OT text, participating in the same work of revelation.

By means of the Holy Spirit, Psalm 95 is brought to bear on the present situation (σήμερον) of the readers (note the present tense λέγει). The words of Psalm 95 are treated as the words of God, and as Peterson notes, it is "God's intention to continue speaking through them to his people .... The same Spirit who inspired the human authors to write the words of God in the first place continues to illuminate, challenge, encourage, and warn through those definitive words once given."[67] It is by the Spirit that the words of God are contextualized to the present situation, yet with no loss of divine authority, but with an even greater sense of urgency and warning. The Spirit "speaks" the ancient word into the eschatological "now."

The "rest" of the land of Canaan is not what is at stake; rather, the eschatological rest of the heavenly Jerusalem (12:22) is at stake for the readers should they fail to persevere. The Spirit warns via Psalm 95 with divine authority. Hughes remarks that this introductory formula tells us something specific about the writer's understanding of Scripture, both that it has an abiding existential significance and a divine origin.[68] Likewise Pamela Eisenbaum concludes that all OT citations in Hebrews are instances of divine utterances.[69] Further, the context of 3:7–4:13 suggests that the "living and active word of God" in 4:12 points back specifically to what the Spirit says in Psalm 95.[70] For Hebrews, the Spirit is divine since he is the author or source of Scripture.[71]

---

[67] Peterson, "God and Scripture in Hebrews," 121.

[68] Hughes, *Hebrews*, 141; cf. Peterson, "God and Scripture in Hebrews," 121–22; 125–26.

[69] Pamela M. Eisenbaum, *The Jewish Heroes of Christian History: Hebrews 11 in Literary Context*, SBLDS 156 (Atlanta: Scholars Press, 1997), 92.

[70] Bruce, *Hebrews*, 111. See esp. Lane, *Hebrews*, 95–105. Contra Mitchell, *Hebrews*, 104, who claims vv. 12–13 begin an excursus on the word of God.

[71] Spicq, *L'Épitre aux Hébreux*, 72; Hagner, *Hebrews*, 63; Bruce, *Hebrews*, 95n93; Marie Isaacs, *The Concept of the Spirit: A Study of Pneuma in Hellenistic Judaism and Its Bearing on the New Testament* (London: Heythrop, 1976), 125.

One final piece of evidence comes from the use of Jeremiah 31. In Heb 10:15–17 the Spirit is the speaker of the prophetic word originally spoken by Yahweh through Jeremiah. In its first appearance (8:8–12), God speaks the prophetic word (λέγει κύριος, v.8). The meaning of how the new covenant has been inaugurated in the death of Christ is the focus of 9:1–10:18.[72] The section concludes with a condensed version of the Jeremiah text,[73] which is brought into the "eschatological now" by means of the testimony of the Spirit.

It is noteworthy that Hebrews sees no conflict attributing the same Scripture to the "Lord" (κύριος), which is most likely a reference to the Father in Hebrews 8:8–12 and to the Spirit in 10:15–17.[74] As he did in 3:7ff., the Spirit plays a unique role in bringing the OT revelation to bear on the eschatological new covenant community. For Hebrews, the Spirit bears witness[75] that the new covenant and its blessings have been inaugurated by the Christ event, and are effective for the community. Indeed, the Spirit speaks these words in 10:15–17 (μετὰ γὰρ τὸ εἰρηκέναι), yet κύριος refers specifically to *Yahweh* (v. 16). P. E. Hughes writes that "the Holy Spirit and Yahweh are one," and this point "is plainly implied by the equation of what the Holy Spirit says with what the Lord (Yahweh) says."[76] Hebrews does not collapse the distinction between the Spirit and God the Father yet sees them participating in the same divine work. This, too, argues for the deity of the Holy Spirit in Hebrews.

The evidence from Hebrews 9:8, 3:7, and 10:15, suggests that the Spirit in Hebrews is divine and shares in the deity of the Father as well as the Son. The Spirit has been assigned a specific eschatological role regarding the divine word and work in, and on behalf of, the new community. On these three occasions, the Spirit specifically brings OT revelation to bear afresh on the new covenant community and does so with all of the authority of the divine.[77] These are not merely the words of a human author; they are the words of deity[78] applied in the new eschatological moment to the readers of this struggling new covenant community. Given the divine nature and source of Scripture, the readers must heed such divine speech lest they find themselves facing eschatological peril.

---

[72] See esp. Joslin, *Hebrews, Christ, and the Law*, 225ff.; Lane, *Hebrews*, 2:268–71; Joslin, "Christ Bore the Sins of Many," 81–83.

[73] Joslin, *Hebrews, Christ, and the Law*, 255–60.

[74] This is the same κύριος that swore to the Son with an oath and "will not change his mind, 'You are a priest forever'" in 7:21, who made the covenant with the fathers of Israel (8:9), who is known from the least to the greatest (8:11) in the new covenant, and who disciplines as a father, the sons whom he loves (12:5, 6).

[75] The use of μαρτυρέω in 10:15 also supports the notion that the Spirit is a trustworthy witness to the divinity and power of the old covenant word. The present active indicative form points to the ongoing nature of the Spirit's ministry.

[76] Hughes, *Hebrews*, 403.

[77] It is for this reason that Emmrich refers to the Spirit's activity as prophetic ("PNEUMA in Hebrews," 60).

[78] While not denying the human author, the focus in Hebrews is on the divine author.

## CONCLUSION

While Hebrews does not specifically assert a Nicene confession of the Trinity, there is sufficient evidence to argue for an implicit Trinitarian theology, much in the same way the church fathers argued from the whole of the Bible.[79] Hebrews demonstrates on a small scale what the early church saw on a canonical scale, namely a "pervasive pattern of divine activity."[80] Such divine activity is, for Hebrews, performed by Father, Son, and Spirit. The totality of God's actions and being in Hebrews cannot be adequately expressed except by articulating the tri-unity of God. The Father, Son, and Spirit are on mission together—a tri-unity of persons in time and history to accomplish the saving mission of God in Christ. In short, Hebrews bears witness to a theology of God that must be understood as trinitarian.

---

[79] A. McGrath, *Christian Theology*, 292–302; cf. 281–84.
[80] McGrath, 293.

*Chapter 10*

# Biblical Types: Revelation Concealed in Plain Sight to be Disclosed—"These Things Occurred Typologically to Them and Were Written Down for Our Admonition"

*by Ardel Caneday*

## INTRODUCTION

*Typology*, a term not within Scripture, implies a developed study of biblical types.[1] Since its coinage it has been a pliable shorthand term used without adequate clarity by divergent interpretative views that conflict.[2] One view represents types as not predictive but as analogies and examples of later things discernible only retrospectively.[3] A more prevalent view sees types as prospective

---

[1] Cf. Daniel J. Treier, "Typology," *Dictionary for Theological Interpretation of the Bible*, ed. Kevin J. Vanhoozer (Grand Rapids: Baker Academic; London: SPCK, 2005), 824. Two pertinent words occur in Scripture—τύπος (type, noun) and τυπικῶς (typologically, adverb).

[2] Richard M. Davidson reasonably points to Johann S. Semler (1721–91) as the one who coined the word *typologie* even as he played a leading role in discrediting what he christened "biblical typology"; Richard M. Davidson, "Typological Structures in the Old and New Testaments" (PhD diss., Andrews University, 1981), 37–38, esp. 38n1, https://digitalcommons.andrews.edu/cgi/viewcontent.cgi?article=1029&context=dissertations.

[3] R. T. France insists, "A type is not a prediction; in itself it is simply a person, event, *etc.* recorded as historical fact, with no intrinsic reference to the future. Nor is an antitype the fulfilment of a prediction; it is rather the re-embodiment of a principle which has been previously exemplified in the type. Richard T. France, *Jesus and the Old Testament: His Application of Old Testament Passages to Himself and His Mission* (London: Tyndale Press, 1971; Grand Rapids: Baker, 1982), 39–40. David L. Baker agrees, "It is only in retrospect that an

foreshadows of things to come rendered clearer by their fulfillment.[4] Many concur: "Typology is 'the interpretation of earlier events, persons, and institutions in biblical history which become proleptic entities, or 'types', anticipating later events, persons, and institutions, which are their antitypes.' It is thus actually a way of looking at history."[5] Definitions that view OT types as prophetic dominate recent literature.[6]

Now a more primal issue than whether types are prophetic needs to be addressed. *Where* we locate our discussion of types, *how* we conceive of Scripture's presentation of them, and *what* we accept as an apt description or definition of biblical types sets us on trajectories that either confuse or clarify. To locate discussion of biblical types principally within the interpretive skills of NT writers and their readers foregrounds the wrong end because it features NT interpretation instead of the revelatory nature of the OT. It inadvertently assumes the conclusion one seeks to prove as this statement does: "Understanding typology is significant because without it we cannot understand the New Testament's interpretation of the Old."[7]

This orientation away from the typological nature of revelation to focus on interpretation as typological may be partially influenced by "reader-response criticism" which arose contemporaneously with burgeoning studies of biblical types. Perhaps more influential is the subtitle of Leonhard Goppelt's book, *The Typological Interpretation of the Old Testament*.[8] He claims that typology "is not a hermeneutical method with specific rules of interpretation" but "a spiritual

---

event, person or institution may be seen to be typical." *Two Testaments, One Bible: The Theological Relationship Between the Old and New Testaments*, 3rd ed. (Downers Grove, IL: InterVarsity Press, 2010), 183.

[4] Following Davidson's lead in "Typological Structures," Paul Hoskins identifies two competing views, both designated "biblical typology." *Jesus as the Fulfillment of the Temple in the Gospel of John*, Paternoster Biblical Monographs (Eugene, OR: Wipf and Stock, 2006), 18–36. The designations "traditional" and "post-critical" are Davidson's. "The Eschatological Hermeneutic of Biblical Typology," *TheoRhēma* 6.2 (2011), 8.

[5] For example, Dan McCartney and Charles Clayton, *Let the Reader Understand: A Guide to Interpreting and Applying the Bible* (Wheaton, IL: Victor Books, 1994), 153. Hermeneutics textbooks tend to categorize biblical types within "special hermeneutics." For example, see Bernard Ramm, *Protestant Biblical Interpretation: A Textbook of Hermeneutics for Conservative Protestants* (Boston: W. A. Wilde, 1956), 196–219; and A. Berkeley Mickelsen, *Interpreting the Bible*, (Grand Rapids: Eerdmans, 1963), 236–264. Citations are from 4th printing, 1972.

[6] Gregory Beale, *Handbook on the New Testament Use of the Old Testament: Exegesis and Interpretation* (Grand Rapids: Baker Academic, 2012), 24. See Richard M. Davidson, "Biblical Typology," 12, 16. He defines typology as "a study of the Old Testament salvation historical realities or 'types' (persons, events, institutions) which God has specifically designed to correspond to, and predictively prefigure, their intensified antitypical fulfillment aspects (inaugurated, appropriated, consummated) in New Testament salvation history."

[7] James Hamilton, "The Typology of David's Rise to Power: Messianic Patterns in the Book of Samuel," *SBJT* 16.2 (2012): 4. His next statement reinforces his begging the question: "If we do not understand the New Testament's interpretation of the Old, we could be led to false conclusions about the legitimacy of the hermeneutical moves made by the authors of the New Testament" (4–5).

[8] Leonhard Goppelt, *TYPOS: The Typological Interpretation of the Old Testament in the New*, trans. Donald H. Madvig (Eugene, OR: Wipf and Stock, 2002).

approach that looks forward to the consummation of salvation and recognizes the individual types of that consummation in redemptive history."[9] Yet, two pages earlier he affirms, "typology is the *method* of interpreting Scripture that is predominant in the NT and characteristic of it."[10] When he defines typology he characterizes it as "typological interpretation" and again of things to be "interpreted typologically."[11]

## BIBLICAL TYPES—MISIDENTIFIED AS A SPECIES OF HERMENEUTICS

Unsurprisingly, scholars who advocate a view like Goppelt's (1) define biblical typology as a species of hermeneutics, (2) tend to identify typology as *typological interpretation* or *figural interpretation*, and (3) present it as a "reading strategy" or "exegetical method."[12] Several examples follow that illustrate how otherwise insightful, instructive, evocative, and even provocative discussions concerning biblical types falter to the degree that they feature *reception* of the OT rather than its *production*.[13] The fruit of their exegesis is regularly enlightening and rewarding even if they may not fully appreciate the nature of the root that yields it.

Theological Interpretation of Scripture (TIS) is a burgeoning but hardly a monolithic movement that endeavors to merge biblical studies and theology with a deference toward precritical exegesis of the patristic, medieval, and

---

[9] Goppelt, 202.

[10] Goppelt, 198. Emphasis added. Goppelt identifies three essential features concerning types: (1) a recognizable correspondence between the OT type and the NT antitype must be present; (2) both the OT type and the NT antitype must be rooted in "historical facts—persons, actions, institutions," not within obscurely concealed meanings of the text; and (3) escalation from the OT type to the superior NT antitype must be evident. Against Goppelt's claim, Henning Graf Reventlow counters, "typology is just one, rather rare, way in which the Old Testament is used in the New." *Problems of Biblical Theology in the Twentieth Century*, trans. John Bowden (Philadelphia: Fortress, 1986), 20.

[11] Goppelt, *TYPOS*, 17–18.

[12] Treier, e.g., prefers "figural reading" for "typological interpretation" and calls it a "reading strategy." "Typology," 825–26. G. K. Beale describes biblical typology both as "typological interpretation" and as an "exegetical method." "Right Doctrine from the Wrong Texts?" 395 and as an "exegetical method." *New Testament Use*, 24. Davidson agrees that typology is a "hermeneutical endeavor" by the writers of the New Testament which entails an "exegetical method" that identifies and draws out the "predictive prefigurations" that are "already in the OT before their NT antitypical fulfillment. "Biblical Typology," 12, 16. He defines typology as "a study of the Old Testament salvation historical realities or 'types' (persons, events, institutions) which God has specifically designed to correspond to, and predictively prefigure, their intensified antitypical fulfillment aspects (inaugurated, appropriated, consummated) in New Testament salvation history."

[13] Credit goes to Richard B. Hays for these helpful terms though he takes the opposite view: "Another way to put this point is that figural reading is a form of intertextual interpretation that focuses on an intertextuality of *reception* rather than of *production*." *Reading Backwards: Figural Christology and the Four Gospel Witness* (Waco, TX: Baylor University Press, 2014), 2.

Reformation eras.[14] Richard Hays, a prominent voice concerning use of the OT in the NT, advocates what he calls "figural interpretation." He builds upon Erich Auerbach's definition.[15] For Hays, "figural interpretation" is "a form of intertextual interpretation," and he contends that there is "a significant difference between *prediction* and *prefiguration*."[16] So, he continues, "Figural reading need not presume that the OT authors—or the characters they narrate—were conscious of predicting or anticipating Christ. Rather, the discernment of a figural correspondence is necessarily retrospective rather than prospective."[17] Hence the title of his book, *Reading Backwards*.

Despite this, Hays's expositions of Scripture usually rise above and break free from this hermeneutical orientation when he claims that the NT Gospels all "declare that the Torah and the Prophets and the Psalms mysteriously *prefigure* Jesus."[18] Again, he affirms, "The Gospels teach us to read the OT for *figuration*."[19] This means that the figuration, the creation of a figure, is not the work of the reader but is actually done by the OT text, which he confirms by saying that the text "becomes the vehicle for latent figural meanings unsuspected by the original author and readers. It *points forward typologically* to the gospel story."[20] One may wonder, "How, then, is prefiguration also not prediction?" Yet, after affirming that the OT type points forward, he lapses back to speak of *figural reading* by claiming that the "figural reading affirms the original historical reference of the text" while leaving "open the possibility of respectful dialogue with other interpretations, other patterns of intertextual reception."[21] Because he diverges from the constraints of his definition of *figural interpretation*, Hays's exegetical insights concerning the OT in the NT are often fruitful, brilliant, and commendable.

Peter Leithart is a scholar in the Reformed tradition who does not associate his textual work with TIS though his trajectory seems quite parallel

---

[14] See Daniel J. Treier, *Introducing Theological Interpretation of Scripture: Recovering a Christian Practice* (Grand Rapids: Baker, 2008); and Kevin J. Vanhoozer, gen. ed., *Dictionary for Theological Interpretation of the Bible* (Grand Rapids: Baker, 2005). Cf. D. A. Carson, "Theological Interpretation of Scripture: Yes, But . . . ," in *Theological Commentary: Evangelical Perspectives*, ed. R. Michael Allen (London: T&T Clark, 2011), 187–207.

[15] Auerbach states, "Figural interpretation establishes a connection between two events or persons in such a way that the first signifies not only itself but also the second, while the second involves or fulfills the first. The two poles of a figure are separated in time, but both, being real events or persons, are within temporality. They are both contained in the flowing stream which is historical life, and only the comprehension, the *intellectus spiritualis*, of their interdependence is a spiritual act." Erich Auerbach, *Mimesis: The Representation of Reality in Western Literature* (Princeton, NJ: Princeton University Press, 1968), 73. See Hays, *Reading Backwards*, 2.

[16] Hays, *Reading Backwards*, 2.

[17] Hays, 2.

[18] Hays, 3. Emphasis added.

[19] Hays, 15.

[20] Hays, 15. Emphasis added.

[21] Hays, 15.

with it. "Typology is deliberate foreshadowing," he affirms, which seems to imply that biblical types as written in the OT are predictive. But he continues, "and the change of meaning from expectation to conclusion is the change from promise to fulfillment. *The original text changes meaning when brought into relation to other texts.*"[22] He explains, "The apostles teach us to recognize that 'how it turned out' exposes dimensions of the original event or text that may not have been apparent, *and perhaps were not even there*, until it turned out as it did. Typological reading is simply reading of earlier texts in the light of later texts and events. *The original text changes meaning* when brought into relation to other texts."[23] This situating of opposing expressions concludes a chapter that poses irresolvable tension.

Peter Leithart illustrates his point with the ram that substituted for Isaac (Genesis 22). He explains, "Once Jesus rises from the dead . . . *that earlier event becomes* something more specific. *It becomes a promise of Jesus*, the crucified and risen Messiah, a type and a foreshadowing of the great deliverance of Golgotha, the final sacrifice."[24] How can a later NT event transform an earlier OT event into a foreshadow of that selfsame latter event? Leithart seems to acknowledge the dilemma: "A somewhat softer version of the thesis: the event does not change, but we do not know what the event was or what it meant until Jesus rises from the dead. That thesis would be sufficient to ground the argument below, but I prefer the stronger version of the thesis."[25] The softer version would satisfy his claim that "Typology is deliberate foreshadowing," but the antinomy remains.

Another scholar in the Reformed tradition, Vern Poythress, expanded the horizons of reading Scripture for many classical dispensationalists with his *Understanding Dispensationalists* and with it may have hastened the rise of Progressive Dispensationalism.[26] As disproportionately impactful as his argument is to the size of the book, it interjects some confusion because he identifies biblical typology as a hermeneutical method, designating it "typological interpretation." To advocate for *typological interpretation* and simultaneously to reject *allegorical interpretation* is not persuasive for others who have been

---

[22] Peter J. Leithart, *Deep Exegesis: The Mystery of Reading Scripture* (Waco, TX: Baylor University Press, 2009), 64. Emphasis added.

[23] Leithart, 74. Emphasis added.

[24] Leithart, 44. Emphasis added.

[25] Leithart, 219n15.

[26] Vern S. Poythress, *Understanding Dispensationalists* (Grand Rapids: Zondervan, 1987). See understated acknowledgments of Poythress's influence in Craig A. Blaising and Darrell L. Bock, eds., *Dispensationalism, Israel and the Church* (Grand Rapids: Zondervan, 1992), 32, 220; and Blaising and Bock, *Progressive Dispensationalism: An Up-to-Date Handbook of Contemporary Dispensational Thought* (Wheaton, IL: Victor Books), 76.

taught to revere grammatical-historical hermeneutics as with classical and progressive dispensationalists.

> So types are a natural starting point for a discussion with dispensationalists. Since grammatical-historical interpretation will find the same symbolic, typological significance within prophecy, it shows how prophecy also has an organically unified relation to New Testament believers. Typological relations cannot merely be dismissed as a secondary application. The major weakness of classic dispensationalist interpretive theory, at this point, has been the neglecting of the integration of *typological interpretation* with grammatical-historical interpretation.[27]

Despite this, his explanation of how biblical types function is excellent when he says that

> the significance of a type is not *fully* discernible until the time of fulfillment. The type means a good deal at the time, but it is open-ended. One can anticipate in a vague, general way how fulfillment might come, but the details remain in obscurity. When the fulfillment does come, it throws additional light on the significance of the original symbolism.[28]

He observes that dispensationalists frequently object to a non-dispensationalist hermeneutic "that it is 'reading the New Testament back into the Old Testament.' That way of putting it makes it sound bad, as if the Old Testament does not really support that 'reading back.'"[29] Yet, to dispensationalists, his call to add *typological interpretation* to *grammatical-historical interpretation* amounts to conceding what he denies doing, namely, "reading the NT back onto the OT." They hear echoes of others who assert that the NT writers *reinterpret* the OT.[30]

---

[27] Poythress, *Understanding Dispensationalists*, 115. Emphasis added.

[28] Poythress, 115–16.

[29] Poythress, 116.

[30] Some seem incautious concerning word choice when they essentially affirm that Christians are to "read the NT back onto the OT." For example, George Ladd argues that "the new redemptive events in the course of *Heilsgeschichte* ('salvation history') have compelled Peter to *reinterpret* the Old Testament. . . . This involves a *radical reinterpretation* of the Old Testament prophecies, but no more so than the *entire reinterpretation* of God's redemptive plan by the early church." George Eldon Ladd, *A Theology of the New Testament*, rev. ed. 1993, ed. Donald A. Hagner (Grand Rapids: Eerdmans, 1975), 373; emphasis added. Likewise, Kim Riddlebarger's conclusions are better than his stark, overstated wording when he reasons that the Old Testament's "eschatological themes are *reinterpreted* in the New Testament, where we are told these Old Testament images are types and shadows of the glorious realities that are fulfilled in Jesus Christ. . . . [T]his means that Jesus Christ is the true Israel. Jesus Christ is the true temple. Jesus Christ is the heir of David's throne, and so on." Kim Riddlebarger, *A Case for Amillennialism: Understanding the End Times* (Grand Rapids: Baker, 2003), 37; emphasis added.

For some dispensationalists, because the NT writers' uses of OT passages sometimes do not fit well into their interpretive scheme, they believe that NT writers "read their fuller NT perspective back onto the OT" and that this is an unreproducible apostolic exegetical practice that derives from receiving direct revelation, a position I once embraced but long ago abandoned. For example, Robert Thomas contends that occasionally a NT writer "goes beyond the grammatical-historical sense in his use of an OT passage" from "a revelatory stance" unique to themselves and unreproducible, which he calls an "inspired *sensus plenior* application."[31] He finds agreement and confirmation in Richard Longenecker's contention that NT writers engage in what he calls *rāz-pesher* exegesis (i.e., μυστήριον) "based upon a revelatory stance," interpretation that is not reproducible.[32] What can be reproduced is what NT writers do when handling the OT in a "more literal fashion," adhering to "what we speak of today as historico-grammatical exegesis."[33]

What follows may seem pedantic. Nevertheless, the point made is consequential, because to identify typology as a hermeneutical term or key locates the discussion within interpretation of Scripture rather than principally within the nature of revelation where it belongs.[34] To categorize typology as the NT writers' "hermeneutical endeavor" and to identify biblical typology with nomenclature such as "typological interpretation" or "exegetical method" seems to subvert the claim that biblical types are prophetic foreshadowings or prefiguring clues of things to come which are recognizable within the OT before they reach fulfillment in their NT antitypes. How?

First, if biblical types are prophetic in nature, to identify typology as a species of hermeneutics rather than of revelation weakens critical responses to those who, like France and Baker, contend that biblical types are not prophetic but are discernible only retrospectively as analogical examples or patterns

---

[31] Robert L. Thomas, "The New Testament Use of the Old Testament," *TMSJ* 13.1 (2002): 91. His appropriation of Longenecker's view resembles Peter Enns's approach: "where we follow the NT writers is more in terms of their hermeneutical goal than in terms of their exegetical methods and interpretive traditions." Peter Enns, ("Fuller Meaning, Single Goal," in *Three Views on the New Testament Use of the Old Testament*, ed. Kenneth Berding and Jonathan Lunde (Grand Rapids: Zondervan, 2008), 216.

[32] See Richard N. Longenecker, *Biblical Exegesis in the Apostolic Period*, (Grand Rapids: Eerdmans, 1999), 216–20; see the second edition, xxi–xxi; also see, Longenecker, "Can We Reproduce the Exegesis of the New Testament?" *TynBull* 21 (1970): 3–38.

[33] Longenecker, *Biblical Exegesis*, 219.

[34] Frances Young locates the discussion in hermeneutics when she claims that typology "is a useful term, and may be employed as a heuristic tool for discerning and describing an interpretive device whereby texts . . . are shaped or read, consciously or unconsciously, so that they are invested with meaning by correspondence with other texts of a 'mimetic' or representational kind. Typology, then, is not an exegetical method, but a hermeneutical key, and taking our cue from where the word 'type' is explicitly used, we may be able justifiably to identify other examples of the procedure where the terminology is not explicit." *Biblical Exegesis and the Formation of Christian Culture* (Cambridge, UK: Cambridge University Press, 1997), 193.

of later things.[35] To feature the NT writers' interpretive skills inadvertently embraces a form of reader response theory that sets one interpretive approach against another in endless disagreements with no authority greater than one's interpretation.[36]

Second, terminology suffers from incautiousness by not properly describing the nature of biblical typology.[37] Many who insist that biblical types are predictive compromise their claim by describing their reading of the OT as "typological interpretation" even as they simultaneously reject "allegorical interpretation" and deny that they superimpose the NT back onto the OT.[38] Greater caution is in order. *Allegorical interpretation* means something different from *interpretation of an allegory*. John Bunyan wrote *The Pilgrim's Progress* as an allegory, but his allegory does not call for *allegorical interpretation*. We do not interpret it allegorically. Rather, we acknowledge that it is an allegory and read it in keeping with its allegorical nature. The same is true concerning allegories in Scripture such as Ezek 17:1–24; Ps 80:8–19; or Matt 22:1–14. Craig Blomberg correctly concludes that all of Jesus's parables are allegories.[39] Yet, they are not suitably subjected to *allegorical interpretation*. Likewise, biblical types do not call for *typological interpretation*. Rather, our role is "to identify types, symbols, and allegories that are in Scripture and not creatively invent them as the phrase 'typological interpretation' suggests."[40]

---

[35] Beale describes biblical typology both as "typological interpretation" and as an "exegetical method" as he counters R. T. France and David L. Baker, who categorize typology not as exegesis but as "theological interpretation of Old Testament history." *New Testament Use*, 24.

[36] Cf. Brent E. Parker, "Typology and Allegory: Is There a Distinction? A Brief Examination of Figural Reading," *SBJT* 21.1 (2017): 66.

[37] By using "allegory" as shorthand for "allegorical interpretation," as if they were identical, which is not at all accurate, many suppress acknowledgment of valid allegories in Scripture. See, for example, Frances Foulkes, *The Acts of God: A Study of the Basis of Typology in the Old Testament* (London: Tyndale, 1958), 36.

[38] For example, James Hamilton, who labels what he is doing as "typological interpretation," cautions, "In spite of the danger of allegory, it is simply not possible to limit our typological interpretation of the Old Testament to those examples explicitly cited in the New Testament." "The Typology of David's Rise to Power: Messianic Patterns in the Book of Samuel," *SBJT* 16.2 (2012): 9. Observe that Hamilton, like Foulkes, uses "allegory" as shorthand for "allegorical interpretation."

[39] On the correlation of parable and allegory see Craig L. Blomberg, *Interpreting the Parables* (Downers Grove, IL: InterVarsity Press, 1990), 29–69. He properly concludes that the parables of the Gospels are allegories (p. 69).

[40] Parker, "Typology and Allegory," 67. For earlier expansion of these points see A. B. Caneday, "Covenant Lineage Allegorically Prefigured: 'Which Things Are Written Allegorically' (Galatians 4:21–31)," *SBJT* 14.3 (2010): 50–77. See also, Caneday, Can You Discuss the Significance of Typology to Biblical Theology?" in "The *SBJT* Forum: Biblical Theology for the Church," *SBJT* 10.2 (2006), 96–98. Cf. the more recent essay by Mathew Y. Emerson, "Arbitrary Allegory, Typical Typology, or Intertextual Interpretation? Paul's Use of the Pentateuch in Galatians 4:21–31," *BTB*, 43.1 (2013): 14–22.

## BIBLICAL TYPES—A SPECIES OF DIVINE REVELATION

The apostle Paul teaches that God reveals invisible things concerning himself through the things that he made (Rom 1:20; 2 Cor 4:18). Early church fathers correctly understood how crucial this is concerning the nature of God's revelation in both creation and Scripture despite their shifting of concerns from revelation to interpretation with their embrace of "allegorical interpretation" of Scripture. Though we ought to distance ourselves from Origen's allegorical interpretation, what he observes here is correct.

> God thus shows that this visible world teaches us about that which is invisible, and that this earthly scene contains certain patterns of things heavenly. Thus it is to be possible for us to mount up from things below to things above, and to perceive and understand from the things we see on earth the things that belong to heaven. On the pattern of these the Creator gave to His creatures on earth a certain likeness to these....[41]

For Origen and other church fathers, this is fundamental to the nature of reality. So, how creation reflects the Creator and how Scripture discloses God are intimately connected.[42] They acknowledge that creation itself is suffused with symbolic representations of invisible things, but they also understood that God imbued his revelatory actions in both creation and redemption with earthly analogies of heavenly realities.[43] Because God reveals himself and his purposes this way, the Fathers realized that proper interpretation of the world and of Scripture entails metaphysics.[44] Correct as Origen's quest is "to perceive and understand from the things we see on earth the things that belong to heaven," he and others took a misstep by laying an external allegorical interpretive grid over the biblical

---

[41] Origen, *Commentary on the Canticles of Canticles*, 3.12, trans. R. P. Lawson, in *The Song of Songs: Commentary and Homilies*, ed. R. P. Lawson, Ancient Christian Writers 26 (New York: Newman, 1957), 218.

[42] For my own extended discussion of this correlation see A. B. Caneday, "Veiled Glory: God's Self-Revelation in Human Likeness—A Biblical Theology of God's Anthropomorphic Self-Disclosure," in *Beyond The Bounds: Open Theism and the Undermining of Biblical Christianity*, ed. John Piper, Justin Taylor, Paul Kjoss Helseth (Wheaton, IL: Crossway, 2003), 149–99.

[43] Irenaeus observes, with God "there is nothing purposeless, nor without signification, nor without design." "Against Heresies," *Ante-Nicene Fathers* (Grand Rapids: Eerdmans, 1950), 4.18.

[44] Hans Boersma, *Scripture as Real Presence: Sacramental Exegesis in the Early Church* (Grand Rapids: Baker Academic, 2017), 5. See also Jonathan Edwards, who affirms, "I am not ashamed to own that I believe that the whole universe, heaven and earth, air and seas, and the divine constitution and history of the holy Scriptures, be full of images of divine things, as full as a language is of words; and that the multitude of those things that I have mentioned are but a very small part of what is really intended to be signified and typified by these things: but that there is room for persons to be learning more and more of this language and seeing more of that which is declared in it to the end of the world without discovering all." *Works of Jonathan Edwards*, vol. 11, *Typological Writings*, ed. Paul Ramsey (New Haven: Yale University Press, 1957), 152.

text, too much resembling Philo's hermeneutic.[45] Their valid observations concerning allegories within the divine revelatory text became muddled and intermingled with their own imaginative allegorical impositions.[46]

Despite differences between the Alexandrian and Antiochene schools, both recognized that "the wording of the Bible carried deeper meanings and that the immediate sense or reference pointed beyond itself."[47] For "the church fathers, the hidden presence of the reality was finally revealed at the fullness of time, in the Christ event—along with everything that this event entails: Christ's own person and work; the church's origin; the believers' new, Spirit-filled lives in Christ; and the eschatological renewal of all things in and through Christ."[48] They saw the whole reality of the new covenant "as the hidden treasure already present in the Old Testament."[49] This Augustine expresses succinctly: "The New Testament is in the Old concealed, and the Old is in the New revealed."[50]

The Bible beckons us to enter the world it portrays and to embrace its presuppositions and affirmations concerning the Creator and his creation, the stage where he reveals his redemptive acts. Throughout the biblical storyline, God is the leading actor but also the scriptwriter, the director, the producer of this grand drama, and the creator and owner of the universal theater in which the drama unfolds. The Bible's storyline spans the history of God's redemption of his creation. Integral to this history of redemption are progressive sequences of God's revelation that reach their completion and fulfillment in the revelation of Jesus Christ.

The entire vast universe is God's creation; it is the canvas of his self-revelation.[51] Therefore the symbolism the Creator suffused into creation is neither artificial nor imposed but is organic and intrinsic to the created world, the visible strata harmoniously reflecting the unseen spiritual strata, the earthly shadowing the heavenly.[52] The OT is filled with symbolism and types that are structural to

---

[45] See D. A. Carson, "Mystery and Fulfillment: Toward a More Comprehensive Paradigm of Paul's Understanding of the Old and the New," in *Justification and Variegated Nomism*, vol. 2, *The Paradoxes of Paul*, ed. D. A. Carson, Peter T. O'Brien, and Mark A. Seifrid (Tübingen, Germany: Mohr Siebeck; Grand Rapids, MI: Baker Academic, 2004), 404.

[46] See 140n30.

[47] Frances Young, "Alexandrian and Antiochene Exegesis," in *A History of Biblical Interpretation*, vol. 1, *The Ancient Period*, ed. Alan J. Hauser and Duane F. Watson (Grand Rapids: Eerdmans, 2003), 352.

[48] Boersma, *Scripture as Real Presence*, 12.

[49] Boersma, 12.

[50] Augustine, *Quaestionum in Heptateuchum*, 2.73.

[51] Herman Bavinck, *Reformed Dogmatics*, vol. 2, *God and Creation*, trans. John Vriend, ed. John Bolt (Grand Rapids: Baker Academic, 2004), 109. Bavinck states, "Because the universe is God's creation, it is also his revelation and self-manifestation. There is not an atom of the world that does not reflect his deity." Pp. 99–110 are of indispensable importance.

[52] Geerhardus Vos convincingly argues that Jesus's parables are not mere illustrations invented for the moment. Rather, the Creator built spiritual symbolism into the very structure of his creation, which is why Jesus's parables work. *Biblical Theology: Old and New Testaments* (Grand Rapids: Eerdmans, 1948), 355. Also, see my development of this Caneday in "Veiled Glory: God's Self-Revelation," 149–99.

Scripture's promise-fulfillment storyline.[53] Types are indispensable to the biblical concept of mystery, what the OT hid for long ages past the NT now reveals.[54] Divine things veiled in plain sight receive greater exposure with the light of the divine word through God's prophets but even greater through Jesus whose acts and parables, whether spoken or dramatized, exploit this divinely imbued symbolism in fulfillment of Scripture: "I will open my mouth in parables; I will utter what has been concealed from creation" (Matt 13:35; Ps 78:2).[55]

## EARTHLY SHADOWS REVEALING HEAVENLY REALITIES—HEBREWS AND JOHN'S GOSPEL

The few times NT writers expressly identify OT types is hardly exhaustive but suggestive and instructive concerning principles by which numerous other OT types are to be "discovered and explained."[56] Of the NT segments, perhaps Hebrews underscores this truth most effectively even though its use of τύπος is distinctive, using τύπος (8:5) as the heavenly original and ἀντίτυπος (9:24) as the earthly copy, opposite other NT writers.[57] The church fathers correctly grasp how the old covenant with all its adornments prefigures the new. The relationship is that the law covenant is "a shadow of the good things about to come [σκιὰ τῶν μελλόντων ἀγαθῶν], not the very image of the things [αὐτὴ εἰκὼν τῶν πραγμάτων]." The heavenly reality casts an earthly shadow which is the law covenant. The law covenant prefigures the good things to come which cohere in the reality itself who is Messiah Jesus. Geerhardus Vos pictorially captures this relationship adapted in the following figure.[58]

---

[53] Vos, *Biblical Theology*, 145. Cf. Edmund P. Clowney, *Preaching Christ in All of Scripture* (Wheaton, IL: Crossway, 2003), 31.

[54] See Carson, "Mystery and Fulfillment," 404–10.

[55] The same can be said of Jesus's signs, both miraculous and non-miraculous. See A. B. Caneday, "The Word Made Flesh as Mystery Incarnate: Revealing and Concealing Dramatized by Jesus as Portrayed in John's Gospel," *JETS*, (forthcoming).

[56] Patrick Fairbairn, *The Typology of Scripture: Viewed in Connection with the Entire Scheme of the Divine Dispensations*, vol. 1, 3rd ed. (Philadelphia: Smith, English, 1857), 41.

[57] It may be that the citation of Exod 25:40—ποιήσεις πάντα κατὰ τὸν τύπον τὸν δειχθέντα σοι ἐν τῷ ὄρει—governs how Hebrews uses τύπος as the heavenly original and ἀντίτυπος as synonymous with ὑπόδειγμα and σκιά to speak of earthly copies. See Geerhardus Vos, *The Teaching of the Epistle to the Hebrews* (Nutley, NJ: P&R, 1975), 55–68.

[58] The sketch is adapted from Geerhardus Vos, *Epistle to the Hebrews*, 55–57. Many argue that biblical types are of two kinds: (1) the more dominant has a horizontal axis, for God designed certain OT persons, events, institutions, and events to foreshadow NT realities; (2) the less common has a vertical axis with correspondences between the heavenly and earthly realms. As my diagrams show, I contend that all biblical types entail both vertical and horizontal axis, though one may be accented over the other in any given passage. Every type is principally an earthly shadow of a heavenly reality and at the same time a foreshadow of the heavenly reality that is to come. No type foreshadows (horizontal axis) apart from shadowing (vertical axis). Hence, observe the implied axes embedded in Paul's recognition of the Adam-Christ typology: (1) horizontal-historical axis: the First Man, Adam, foreshadows the Second Man, Christ Jesus; (2) the vertical-spatial axis: the Earthly Man, Adam, shadows the Heavenly Man, Christ Jesus (1 Cor 15:45–49).

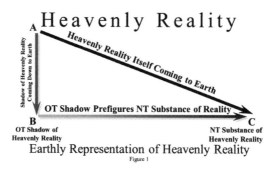

Earthly Representation of Heavenly Reality
Figure 1

Indeed, the NT writers are readers of the OT. As readers of the OT, Messiah's witnesses testify that their understanding comes only because the resurrected Jesus opens eyes to understand the Scriptures (Luke 24:31, 45). John testifies that Jesus's disciples misunderstand when he purposefully tells his riddle in the temple: "Destroy this temple and in three days I will raise it up again." Later, they come to understand: "Therefore, when he was raised from the dead his disciples remembered that he said this and they believed the Scripture and the saying that Jesus had uttered" (John 2:22). With no mention of τύπος in John 2, Jesus's riddle turns on both the implicit spatial and historical axes. The temple both shadows the heavenly one and foreshadows its coming to earth. Thus, Jesus is the fulfillment of Israel's tabernacle which was but an earthly copy of the heavenly one made evident in what Moses says concerning the Lord's directives about its construction: "See that you make everything according to the pattern [τὸν τύπον] shown to you on the mountain" (Heb 8:5, citing Exod 25:40).

Vos refers readers to art and philosophy as realms that explain the conception of biblical types. Scripture seems to draw upon God's creation itself within which objects and shadows ubiquitously resemble heavenly realities that cast earthly shadows. Of course, the creation of humanity in God's image, after his likeness, is also noteworthy.

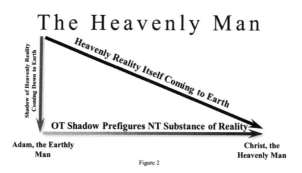

Figure 2

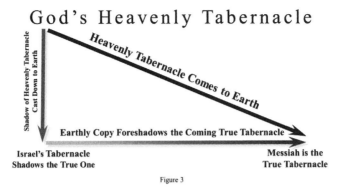

God's Heavenly Tabernacle

Figure 3

The tabernacle's unified functions served as a divinely cast earthly copy and shadow of the heavenly sanctuary to instruct the Israelites concerning the heavenly sanctuary and the kind of sacrifice God requires (Heb 8:1–6). It signifies the sacrificial system's ineffectiveness to absolve the conscience of guilt before God, for the conscience is not made habitable for God by external regulations that concern food, drink, and ceremonial washings.

The NT writers' recognition of OT types that are embedded within Scripture is due to Messiah's revelatory act that both exposes the types with sharper clarity and illumines eyes to see what was concealed within plain sight in Scripture's text. Thus, they see that Scripture is pregnant with types, prefigurements, and foreshadows of the Christ, but none of this suggests that they engage in *typological interpretation* nor *figural reading* nor *Christotelic interpretation*, the categories that contemporary scholars attribute to them.

Divine revelation, not human interpretation, is *where* we ought to locate our discussion of types. The apostle Paul instructs us *how* to conceive of Scripture's presentation of types. They are both divinely appointed to occur and divinely authorized as written. Revelatory foreshadowing divine appointments of correlative NT persons, events, institutions, and places is *what* we should accept as an apt description of biblical types.

Douglas Moo offers helpful guidance concerning biblical typology by steering away from hermeneutics to view types as "a specific form of the larger 'promise-fulfillment'" motif and framework of how the OT and NT correlate.[59] The two testaments harmoniously bear "witness to the unfolding revelation of God's

---

[59] Moo, "The Problem of *Sensus Plenior*," in *Hermeneutics, Authority, and Canon*, ed. D. A. Carson and John D. Woodbridge (Grand Rapids: Zondervan, 1986), 196. An update of this essay reads slightly different: "Typology is a specific form of the larger 'promise-fulfillment' framework essential for understanding the OT and NT's relationship; it is a core component of the canonical approach." Douglas J. Moo and Andrew David Naselli, "The Problem of the New Testament's Use of the Old Testament," in *The Enduring Authority of the Christian Scriptures*, ed. D. A. Carson (Grand Rapids, MI: Eerdmans, 2016), 726.

character, purpose, and plan."[60] The salvation that Christ brings fulfills the entire OT—its historical, legal, and prophetic features—which to preach and teach correctly is to proclaim Christ Jesus. So, the symbolism God imprinted upon OT persons, events, settings, and institutions reaches profound and climactic fulfillment in corresponding NT persons, events, settings, and institutions.[61]

## OT EVENTS OCCURRED TYPOLOGICALLY—1 CORINTHIANS 10:1–13

We rightly use the adjective *typological* of God's revelation embedded in persons, events, institutions, and places as recorded in Scripture but not of our interpretation of these.[62] This should be evident from the apostle Paul's pastoral appeal where modern versions insufficiently translate τύποι and τυπικῶς "as examples" (NIV; ESV). "Now these things *took place as types* of us lest we crave evil as they did. . . . Now these things *occurred typologically* to them and they were written down for our admonition, on whom the ends of the ages have come" (1 Cor 10:6, 11; emphasis added). Paul's statements distinguish two emphases. Concerning everything "our forefathers" experienced (10:1–5): (1) they *"took place as types* **of us**" and (2) *"these things occurred typologically* **to them.**"[63] When the events "took place" in Israel's history God already imbued them "as types of" Messiah and of his latter-day people.[64] What Paul initially states, "these things took place as types of us" (ταῦτα τύποι ἡμῶν ἐγενήθησαν, 10:6), he reinforces by saying, "these things occurred typologically to them" (ταῦτα τυπικῶς συνέβαινεν, 10:11). They do not become types retrospectively by way of subsequent analogous events. Rather, concerning all the events Israel experienced, Paul calls them *types*. The events themselves were predictive in nature, foreshadowing things at the end of the ages in Messiah and his people, the goal toward which God has directed his redemptive and revelatory deeds throughout history.

Paul insists that when God caused Israel to pass under the cloud and through the sea, to eat food provided in the wilderness, to drink water from

---

[60] Moo and Naselli, "New Testament's Use of the Old,", 726. In updated edition reads, "Both the OT and NT unfold God's character, purpose, and plan, but God's salvation through Christ fulfills OT history, law, and prophecy" (726–27).

[61] Moo and Naselli, 727.

[62] Caneday, "Can you discuss the Significance of Typology," 96–97.

[63] For detailed exegesis of 1 Cor 10:1–13, see Richard M. Davidson, *Typology in Scripture*, 250–80. See also Thomas R. Schreiner and Ardel B. Caneday, *The Race Set Before Us: A Biblical Theology of Perseverance & Assurance* (Downers Grove, IL: IVP Academic, 2001), 222–26.

[64] David Garland objects, "But this meaning is unlikely here because that would entail that the Corinthians will also displease the Lord and perish, and Paul writes to *prevent* this from happening." *1 Corinthians*, BECNT (Grand Rapids: Baker Academic, 2003), 459. Davidson answers this objection as he makes the convincing case that τύποι ἡμῶν (11:6) should be translated "of us" not "for us." *Typology in Scripture*, 252–56.

the rock, and for unfaithful Israelites to perish in the wilderness, God infused all these events with symbolism, which is what Paul means when he states that they took place *typologically to them*. Hence, he writes, "They all ate the same spiritual food and drank the same spiritual drink, for they drank from the spiritual rock that followed them, and the rock was Christ" (10:4–5). The manna and the water signify the spiritual vitality God provides in Christ alone.

Paul distinguishes the *events* themselves as *they occurred typologically to them* from their being *written down for our admonition* (τυπικῶς συνέβαινεν ἐκείνοις; ἐγράφη πρὸς νουθεσίαν ἡμῶν, 10:11). Neither Paul, who reads the accounts, nor Moses, who wrote the Pentateuch, which the apostle cites, cast Israel in her role to experience types of us on whom the ends of the ages have come.[65] God orchestrated the whole of it. God imbued both Israel and her experiences with typological significance to foreshadow corresponding things of the last days.[66] God authorized Moses to inscribe these typologically infused events for our instruction at the ends of the ages.

## The Heavenly Rock

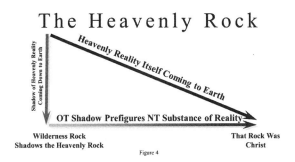

Figure 4

The composition of Scripture's mystery that attains resolution with the multifaceted coming of Messiah Jesus is analogous to a well-crafted mystery novel with the story's climax that provides no simplistic resolution but obliges readers to return to earlier chapters to trace clues among the characters, events, settings, and plotted conflict.[67] This analogy is inverted, of course, because God does not replicate mystery writers; rather, writers of mystery novels who are

---

[65] Davidson correctly affirms, "Paul is not saying that the events can now be seen to be τυπικῶς—as if they *became* τύποι as a result of some later occurrence or factor. Rather, Paul insists that in their very happening, they were happening τυπικῶς." *Typology in Scripture*, 268.

[66] On Paul's use of εἰς οὓς τὰ τέλη τῶν αἰώνων κατήντηκεν see Gordon D. Fee, *The First Epistle to the Corinthians*, NICNT (Grand Rapids: Eerdmans, 1987), 458–59; also, Roy E. Ciampa and Brian S. Rosner, *The First Letter to the Corinthians*, PNTC (Grand Rapids: Eerdmans, 2010), 465. Cf. C. Marvin Pate, *The End of the Age Has Come: The Theology of Paul* (Grand Rapids: Zondervan, 1995), 105–8.

[67] I do not borrow the idea from Peter Enns, though he argues similarly; but his analogy is from the reader's vantage point, not the author's, and this agrees with his conclusions concerning uses of the OT in the NT that I do not share. He illustrates his "Christotelic" reading of the OT: "To read the OT 'Christotelicly' is to read it *already knowing* that Christ is somehow the *end* (*telos*) to which the OT story is heading; in other words, to read the OT in light of the exclamation point of the history of revelation, the death and

made in God's image mimic the writing of God's grand mystery. God's authoring of Scripture's mystery embeds presaging clues throughout the OT, concealing the gospel in advance within his revelatory acts and words which emerge from Scripture's penumbras with the arrival of God's Messiah.[68]

## CONCEALING AND REVEALING—LUKE 24:13–35

To the chagrin of many, Luke's Emmaus Road narrative includes no transcript of Jesus's commentary on the OT when "beginning with Moses and all the Prophets he thoroughly explained what was said concerning him in all the Scriptures" (24:27). Yet, the account is instructively rich because Luke replicates for readers the experience of two disciples as they walk with Jesus unaware. Readers who know that Jesus is risen from the dead need to inquire, "Why does Jesus not show himself plainly and suddenly to the two disciples as he later does to Paul on the Damascus Road? Why does he prevent them from recognizing him until after he expounds the Scriptures that portend that Messiah had to suffer and die before being glorified?" Not to ask is to run the risk of becoming satisfied with shortsightedness in two significant ways. One is the notion that sight of the resurrected Messiah adequately accounts for Paul's appeals to the OT to ground his gospel without the need to trace OT warrants that validate his uses. A second that reinforces the first is to overlook an essential detail Jesus dramatizes and Luke narrates by juxtaposing two distinguishable but inseparable dimensions of concealing and revealing: (1) interpretation—perception prevented and given; and (2) revelation—the OT shrouded and uncovered.

The more obvious dimension of concealing and revealing is the one on which the whole episode turns. It hinges on the dramatic element of eyes prevented from recognizing Jesus (ἐκρατοῦντο, 24:16), followed by divine opening of eyes enabling recognition (διηνοίχθησαν, 24:31), at which time Jesus suddenly becomes invisible to his two disciples (ἄξαντος ἐγένετο).[69] In the presence of these two men, Jesus dramatizes the beatitude he speaks to Thomas: "Because you saw me, you believed; *blessed are those who do not see but believe*" (John 20:29). Similarly, for the two disciples on the Emmaus Road

---

resurrection of Christ.... [I]t is like reading a story and finally grasping the significance of the climax, and then going back and reading the story in light of the end." ("Fuller Meaning, Single Goal," 214).

[68] On this theme see G. K. Beale and Benjamin L. Gladd, *Hidden But Now Revealed: A Biblical Theology of Mystery* (Downers Grove, IL: InterVarsity Press, 2014). See also D. A. Carson, "Mystery and Fulfillment," 393–426.

[69] I. Howard Marshall correctly observes that the passive verb, "their eyes were prevented" (οἱ δὲ ὀφθαλμοὶ αὐτῶν ἐκρατοῦντο) "so that they could not recognize him" (τοῦ μὴ ἐπιγνῶναι αὐτόν) refers to an "action by God ... rather than Satan." *Commentary on Luke*, NIGTC (Grand Rapids: Eerdmans, 1978), 893. This divine concealing anticipates God's act of revealing by opening their eyes to recognize Jesus (αὐτῶν δὲ διηνοίχθησαν οἱ ὀφθαλμοὶ καὶ ἐπέγνωσαν αὐτόν, Luke 24:31).

Jesus reverses the order experienced by the disciple whom Jesus loved, who ran to the tomb and arrived there ahead of Peter. Upon entering the empty tomb "he saw and believed," but John's editorial comment explains that both disciples "still did not understand from Scripture that Jesus had to rise from the dead" (John 20:8–9).

For his two disciples on the Emmaus Road, Jesus prevents their eyes from recognizing him because he purposes to ground their belief concerning the resurrected Messiah in the Scriptures before he authorizes them to be eyewitnesses of his climactic resolution of redemption's story. Thomas, Peter, and John first believe and later come to understand from Scripture that Messiah had to die and then rise from the dead. However, for these other two disciples, Jesus reorders belief that is inherent in seeing him and belief that he is the promised Messiah grounded in what the Scriptures say concerning him. So, first Jesus elicits them to believe that Scripture's promised Messiah had to die and rise from the dead. Then he bequeaths belief to them by causing them to recognize him as the risen Messiah. Thus, Jesus constrains them to play a noteworthy role in redemption's dramatic climax. Unbeknownst to them, Jesus casts these two as types of others who, without the benefit of being eyewitnesses after his brief period of resurrection appearances, will be called upon to see Messiah foreshadowed throughout the OT. Jesus casts them as types of us, who, though we have not seen him we love him, and though we do not see him now, we believe in him (cf. 1 Pet 1:8).

No one who will be Messiah's disciple and receive the glory of the age to come can circumvent the sorrows of the cross. Suffering precedes glory for Messiah and for all his disciples (Luke 9:23–27; 14:25–35; 24:26, 46). Because belief must rest in Scripture's testimony concerning the full measure of Messiah's mission, including his sufferings, Jesus does not banish his disciples' sorrow by disclosing to them his resurrected glory.[70] Instead, he resolves the puzzling mystery that his crucifixion causes the two disciples by rehearsing the OT plotline that features Messiah's suffering and death, "beginning with Moses and all the Prophets he thoroughly explained what was said concerning him in all the Scriptures" (24:17).

Later, at his breaking of bread, an act designed to trigger reminiscence of the symbolic meal he recently instituted, Jesus imparts unimpaired vision

---

[70] Richard Hays expresses it this way: "It is essential to teach them about Scripture because Scripture forms the hermeneutical matrix within which the recent events in Jerusalem become intelligible. Understanding can dawn only when these shattering events are brought into an interpretive dialectic with Israel's story: '[A]s Jesus cannot be understood apart from Jewish scripture, Jewish scripture cannot be understood apart from Jesus; what is needed is an interpretation which relates the two—and it is this that Jesus provides (v. 27)." "Reading Scripture in Light of the Resurrection," in *The Art of Reading Scripture*, ed. Ellen F. Davis and Richard B. Hays (Grand Rapids: Eerdmans, 2003), 230.

which signifies belief (24:31, 35).[71] Their capabilities of perception are suddenly opened by God so that now they realize that the crucified Jesus they mourned is the promised Messiah raised from the dead and they are in his presence, at which point Jesus abruptly becomes invisible, again concealing himself from their vision.[72]

Now a second dimension of concealing and revealing becomes implicit in Luke's narrative, for when Jesus reveals his identity by way of his reminiscent act of breaking bread Cleopas and his friend speak of another *opening*: "Were not our hearts burning within us while he was speaking to us on the road as he *opened* the Scriptures to us?" (24:32). This implies that to the degree the Scriptures required *opening* to that same degree they were *concealed*. This concealing and opening is not of eyes but of Scripture itself. Not to put too fine a point on this *opening of the Scriptures*, it features the OT as *revelatory* more than the OT *interpreted*. Though inseparable, these are distinguishable. The OT is like a fully furnished but dimly lit room which when light is brought into it, nothing is added that was not already there, but the light dispels dark shadows and things shrouded begin to emerge with clarity even as shadows linger.[73] Scriptures' shadows yield discernible shapes illumined by the resurrected Messiah. What was there all along is now made clear, for the OT coheres in Messiah. Thus, Luke's account instructs both how to read the OT and how the OT reveals Messiah by foreshadowing him. Jesus expounds the Scriptures not backward by projecting Messiah back onto the OT or by reinterpreting the text, but forward by proceeding through the OT and climaxing upon himself to demonstrate that at many times and in numerous ways it foretells of both Messiah's sufferings and glory.

Like their old covenant forebears, Cleopas and his companion are characters in God's unfolding drama of redemption that simultaneously elicits their believing inquiry but eludes their understanding. They anticipate the promised Messiah who is veiled in types, foreshadows, and prophecies that await greater illumination. As Jesus expounds Messiah's fulfilling of Scripture's portents,

---

[71] Marshall observes that the language "points irresistibly" both to Jesus's actions at the last supper and to his feeding the multitude—λαβὼν δὲ τοὺς πέντε ἄρτους . . . εὐλόγησεν αὐτοὺς καὶ κατέκλασεν καὶ ἐδίδου τοῖς μαθηταῖς, 9:16; καὶ λαβὼν ἄρτον εὐχαριστήσας ἔκλασεν καὶ ἔδωκεν αὐτοῖς, 22:19, and λαβὼν τὸν ἄρτον εὐλόγησεν καὶ κλάσας ἐπεδίδου αὐτοῖς, 24:30. *Luke*, 898. Though Darrell Bock acknowledges language similarities, he downplays connections contrary to others who call this a reenactment of the Lord's Supper. *Luke*, BECNT (Grand Rapids: Baker, 1996), 2.1919. Against this, Robert Stein affirms that "Jesus was recognized in the 'breaking of bread' (24:35), which for Luke meant the breaking of bread in the Lord's Supper." *Luke*, NAC (Nashville: Broadman, 1992), 613.

[72] In Luke 24 faculties of perception are *eyes* that are opened (αὐτῶν δὲ διηνοίχθησαν οἱ ὀφθαλμοί, 24:31) and *minds* that are opened, "Then he opened their minds to understand the Scriptures" (τότε διήνοιξεν αὐτῶν τὸν νοῦν τοῦ συνιέναι τὰς γραφάς, 24:45).

[73] The illustration of how divine revelation within the two testaments relates is from Benjamin B. Warfield, *Biblical Doctrines* (Oxford, England: Oxford University Press, 1929; Grand Rapids: Baker, 1981), 141.

his two disciples occupy roles they do not comprehend during an encounter that bristles with divine mystery. Jesus dramatizes the mystery nature of divine revelation for the two men by veiling recognition of himself while in the act of unveiling his messianic identity from Scripture. Jesus's revelatory actions replicate Scripture's concealing and revealing of Messiah. The truth about Messiah concealed in plain sight both *objectively* within Scripture (24:25–27) and *subjectively* within the disciples' vision (24:16) is now revealed plainly to the two whose eyes are divinely opened (24:31) to recognize Jesus as the glorified Messiah announced in advance by Scripture (24:32).

Luke's literary replication calls for readers to anchor their belief concerning the resurrected Messiah within the biblical story line's mystery, the tension of revealing that entails concealing. Jesus forbids contentment with accessing the climactic resolution of redemption's mystery as if the countless divinely hidden disclosures throughout the OT that foreshadow Messiah's suffering and subsequent glory were inconsequential to the grand story's dramatic climax. By expounding Scripture's plotline concerning Messiah's suffering and death, Jesus obligates his two disciples to ponder the mystery's presaging clues embedded throughout the OT before revealing to them the reversal of circumstances they failed to anticipate from Scripture. Divine concealing and revealing resolve in Messiah's self-disclosure, for in him converge (1) two covenants—promise and fulfillment, (2) two ages—the old and the new, (3) two realms—the earthly and the heavenly, and (4) two forms of revelation—objective unveiling of Messiah and subjective clearing of occluded vision.

## CONCLUSION

Accumulating revelation brings clarity to prior revelation that came in various forms—trope, type, foreshadow, parable, allegory, etc. Dimness recedes as the dramatic escalation of the biblical plotline unfolds but especially when the climactic finale emerges from the shadows and light breaks forth from death's tomb. As expressed earlier, the analogy is backward but instructive; μυστήριον, biblically conceived, is akin to how writers craft mystery novels. Within characters, events, settings, and plotted conflicts throughout the story line of mystery novels, authors embed hints, foreshadows, prefigurements, harbingers, and portents that incite anticipation of full and final resolution to be revealed with surprises, invoking belief that seeks understanding. It is this way with Scripture's unfolding story line, not for readers only but first for characters who inhabit the story, including Adam, Noah, Abraham, Sarah, Hagar, Isaac, Moses, Ruth, David, Mary, and Jesus with Cleopas and his fellow disciple on the Emmaus Road. As they perform their redemptive-historical roles, for each of them, the unfolding story engenders hope that anticipates the promised Seed who brings salvation (cf. Hebrews 11).

For the Bible's characters and readers alike, integral to the plotted conflict of escalating hope are other cast members, events, places, and institutions laden with symbolism, sometimes layered, and posing as puzzling shadows, enigmas, riddles, conundrums that tantalize, and prefiguring types of things to come, yet veiled from full comprehension as they await further disclosures. All build toward the plot line's climactic resolution. When the time is fulfilled and the mystery is at last revealed with its variegated culmination converging in Messiah, Jesus of Nazareth, readers of Scripture, like the two disciples on the Emmaus Road, palm their foreheads and exclaim, "Did not our hearts burn within us? There he was all along on the pages of the OT. He was right there before our eyes from the beginning. How could we have missed him? How could we not have seen him until he made himself obvious to us?"

What is now revealed is what was always hidden in plain sight, seen by both Scripture's characters and readers though dimly. This is how the OT reveals Messiah. This is how Scripture bears witness to him. This is how Jesus reveals himself. Throughout his ministry, even to the end, Jesus, veiled in flesh, replicates Scripture, concealing even while revealing with his incarnation, with symbolic acts (miraculous or not), with teachings (parabolic or not), and with his passion and resurrection. How could it be otherwise, the Creator making himself known to his creatures?

If we persist in viewing the function of biblical types principally as a species of interpretation, we perpetuate confusion. To attach *typological, figural, figurative,* or *literal* as modifiers of *interpretation* improperly fixates the clash of ideas on hermeneutics rather than on the typological or prefiguring nature of divinely given revelation which the discussion should feature. The NT writers do not interpret the symbol-laden OT allegorically, figurally, figuratively, or typologically. None of these modifiers properly represents the interpretive activity of the NT writers nor should we use them to describe how NT writers read the OT. Rather, they are terms that properly describe *how God conveys his revelatory acts in history to foreshadow his consummating acts in Messiah,* revelatory acts that he authorized holy men of old to inscribe in Scripture for us on whom the ends of the ages have come.

The OT's types are divinely imbued revelatory foreshadows concealed within plain sight, some disclosed more fully than others, designed to tutor the first recipients concerning heavenly things but also written down in Scripture, pointing forward to greater disclosures in the fullness of time with the coming of Messiah as expounded in the apostolic proclamation of the gospel for the instruction of God's people in the last days. So, the same Scriptures that conceal while simultaneously revealing foreshadowing types now make them known to us at the ends of the ages, a divine wonder the apostle Paul identifies as "mystery" (μυστήριον; Rom 16:25–27). Instructive concerning the nature and function of biblical types is the apostle Paul's double admonition derived from Israel's divinely arranged experiences under the old covenant: "Now these things *took place as types* for us lest we desire evil as they did. . . . Now these things *occurred typologically* to them and they were written down for our admonition, on whom the ends of the ages have come" (1 Cor 10:6, 11; emphasis added).

*Chapter 11*

# "Particular Medicine:" Faithful Pastoral Ministry and τῇ διακονίᾳ τοῦ λόγου in Acts 6:4[1]

*by Ray Van Neste*

S ince the apostolic age, Acts 6:4 has been a seminal text for understanding the priorities of pastoral ministry. The dramatic growth of the early Jerusalem church precipitated a crisis for the apostles and their ministry. The needy widows of a minority group within the church (Greek-speaking Jews) were being neglected. In sorting out this problem, as Luke records in Acts 6, the apostles declared their two central and irreducible tasks: prayer and the ministry of the word.[2] Recently, some Bible translators have rendered the Greek phrase τῇ διακονίᾳ τοῦ λόγου (literally, "the ministry of the word") from 6:4 as "preaching," "the preaching ministry," or similar phrases. Undoubtedly, the intention of these translations was to clarify or simplify a phrase thought to be ambiguous or complex. Translating the apostolic priorities in Acts 6:4 as "prayer and preaching,"[3] however, rather than the more common "prayer and ministry of the word" is misleading. Something is lost in this interpretive simplification.

---

[1]  It is an honor to have the privilege of contributing this essay in appreciation of Tom Schreiner, who has so faithfully engaged in the ministry of the word for so many years. In a challenging time, I was blessed to be the recipient of his private ministry of the word as he took time to meet with me and to help me sort through various ideas as I sought the will of God.

[2]  This mandate was in contrast to that of the newly formed group of "deacons" who would serve tables and meet the practical needs of the widows.

[3]  Holman Christian Standard Bible (1999) has translated the phrase in this way. This has been changed to the traditional "prayer and ministry of the word" in the substantial revision of the translation published as the Christian Standard Bible (2017).

The more literally rendered "ministry of the word" connotes a broader semantic range than "preaching." For most contemporary English readers, "preaching" refers to ministry to the gathered church in public proclamation. However, when Paul describes his "ministry of the word" among the Ephesian elders he says he taught them both "publicly and from house to house" (Acts 20:20).[4] The translation "preaching" in Acts 6:4 improperly limits the idea to public proclamation, which, I would argue, provides a basis for neglecting the private and personal *ministry of the word* today.

To pursue this thesis, I will first examine the way Acts 6:4 has been translated across the spectrum of English translations. Such a survey demonstrates that the translation "preaching" is a more recent variation. Secondly, I will argue that the context of the rest of the book of Acts suggests a broader understanding of "ministry of the word" than is connoted by "preaching" as understood by most English readers today. Third, I will illustrate how Acts 6:4, particularly with the translation "preaching," affirms a view of pastoral ministry which is almost exclusively given to public proclamation. I will discuss the deleterious effects upon the church's ministry brought about by this understanding. Lastly, I will draw some implications from this study for our philosophy of translation.

## SURVEY OF ENGLISH TRANSLATIONS

In Acts 6:4 the phrase we are concerned with is τῇ διακονίᾳ τοῦ λόγου. The word διακονία is used in Luke and Paul to refer to serving others generally (Luke 10:40), specifically to meeting physical needs (Acts 11:29; 2 Cor 8:4; 9:1, 12) and to apostolic ministry (Rom 11:13; 2 Cor 4:1; 6:3; 1 Tim 1:12). In Acts 6:1 the same word is used to refer to the daily distribution of food. This regular "ministry" of food distribution is delegated to the appointed seven men (the first deacons I believe),[5] while prayer and the "ministry" of the distribution of the "word" will be the focus of the apostles.

Our concern here is what is meant by this "ministry of the word." Is the *distribution of the word* in view here limited to public proclamation? Here is a listing of some of the leading translations and how they rendered this verse:

---

[4] This follows Luke's description of the apostles' activity prior to the crisis with the Grecian Jews. Acts 5:42 reads, "And every day, in the temple and from house to house, they did not cease teaching and preaching that the Christ is Jesus" (ESV). Luke's narrative and Paul's description follow the same formula.

[5] Joseph B. Lightfoot states, "Universal tradition . . . connects the establishment of the 7 with the diaconate of later times." *The Acts of the Apostles* (Downers Grove, IL: InterVarsity Press, 2014), 106. Richard Pervo notes, "Since Irenaeus (A.H. 1.26.3; 3.12.10; 4.15.1), followed by most of the tradition, this passage has been understood as the foundation of the diaconate." *Acts* (Minneapolis: Fortress, 2009), 161.

# "MINISTRY OF THE WORD" (OR EQUIVALENT)

King James Version: But we will give ourselves continually to prayer, and to the ministry of the word.

American Standard Version: But we will continue steadfastly in prayer, and in the ministry of the word.

Christian Standard Bible: But we will devote ourselves to prayer and to the ministry of the word.

Douay-Rheims American Edition: But we will give ourselves continually to prayer, and to the ministry of the word.

English Standard Version: But we will devote ourselves to prayer and to the ministry of the word.

Geneva Bible: And we will give ourselves continually to prayer, and to the ministration of the word.

Phillips New Testament: Then we shall devote ourselves whole-heartedly to prayer and the ministry of the Word.

Lexham English Bible: But we will devote ourselves to prayer and to the ministry of the word.

New American Standard Bible: But we will devote ourselves to prayer and to the ministry of the word.

New English Translation: But we will devote ourselves to prayer and to the ministry of the word.

New International Version: and will give our attention to prayer and the ministry of the word.

New King James Version: but we will give ourselves continually to prayer and to the ministry of the word.

New Revised Standard Version: while we, for our part, will devote ourselves to prayer and to serving the word.

Revised Standard Version: But we will devote ourselves to prayer and to the ministry of the word.

## PREACHING (OR EQUIVALENT)

Common English Bible: As for us, we will devote ourselves to prayer and the service of proclaiming the word.

Contemporary English Version: We can spend our time praying and serving God by preaching.

Good News Translation: We ourselves, then, will give our full time to prayer and the work of preaching.

Holman Christian Standard Bible: But we will devote ourselves to prayer and to the preaching ministry.

New Living Translation: Then we apostles can spend our time in prayer and teaching the word.[6]

## THE CONTEXT OF THE BOOK OF ACTS

The book of Acts provides further context for considering the scope of the "ministry of the word" to which the apostles devoted themselves. First, Luke has already described the pattern of the apostles' teaching ministry in the previous chapter this way: "And every day, *in the temple and from house to house*, they did not cease teaching and preaching that the Christ is Jesus" (Acts 5:42 ESV, emphasis added). This is simply a continuation of the practice of the church immediately following Pentecost where they met in the temple and in homes (Acts 2:46). Thus, when "ministry of the word" is mentioned in Acts 6 we should already be prepared to think of this as including public ministry (such as to crowds in the temple) and private ministry, "from house to house."[7]

Alongside Acts 6:4, one of the most significant texts for pastoral ministry is Paul's description of his ministry to the Ephesians in Acts 20:17–35.[8] In this text Paul gives a farewell address to the pastors of the Ephesian church, summarizing his ministry among them as an example of proper ministry. Among other aspects of his ministry, Paul says he did not shrink back from declaring anything profitable but proclaimed to them the whole counsel of God. So, Paul engaged in a significant and comprehensive teaching ministry. But where or

---

[6] "Teaching the word" might be understood broadly enough to encompass more than pulpit ministry.

[7] Craig Keener also interprets these as marking public and private instruction. *Acts: An Exegetical Commentary*, 2:1, 2–44 (Grand Rapids: Baker Academic, 2012). Also Carl Holladay, *Acts* (Louisville: Westminster John Knox Press, 2016), 149. See Keener further for discussion on the two verbs, *preaching* and *teaching*, as he demonstrates that they do not connote distinct activities but are used together to describe comprehensively the communication of God's message.

[8] David Peterson, *The Acts of the Apostles* (Grand Rapids: Eerdmans, 2009), 234, points to Paul's message in Acts 20 as exemplifying what was meant by "ministry of the word."

in what context did this teaching take place? He makes this explicit by stating that he taught them publicly and from house to house (20:20). Thus, when Paul describes his teaching ministry, in an especially important setting where he is using his own labors as an example for other pastors, he makes the point of noting that his teaching ministry included both public and private teaching of the word.[9]

On the significance of Paul's mention of both public and private ministry, Calvin[10] is worth quoting at length:

> [Paul] did not only teach all men in the congregation, but also every one private-ly, as every man's necessity did require. For Christ hath not appointed pastors upon this condition, that they may only teach the Church in general in the open pulpit; but that they may take charge of every particular sheep, that they may bring back to the sheepfold those which wander and go astray, that they may strengthen those which are discouraged and weak, that they may cure the sick, that they may lift up and set on foot the feeble, (Ezekiel 34:4) for common doctrine will oftentimes wax cold, unless it be helped with private admonitions.
>
> Wherefore, the negligence of those men is inexcusable, who, having made one sermon, as if they had done their task, live all the rest of their time idly; as if their voice were shut up within the church walls, seeing that so soon as they be de-parted, thence they be dumb. Also, disciples and scholars are taught, that if they will be numbered in Christ's flock, they must give place to their pastors, so often as they come unto them; and that they must not refuse private admonitions. For they be rather bears than sheep, who do not vouchsafe to hear the voice of their pastor, unless he be in the pulpit; and cannot abide to be admonished and reproved at home, yea, do furiously refuse that necessary duty.[11]

Calvin reiterates this in his commentary on 1 Thess 2:11: "It is not enough that a pastor in the pulpit teach all in common, if he does not add also partic-ular instruction, according as necessity requires, or occasion offers. Hence Paul himself, in Acts 20:26, declares himself to be *free from the blood of all men*, be-cause he did not cease to admonish all publicly, and also individually in private

---

[9] Affirming that public and private is the sense here, see also, Eckhard Schnabel, *Acts* (Grand Rapids: Zondervan, 2012), 840; Holladay, *Acts*, 397; Pervo, *Acts*, 520.

[10] Lest anyone believe that Calvin was a pastor of a small declining church, see Elsie Anne McKee's *The Pastoral Ministry and Worship in Calvin's Geneva* (Geneva: Droz, 2016), and Scott Manetsch's *Calvin's Company of Pastors: Pastoral Care and the Emerging Reformed Church, 1536–1609* (Oxford: Oxford University Press, 2013). Their studies of the archival record of Geneva, both city and parish, make it clear that Calvin himself and his fellow pastors were much exercised in active pastoral ministry (this included home visits and constant vigilance for the hundreds of souls in Geneva as well as upwards of 260 sermons each year by Calvin).

[11] John Calvin, *Commentary upon the Acts of the Apostles* (Grand Rapids: Baker, 2003), 19:244.

in their own houses. For instruction given in common is sometimes of little service, and some cannot be corrected or cured without particular medicine."[12] In fact, even in preaching on Acts 6, Calvin makes clear that private teaching is also in view, stating that God "wants the charge kept inviolate until the end of the world so that preachers of the gospel will be able to accommodate the teaching according as they see a need and proclaim the word both in public and in private."[13]

Calvin's fellow reformer Martin Bucer also emphasizes the importance of private teaching, addressing Acts 20:26:

> Those pastors and teachers of the churches who want to fulfill their office and keep themselves clean of the blood of those of their flocks who are perishing should not only publicly administer Christian doctrine, but also announce, teach and entreat repentance toward God and faith in our Lord Jesus Christ, and whatever contributes toward piety . . . even at home and with each one privately.[14]

More recently, Paul Beasley-Murray assessed the Apostle Paul's work as a pastor:

> Paul was concerned not just for the corporate health of the churches in his care, but also for the well-being of individuals. People mattered to Paul. . . . In 1 Thessalonians 2:11 Paul declared: "We dealt with each one of you like a father with his children," implying that he had concerned himself with his converts on an individual basis. Similarly, Paul emphasized the personal character of his work in Colossians 1:28: he sought to promote individual maturity by "warning and teaching everyone in all wisdom." All this is in line with Luke's account of Paul's speech to the Ephesian elders, which suggests that his normal practice was to combine preaching to the church at large together with the visiting of individual church members (Acts 20:20).[15]

In the context of the book of Acts it becomes clear that the apostolic priority of "the ministry of the word" cannot be limited to public proclamation. With this conclusion in view, let us return to the range of terms used in English translations. The literal "ministry of the word" leaves open the possibility of private and public proclamation. "Teaching" or "speaking God's word" are both

---

[12] John Calvin, *Commentary on the First Epistle to the Thessalonians* (Grand Rapids: Baker, 2003), 21: 254–55.

[13] John Calvin, *Sermons on the Acts of the Apostles: Chapters 1–7*, trans. Rob Roy McGregor (Edinburgh: Banner of Truth, 2008), 329.

[14] Martin Bucer, *De Regno Christi*, in *Melanchthon and Bucer*, ed. Wilhelm Pauck (Philadelphia: Westminster Press, 1969), 235.

[15] Paul Beasley-Murray, "Paul as Pastor," in *Dictionary of Paul and His Letters*, ed. Gerald F. Hawthorne, Ralph P. Martin, and Daniel G. Reid (Downers Grove, IL: InterVarsity Press, 1993), 657.

also likely to be understood as potentially involving public and private settings. However, "preaching" (CEV) or "preaching ministry" (HCSB) is likely to be understood only in terms of public ministry.[16]

## PROBLEMATIC IMPLICATIONS FOR PASTORAL MINISTRY

The Christian church, generally, has historically understood pastors to be carrying on the apostles' work, especially their ministerial labors in prayer and the Word. As I teach pastoral ministry or speak to pastors about their labors, I seek to counter the idea that public ministry is the sum of pastoral ministry. Drawing from numerous NT texts and historical examples I argue that the soul of pastoral work is the oversight of souls, which includes but goes well beyond preaching.[17] I argue for the necessity of pastoral visitation, keeping up with the needs and spiritual state of congregants. In such settings, someone will typically point to Acts 6:4 as a text which seems to contradict what I am saying. "But didn't the apostles just devote themselves to prayer and preaching?" The answer is no, they did not, at least not if by "preaching" you mean simply public proclamation. I point them to Acts 20:20, as I have discussed above, but translating "ministry of the word" in Acts 6:4 as "preaching" or "preaching ministry" short circuits such a conversation. The reader is inadvertently prevented from thinking of the *ministry of the word* in any broader terms. When we already have cultural currents pushing us away from the private side of pastoral ministry, the last thing we need is a translation that obscures it.

Julia Duin conducted wide and varied interviews seeking reasons why otherwise mature believers were deeply disaffected with the church. Among those reasons she discovered was the lack of pastoral care. She wrote, "My research suggested that people simply were not being pastored. Often ministers are out of touch with what's happening on the ground." She cited difficulties people had getting in touch with their pastors or in finding care and guidance for their souls. People often felt they were just supposed to attend mass meetings, fill their cog in the machine and not expect anything more. They did not feel shepherded, or that anyone was engaging their day-to-day world.[18]

Certainly, the celebrity culture, which has infected even the church, does not help us here. Individual work with people cannot be seen or distributed

---

[16] See Peter Adam's excellent book on preaching, *Speaking God's Words: A Practical Theology of Expository Preaching* (Downers Grove, IL: InterVarsity Press 1996), esp. chap. 4, "Preaching as a Ministry of the Word" (emphasis added).

[17] See further, Ray Van Neste, "The Care for Souls: Reconsidering Pastoral Ministry in Southern Baptist and Evangelical Contexts," in *Southern Baptists, Evangelicals, and the Future of Denominationalism*, ed. David S. Dockery, with Ray Van Neste and Jerry Tidwell (Nashville: B&H, 2011), 113–34.

[18] Julia Duin, *Quitting Church: Why the Faithful Are Fleeing and What to Do about It.* (Grand Rapids, MI: Baker, 2009), 22–23.

and, thus, does not promote a platform. As Calvin Miller stated, "No one ever gets his or her picture in an evangelical magazine simply because they visited the sick."[19] People are messy and individual work is complicated, tangled, and slow. Henry Scougal (1650–1678), a prominent Scottish pastor and theologian who profoundly influenced George Whitefield and John and Charles Wesley, pleaded with a regional gathering of pastors in Aberdeen:

> But certainly the greatest and most difficult work of a minister is in applying himself particularly to the various persons under his charge; to acquaint himself with their behavior and the temper of their souls; to redress what is amiss and prevent their future miscarriages. Without this private work, his other endeavors will do little good. . . . Now this supposes a great deal of care, to acquaint ourselves with the humors and conversation of our people; and the name of 'watchmen' that is given to us implies no less.[20]

Along these lines, Christian counselor Larry Crabb has provocatively written:

> There is an awful assumption in evangelical circles that if we can just get the Word of God into people's heads, then the Spirit of God will apply it to their hearts. That assumption is awful, not because the Spirit never does what the assumption supposes, but because it has excused pastors and leaders from the responsibility to tangle with people's lives. Many remain safely hidden behind pulpits, hopelessly out of touch with the struggles of their congregations, proclaiming the Scriptures with a pompous accuracy that touches no one.[21]

The implications of the broader *ministry of the word* are missed far too often. We need the breadth of this ministry highlighted, not obscured by translation. Individualized ministry is the norm across the New Testament even if we are conditioned today by experience to miss it. Below are just a few examples.

In Col 1:28, one of Paul's summary statements about his ministry, he states, "[Christ] we proclaim, warning everyone and teaching everyone with all wisdom, that we may present everyone mature in Christ" (ESV). Paul is not focused simply on a large crowd but is concerned that his teaching reach and shape each member of the congregation. Commenting on Paul's repeated use of "everyone" here, Peter O'Brien states, "The singular is used to show that each person individually . . . was the object of the apostle's care."[22]

---

[19] Calvin Miller, *O Shepherd, Where Art Thou?* (Nashville, TN: B&H, 2006), 42.
[20] "On the Importance and Difficulty of the Ministerial Function," in *The Works of the Rev. Henry Scougal* (1765), reprint, ed. Don Kistler (Morgan, PA: Soli Deo Gloria, 2002), 241, 252.
[21] Larry Crabb, *Inside Out* (Colorado Springs, CO: Navpress, 1988), 160.
[22] Peter O'Brien, *Colossians, Philemon* (Waco, TX: Word Books, 1982), 88.

Peter, speaking to other pastors, says, "I exhort the elders among you, as a fellow elder and a witness of the sufferings of Christ, as well as a partaker in the glory that is going to be revealed: shepherd the flock of God that is among you, exercising oversight" (1 Pet 5:1 ESV). The key command here is to shepherd, which cannot be reduced to sermons from afar. Sermons play a key role, but they do not exhaust the work of the pastoral office. The use of shepherd imagery is rooted in the work and example of Jesus as the Great Shepherd (cf. Heb 13:20), who said:

> I am the good shepherd. The good shepherd lays down his life for the sheep. He who is a hired hand and not a shepherd, who does not own the sheep, sees the wolf coming and leaves the sheep and flees, and the wolf snatches them and scatters them. He flees because he is a hired hand and cares nothing for the sheep. I am the good shepherd. I know my own and my own know me, just as the Father knows me and I know the Father; and I lay down my life for the sheep. (John 10:11–15 ESV)

Alexander Maclaren, commenting on this passage, wrote: "Individualising care and tender knowledge of each are marks of the true shepherd. To call by name implies this and more. To a stranger all sheep are alike; the shepherd knows them apart. It is a beautiful picture of loving intimacy, lowliness, care, and confidence, and one which every teacher should ponder."[23]

Lastly, and perhaps most significantly, Heb 13:17 summarizes the pastoral role stating that pastors "are keeping watch over your souls, as those who will have to give an account" (ESV). It is hard to imagine this accounting as being anything other than individual and particular. If we must give account for each one, we surely must minister to each one in addition to speaking to the whole congregation. It will be difficult to give account to God for souls whose names we do not know.

So, nineteenth-century Baptist pastor Hezekiah Harvey stated of pastors,

> "Each member of his flock is a soul entrusted to his care by the Lord; and if true to his trust, he is one of those who 'watch for souls as they must give account.' Paul, when in Ephesus, taught not only publicly, but 'from house to house;' and in his farewell charge to the elders of that city he said, 'Watch, and remember that, by the space of three years, I ceased not to warn every man night and day with tears' (Acts 20:31)."[24]

---

[23] Alexander Maclaren, *The Gospel of St. John*, Bible Class Expositions (London: Hodder and Stoughton, 1893), 106.

[24] Hezekiah Harvey, *The Pastor: His Qualifications and Duties* (Philadelphia: American Baptist Publication Society, 1879), 78

This is a significant aspect of ministry, significant in terms of the impact on people, its importance to kingdom growth, and in terms of the percentage of a pastor's time it will take. We ought not have pastors in training thinking that the sum of their labors will be preaching and sermon preparation. We are setting them up for failure and setting our churches up for harm. This line of thinking impoverishes preaching as the pastor lacks the close knowledge of his people required in order to apply the text most helpfully, most graciously, and most directly. John Angell James stated well, "He who can only generalize in the pulpit, but has not ability to individualize out of it . . . may be a popular preacher, but he is little fitted to be the pastor of a Christian church."[25] Indeed, Richard Baxter wrote, "I fear most those ministers who preach well, and who are unsuited to the private nurture of their members."[26]As Peter Adam has stated,

> Those of us who are committed to preaching need to be committed to a wider ministry of the Word as well. We need to see preaching as part of that ministry of the Word. Otherwise we shall try to make preaching do what it cannot easily achieve. Not only will God's people suffer because they do not receive other ministries of the Word, but our preaching will suffer as we force it into an alien mould. Our ministry may be pulpit-centered, but it should not be pulpit-restricted, for such a ministry of the Word will suffer severe limitations.[27]

Yet, translations which render τῇ διακονίᾳ τοῦ λόγου simply as "preaching" (or its equivalent) obscure this point. They prevent people from seeing this component of a pastor's work, helping pastors to overlook this work and helping church members miss this aspect of ministry they should expect.

## IMPLICATIONS FOR TRANSLATION WORK

What then are the implications of this study for the way we approach Bible translation? Of course, there is no strictly literal translation. Interpretation is always in view. But we must be careful not to over interpret. We must be very careful that our well-intended clarifications do not obscure connections elsewhere in the text. Of course, there will be difficult decisions and balancing acts, but I believe it will be safer to err on the side of literal, even allowing people to wrestle with some ambiguity. We ought not make interpretive decisions for the reader unnecessarily. We do want clarity in translations, but we do not want

---

[25] John Angell James, *An Earnest Ministry: The Want of the Times* (1847; repr., Carlisle, PA: Banner of Truth, 1993), 151.
[26] Richard Baxter, *The Reformed Pastor* (1656), rev. ed., ed. James M. Houston (Portland, OR: Multnomah, 1982), 7.
[27] Adam, *Speaking God's Words*, 74–75.

simplification which removes the opportunity to see broader aspects of what is in view. In some cases, like this one in Acts 6:4, the restriction of interpretive options is harmful.

# BACKGROUND ISSUES AND BIBLICAL THEOLOGY

*Chapter 12*

# "Do We Really Need to Reconstruct the Background of Colossians to Understand the Letter?"

*by Clinton E. Arnold*

The issue of identifying the precise nature of the problem looming large in the background of Paul's letter to the Colossians remains a conundrum in the history of the interpretation of the letter. What exactly was the so-called "Colossian heresy"?[1]

In the past century, dozens of different proposals have been put forward. And in the past thirty years, several newer ideas have emerged. Some scholars have taken their lead from the term "philosophy" (Col 2:8) and have proposed that the problem was due to the influence of a philosophical system, such as Platonism,[2] Cynicism,[3] or Neo-Pythagoreanism.[4] Others have emphasized the Jewish elements—such as the references to sabbaths, festivals, new-moon celebrations, and food laws (Col 2:16)—and have argued that the competing

---

[1] I am deeply grateful for my friendship with Dr. Thomas Schreiner over the years and the opportunity to serve together with him in a variety of ways. I have fond memories of extended meetings with Tom and a group of others beginning in 2001 where we envisioned and planned the Zondervan Exegetical Commentary series. We also enjoyed a period of working together on the executive board of the Evangelical Theological Society. Tom has also been a great dialogue partner. I am grateful for his participation in a panel that reviewed my monograph on Colossians in a Pauline Studies group meeting at ETS in 1998 and for his extensive review that appeared in *Trinity Journal* 20 (1999), 100–105.
[2] Richard E. DeMaris, *The Colossian Controversy: Wisdom in Dispute at Colossae*, JSNTSS 96 (Sheffield: JSOT Press, 1994).
[3] Troy W. Martin, *By Philosophy and Empty Deceit: Colossians as Response to a Cynic Critique*, JSNTSS 118 (Sheffield: JSOT Press, 1996).
[4] See Eduard Schweizer, *The Letter to the Colossians* (Minneapolis: Augsburg, 1982),132.

teaching at Colossae was some form of Jewish influence, either from the local synagogue down the road or from a Jewish Christian leader within the church.[5] Many have pointed to visionary experience as part of the problem (see Col 2:18) and link the errant teaching to Jewish mysticism and ascent to heaven experiences.[6] Still others have noticed that there are words and practices that come from local pagan religions, such as the term *embateuō* ("entering," which could be a technical term from ritual initiation practices; Col 2:18) and have argued that the Colossian problem is a combination of pagan and Jewish practices—a syncretism.[7] Some then point to Gnosticism or proto-Gnosticism as the most likely explanation for such syncretistic practices. And, in the interest of full disclosure, I, too, have contributed a possible reconstruction for these various elements of the teaching and practice that comprise the Colossian "philosophy."[8] I have argued that the competing teaching is syncretistic (combining Jewish and elements from local religions and magical practices), but that the overarching context is folk belief and shamanistic practices.

There is a bewildering variety of options and the interpreter is hard-pressed to determine which one best accounts for all the evidence. But just how important is it to come to a settled conclusion in order to interpret the letter? Is a decision on this interpretive puzzle essential for understanding the letter or is it simply a matter of historical interest and the satisfaction of scholarly curiosity? Can we understand the theology of the letter without attending to the historical matters? Is it possible to achieve an accurate understanding of the message of the letter without reconstructing the precise contours of the historical situation?

## GRAMMATICAL *AND HISTORICAL* EXEGESIS

Evangelicals have typically practiced a form of grammatical-historical exegesis.[9] The text is primary, but we also acknowledge a necessary role for historical

---

[5] See James D. G. Dunn, "The Colossian Philosophy: A Confident Jewish Apologia" *Bib* 76 (1995), 153–81.

[6] See, for example, Ian K. Smith, *Heavenly Perspective: A Study of the Apostle Paul's Response to a Jewish Mystical Movement at Colossae*, LNTS 346 (London: T&T Clark, 2006); Thomas J. Sappington, *Revelation and Redemption at Colossae*, JSNTSup 53 (Sheffield: JSOT Press, 1991).

[7] M. Dibelius, "The Isis Initiation in Apuleius and Related Initiatory Rites," in *Conflict at Colossae*, eds. Fred O. Francis and Wayne A. Meeks, SBLSBS 4 (Missoula: Scholar's Press, 1973), 61–121; William M. Ramsay, "The Mysteries in their Relation to St. Paul," *Contemporary Review* 104 (1913): 198–209; Eduard Lohse, *Colossians and Philemon*, Hermeneia (Philadelphia: Fortress Press, 1971), 128–29.

[8] See Clinton E. Arnold, "Initiation, Vision, and Spiritual Power: The Hellenistic Dimensions of the Problem at Colossae," in *The First Urban Churches*, eds. James R. Harrison and Lawrence L. Welborn, vol. 5, *The Lycus Valley*, Writings from the Greco-Roman World Supplement Series (Atlanta: SBL Press, forthcoming); Arnold, "Sceva, Solomon, and Shamanism: The Jewish Roots of the Problem at Colossae," *JETS* 33 (2012): 7–26; Arnold, *The Colossian Syncretism. The Interface between Christianity and Folk Belief at Colossae*, WUNT 2/77 (Tübingen: Mohr Siebeck, 1995; repr., Wipf and Stock, 2015).

[9] In the post-Reformation era, conservative scholarship began referring to this interpretive approach as the "grammatico-historical method." In the mid-1700s, the eminent German historian Johann August Ernesti (1707–81) elaborated on this method in his *Institutio interpretis Novi Testamenti* noting, "the object in using

background study to provide us with context, understanding of certain words, images, and phrases, and to understand the contingent setting of the letters. In his *New Testament Exegesis* text, Gordon Fee rightly asserts, "The very nature of Scripture demands that the exegete have some skills in investigating the historical-cultural background of NT texts."[10] But what do we lose if we neglect the historical component? Or, to put it more positively, surely we can understand the substance of what the text has to say without historical research. Right?

We must frame the question in more specific terms when it comes to interpreting a document like Colossians. We must first of all understand that Colossians is a letter and that it shares many of the literary conventions of first-century letters. But we must also realize that by reading someone else's mail, we are eavesdropping on a piece of communication in which the letter writer and his readers share a set of assumptions and mutual understandings that are reflected in the letter. Because of this, the letter writer can simply make an allusion to something that is understood by both parties and does not need to provide a full explanation of what he is referring to.

We do this commonly in our letter writing and email communication. For instance, imagine I wrote to a friend here in the Los Angeles area and included the line, "I still can't believe how he swung on that inside fast ball in the bottom of the ninth and missed." If this piece of communication were discovered 2,000 years from now, it could create confusion and may very well be unintelligible unless one did historical research. What is the time reference, "bottom of the ninth?" Why would someone swing at a ball? And with what? Why was this miss so important to these individuals? Of course, the context is a sport called "baseball" and the reference is to a particular game at Dodger stadium in 2017. The various terms and expressions as well as the statement itself are meaningless without this historical context.

Consider another example. I am writing this at the beginning of a new semester at the university where I serve. Given some recent developments in our area, I could imagine the provost of our university writing a note like the following:

> To Our Faculty: Welcome back to the start of a new semester! I hope you have all had an enjoyable and refreshing summer break. I can't believe that classes begin in less than a week. It will be great to be with our students again as they arrive back on campus. As we anticipate the beginning of the semester, please be sure to warn your students to keep their arms and legs covered, especially at

---

this compound name is to show that both grammatical and historical considerations are employed, in making out the sense of a passage."

[10] Gordon D. Fee, *New Testament Exegesis: A Handbook for Students and Pastors,* 3rd ed. (Louisville: Westminster John Knox, 2002), 96.

dusk. Please encourage them to use Off or a similar repellent. Everyone simply needs to be particularly cautious right now and to be vigilant to avoid these pests. This is a very dangerous situation right now for all.

Much of this letter would be understandable by someone from a different cultural location or by someone in the distant future. The term "faculty" defines the addressees as members of an institution of learning. The terms "semester," "classes," "students," and "campus" are consistent with this and would require little or no historical or contextual research to interpret. Yet what are the "pests" referred to in the latter part of the note? Why would they attack arms and legs? What is "Off"? The capitalization of this term would suggest that it is a technical term. One clearly needs to know the historical context to understand the full meaning of this paragraph. Careful historical investigation would reveal that certain areas of southern California were threatened by mosquitoes carrying the West Nile virus and the Zika virus in the summer of 2017.

Paul's letter to the Colossians warns of a very serious problem threatening the church in that area. He uses very strong language to underline the gravity of the problem: "see to it that no one takes you captive" (Col 2:8 ESV); "let no one pass judgment on you" (Col 2:16 ESV); "let no one disqualify you" (Col 2:18 ESV). He then makes allusions to the competing and dangerous teaching without ever explaining himself. We are distant in both time and culture and find it difficult to know precisely what he is talking about. Elements of the letter may very well be inscrutable to us without knowing the historical context and circumstances.

As Wright notes, in principle, "history sets the context for exegesis, and must always remain in close dialogue with it; history and exegesis together must always remain in dialogue with theology itself."[11] But this leads us back to our original question: can we interpret and understand the theology of the letter without having to reconstruct the Colossian "philosophy"? This is a more complex question than it may appear at first blush. And the answer is both yes and no. We will explore below in what sense the answer is yes and in what sense it is no.

## YES, WE CAN UNDERSTAND THE THEOLOGY

There is much in Colossians that is not part of the polemic against the competing teaching. The introductory thanksgiving (1:3–8), the intercessory prayer report (1:9–14), the poetic praise of Christ (1:15–20), the teaching on reconciliation (1:21–23), Paul's reflections on his ministry (1:24–2:3), the admonition to focus on Christ (3:1–4), the section on putting away sinful behaviors

---

[11] N. T. Wright, *Paul and His Recent Intepreters* (Minneapolis: Fortress Press, 2015), 23.

and appropriating virtues (3:5–17), the instructions to various members of the household (3:18–4:1), the final admonitions (4:2–6), the extensive personal greetings (4:7–17), and the letter closing (4:18) are not dependent upon any particular reconstruction of the false teaching to be readily understood. This is by far the bulk of the letter. To be sure, there are aspects of each of these sections that can and need to be illuminated through historical research. And the question of why Paul selected certain themes and doctrines to communicate to the Colossians still remains to be answered. But the theological affirmations reflected in these passages can be grasped without much difficulty.

The interpretive situation becomes substantially more complicated within the polemical core of the letter (2:4–23, and, especially, 2:16–23). Throughout this section, theological statements are interwoven with rhetoric, polemic, "catchwords" from the erroneous teaching, and abbreviated descriptors. Yet within this context, the meaning of key theological affirmations can be clearly apprehended without recourse to a particular reconstruction of the competing teaching.

For instance, at the heart of Paul's teaching here is a strong affirmation of the identification of believers with Christ in his burial, resurrection, and newness of life (2:12–13). Paul stresses this threefold identification through a rhetorical emphasis by means of compounding each verb with the preposition, *sun* ("together with"). This theological teaching was very important to the Colossians in their distinctive situation, yet these statements can easily be interpreted apart from the situation.

The same can be said of the magnificent portrayal of the implications of Jesus's death on the cross for the principalities and powers (2:15). God has stripped these spirits of their power and authority, publicly exposed them, and triumphed over them through the work of Christ on the cross. Once again, this teaching is very relevant to the Colossians in the exigencies of their setting, but the theological teaching of the defeat of the powers by the cross is crystal clear.

Finally, Paul's most important critique of the leader of the factional teaching is that "he is not holding tight to the Head" (2:19).[12] Of course, this is the problem with most any deviant teaching within the church. The false teacher is not in close connection with the fountain of truth and the source of all that is conducive for the growth and health of the church. We do not need to make an appeal to a particular reconstruction of the false teaching to know that Christ is Lord and that submitting to his lordship is crucial for our well-being.

There are a few other positive theological statements made throughout 2:4–23, such as, "all the fullness of the Godhead lives in him bodily" (2:9), "you have been filled in him" (2:10), "he is the head over every principality and

---

[12] Unless otherwise noted, biblical translations are the author's own.

authority" (2:10), "in him you have been circumcised" (2:11), "you were dead in your transgressions" (2:13), "he forgave us all our transgressions" (2:13), and more. There are fewer in 2:16–23 since this contains most of the direct polemic. Yet all of these rich theological affirmations can be interpreted on their own in a manner that is not contingent upon discerning the precise nature of the so-called "Colossian heresy."

This is encouraging news and reinforces the Protestant notion of the perspicuity of Scripture. One does not need to have a PhD in history and spend countless hours researching the historical background of the letter to grasp the main elements of its theological message.

## NO, WE CANNOT UNDERSTAND CERTAIN PASSAGES

Nevertheless, not all of the letter can be completely understood without historical study. Some aspects of the letter remain opaque or even inscrutable without an accurate grasp of the historical context. There is also an array of interpretational issues with scholars on two or more sides of the interpretive divide that cannot be resolved without historical information. These can be sorted into two different types of issues: (1) those related to the overall polemical situation, and (2) specific words, phrases, and images that require historical information to be grasped.

At the outset of his polemical section, Paul warns, "watch out that someone does not take you captive through the philosophy or empty deceit" (2:8). The obvious question to ask is, what is "the philosophy" that threatens to take them captive? There is no way to answer this question apart from careful historical study in light of the composite details that emerge from the text of Colossians.

In some ways, assembling a portrait of the situation at Colossae resembles a thousand-piece puzzle with a few hundred pieces missing and most of the pieces mixed up. Neither do we have the cover of the box to see what it is to look like once it is assembled. This suggests that, at the minimum, we all need to be somewhat tentative in our reconstructions of the problem. We need to assert our results with a degree of humility commensurate with the complexity of the issue. As we have noted, however, an inability to reconstruct the issue does not mean that we are at a loss for understanding the positive theological statements of the letter. We can grasp these and interpret them, albeit with a less than precise understanding of why Paul thought they were relevant to the Colossians and how they were relevant.

Yet we need to be cautious of giving up the historical quest prematurely or pleading that it is a hopeless case when there is relevant historical data that can help to illuminate the matter. For example, I have argued that there is an abundance of inscriptional data that is now available for correlation with the expression "worship of angels" (*thrēskeia tōn aggelōn*) in Col 2:18. Much of this information has become available only in the past fifty years and is also now much more accessible because of its availability digitally. In looking at the abundance of angel inscriptions from western Asia Minor, I have observed that the vast majority of occurrences are in the context of folk belief, magic, and shamanistic practices in which angels are called upon for help or protection from evil spirits or dangers of various sorts.[13] For instance, a few years ago, archaeologists discovered a bronze scroll in a silver tube in the necropolis of Hierapolis, a city very close to Colossae. The text reads, "I adjure you by God who founded the earth and the heavens; I adjure you by the angels, Cherubim, the harmony above, Michael, Raphael, Abrasax [at this point the text breaks away and no other names are legible] to be averted from injury."[14] This information is potentially very relevant for interpreting the situation at Colossae and needs to be taken into account by all commentators. This text and others like it suggest to me that the genitive case of the Greek expression, *tōn aggelōn*, should be interpreted as objective and that the angels are the objects of the rituals or veneration and that it is not subjective, namely people are joining angels in worshipping [God].

There are many other pieces of historical information that can, and should, be correlated to what we know of the problem at Colossae as part of an effort to fill out the picture of the precise contours of the problem afflicting the church. I would go so far as to say that most of Col 2:16–23 is incomprehensible without engaging in this kind of historical research.

Another explicit indicator of the nature of "the philosophy" at Colossae is the term *embateuō* in Col 2:18. The term occurs in a clause immediately after the phrase "worship of angels" and could be translated "entering what he has seen." Like other elements of Paul's discussion of the problem, the readers would know precisely what he was referring to because of their shared knowledge with Paul (like we know that "bottom of the ninth" refers to an inning in baseball). Yet we need to try to uncover the proper religious-cultural context for this expression. Interpreting *embateuō* is made all the more difficult by the rarity of the term; it never appears elsewhere in the NT and seldom occurs in the Septuagint (only twice in the canonical OT). It appears four times in the text of 1 Maccabees in the sense of "invading" a territory (1 Macc 12:25; 13:20; 14:31; 15:40)—an idea that does not fit the context here. Yet archaeologists have found the term in a series of inscriptions at the famous temple of Apollo at Claros (just north of Ephesus; about one hundred miles due west of Colossae). Here it is used as a technical term for the second (and higher) stage

---

[13] See my *Colossian Syncretism*, 8–102.

[14] Murat Aydaş, "New Inscriptions from Asia Minor," *Epigraphica Anatolica* 37 (2004), 124.

of ritual initiation into the mysteries of Apollo. The plausibility of the term being known at Colossae is enhanced by the fact that delegations came from the area around Colossae and consulted the Clarian Apollo. Once again, this information needs to be consulted and correlated for how it may shed light on this lexical item and for an overall reconstruction of the problem at Colossae. If it is relevant, as I think it is, it would suggest that the competing teaching was syncretistic—a mix of Jewish and Hellenistic ideas. Without historical investigation, Bible translators and commentators are very much left in the dark about how to translate and understand this Greek word.

There are many features of the problem at Colossae that Paul reveals. These each need to be interpreted before a composite picture can be postulated. But this is done by moving back and forth from an overall explanatory hypothesis and the individual elements. The end result must be a coherent picture based upon the explicit and implicit indicators of the false teaching.

The danger of not doing this historical work is that it is easy to unwittingly allow modern assumptions to sneak into the interpretation of the text. For instance, one might be tempted to see Col 2:8 as a condemnation of the academic discipline of philosophy or assume that it refers to some school of philosophy. There is definitely the possibility of many wrong-headed applications from this text.

## RECONSTRUCTION HELPS WITH UNDERSTANDING THE WHY?

The Apostle Paul was certainly capable and well equipped to write an extensive systematic theology covering all of the theological loci in great depth. Yet when he wrote to the Colossians, he limited himself to 1,582 words in four chapters. The reason for this is that his thirteen letters are occasional, *ad hoc* documents written to address specific situations and matters in the life of the churches. Paul was necessarily selective in the theology he chose to present in his letters. For the most part, his selectivity is informed by what he considers most relevant and important for his readers to receive at that particular instance in their history. As a wise and caring pastor, he relates to them theological truths that they most needed to hear given what they were facing. Dean Fleming aptly notes, "Paul's letters are models of doing context-oriented theology for the diverse churches and situations he addressed."[15]

In the process of interpreting Paul's letters, it is instructive for us to ask the question, out of all the things that Paul could have said to this group, why did he choose to say these particular things at this point in time? The answer to

---

[15] Dean Fleming, *Contextualization in the New Testament: Patterns for Theology and Mission* (Downers Grove, IL: InterVarsity Press, 2005), 15.

this question will not necessarily help us in understanding the meaning of the theology of the letter, but it will assist us in understanding its *relevance*. It will provide us with insight into Paul's pattern of contextualizing theology, namely what theology Paul deemed relevant for addressing a particular situation or set of needs in the church. We also see how Paul expressed and communicated that theology for that setting. In essence, we learn from Paul not only as theologian but *as pastor*. He models an approach to ministry that we can emulate and follow.

This principle can be illustrated by exploring two prominent theological themes in Colossians: Jesus as Lord of all and the participation of believers in Jesus's death, resurrection, and newness of life.

### *Jesus as Lord of All*

There is a strong emphasis on the Lordship of Christ throughout Colossians. This is expressed not only through the fourteen references to Jesus as Lord (*kyrios*) in the letter and his role as "head" (*kephalē*), but also through a variety of other terms and concepts that convey this teaching. Paul pens (or cites) a moving and eloquent poem of praise to Christ as Lord at the outset of the letter (without ever actually using the term "Lord"). In Col 1:15–20, he portrays Christ as the image of the invisible God, the one who possesses all the fullness of God, the creator of heaven and earth, the goal of all creation, the one who holds all of creation together, sovereign over all of creation, the one who is preeminent over all, and the one who will reconcile all of creation. Within this hymn, however, he lays stress on the invisible side of creation—the principalities, authorities, thrones, and lordships. These angelic beings are "the invisible realm" and "the things in heaven" over whom Christ reigns supreme and who will one day be pacified.

The theme of Christ's lordship over this realm continues through the letter. Paul describes salvation as a rescue act in which God delivers us from "the authority of darkness" and transfers us to the kingdom of his Son (1:13). We learn that the false teaching at Colossae is ultimately due to the influence of "the elemental spirits of the world" (2:8).[16] But the readers are assured that Christ is "the head over every ruler and authority" (2:10). Part of the reason for this (in addition to all that was proclaimed in the hymn of 1:15–20) is that Christ's work on the cross has resulted in a dramatic and decisive defeat of the principalities and authorities (2:15). Christ's death renders their influence ineffective (2:20).

---

[16] Interpreting the meaning of τὰ στοιχεῖα τοῦ κόσμου (2:8, 20) is a notoriously difficult interpretive issue. It must be solved, in part, by careful historical research. I have discussed this problem in depth in *Colossian Syncretism*, 158–94.

It is crucial to see that the lordship of Christ in Colossians is affirmed over and against the realm of demonic forces. Paul wants his readers to know beyond any shadow of a doubt that Jesus is Lord over this realm. But why does Paul choose this occasion to assert this truth about Jesus's lordship? It has everything to do with the setting. The theme of hostile spirit powers is prominent in Colossians and Paul has already mentioned that their fingerprints are on the teaching that is threatening the church at Colossae (2:8). But what is this teaching? This takes us back to our original question of the importance of reconstructing the nature of the teaching for interpreting the letter. We do not need to identify the precise nature of "the philosophy" to interpret the theological statements. But knowing what the deviant teaching was all about would help to see the relevance of the theology. We will examine one other prominent theological theme in the letter before correlating it to the problem at Colossae.

### *The Participation of Believers in Jesus's Death, Resurrection, and Newness of Life*

There is a strong emphasis on participation with Christ in Colossians—not only in his death, but especially in his resurrection and new life (Col 2:11–13; 3:1–4). This theme is also present elsewhere in Paul, most notably Rom 6:1–14, but with a less pronounced emphasis on co-resurrection and participation in newness of life. The emphasis on co-resurrection is so strong in Colossians (and Ephesians) that some have used this as an argument against the Pauline authorship of the letter.[17]

This theme is developed as a prelude to Paul's polemic against the false teaching and the theme of co-resurrection is taken up by Paul immediately after the polemic. Co-resurrection thus functions as a literary inclusio to the polemical section.

It is instructive also to trace the flow of Paul's argument leading up to and through this section. In 2:8, Paul issues his stern warning to "watch out that no one takes you captive through the philosophy" which, ultimately, is inspired by demonic forces and is out of sync with Christ and his purposes. The causal conjunction, "because" (*hoti*), indicates that the theological reasons that will then be introduced provide the basis for resisting the influence of this dangerous teaching and practice. Verses 2:9–10 then serve as the heading for the theological teaching that follows (extending through 2:15). There are an opening and a closing statement about Christology that sandwich a statement about the participation of believers in Christ:

---

[17] See, for example, Lohse, *Colossians and Philemon*, 180–181, and Hans Hübner, *An Philemon, An Die Kolosser, an Die Epheser*, HzNT 12 (Tübingen: Mohr Siebeck, 1997), 84.

Christology: "In him dwells all the fullness of the deity bodily."

Participation: "And you have been filled in him."

Christology: "He is the head over every principality and authority."

The Christological statements are strong affirmations of Jesus's lordship and even his deity. But most shocking is the statement about the extent of the participation of believers in Christ. The emphasis of the text is upon the participation of believers in Jesus's lordship over the principalities and powers. The overt teaching of this passage is that believers share in his power and authority over this realm.

Why is this important? In terms of the explicit teaching of Colossians, it is crucial to note three things: (1) the powers have inspired the false teaching (2:8); (2) the powers continue to influence believers through false teaching, the flesh, and other means; and, (3) although defeated by Christ (2:15), the powers continue to reign over a dominion and to oppose the kingdom of Christ (1:13). This much can be discerned without recourse to a reconstruction of the specific teaching of "the philosophy" at Colossae.

Yet by interpreting the precise nature of the problem, we can gain a deeper and better appreciation of *the relevance* of the theology to the real-life situation. The difficulty, however, is that there are competing reconstructions of the false teaching, as I recounted at the outset of this chapter.

## RECONSTRUCTION HELPS WITH APPLICATION

The good news is that we can understand the theology of the letter without having a right understanding of the false teaching. But for preaching and teaching this letter, having a grasp of the contours of the problem would help in knowing how to apply the text.

I would encourage interpreters not to give up on discerning the historical situation behind Colossians. The process of researching this question will yield insights that are helpful in communicating the text. Also, new discoveries and new historical information help in moving past the lack of consensus among scholars in years past.

Most scholars have moved past the *Gnostic* explanation of a generation ago. This is largely because there is increasing evidence that Gnosticism even existed as a religion of redemption in the first century. For applying the text, this is perhaps a good thing. Most contemporary churchgoers have little idea of what Gnosticism was and would have even more difficulty finding any point of connection between their convictional world and Gnosticism.

Many scholars still find the *Jewish Mysticism* explanation of the false teaching to be the most compelling. Yet I find that the local evidence from Asia Minor does not support this view. Nevertheless, if this were the correct view, it is difficult for contemporary readers to find correspondences with their experiences because it is such a unique problem. Few groups today practice asceticism as a way to prepare themselves for a mystical ascent-to-heaven experience whereby they can catch a vision of God at his heavenly throne and join angels in worshipping him.

If I am correct, however, in affirming that the problem has to do with religious syncretism and shamanistic practice in the context of a fear of the demonic, it is much easier to see the relevance of Colossians for similar settings today. The declaration that Jesus is Lord of all—everything in heaven and on earth, visible and invisible—becomes profoundly encouraging and freeing. The participation of believers with Christ in his death, resurrection, and newness of life empowers believers by affirming that they share in Christ's authority over the realm of darkness. Consequently, they do not need to rely on magic, rituals, invocations, or any other kind of formulas for resisting evil spiritual forces. Christ is supreme, he is sufficient, and he will help. As Fleming notes, "it is hard to miss the similarities between the context Paul addressed in Colossae and that of many non-Western worldviews and cultures, where established religions, popular folk beliefs and Christianity routinely share the same quarters."[18]

## CONCLUSION

Evangelicals have long affirmed the importance of the historical component in the exegetical process. One needs to understand the historical context of usage for terms, phrases, and images to grasp their intended sense. For instance, knowing something about Roman triumphal processions helps the reader to understand and appreciate Paul's use of *thriambeuō* in Col 2:15. And the issue of how to interpret the *stoicheia tou kosmou*, "elementary spirits of the world" (Col 2:8, 20) cannot be resolved apart from historical study. Numerous similar examples could be given.

But does the interpreter need to have an accurate understanding of the Colossian "philosophy" to understand the letter. The answer to this question turns out to be rather complex. On the one hand, no, understanding the theological affirmations of the letter can be grasped without reconstructing the precise contours of the historical setting and, in particular, the nature of the so-called Colossian heresy. One could also say that having an erroneous view of the Colossian problem will not necessarily result in misinterpretation of the theological teaching of the letter.

---

[18] Fleming, *Contextualization*, 231–32

Yet there is indeed something lost without doing historical work on the background of Colossians. Portions of the letter cannot be interpreted and understood apart from historical investigation. This is particularly true at the points in the letter where Paul engages in explicit polemic against the opposing teaching as, for instance, in 2:16–23.

But another significant benefit of doing careful research into the setting of the letter is that it enables the interpreter to understand the contextualization strategy of the apostle. There is much to learn from Paul on *how* he applies theology to real-life situations facing his churches. This kind of investigation helps pastors and teachers today to discern how to apply theology in their settings. One of the blessings in the way that God has given us the Scripture, and, in particular, the NT letters, is that we see theology applied. We thus learn from the Scripture not only content, but strategy.

*Chapter 13*

# The Importance of Reading Second Temple Jewish Literature for New Testament Studies

*by Jarvis J. Williams*

## INTRODUCTION

New Testament scholars generally agree on the importance of reading extra-biblical literature for the study of the New Testament.[1] We know the New Testament was not written in a historical vacuum.[2] And, by setting

---

[1] By extra-biblical literature, I specifically mean the Old Testament Apocrypha, the Old Testament Pseudepigrapha, the Dead Sea Scrolls, Josephus, and Philo. The term *extra-biblical* could refer to ancient sources that have not been recognized as Scripture. These kinds of sources would include, but would not be limited to, the Apocryphal Gospels and other Greco-Roman sources. In this essay, I focus on Second Temple Jewish literature. For a few helpful resources to expose students of the New Testament to Second Temple Jewish literature, see James C. Vanderkam, *An Introduction to Early Judaism* (Grand Rapids: Eerdmans, 2001); Martin Goodman, ed., *The Apocrypha*, Oxford Bible Commentary (Oxford: Oxford University Press, 2001, 2012, 2013); David A. DeSilva, *Introducing the Apocrypha: Message, Context, and Significance* (Grand Rapids: Baker, 2002); Everett Ferguson, *The Background to Early Christianity* (Grand Rapids: Eerdmans, 2003); John J. Collins and Daniel C. Harlow, eds., *The Eerdmans Dictionary of Early Judaism* (Grand Rapids: Eerdmans, 2010); Lawrence H. Schiffman, *Qumran and Jerusalem: Studies in the Dead Sea Scrolls and the History of Judaism* (Grand Rapids: Eerdmans, 2010); Craig Evans, ed., *Ancient Texts for New Testament Studies* (Grand Rapids: Baker, 2012); John J. Collins and Daniel C. Harlow, ed., *Early Judaism: A Comprehensive Guide* (Grand Rapids: Eerdmans, 2010, 2012); Louis H. Feldman, James L. Kugel, and Lawrence H. Schiffman, eds., *Outside the Bible: Ancient Jewish Writings Related to Scripture* (Philadelphia: The Jewish Publication Society, 2014); Susan Docherty, *The Jewish Pseudepigrapha: An Introduction to the Literature of the Second Temple Period* (Minneapolis: Fortress, 2014).

[2] Ironically, my first encounter with Second Temple Jewish literature was as a Master of Divinity student in 2001 in Tom Schreiner's Greek exegesis class of Romans. My first serious engagement with the primary Jewish literature was as a Master of Theology student in Brian Vickers's PhD New Testament colloquium on Second Temple Judaism. These two men introduced me to this rich and important literature that has guided my studies and everything I've written.

the New Testament alongside contemporary ancient sources, New Testament scholars have shown many of the ideas in the New Testament are not unique to the New Testament.[3] Words like grace, justification, righteousness, sin, etc., take on a life of their own in different extra-biblical sources apart from the New Testament.[4] In fact, the New Testament uses and discusses many of the same words and concepts in ancient, extra-biblical sources. They often simply attach different nuances of these terms in their New Testament contexts since the authors interpret them in light of the cross and resurrection of Jesus Christ.[5] Yet, many concepts and words in the New Testament still find their roots in the Greco-Roman and Jewish culture in which the New Testament was written.[6] The importance of this context is evident in the many New Testament monographs and grammatical-historical exegetical commentaries that interact with extra-biblical literature or that read New Testament texts or ideas comparatively alongside of Second Temple Judaism.[7]

In this essay, I argue a basic and rather pedestrian thesis for most New Testament scholars in the academic guild.[8] Namely, a basic understanding of Second Temple Jewish literature can help New Testament readers become more familiar with the cultural context of the New Testament and help shine a ray of light onto their reading of the New Testament. I support this thesis by simply offering a comparative reading of MT Psalm 110 (LXX Psalm 109), the Pseudepigraphal texts of the Psalms of Solomon 17–18, and selected texts in the New Testament that cite LXX Ps 109:1 (MT Ps 110:1). This analysis endeavors to show the reader that reading these New Testament texts in front of their Second Temple Jewish background can give readers insight into the

---

[3] For a few examples of work demonstrating the importance of reading Paul in his Second Temple Jewish context, see Simon J. Gathercole, *Where Is Boasting: Early Jewish Soteriology and Paul's Response in Romans 1–5* (Grand Rapids: Eerdmans, 2002); David Lincicum, *Paul and the Early Jewish Encounter with Deuteronomy* (Grand Rapids: Baker, 2010); Preston M. Sprinkle, *Paul and Judaism Revisited: A Study of Divine and Human Agency in Salvation* (Downers Grove, IL: InterVarsity Press, 2013); Kyle B. Wells, *Grace and Agency in Paul and Second Temple Judaism: Interpreting the Transformation of the Heart* (Leiden: Brill, 2014); Ben C. Blackwell, John K. Goodrich, and Jason Maston, eds., *Reading Romans in Context: Paul and Second Temple Judaism* (Grand Rapids: Zondervan, 2015).

[4] For example, see the concept of justification in the Dead Sea Scroll (DSS) 4QMMT. See also the concept of divine agency in the DSS 1QH.

[5] Just compare, for example, the concept of grace in Philo and in Romans and Galatians.

[6] For an example of this with respect to grace in Paul, see John Barclay, *Paul and the Gift* (Grand Rapids: Eerdmans, 2016).

[7] For a few examples, see arguments and bibliography in Jarvis J. Williams, *For Whom Did Christ Die? The Extent of the Atonement in Paul's Theology*, Paternoster Biblical Monographs Series (Milton Keynes, UK: Paternoster, 2012); Williams, *Christ Died for Our Sins: Representation and Substitution in Romans and Their Jewish Martyrological Background* (Eugene, OR: Pickwick, 2015). For examples from commentary series, see Hermeneia, Baker Exegetical, Zondervan Exegetical Commentary of New Testament, Word Biblical Commentary, the New Covenant Commentary, the New International Greek Text Commentary, among many others.

[8] This essay is for the non-specialist with a basic knowledge of Greek and Hebrew.

way in which Jesus's messianic identity in selected New Testament texts that cite LXX Ps 109:1 (MT Ps 110:1) fits into the Second Temple Jewish context in which these New Testament texts were written.[9]

### The LORD and the Lord in MT Psalm 110

1 לְדָוִד מִזְמוֹר נְאֻם יְהוָה | לַאדֹנִי שֵׁב לִימִינִי עַד־אָשִׁית אֹיְבֶיךָ הֲדֹם לְרַגְלֶיךָ:

2 מַטֵּה־עֻזְּךָ יִשְׁלַח יְהוָה מִצִּיּוֹן רְדֵה בְּקֶרֶב אֹיְבֶיךָ:

3 עַמְּךָ נְדָבֹת בְּיוֹם חֵילֶךָ בְּהַדְרֵי־קֹדֶשׁ מֵרֶחֶם מִשְׁחָר לְךָ טַל יַלְדֻתֶיךָ:

4 נִשְׁבַּע יְהוָה | וְלֹא יִנָּחֵם אַתָּה־כֹהֵן לְעוֹלָם עַל־דִּבְרָתִי מַלְכִּי־צֶדֶק:

5 אֲדֹנָי עַל־יְמִינְךָ מָחַץ בְּיוֹם־אַפּוֹ מְלָכִים:

6 יָדִין בַּגּוֹיִם מָלֵא גְוִיּוֹת מָחַץ רֹאשׁ עַל־אֶרֶץ רַבָּה:

7 מִנַּחַל בַּדֶּרֶךְ יִשְׁתֶּה עַל־כֵּן יָרִים רֹאשׁ:

MT Psalm 110 is a messianic psalm. New Testament authors interpret this psalm messianically and apply it to Jesus (cf. Matt 22:42–46; Mark 12:35–37; Luke 20:41–43; Acts 2:34–35; Heb 5:6).[10] In MT Ps 110:1, the psalm begins with the words, "To David, a song. A declaration of the LORD (=Heb. Yahweh) to my Lord (=Heb. Adonai)." The psalm positions Yahweh as the primary speaker. His speech is directed to someone who shares his authority and who is likewise identified as the Lord (Adonai). The content of Yahweh's speech in the following verses of MT Psalm 110 confirms this.

In MT Ps 110:1, Yahweh says to the Lord (=Adonai): "Sit at my right hand until I (=Yahweh) appoint your (=Adonai/Lord) enemies to be a footstool at your (=Adonai/Lord) feet" (emphasis mine). Yahweh appoints the Lord's enemies to be a footstool at the Lord's feet. This appointment of the LORD speaks to his authority, and the subjugation of the enemies under the feet of the Lord speaks to both Lords' authority over their enemies. MT Ps 110:2 says "The LORD will stretch out from Zion [the] rod of your strength to

---

[9] This essay is not intended to make a fresh contribution to messianic studies, but rather to show the non-specialist a benefit of reading the New Testament against the background of Second Temple Jewish sources. Thus, I will spend the vast majority of my time interacting with primary texts from MT Psalm 110, LXX Psalm 109, the Psalms of Solomon 17–18, and selected New Testament texts. For critical interaction with the relevant scholarship on the issues discussed or briefly mentioned in this essay, see critical monographs and critical New Testament commentaries. Finally, a basic point readers should keep in mind is Second Temple Judaism was complex and differed in practice depending on location and group. For examples of this complexity, see D.A. Carson, Peter O'Brien, and Mark Seifrid, eds., *Justification and Variegated Nomism: The Complexities of Second Temple Judaism*, 2 vols. (Grand Rapids: Baker, 2001–2004).

[10] As common with major English translations, I spell LORD in all caps to emphasize the Hebrew word is Yahweh.

rule in the presence of your enemies" (brackets mine). The sharing of authority between the LORD and the Lord is evident in the rule of both the LORD (Yahweh) and the Lord (Adonai) from Zion as the LORD stretches out the Lord's strength in the presence of the Lord's enemies.

In MT Ps 110:3, the text continues "Your (=Adonai's/Lord's) people will offer themselves freely in the day of your (=Adonai's/Lord's) power in the glories of holiness from the womb of the dawn, to you (=Adonai/Lord) [will be] the dew of your (=Adonai's/Lord's) descendants" (brackets and emphasis mine). In MT Ps 110:4, Yahweh promises with an oath to execute his authority through the reign of the Lord ("The LORD [=Yahweh] has sworn and he [=Yahweh] will not change his [=Yahweh's] mind.") (brackets and emphasis mine). In MT Ps 110:5, the Psalm identifies the Lord as a king of righteousness in accordance with the LORD's word ("Thus, you [=Adonai/the Lord] [are] a king of righteousness according to my [Yahweh's]word.") (brackets and emphasis mine).

In MT Ps 110:5–6, David confesses the Lord is at the LORD's right hand ("My [=David] Lord [=Adonai] [is] at your [=Yahweh's] right hand") (brackets and emphasis mine). The Lord's position at the LORD's right hand speaks to shared authority between both the LORD and the Lord and shared divine exaltation over everything beneath the feet of both the LORD and the Lord. MT Ps 110:6 confirms this point when David asserts the Lord will crush his enemies ("He [=Adonai/Lord] will crush kings in the day of his [=Adonai/Lord] burning nostrils. He [=Adonai/Lord] will punish nations. He [=Adonai/Lord] will fill up corpses [in the nations]. He [=Adonai/Lord] will crush a head over the abundant land.") (brackets and emphasis mine). Finally, in MT Ps 110:7, David says the Lord triumphantly reigns in victory over his crushed enemies on earth as he lifts up his head ("He [=Adonai/Lord] will drink from the valley in the way. Therefore, he [=Adonai/Lord] will lift up [a] head.") (brackets and emphasis mine).

### *The LORD and the Lord in LXX Psalm 109 (=Hebrew/English Psalm 110)*

1 τῷ Δαυιδ ψαλμός εἶπεν ὁ κύριος τῷ κυρίῳ μου κάθου ἐκ δεξιῶν μου
   ἕως ἂν θῶ τοὺς ἐχθρούς σου ὑποπόδιον τῶν ποδῶν σου

2 ῥάβδον δυνάμεώς σου ἐξαποστελεῖ κύριος ἐκ Σιων καὶ κατακυρίευε
   ἐν μέσῳ τῶν ἐχθρῶν σου

3 μετὰ σοῦ ἡ ἀρχὴ ἐν ἡμέρα τῆς δυνάμεώς σου ἐν ταῖς λαμπρότησιν τῶν
   ἁγίων ἐκ γαστρὸς πρὸ ἑωσφόρου ἐξεγέννησά σε

4 ὤμοσεν κύριος καὶ οὐ μεταμεληθήσεται σὺ εἶ ἱερεὺς εἰς τὸν αἰῶνα κατὰ τὴν τάξιν Μελχισεδεκ

5 κύριος ἐκ δεξιῶν σου συνέθλασεν ἐν ἡμέρᾳ ὀργῆς αὐτοῦ βασιλεῖς

6 κρινεῖ ἐν τοῖς ἔθνεσιν πληρώσει πτώματα συνθλάσει κεφαλὰς ἐπὶ γῆς πολλῶν

7 ἐκ χειμάρρου ἐν ὁδῷ πίεται διὰ τοῦτο ὑψώσει κεφαλήν

MT Psalm 110 is Psalm 109 in the Septuagint (=LXX). The goal here is not to comment on each verse of LXX Psalm 109. Instead, I mention in passing the verses in LXX Psalm 109 that highlight the shared authority and identity of both the LORD (Yahweh) and the Lord (Adonai) from MT Psalm 110 and the Greek terms used to refer to the LORD and to Jesus in the New Testament.

LXX Psalm 109 translates יְהוָה and אֲדֹנִי from MT Psalm 110 as κύριος. The LORD (ὁ κύριος) speaks to David's Lord (τῷ κυρίῳ μου) (LXX Ps 109:1). The LORD (κύριος) sends forth the Lord's (Adonai's) rod with power from Zion (LXX Ps 109:2). The LORD (κύριος) made an immutable oath regarding the Lord's priesthood (LXX Ps 109:4). The LORD (κύριος) will crush kings at the Lord's right hand in the day of his wrath (LXX Ps 109:5). In LXX Psalm 109, the term κύριος refers to both the LORD and the Lord (cf. LXX Ps 109:1). This translational move at least demonstrates the translators of the LXX identified both יְהוָה and אֲדֹנִי as κύριος.[11] This suggests that these Jews already understood Yahweh as a complex plurality. The preceding is not making a claim about the Trinity in early Judaism. Rather, the point is simply the translators of LXX Ps 109:1 and of MT Ps 110:1 show a willingness to merge the identities of יְהוָה and אֲדֹנִי into the singular identity of κύριος. This translational move is also evident in the Psalms of Solomon 17–18 and in the New Testament's use of LXX Ps 109:1.

### *The LORD and the Lord in the Psalms of Solomon 17–18*

The Psalms of Solomon are eighteen extra-biblical psalms in both the Pseudepigrapha and in Rahlfs's critical edition of the LXX.[12] According to some scholars, these psalms record the response of pious Jews to Rome's sacking

---

[11] I realize critical and translational issues of (what we have come to know as) the LXX are complex.

[12] For a critical English translation of the Psalms of Solomon, see R.B. Wright, "Psalms of Solomon," in *The Old Testament Pseudepigrapha*, vol. 2, ed. James H. Charlesworth (New York: Doubleday, 1985) , 639–70. For a critical Greek edition, see *Rahlfs-Hanhart Septuaginta*, ed. Alfred Rahlfs and Robert Hanhart (Stuttgart: Deutsche Bibelgesellschaft, 2006).

of Jerusalem in 63 BC (cf. Pss Sol 1, 2, 8, 17).[13] Psalms of Solomon 17–18 talk about the Messiah. The psalmists cry out to the LORD asking him to send the Messiah to crush their enemies and to vindicate Jerusalem. According to R.B. Wright, Psalms of Solomon 17 has specifically been identified as an "extended messianic hymn, describing the reign of this king, the anointed son of David."[14] Wright suggests these psalms were originally penned in Hebrew and translated into Greek and later in Syriac.[15]

In the Greek version of the Psalms of Solomon 17, certain words and concepts are similar to LXX Psalm 109 (MT Psalm 110).[16] Κύριος refers to both Yahweh (Pss Sol 17:1) and to the Messiah/seed of David (Pss Sol 17:22–24). The psalm identifies Yahweh as the Lord (κύριος), God, and king (Pss Sol 17:1, 3, 7–10, 13, 21, 34, 39, 44–46). Likewise, the psalm refers to the Messiah/ seed of David as the Lord (κύριος), king, and son of David (Pss Sol 17:21–43). The people of God ask the Yahweh-κύριος to send the seed of David-κύριος to crush their enemies (Pss Sol 17:22–24). Yahweh-κύριος and seed of David-κύριος are distinct but share authority and identity.

The distinction between the two Lords emerges when Israel confesses Yahweh-κύριος made an oath concerning David's seed so that his kingdom would never end (Pss Sol 17:4). That Yahweh-κύριος and seed of David-κύριος share identity and authority while being distinct in the psalm is apparent throughout the psalm but appears most forthrightly at the end of the psalm (cf. Pss Sol 17:1, 3, 7–10, 13, 21, 34, 39, 44–46 with 17:21–33–43). Israel says "The Lord himself is king" at the end of the psalm (Pss Sol 17:46) after they've already asked Yahweh-κύριος to raise up the Messiah to reign (kingship) over Israel (Pss Sol 17:21). The phrase "the Lord himself is king" refers to Yahweh-κύριος since Israel's prayer urges Yahweh-κύριος to send seed of David-κύριος to reign over and to crush their enemies (Pss Sol 17:21–24).

Prior to identifying Yahweh-κύριος as king in Pss Sol 17:46, Israel confesses the servant of David will be a king taught by God in the days of the Messiah's reign on earth (Pss Sol 17:32). The psalm further says Israel's king (βασιλεὺς) will be Christ, namely, the Lord or will be the Lord's Christ (χριστὸς κυρίου) (Pss Sol 17:32).[17] Regardless of how one takes the grammar

---

[13] Wright, "Psalms of Solomon," 639. The date and composition of Psalms of Solomon 17 are matters of debate in critical scholarship. For an introduction to critical issues in the Psalms of Solomon and for argument in favor of a date after 63 BC, see argument and bibliography in Kenneth Atkinson, "On the Herodian Origin of Militant Davidic Messianism at Qumran: New Light from Psalm of Solomon 17," *JBL* 118/3 (1999): 435–60.

[14] Wright, 639.

[15] Wright, 640.

[16] The above statement simply affirms similarities between Psalms of Solomon 17–18 and LXX Psalm 109. I'm not arguing for a genealogical connection but providing an analogical reading of these texts.

[17] The grammar could work either way.

(χριστὸς κυρίου), the psalm identifies the seed of David as a king and the Christ in close association with the Lord, while also distinguishing Yahweh-κύριος from the seed of David-κύριος in the psalm.

Psalms of Solomon 18 has similarities with Psalms of Solomon 17 in this regard. The terms κύριος (Pss Sol 18:1) and God refer to Yahweh (Pss Sol 18:5, 6, 8–9, 10, 11, 12). Psalms of Solomon 18:7 uses κύριος to refer to the Messiah (χριστός). In this psalm, the Messiah is both distinct from Yahweh-κύριος (Pss Sol 18:1) and yet shares in the divine identity of Yahweh-κύριος (Pss Sol 18:7).[18] Statements about the reign of the Messiah (18:5), the mercy of Yahweh-κύριος reigning upon his people (18:1–7), and the statement that the people will see the good things of Yahweh-κύριος when the Messiah reigns (18:6–7) support the preceding premise.

MT Psalm 110, LXX Psalm 109, and Psalms of Solomon 17–18 speak of the identity of Yahweh with complexity. This complexity allows for a plurality. LXX Psalm 109 and Psalms of Solomon 17–18 speak of Yahweh's identity with the same or similar vocabulary and concepts as the New Testament authors, but they explicitly identify Jesus as the other Lord in MT Ps 110:1 and LXX Ps 109:1 who shares Yahweh's identity and authority. That is, the unnamed κύριος, who shares in the authority and identity of Yahweh-κύριος in LXX Ps 109:1 and the unnamed Messiah-seed of David-κύριος in the Psalms of Solomon 17–18 is identified as the κύριος Jesus Christ in the Gospels and Acts.

### *The LORD and the Lord in Selected Texts in the New Testament*

The Synoptic Gospels quote Psalm 110:1 (MT Ps 110:1; LXX Ps 109:1) in response to a question posed to Jesus about the identity of the Christ by the Pharisees (Matt 22:42–46) and by the scribes (Mark 12:35–37; Luke 20:41–43). Jesus's answer accentuates the Christ cannot be David's son since David calls him Lord (κύριος). Then, with the exception of one word,[19] Matthew's Gospel records Jesus's words with an exact quotation of LXX Ps 109:1 (MT Ps 110:1) ("The Lord said to my Lord: 'sit at my right hand until I appoint your enemies under your feet'"). Both Mark 12:35–37 and Luke 20:41–43 quote LXX Ps 109:1 verbatim. With an appeal to what we've come to know as MT Ps 110:1 and LXX Ps 109:1, Jesus's response highlights the Christ is greater than David.

---

[18] I borrow the phrase, "divine identity" from Richard Bauckham. For his important work on this, see his seminal essay *God Crucified: Monotheism and Christology in the New Testament* (Grand Rapids: Eerdmans, 1999). For his recent work on Christology, see Richard Bauckham, *Jesus and the God of Israel: God Crucified and Other Studies on the New Testament's Christology of Divine Identity* (Grand Rapids: Eerdmans, 2008).

[19] τῷ Δαυιδ ψαλμός εἶπεν ὁ κύριος τῷ κυρίῳ μου κάθου ἐκ δεξιῶν μου ἕως ἂν θῶ τοὺς ἐχθρούς σου ὑποπόδιον τῶν ποδῶν σου (LXX Ps 109:1).

In the citation of LXX Ps 109:1 in Acts 2:32–36, that Jesus shares in Yahweh's identity and authority while remaining distinct from him is even more apparent than in the Synoptic Gospels' citation of the verse. On the day of his great Pentecostal sermon (Acts 2), Peter quotes verbatim LXX Ps 109:1 (cf. Acts 2:35). As an explanation to why diverse people heard diverse languages speaking in their own tongues (Acts 2:1–34), Peter states God inaugurated Jesus as both Lord (κύριος) and Christ/Messiah (χριστὸς) at his resurrection (Acts 2:34; cf. with Pss Sol 17:32 and 18:7). He makes this statement after citing a portion of a Davidic psalm (Eng. Ps 16:8–11) in which David prays to the LORD (יְהוָה in the MT, but κύριον in the LXX) about not suffering decay. Peter cites this text to accentuate David spoke about the Christ's resurrection instead of himself (Acts 2:25–34). Peter's evidence of this is both the tongues spoken at Pentecost in fulfillment of Joel 2:28–32 and the presence of David's tomb (Acts 2:29).

Then, in Acts 2:35, Peter cites LXX Ps 109:1 verbatim in support of his statement that David foresaw the resurrection of Jesus Christ (Acts 2:31; cf. LXX Ps 16:8–11). As a climax to his sermon, Peter says God made Jesus to be both Lord (κύριος) and Christ (χριστὸς). Peter's remarks distinguish Jesus from the κύριος but identifies him as κύριος, while stating that God appointed him to be both Lord (κύριος) and Christ (χριστὸς) at the resurrection. Peter's citation of Joel 2 and two Davidic psalms in the context of defending the resurrection of Jesus suggests Jesus fulfills MT Ps 110:1 and LXX Ps 109:1.

In addition, Peter suggests God did at the resurrection of Jesus Christ what Psalm 110 and Psalms of Solomon 17–18 ask Yahweh-κύριος to do with respect to the Messiah. Israel's Messiah was inaugurated as king and began to reign as the Messiah at the right hand of God at the resurrection of Jesus Christ, and Jesus Christ is κύριος. Similar to MT Ps 110:1, LXX Ps 109:1, and Psalms of Solomon 17–18, Yahweh's identity is discussed in a complex plurality. However, the Gospels and Acts make an even bolder statement. They explicitly identify Jesus as the Messiah-κύριος who shares the identity and authority of Yahweh-κύριος as the seed of David-κύριος. The Lord Jesus Christ was the Davidic seed anticipated in MT Ps 110:1 and LXX Ps 109:1 and for which Israel prays in Psalms of Solomon 17–18.

## CONCLUDING THOUGHTS

Reading the above New Testament texts that cite LXX Psalm 109 (MT Psalm 110) against Psalms of Solomon 17–18 shines a ray of light onto what the New Testament authors are saying with respect to Jesus's identity in the Synoptic Gospels and Acts. MT Psalm 110 and LXX Psalm 109 mention the reign of the Messiah and identify the Messiah as the Lord who shares in the LORD's identity and authority (MT Ps 110:1; LXX Ps 109:1). Psalms of Solomon 17–18 identify both Yahweh and the seed of David as the Lord and king; Israel asks the Lord to send the Messiah to crush her enemies, and the Lord shares the identity and the authority of the LORD in Psalms of Solomon 17–18.

The Synoptic Gospels and Acts explicitly identify Jesus of Nazareth as the Lord and Messiah mentioned in MT Psalm 110 and LXX Psalm 109 and the seed of David and the Lord and king in Psalms of Solomon 17–18. The New Testament authors highlight Jesus as the fulfillment of Israel's long-awaited son of David who shares in Yahweh's identity and authority. They don't create *de novo* the concept of a Messiah who rules on earth as a man and who shares Yahweh's identity and authority. Rather, their understanding of Jesus's identity and authority is in continuity with the Hebrew Scriptures and certain Second Temple Jewish ideas about Yahweh, the Messiah, and the seed of David. The New Testament authors are novel in that they identify Jesus of Nazareth, a crucified and resurrected and exalted Jewish man, as Yahweh and as the one and only promised hope of Israel in fulfillment of MT Psalm 110 and LXX Psalm 109.

Similar to when New Testament readers with a working knowledge of Greek can gain insights from reading the Greek New Testament, Second Temple Jewish literature can help New Testament readers see cultural reasons behind the foolishness, the scandal, and the power of the gospel of Jesus Christ. This literature can also help New Testament readers understand the cultural context in which the ministry of Jesus took place and in which the authors wrote the New Testament.[20] May New Testament readers take up Josephus, Philo, the Apocrypha, the Pseudepigrapha, and the Dead Sea Scrolls and read!

---

[20] The above comparative analysis reveals at least the following conclusions. First, Jews in the pre–Second Temple period and during the Second Temple period understood Yahweh's identity in terms of a complex plurality. Second, Jesus shares Yahweh's divine identity and authority. Third, Jesus is Yahweh, while remaining distinct as the son of David. Fourth, Jesus is the Messiah. Fifth, Jesus is not the Father, but he shares the divine identity and authority of the Father. Sixth, when Christians worship the Lord Jesus Christ, we worship and honor Yahweh (cf. John 5:22–23).

*Chapter 14*

# The Old Testament in the Gnostic and Valentinian Gospels

*by Simon Gathercole*

Recently, Notger Slenczka, a professor of Protestant theology in Berlin, published an article arguing that the Old Testament should no longer have authoritative canonical status for the church.[1] In early Christianity as well, one of the key fault lines in debates between mainstream Christians and heretics was over this question of the Old Testament. This debate was reflected in their written accounts of Jesus. Some maintained that the Old Testament was part of the DNA of the good news about Christ, while others produced their accounts of the saving activity and message of Jesus with a negative or ambiguous stance towards Israel's scriptures. These rival accounts of Jesus are going to be the focus of discussion here. The most notorious case of this was Marcion, who did not, as is sometimes thought, straightforwardly *reject* the Old Testament but rather saw it as true testimony to the inferior creator god and his messiah.[2] The focus here in this essay will not be on Marcion, but on the Gospel productions of two other movements, the Gnostics and the Valentinians, and the way in which each treats the Old Testament.

---

[1] Notger Slenczka, "Die Kirche und das Alte Testament," in Elisabeth Gräb-Schmidt and Reiner Preul, eds. *Das Alte Testament in der Theologie*, Marburger Jahrbuch Theologie XXV (Leipzig: Evangelische Verlagsanstalt, 2013), 83–119. The essay is accessible online at: https://www.theologie.hu-berlin.de/de/st/vortragkolnendgestalt.pdf.

[2] See e.g., Judith M. Lieu, *Marcion and the Making of a Heretic: God and Scripture in the Second Century* (Cambridge: Cambridge University Press, 2015), 398–432.

# 1. THE OLD TESTAMENT IN THE GNOSTIC GOSPELS OF *JUDAS* AND THE *EGYPTIANS*

The first selections of extra-canonical literature to be examined here are, in the proper sense of the word, "Gnostic." Although the word is used in common parlance and even among scholars in a rather vague way to refer to almost any heretical movement or text, in antiquity at least initially it was used in a more specific sense. The neo-Platonic circle in Rome in the mid-third century AD which centred on the philosopher Plotinus, for example, is quite specific about who "the Gnostics" are. A particular section of Plotinus's corpus (*Ennead* 2.9) is titled by Plotinus's student Porphyry both "Against the Gnostics" (Πρὸς τοὺς γνωστικούς) and "Against those who say that the creator of the cosmos is evil and that the cosmos is evil" (Πρὸς τοὺς κακὸν τὸν δημιουργὸν τοῦ κόσμου καὶ τὸν κόσμον κακὸν εἶναι λέγοντας).[3] This clearly implies a distinctive theology and cosmology. Similarly, the more careful of the church fathers distinguish between "those who call themselves Gnostics" and others, such as the Valentinians (whose works will be treated in the section below). Irenaeus refers to "the so-called Gnostic school" (ἡ λεγομένη Γνωστικὴ αἵρεσις), indicating that the name was a conventional one in the late second century.[4] There is therefore a coincidence of usage between the school of Plotinus and the church fathers who both independently and for some of the same reasons engaged with the Gnostics (both found rebarbative the idea that God and the world were evil).[5] The two sample texts to be treated here are the *Gospel of the Egyptians* from Nag Hammadi and the *Gospel of Judas* from Codex Tchacos.

## 1.1 *The Gospel of the Egyptians*

According to the *Gospel of the Egyptians*, the event of salvation comes through a union of the heavenly Seth with a spiritual Jesus, which results in the institution of the Gnostic baptism which is perhaps the main focus of this Gospel. According to the version in Codex III from Nag Hammadi,[6] the great heavenly figure Seth goes through a series of tribulations. His third and final tribulation, the "judgement of the rulers, powers and authorities," consists of his undergoing baptism through a Logos-begotten body, a body which he himself had

[3] Porphyry, *Life of Plotinus* 5 and 24.

[4] Irenaeus, *Against Heresies* 1.11.1. "School" (αἵρεσις) here has the sense not of a physical institution but of a "school of thought."

[5] On the whole question see especially M.J. Edwards, "Gnostics and Valentinians in the Church Fathers," *JTS* 40 (1989), 26–47, and Edwards, "Neglected Texts in the Study of Gnosticism," *JTS* 41 (1990), 26–50.

[6] There are two versions of the *Gospel of the Egyptians* at Nag Hammadi (in codices III and IV), both of which are fragmentary, but the Codex III text is in the main better preserved. For the texts and translations, see Alexander Böhlig and Frederik Wisse, eds. *Nag Hammadi Codices III, 2 und IV: 2. The Gospel of the Egyptians - The Holy Book of the Great Invisible Spirit* (Leiden: Brill, 1997), 52–167.

produced through the virgin (*Gos. Egy.* 63.10–13). Baptism is thus established by the Father, through the incorruptible and Logos-begotten living Jesus: this Jesus figure is the one whom Seth had "put on," through whom Seth nailed the powers of the thirteen aeons, and secured the position of his elect. This nailing of the thirteen aeons and establishment of the seed, in the climactic third descent, are of clear soteriological significance in the book. So there is in a sense a "history of salvation" in this work. What is noteworthy, though, is the relation which this *Heilsgeschichte* has to the Old Testament.

At the end of the book we have a postscript by the author:

> This is the book which the great Seth wrote, and placed in high mountains on which the sun has not risen, nor can it. And since the days of the prophets and the apostles and the preachers, the name has not at all risen upon their hearts, nor can it. And their ear has not heard it. The great Seth composed this book in writing in one hundred and thirty years. He placed it in the mountain that is called Charaxio . . . (*Gos. Egy.* III 68.1–14)

The author of this Gospel is allegedly Seth, then, who laboured over its composition for 130 years and then hid it. This hiddenness means that there is a polemic here against the notion that there may have been scriptural witness to Jesus before him (in its reference to the "prophets"), or any other true testimony after him (in its statement about the "apostles and preachers"). Far from acknowledging Jesus's fulfilment of Scripture, this Gospel argues against it, because the OT prophets had the truth hidden from them, as did the apostles. Part of the claim in making Seth the author could be that the text would then be much older than the Old Testament, and correspondingly much more authoritative. In some ways, however, the polemic is perhaps more muted than we find in other Gnostic texts.

### 1.2 The Gospel of Judas

The *Gospel of Judas* is the most recently known of these Gospels, only made widely available to scholars and the general public in April 2006.[7] Like some other Gnostic works, the *Gospel of Judas* is also a protest Gospel. It is bitterly hostile to the mainstream church. In fact, it devotes almost as much space to its criticism of apostolic Christians as it does to telling us what its 'good news' is.

The most surprising element in it is that Judas is transformed *from* being a treacherous plotter *into* a trusted recipient of Jesus's special revelation. Judas alone knows the good news. What is that "good news"? It centres on two

---

[7] For the Coptic text and English translation, see Lance W. Jenott, *The Gospel of Judas: Coptic Text, Translation, and Historical Interpretation of "the Betrayer's Gospel"* (Tübingen: Mohr Siebeck, 2011). Cf. further Simon J. Gathercole, *The Gospel of Judas* (Oxford: University Press, 2007).

things: understanding who Jesus is, and understanding the world and the place of the true "Gnostic" in that world.

On the first point, Judas alone reveals who Jesus is:

> Judas [said] to him (to Jesus), "I know who you are and from where you have come. You have come from the immortal aeon of Barbelo and the one who sent you is the one whose name I am not worthy to speak." (*Gos. Jud.* 35.14–21)

Jesus's origins, then, lie in the "aeon of Barbelo," Barbelo being one of the highest figures in the heavenly realms. Moreover, Jesus does not really take on flesh but remains a discarnate spirit. Near the end of Judas's Gospel, Jesus says to him:

> "Truly, [I] say to you, Judas . . . you will be greater than them all. For you will sacrifice the man who carries me about." (*Gos. Jud.* 56.11–21)

The point, then, is that we have no embodied Jesus who will give his life as a ransom for many or lay down his life for his friends. Jesus does not save by coming into the world and dying. There is also no reference to "love."[8] No love of God, no love from Jesus, and no love for his disciples to practice. The *Gospel of Judas* is a rather bitter work, with a strong emphasis on criticizing the church. That the church and the world are doomed is an essential part of the good news of saving revelation according to this Gospel.

The *Gospel of Judas* is replete with scriptural characters and locations. The text begins with the action defined chronologically in relation to the Passover festival (*Gos. Jud.* 33.3–6). Biblical categories of "righteousness" and "transgression" are introduced in the extended prologue (*Gos. Jud.* 33.10–13). The theogony and cosmogony is introduced with the formula "Let there be . . ." (e.g., *Gos. Jud.* 47.16–17), with a corresponding "And there came into being . . ." (e.g., 47.21–22). The creations, or rather, emanations, include light, two luminaries, heavens, firmaments, and a cosmos. These heavenly aeons are populated by Adamas, Seth and his generation, Nimrod, "Christ," "Yobel" (Hebrew for "Jubilee"), "Adonaios," Michael, and Gabriel.[9] Adam and Eve are created as follows:

---

8  See Gathercole, *Gospel of Judas*, 163–68.

9  Adamas, Seth and his generation: *Gos. Jud.* 48.21–49.6; "Christ," "Yobel," and "Adonaios": 52.6–11; Michael and Gabriel: 53.20, 23. Nimrod appears in *Gos. Jud.* 51.12–13, 17 as one of Saklas's demonic associates: the spelling "Nebro" in the *Gospel of Judas* reflects the Greek spelling Νεβρωδ in the LXX of Gen 10.8–9; 1 Chr 1.10; Mic 5.6.

> Then Saklas said to his angels, "Let us make man according to the likeness and according to the image." And they created Adam and his wife Eve, who in the cloud is called Zoë. (*Gos. Jud.* 52.14–21)

There is clear reference to Genesis 1 here, as well as a subversion of it, given the nature of Saklas (on which more anon). Further allusions to the OT are seen in the fact that the earth is populated by "the twelve tribes of Israel" (*Gos. Jud.* 55.8–9) and in general by "Adam with his generation" (*Gos. Jud.* 53.11–12).[10]

There is even a notion of fulfilment:

> Jesus said, "Truly I say to you, when the stars over them all have completed their courses, and when Saklas has completed the times which have been appointed for him, their leading star will come with the generations, and the things which have been spoken of will be fulfilled.

> "Then they will commit adultery in my name and they will kill their children and . . . evil and [almost 3 lines missing] the aeons which bring their generations, presenting them to Saklas. And after that, [Is?]rael will come bringing the twelve tribes of Israel from . . . and all the generations which sinned in my name will serve Saklas. And your star will ru[le] over the thirteenth aeon." After this, Jesus laughed.

> Judas said, "Master, wh[y are you laughing?]"

> [Jesus] replied [and said], "I am not laughing [at yo]u (pl.), but at the error of the stars, because these six stars were deceived with these five warriors, and all these will perish with their creations." (*Gos. Jud.* 54.15–55.20)

In this passage, there is a sense, perhaps surprisingly given the picture of the cosmos elsewhere in the book, of the stars following an orderly pattern. Parallel to this, Saklas has a limited time of activity, after which his power will presumably be annulled. After the stars and Saklas have run their courses, "the things which have been spoken of will be fulfilled" (*Gos. Jud.* 54.23–24). This may be a reference to the speech of the generations which have just been mentioned, hence the Kasser-Meyer-Wurst translation: "they will finish what they said they would do."[11] Perhaps more likely is a reference to the fulfilment of some of Jesus's own speech. He has previously spoken of eschatological events which would fit into this context, such as the disciples' visions of the outbreak of sin interpreted by Jesus (*Gos. Jud.* 38.1–40.26). These match closely what

---

[10] Cf. *Gos. Jud.* 56.5–6: "the whole generation of the earthly Adam."
[11] Rodolphe Kasser, Marvin Meyer, and Gregor Wurst, eds., *The Gospel of Judas* (Washington: National Geographic, 2006), 42.

immediately follows the reference to fulfilment: "Then they will commit adultery in my name and they will kill their children and . . . evil and . . ." (*Gos. Jud.* 54.24–55.1). Or again, the teaching about the stars and the kingdom (*Gos. Jud.* 45.12–46.2), or Judas's destiny (46.18–47.1), are other possibilities.

There is no indication, however, of any reference to the fulfilment of Old Testament Scripture, and it would be very surprising if there were, given the picture of the creator god Saklas and his minions: Saklas is probably related to the Aramaic word *sakla*, meaning "stupid." He is an evil deity, a recipient of sacrifice from his sinful servants (*Gos. Jud.* 55.10–56.13). Certainly, there is no sense that the Old Testament, as we know it, is authoritative Scripture of any sort. Unlike the *Gospel of the Egyptians*, which does have its reference to the "prophets" as not having attained to the truth, the *Gospel of Judas* does not have anything like a programmatic or explicit statement about the Old Testament. It rejects the Old Testament by its silence (and its subversive rereading) rather than by any explicit or implicit polemic.

### 1.3 Gnostic Gospels: Conclusion

The silence in the *Gospel of Judas* and the claim of the *Gospel of the Egyptians* that the prophets had no access to the truth are only two strategies in Gnostic texts for dealing with the Old Testament. Other works are more outspoken. The *Apocryphon of John*, for example, is similar to the *Gospel of Judas* in identifying the OT God with the weak archon "Yaltabaoth-Saklas-Samael," but goes further and also more explicitly identifies Moses's words four times as mistaken:

> But he [sc. the Saviour] smiled and said, "Do not think it is, as Moses said, 'above the waters.' No, but when she had seen the wickedness which had happened, and the theft which her son had committed, she repented." (*Ap. John* II 13,18–23)

> And he [sc. the Saviour] said, "It is not the way Moses wrote (and) you heard. For he said in his first book, 'He put him to sleep' (Gen 2:21), but (it was) in his perception. For also he said through the prophet, 'I will make their hearts heavy, that they may not pay attention and may not see.'" (Isa 6:10) (*Ap. John* II 22,22–25)

> And he made another creature, in the form of a woman, according to the likeness of the Epinoia which had appeared to him. And he brought the part which he had taken from the power of the man into the female creature, and not as Moses said, his "rib." (Gen 2.22) (*Ap. John* II 23,3–4)

It is not as Moses said, "They hid themselves in an ark" (Gen 7:7), but they hid themselves in a place, not only Noah, but also many other people from the immovable race. They went into a place and hid themselves in a luminous cloud (*Ap. John* II 29,6–10).

The clear sense here is that the Pentateuch is wrong in its assertions. In *Ap. John* II 22,22–25, Genesis 2 is corrected from Isaiah, and the details of the creation and flood accounts need to be corrected from the Gnostic myth. Similarly, the *Second Treatise of the Great Seth* identifies the prophets as counterfeit, and fit only to be mocked (62,27–64,1).

## 2. THE OLD TESTAMENT IN THE VALENTINIAN GOSPELS OF *TRUTH* AND *PHILIP*

The *Gospel of Philip* and the *Gospel of Truth* both emerge from a movement spearheaded by a second-century leader called Valentinus (and whose disciples with their writings are usually called "Valentinian").[12] They are not in the proper sense of the word "Gnostic." Unlike the Gnostics, they do not take the line that the world is simply evil along with the "demiurge," its creator: in the *Gospel of Philip*, for example, the creator is misguided and his creation intrinsically subject to decay, but they are not thereby evil (*Gos. Phil.* 75.2–14). The Valentinian school had a relatively clearly defined theological outlook, rooted in three different modes of theological discourse. Some of these will be elucidated further as we proceed, but they can be summarized at the outset here. First, there is a protological mode, in which salvation is described as taking place to some degree in God's own self prior to the existence of the material creation, in mythological terms. Secondly, a historical mode describes—in terms strongly reminiscent of the New Testament and often employing New Testament language and ideas—the action of Jesus in history, with his disciples, in interaction with opponents, in his crucifixion, and so on. Thirdly, a ritual mode speaks of the recapitulation of the protological and historical events in the life of the community and the salvation of the individual. As we shall see, the *Gospel of Truth* focuses on the first two, with occasional allusion to the last, and the *Gospel of Philip* alludes briefly to the first, focusing on the second and third.

---

[12] For a biography of Valentinus and his theological outlook, see Christoph Markschies, *Valentinus Gnosticus? Untersuchungen zur valentinianischen Gnosis mit einem Kommentar zu den Fragmenten Valentins* (Tübingen: Mohr Siebeck, 1992).

## 2.1 The Gospel of Truth

The *Gospel of Truth*, as we would expect from its title, is about its version of "the good news."[13] The work is a powerful, vivid sermon which largely on the grounds of its literary quality has even been attributed to Valentinus himself, and this has led to debate over the question of whether the theological content of the *Gospel of Truth* corresponds sufficiently closely to the fragments of Valentinus's writings preserved in the church fathers. In any case, it comes from the middle of the second century, as we can tell from the fact that Irenaeus writing around the 180s refers to it as something written recently.[14] The *Gospel of Truth* begins with the words: "The gospel of truth is joy to those who have received from the Father of truth the gift of knowing him by the power of the Word" (*Gos. Tr.* 16.31–34).[15] The work focuses on two main Christological themes, Jesus's revelatory teaching and his suffering. The "Word appeared" and "became a body," and so:

> Jesus Christ enlightened those who were in darkness through oblivion. He enlightened them; he showed a way; and the way is the truth which he taught them. For this reason, error grew angry with him, persecuted him, was distressed at him, and was brought to nothing. He was nailed to a tree and became the fruit of the knowledge of the Father. That fruit did not, however, cause destruction because it was eaten, but to those who ate it, it gave cause for rejoicing at the discovery, and he discovered them in himself, and they discovered him in themselves. (*Gos. Tr.* 18.16–31)

Alongside this portrayal of Jesus's earthly ministry in the *Gospel of Truth* is a stronger focus on a mythological backdrop to the Gospel history.[16] In this myth, there is a primordial fall of "the All," which becomes separated from the Father and lapses into ignorance and deficiency. The Father reveals himself as and in the Son; this revelation is also expressed as the Word coming forth from the mind of the Father. The restoration of the All happens when the Son brings

---

[13] For text and translation, see Harold Attridge, ed., *Nag Hammadi Codex I: Introductions, Texts, Translations, Indices v. 1: The Jung Codex* (Leiden: Brill, 1985), 82–117.

[14] Irenaeus, *Against Heresies* 3.11.9.

[15] Conventionally, the *Gospel of Truth* and the other works described below are labeled by the page and line numbers in the ancient manuscripts where they appear. Hence this apparently odd "chapter and verse" for the beginning of a work.

[16] On the theology of the myth, see e.g., Anne McGuire, "Conversion and Gnosis in the 'Gospel of Truth,'" *NovT* 28 (1986), 338–55 (esp. 344–53); Barbara Aland, "Gnosis und Christentum," in Bentley Layton, ed., *The Rediscovery of Gnosticism: Proceedings of the International Conference on Gnosticism at Yale, New Haven, Connecticut, March 28–31, 1978*, vol. 1, *The School of Valentinus* (Leiden: Brill, 1980), 330–50 (including the fascinating discussion appended to the paper); Einar Thomassen, *The Spiritual Seed: The Church of the 'Valentinians'* (Leiden: Brill, 2006), 146–65.

revelation to supply knowledge to the ignorant All, and this is simultaneous with the filling up of the All's deficiency by Jesus: "Since deficiency came because the Father was not known, when the Father comes to be known, there will no longer be deficiency" (*Gos. Tr.* 24.28–32). When the All is brought back to the Father, it receives its necessary replenishment, which the Father had retained in himself all along.

This myth corresponds in some way to Jesus's earthly activity, especially in these central soteriological motifs of (1) the filling up of deficiency to bring plenitude, and (2) the revelation leading to knowledge in place of ignorance. His death accomplishes salvation 'because he is knowledge and fullness' (*Gos. Tr.* 20.38–39).

There is no hint of scriptural fulfilment here or elsewhere in the *Gospel of Truth*. This is not to say that this Gospel rejects other texts; it contains dozens of allusions to the New Testament. As far as the Old Testament is concerned, though, there is little or no interest in it. There are only a couple of allusions to Old Testament language, including in the passage quoted earlier some sort of implied contrast between the tree of the knowledge of good and evil in Genesis and the tree of the cross.[17] But there is certainly nothing like fulfilment. There are no negative statements of the kind we find in the *Gospel of the Egyptians*, but there is nothing positive about the Old Testament either. In a sense this is understandable in the *Gospel of Truth*, because there is no need of a prior revelation. The *Gospel of Truth* after all contains *within itself* the protological backdrop to the gospel events of Jesus's crucifixion and exaltation. This backdrop is not a historical backdrop like the Old Testament, but a kind of projection of the small film strip of history onto the larger screen of the primordial divine realm. We learn, for example, from other accounts of Valentinian theology that the events of the earthly realm have their heavenly counterparts in what goes on above. For example, in Valentinian exegesis, Jairus's daughter is an earthly type of "Achamoth"—one of the names of cosmic Sophia or "Wisdom;" Judas's defection is an earthly type of the heavenly reality of Sophia's fall, and Jesus's cry of dereliction points to Achamoth's sufferings.[18] Or again, in the fragments of Heracleon's commentary on John (the first commentary on a New Testament book was by a Valentinian!), Jerusalem is imaged in the psychic sphere, the realm of soul (fr. 13), whereas Capernaum represents specifically the lower part of the psychic realm of soul, near to the material realm (fr. 40).

This protological, heavenly myth is not "promise" or precursory testimony in some other way, but rather part of the Gospel itself, the "back story" to the activity of the incarnate Jesus in history. Nor is the myth only rhetorical

---

[17] The fruit of the cross "did not cause destruction," in contrast presumably to the tree of knowledge in Genesis, which did.

[18] Respectively, Epiphanius, *Pan.* 31.25.3, 31.35.4, and 31.25.6.

flourish or ornamental illustration. As is recognised by Thomassen and others, the protological discourse is not parabolic or *mere* myth, but real.[19] How exactly the reality of this myth was conceived remains elusive. Nevertheless, just as in Heb 8:5 the heavenly tabernacle is a *real* preexistent thing upon which Moses's earthly tabernacle is patterned, so the myth in the *Gospel of Truth* is a real primeval drama. Unlike the material tabernacle in Hebrews, however, the historical drama of Jesus in the *Gospel of Truth* is not an inferior copy of the mythic drama, but a recapitulation of it. Unlike the canonical Gospels, where the promissory scriptural testimony is *external* to the Gospel texts (in the Old Testament), in the *Gospel of Truth* the back story is internal to the work itself.

### 2.2 *The Gospel of Philip*

The *Gospel of Philip* focuses not on the protological myth but instead on Jesus's ministry and the ritual application of Jesus to Valentinian disciples. In the historical realm, Jesus has male and female disciples, including the three Marys: his mother, his sister, and Mary Magdalene (e.g., *Gos. Phil.* 58.5–10). He teaches, goes to different places (including into a dyeing works), and is crucified.[20] In the ritual realm, those who are baptised go through two baptisms, the traditional Christian water baptism as well as an anointing with oil which is designated as the baptism in light (e.g., *Gos. Phil.* 74.12–17). This is the saving event for the Christian. In a similar way to Paul's theology in Romans 6, baptism is seen as a recapitulation of the events in the historical realm. The ritual of baptism opens up to the disciple the higher realm, in which the soul is united with Jesus in the saving location of the bridal chamber (e.g., *Gos. Phil.* 67.2–9).

The *Gospel of Philip* has a good deal in common theologically with the *Gospel of Truth*. They share the idea, for example, that creation is the result of a mistake (*Gos. Phil.* 75.2–14). Because we inhabit this substandard creation, the truth of the divine realm is inaccessible to us. Hence the *Gospel of Philip* says that heavenly realities cannot be described as they really are; instead this Gospel presents to us metaphors and analogies. This is possible because truth has been dispersed into the world in fragments:

> Truth, which has existed from the beginning, is sown everywhere, and many see it being sown but few see it being reaped. (*Gos. Phil.* 55.19–22)

On the other hand, the truth is not easily accessible, because the names which things currently possess are treacherous:

---

[19] See the definitive study in Thomassen, *Spiritual Seed*.
[20] For the visit to the dyeing works, see *Gos. Phil.* 63.25–28, and for the crucifixion see 68.26–29.

Names given to worldly things are very deceptive, for they divert our thoughts from what is correct to what is incorrect. (*Gos. Phil.* 53.23–27)

This poses a potential problem for interpreting what *Philip* calls the "types and images" in this world (*Gos. Phil.* 84.14–21).[21] These types and images only have a distorted relationship to "the mysteries of the truth" in the supra-mundane realm, but they do have some relationship: "The mysteries of truth are manifest as types and images" (*Gos. Phil.* 84.14–21).

These types and images include institutions like human fatherhood, marriage, and sex, but some of them are also distinctively scriptural. Abraham's circumcision was "teaching us" the destruction of the flesh (*Gos. Phil.* 82.26–29). One of the most elaborated images is the temple, and its layout is seen as significant. According to the *Gospel of Philip*, there were three buildings for sacrifice in Jerusalem, each a "house": the "holy," the "holy of holy," and the "holy of holies" (*Gos. Phil.* 69.14–22). The curtain appears in two passages which echo the New Testament tradition of the tearing of the veil (*Gos. Phil.* 69.35–70.4; 84.23–29). The second of these passages also mentions the ark, suggesting a connection between the wings (of the cherubim) over the ark and the "wings of the cross." In two passages, animal sacrifice is mentioned, as characteristic of the time before the revelation of Christ; the sacrificial system is cast in negative terms as involving offerings to animal-deities and those who are not gods (*Gos. Phil.* 55.1–2; 63.1–4). In this respect, the temple and its "places of sacrifice" (*Gos. Phil.* 69.14–15) might be a good example of a fragment of truth sown in the world but distorted: it has elements which point to the ultimate reality of salvation, but it also functioned as a centre for idolatrous worship. There is antecedent revelation in it, as there is everywhere else, but its light has been seriously refracted by the influence of the demonic powers, or "archons."

Finally, there is a good deal of material in the *Gospel of Philip* about Adam and Eve in Paradise from the early chapters of Genesis.[22] There is a Paradise with two significant trees, one bearing foul fruit and the other fair—"one bears animals and the other bears humans" (*Gos. Phil.* 71.22–29). The negatively valued tree is the tree of knowledge, which brought death for Adam, and the saving tree is the tree of life in the middle of the garden: this is an olive tree whence comes the oil of chrism in the Valentinian rite (*Gos. Phil.* 73.15–19).

---

[21] For example, the "cup of prayer," which contains wine and water, is a "type" (*tupos*) of the blood (75.14–25), and image language (*eikôn*) is used to describe the physical, earthly person in contrast to their heavenly angelic counterpart (65.1–26).

[22] Other possible Old Testament allusions include, in Meyer's version, Sophia called a "pillar of salt," echoing Lot's wife, but this translation is based on a restoration (*Gos. Phil.* 59.33–34). There is also a fleeting reference to Sabbath but again in a lacunose passage (*Gos. Phil.* 52.34).

In all this discussion, however, there is little sense of what we think of as the Old Testament being treated as *Scripture*. Instead, just like the world in general, the OT according to the *Gospel of Philip* contains various distorted fragments of the truth, which can only be decoded by the virtuoso Valentinian *savants* who "have come to know what is correct" (*Gos. Phil.* 53.34–35).

## CONCLUSION

As we have seen here, there is a good deal of variety in how these non-canonical Gospels approach the Old Testament, both in their programmatic statements and in their usage of particular passages. Other non-canonical Gospels not treated here are more positive towards the Old Testament. The *Protevangelium of James* is immersed in the Old Testament world, with a feel akin to that of Luke 1–2. The *Gospel of Peter* has an ambiguity which means that it is neither like the canonical Gospels, nor particularly negative like the *Gospel of the Egyptians*.

The non-canonical Gospels of the Gnostics and Valentinians surveyed here, however, mark a key departure from the earliest apostolic proclamation in their neglect of, or hostility to, Israel's Scripture. One important lesson these non-canonical Gospels show us today is that if we set aside the Old Testament as the framework for understanding Jesus and the gospel, we are left to our own cultural presuppositions as the framework of understanding. This is a key characteristic of liberal theology, which gives us a Jesus cut off from the Old Testament and turned into someone palatable to our own culture's sensibilities. But this will hardly be the Jesus who reveals the true God to us, and the gospel message which results will hardly be a true one either.

In the gospel preached by the apostles, the Old Testament provides the whole framework for understanding Jesus's life, death, and resurrection. This is made clear by Paul's comment about the preaching of the apostles in 1 Corinthians 15 (vv. 3–4, and 11) where the Old Testament is the framework ("according to") for understanding both Jesus's death for our sins and his resurrection. And it is the New Testament Gospels, in contrast to those others discussed here, which have truly captured this earliest apostolic preaching. These canonical Gospels demand from us, just as they did in the first century, that we understand, confess, and proclaim the good news of Jesus Christ "according to the Scriptures."

As one modern-day successor to Paul has written:

> The Old Testament clearly leaves us with an unfinished story. The serpent was not crushed. The promise that Israel would dwell in the land was contradicted by the exile, and even when Israel repossessed the land, they were either under the thumb of foreign powers or barely hanging on to independence. The promises

of the new covenant, the new exodus, the new creation and the new David obviously were not realized. Yahweh ruled as the sovereign king over the entire earth, but his saving promises for Israel and the world remained unfulfilled. The New Testament witness claims that the promise of a kingdom, anticipated in the Old Testament, is fulfilled in Jesus Christ. The new creation, the new covenant, and the new exodus have arrived in Jesus Christ.[23]

The author of this statement, a certain Tom Schreiner, has done a great service to the church in his championing of the unity of Old and New Testaments as essential to our understanding of the gospel.[24] *Ad multos annos!*

---

[23] For the quotation, see Thomas R. Schreiner, *The King in his Beauty: A Biblical Theology of the Old and New Testaments* (Grand Rapids: Baker, 2013), 428.

[24] I am personally very grateful to Tom for his friendship over the years, which I think dates back to around 2002 or 2003 when we first met at SBL before my visit to Southern Seminary in 2004.

# APPLICATIONS

# Chapter 15

# Transgenderism and Three Biblical Axioms

*by Denny Burk*

Few men have made as deep an impact on me as Tom Schreiner—first as a doktorvater and then as a friend and colleague. Tom played a significant role in two of the major turning points in my life. The first was the decision to pursue a PhD at Southern Seminary. In 1998, I found myself perusing stacks of new titles in the bookstore at Dallas Theological Seminary where I spied a new commentary on Romans by Tom Schreiner. As I thumbed through the pages, it was immediately clear to me that this was a Reformed expositor who proclaimed the supremacy of God in all things. His was a Reformed vision of the faith that resonated deeply with me. But the part that really surprised and stunned me was his bio, which indicated that he served as a professor at The Southern Baptist Theological Seminary. This was stunning because I was in a non-denominational seminary and had begun to think that there may be no place for me in the denomination of my youth—the Southern Baptist Convention. I knew that was not true after seeing Tom's Romans commentary. I knew something special was happening at Southern and that I wanted to be a part of it. And that's what led me to Louisville.

Tom also had a direct influence over what would become my chief focus as a writer—the Bible's teaching about gender and sexuality. In 2007, I called Tom to ask his advice about an opportunity I had to become editor of *The Journal for Biblical Manhood and Womanhood*. I had only been a professor for three years and was still wet behind the ears professionally. I wanted to edit the journal but was concerned about how such a controversial position might marginalize me in the scholarly guild. I will never forget what Tom told me. "If you lose opportunities because you proclaim God's truth, then you should accept that as the reproaches of Christ." He was so matter-of-fact about it, but it changed my life. And it certainly provided focus to my work over the last eleven years. I have never looked back.

Eleven years ago in that conversation with Tom, neither one of us could have anticipated the twists and turns that would come to characterize the evangelical gender debate. To be sure, the old differences between complementarians and egalitarians are still with us. Tom has made his own enormous contribution to that conversation.[1] But in recent years, evangelicals have had to face even more fundamental questions than they ever have before. Almost immediately after gay marriage became legal in the United States in 2015, our culture seemed to turn immediately to the normalization of transgenderism.[2] Our questions now are not merely about male and female roles in the church and the home. Our questions now also include uncertainty about what a man and a woman even are. The sexual revolution has forced a crisis of belief for evangelicals concerning manhood and womanhood.

It is no secret that the church's deepest commitments are often clarified and expressed in the midst of such crises. Time and again throughout history, assaults on the faith have led to clarifications of the faith. Sometimes the challenges become so acute and so fundamental that faithfulness to Christ requires explicit declaration of biblical conviction in the face of error. In his own time, Dietrich Bonhoeffer believed the church in Germany was facing such a threat. Jill Carattini has described the situation this way:

> Dietrich Bonhoeffer declared a state of *status confessionis* for the church under Nazi Germany. Status confessionis, literally "a state of confessing," is a dire situation in which the church must stand up for the integrity of the gospel and the authority of the God it confesses. For Bonhoeffer and others, the Nazification of the church was an issue so threatening to the veracity of their confession of Christ that no dissimulation or concession was possible. Bonhoeffer recognized that the Nazi persecution of Jews demanded a serious response from the church. But more so, he recognized that the church was called "not only to bandage the victims under the wheel, but to jam a spoke into the wheel itself" and bring the

---

[1]  Andreas J. Köstenberger and Thomas R. Schreiner, eds., *Women in the Church: An Analysis and Application of 1 Timothy 2:9–15*, 3rd ed. (Wheaton, IL: Crossway, 2015); Thomas R. Schreiner, "Head Coverings, Prophecies, and the Trinity: 1 Corinthians 11:2–16," in *Recovering Biblical Manhood & Womanhood: A Response to Evangelical Feminism* (Wheaton, IL: Crossway, 1991), 124–39; Thomas R. Schreiner, "Women in Ministry: Another Complementarian Perspective," in *Two Views on Women in Ministry*, ed. James R. Beck, rev. ed., Counterpoints (Grand Rapids: Zondervan, 2005), 263–322; Thomas R. Schreiner, "Much Ado about Headship: Rethinking 1 Corinthians 11:3," in *Scripture and the People of God*, forthcoming, 200–215.

[2]  It was already clear in 2014 that transgenderism would be the next phase of the LGBT revolution. See for example, Katy Steinmetz, "The Transgender Tipping Point: America's Next Civil Rights Frontier," *Time*, June 9, 2014.

engine of injustice to a halt. Confessing Christ was a theology that could not be held without obligation.[3]

When we think of the situation that Bonhoeffer faced and the situation that we are facing in the wake of the sexual revolution, is our situation any less dire? To be sure, we are not facing anything like Nazi Germany in our moment. But that doesn't mean that we aren't facing a dire threat to the church's integrity and witness. The threat we face is not due merely to influences from outside the church. Even within the evangelical movement, we are not all on the same page when it comes to a biblical understanding of transgenderism.

Mark Yarhouse's 2015 book *Understanding Gender Dysphoria* has been regarded by many as the most comprehensive response to the transgender question by someone within the evangelical movement. *Christianity Today* had Yarhouse write a feature-length piece on transgenderism and gender dysphoria after Bruce Jenner made his transition in the summer of 2015.[4] The review of Yarhouse's book on The Gospel Coalition website says that this book "marks a step forward in Christian engagement with gender issues."[5] And yet, Yarhouse says that cross-dressing might in some cases be the best prescription for a gender-confused child.[6] Yarhouse also contends that sex-change surgery might in some cases be the best prescription for transgender adults.[7] I contend that if Christians are unable to discern that cross-dressing children and sex-change are out of step with the gospel, then we are indeed in a state of confession, a *status confessionis*.

*Transgender* is a catch-all term that refers to the many ways that people might perceive their gender identity to be out of sync with their biological sex. Until recently, *The Diagnostic and Statistical Manual of Mental Disorders* (DSM), had classified this experience as Gender Identity Disorder. But in 2013, the DSM-5 removed this experience from its list of disorders and replaced it with the term Gender Dysphoria.[8] They did this in part to remove the stigma from the transgender experience—so that transgender people wouldn't have to say

---

[3] Jill Carattini, "Status Confessionis," *RZIM* (blog), June 24, 2016, https://rzim.org/a-slice-of-infinity/status-confessionis-2/.

[4] Mark Yarhouse, "Understanding Gender Dysphoria: The Leading Christian Scholar on Transgender Issues Defines the Terms and Gives the Church a Way Forward," *Christianity Today* 59, no. 6 (July 2015): 44–50.

[5] Sam Ferguson, "Understanding Gender Dysphoria: Navigating Transgender Issues in a Changing Culture," TGC - The Gospel Coalition, July 15, 2015, https://www.thegospelcoalition.org/article/book-reviews-understanding-gender-dysphoria-transgender-mark-yarnhouse.

[6] Mark A. Yarhouse, Understanding Gender Dysphoria: Navigating Transgender Issues in a Changing Culture (Downers Grove, IL: InterVarsity Press, 2015), 107.

[7] Yarhouse, 123–24.

[8] American Psychiatric Association, *Diagnostic and Statistical Manual of Mental Disorders: DSM-5* (Washington, DC: American Psychiatric Association, 2013), 451–59.

they had a psychological disorder. Instead, the DSM-5 focuses on those who experience "Dysphoria" (or mental distress) as a result of their perceived gender identity being out of sync with the gender they were assigned at birth.

This clinical approach to the transgender experience relies on an understanding of the human condition that is foreign to both natural law and Christian Scripture. Others have ably shown how natural law teaches us to see complementary differences between male and female.[9] I agree with such perspectives, but my aim in this essay is to outline how God's special revelation also shows us a distinction between male and female. The Bible teaches what every faithful Christian must believe about this distinction. We can summarize this teaching under three headings: (1) the distinction between male and female is *biological*, (2) the distinction between male and female is *social*, and (3) the distinction between male and female is *good*.

## THE DISTINCTION BETWEEN MALE AND FEMALE IS BIOLOGICAL

Genesis 1:26–28 provides the Bible's foundation for understanding male-female difference. These verses not only assert the fact of difference, but also the nature of the difference.

> [26] Then God said, "Let Us make man in Our image, according to Our likeness; and let them rule over the fish of the sea and over the birds of the sky and over the cattle and over all the earth, and over every creeping thing that creeps on the earth." [27] And God created man in His own image, in the image of God He created him; male and female He created them. [28] And God blessed them; and God said to them, "Be fruitful and multiply, and fill the earth, and subdue it; and rule over the fish of the sea and over the birds of the sky, and over every living thing that moves on the earth." (NAS 77)

Verse 26 accents what the man and the woman have in common. They are *both* classified as אָדָם. They are *both* created in God's image, and they are *both* given the responsibility to rule over God's good creation. They are to be, as it were, God's vice-regents ruling on his behalf over the world that God has made. In verse 27, however, the accent is on difference, "male and female He created them." Here we discover that these divine image-bearers come in two distinct genres—male and female. If these words mean anything, they mean that there is a distinction between male and female. As Alastair Roberts observes,

---

[9] E.g., J. Budziszewski, *On the Meaning of Sex* (Wilmington, DE: ISI, 2012).

The difference between the sexes is a central and constitutive truth about humanity, related to our being created in the image of God. Humanity has two distinct kinds: a male kind and a female kind. Sexual dimorphism, the fact that we come in these two distinct kinds, is a fundamental fact about humanity.[10]

The fact of male-female difference is clear in this text, but what is the nature of their difference? Is it a biological thing, a self-concept, or something else altogether? This is where the biblical revelation offers an answer that contradicts the one coming from transgender advocates.

A few years ago, I received a heart-breaking letter from two transgender advocates—a married couple who were parents of a transgender child, a son who had grown up with gender-conflicted feelings.[11] As an adult their son married a woman and had children. After being married for a number of years, he decided to end his marriage and to "transition" his appearance to that of a female. Eventually, he even underwent so-called "sex-change" surgery.[12] The parents informed me that they support the transition and the surgery because they believe their son's transgender identity is the result of his brain-sex being mismatched with his biological sex. They believe his mind has always been female, even though his body has always been male. Because the brain is the "most important human sex organ," they believe that he was simply born with the "wrong genitals." Furthermore, they claim that Scripture is silent about the biological factors that distinguish male from female and that there is no scriptural authority for prioritizing genital anatomy over brain structure and function. For this reason, they feel that their child's body needed to be transformed through surgery so that it would match his mind. That is why they support their child's gender-reassignment surgery, even though it cost him his marriage and family.

These parents have adopted what psychologists call a "Brain-Sex Theory."[13] Brain-sex theory says that our brains "script" us toward male or female behaviors

---

[10] Alastair Roberts, "The Music and Meaning of Male & Female," *Primer*, no. 3 (2016): 36.

[11] I previously shared this anecdote in Denny Burk, "The Transgender Test," in *Beauty, Order, and Mystery: A Christian Vision of Human Sexuality*, ed. Gerald Hiestand and Todd Wilson (Downers Grove, IL: InterVarsity Press, 2017), 87–89.

[12] "So-called" because it is a physical impossibility to change one's sex. See Roberts, "Music and Meaning," 40: "Sexual reassignment surgery may create the appearance of the other sex's physicality, but lacks any connection to the procreative *telos* (goal) or capacity of the sexed body. It cannot be more than a hollow simulation of the reality. For this reason alone, changing one's sex can only ever be a fiction."

[13] Brain-sex theory is not monolithic but is an umbrella term for a variety of theories that share in common a focus on the brain differences between male and female. See Yarhouse, "Understanding Gender Dysphoria," 67–74. Brain-sex theory has not garnered a consensus in the scientific community. Lawrence Mayer and Paul McHugh conclude, "Studies comparing the brain structures of transgender and non-transgender individuals have demonstrated weak correlation between brain structure and cross-gender identification. These correlations do not provide an evidence for a neurobiological basis for cross-gender identification." See Lawrence

and dispositions.[14] Normally these scripts correspond with biological sex, but sometimes they don't. When that is the case, proponents of "brain-sex theory" believe that what a person *thinks* about him- or herself should trump what God has *revealed* through biological sex. And that is why the aforementioned parents wrote to me saying, "You have chosen, *without any scriptural authority that I can find*, to prioritize genital anatomy over brain structure and function in determining sex and gender" (emphasis mine).

This unsubstantiated claim occurs with great frequency in popular culture, and this perspective has exerted influence on many Christians as well. Christians are being told that *brain structures* determine a person's "sex and gender," not their reproductive anatomy. While we do not deny evidence showing neurological differences between male and female,[15] neither do we accept that such differences are the foundation of male-female difference. A careful reading of Genesis 1 will not allow such a conclusion. Genesis 1:28 says: "And God blessed them; and God said to them, "Be fruitful and multiply, and fill the earth, and subdue it..." (NAS 77). It is obvious that this creation mandate requires procreation within the covenant of marriage.

The procreative purpose of Adam's and Eve's union has implications for our understanding of brain-sex theory. Does God use the terms *male* and *female* to refer to "brain structures"? Or do *male* and *female* refer to differences in the reproductive systems of the man and the woman? The answer to this is clear. Human beings do not procreate with their brains but with their reproductive structures. Male and female, therefore, have a primary reference to the latter rather than the former. As Ryan Anderson explains, "The fundamental conceptual distinction between a male and a female is the organism's organization for sexual reproduction."[16] That is what is reflected in nature, and it is certainly what is reflected in Moses's creation account in Gen 1:26–28.

That means that if a body says *male* but the brain is saying *female*, the brain is wrong. In a fallen world where the noetic effects of sin still prevail, what we think about ourselves is often mistaken. And that is certainly the case with transgender experience. The distinction between male and female is first of all *biological*, and the biological distinction in view has to do with a body's organization for reproduction—quite apart from any consideration of brain structures.

---

S. Mayer and Paul R. McHugh, "Sexuality and Gender: Findings from the Biological, Psychological, and Social Sciences," *The New Atlantis* 50 (Fall 2016): 8.

[14] Yarhouse, *Gender Dysphoria*, 67.

[15] Budziszewski, *Meaning of Sex*, 38–40.

[16] Ryan T. Anderson, *When Harry Became Sally: Responding to the Transgender Moment* (New York: Encounter Books, 2018), 79. See also J. Budziszewski's discussion of "polaric complementarity" in Budziszewski, *Meaning of Sex*, 41ff.

If this is true, then there are massive implications for how Christians ought to minister the gospel to people dealing with gender-confused feelings. It means that Christians must tell them on the authority of God's word that their body isn't lying to them.[17] A person's maleness or femaleness isn't socially constructed or self-constructed, but God-constructed. Sex is not something that is *assigned* at birth. It is something that is revealed by God in his special distinct design of male and female bodies.

The world is telling gender-confused people that if they perceive themselves to have a gender identity at odds with their bodily identity, then the mind takes precedence over the body. The world is telling them to take steps to conform the body to the gender-confused mind rather than to conform the gender-confused mind to what is clearly revealed by the body. If that means dressing the body in clothing associated with the opposite sex, then so be it. If that means reshaping the body through amputation of healthy sexual organs, then so be it. The fallen mind trumps the Creator's design of the body. On this view, what God has revealed about maleness and femaleness through the body can and must be set aside. But this lie is precisely what Christians must prepare people to resist by pointing them to Scripture and to nature, both of which teach that the distinction between male and female is *biological* according to the body's organization for reproduction.

## THE DISTINCTION BETWEEN MALE AND FEMALE IS SOCIAL

While the basic biological differences between male and female may be clear, such is often not the case with social roles that stem from biological differences. At the very least, such differences are fiercely contested. And yet, scriptural revelation clearly teaches a social distinction between male and female. The foundational text on this point is Gen 2:18–25:

> Then the LORD God said, "It is not good that the man should be alone; I will make him a helper fit for him." . . . So the LORD God caused a deep sleep to fall upon the man, and while he slept took one of his ribs and closed up its place

---

[17] What about people who have an intersex condition? Are their bodies lying to them? I have a chapter dealing with intersex in my book *What Is the Meaning of Sex?* in which I argue that for many intersex persons there still remains an underlying chromosomal binary based on the presence or absence of at least one Y chromosome. Intersex conditions result from living in a fallen world east of Eden. In other words, the fall has obscured in some people what would otherwise be clear about biological sex. This doesn't disprove a sexual binary. It shows that the fall is pervasive in the human condition, even sometimes obscuring the binary norm. Nevertheless, the sexual binary norm remains and will be renewed in the new creation. See Denny Burk, *What Is the Meaning of Sex?* (Wheaton, IL: Crossway, 2013) For a view on intersex contrary to my own, see Megan K. DeFranza, *Sex Difference in Christian Theology: Male, Female, and Intersex in the Image of God* (Grand Rapids: Eerdmans, 2015).

with flesh. And the rib that the LORD God had taken from the man he made into a woman and brought her to the man. Then the man said, "This at last is bone of my bones and flesh of my flesh; she shall be called Woman, because she was taken out of Man." Therefore a man shall leave his father and his mother and hold fast to his wife, and they shall become one flesh. And the man and his wife were both naked and were not ashamed. (ESV)

In verse 18, the word "helper" corresponding to Adam designates a *social role* for Eve within her marriage to Adam—a role that is inextricably linked to her biological sex. Adam's creation before Eve designates a *social role* within his marriage to Eve—a role that is inextricably linked to his biological sex. He is to be the leader, protector, and provider within this marriage covenant. And these social roles within the covenant of marriage are not only creational realities, they are also commanded in Scripture.

Tom Schreiner has written at length arguing that Genesis 2 establishes headship and helper-ship as roles that are a part of God's good creation design. God's appointment of Adam as leader and Eve as follower comes out in at least five ways in Genesis 2.[18] First, God creates Adam before he creates the woman.[19] This order of creation establishes a primogeniture relation that would have been apparent to first-century readers of the Old Testament (e.g., 1 Tim 2:13; 1 Corinthians 8–9).[20] Second, God holds Adam accountable first for breaking God's word, even though Eve was the one who sinned after being deceived by the serpent. Third, God designates the woman to be a "helper"[21] to Adam. In Gen 2:18, Adam and Eve's roles cannot be exchanged. Eve's helping is oriented toward Adam's leadership.[22] Fourth, Adam names Eve (cf. Gen 2:19–20). When Adam "called" her name to be "Woman" (Gen 2:23; and later

---

[18] The arguments enumerated below are an adaptation from Schreiner, "Women in 289–97. These six arguments could be expanded. E.g., Wayne Grudem identifies ten arguments showing male headship before the fall. See Wayne Grudem, *Evangelical Feminism and Biblical Truth: An Analysis of More Than 100 Disputed Questions* (Sisters, OR: Multnomah, 2004), 30–42.

[19] So Schreiner, "Women in Ministry," 291. Contra Richard S. Hess, "Equality with and without Innocence: Genesis 1–3," in *Discovering Biblical Equality: Complementarity without Hierarchy*, ed. Ronald W. Pierce, Rebecca Merrill Groothuis, and Gordon D. Fee (Downers Grove, IL: InterVarsity Press, 2004), 84.

[20] Thomas R. Schreiner, "An Interpretation of 1 Timothy 2:9–15: A Dialogue with Scholarship," in *Women in the Church: An Analysis and Application of 1 Timothy 2:9–15*, ed. Andreas J. Köstenberger and Schreiner, 2nd ed. (Grand Rapids: Baker, 2005), 106. "The notion of the firstborn having authority would be easily understood by Paul's readers" (Schreiner, 107). Contra William J. Webb, *Slaves, Women & Homosexuals: Exploring the Hermeneutics of Cultural Analysis* (Downers Grove, IL: InterVarsity Press, 2001), 257–62.

[21] HALOT, "1", נֶגֶד: "that which corresponds." So Gordan J. Wenham, *Genesis 1–15*, Word Biblical Commentary, vol. 1 (Nashville: Thomas Nelson, 1987), 68: "It seems to express the notion of complementarity rather than identity."

[22] Kenneth Matthews, *Genesis 1–11:26*, New American Commentary, vol. 1A (Nashville: Broadman & Holman, 1996), 221.

"Eve," 3:20), he was exerting a leadership role that God gave to him alone.[23] Fifth, the serpent's attack represented a subversion of God's pattern of leadership. The apostle Paul confirms that it was indeed the undoing of the order of creation that was the basis for the fall of humanity into sin (1 Tim 2:13–14).[24] In all of these ways, the text of Genesis 2 establishes the distinct, complementary social roles of male and female in marriage. The text sets this first man and woman forth as the paradigm for all marriages that follow.

Some readers will object to this construal of social roles by observing that Adam's headship and Eve's helper-ship are covenantal obligations that apply to marriage, not creational distinctions that apply to every male and every female regardless of marital status. That objection is partially correct and partially incorrect. Yes, *headship* and *helper-ship* are covenantal obligations that apply primarily to marriage. No, it is not correct to deny creational distinctions that make male and female fitted for such covenantal roles. As Bobby Jamieson has argued,

> The Bible's prescriptive teaching flows from a descriptive vision of the divinely created differences between men and women. The less attention we pay to the descriptive, the more arbitrary and constraining the prescriptive will appear. When Scripture instructs husbands to lead their families and wives to submit to their husbands, or limits pastoral leadership of the church to men, it formalizes, codifies, and extends what is already written into our nature.[25]

There are creational differences of temperament and disposition that reflect the reproductive distinctions between male and female and that make male and female fitted for the covenantal obligations of marriage. In other words, the biological differences between male and female have social consequences. And those differences must be celebrated, not denigrated or ignored or dismissed as a social construct.

Genesis 2:18–25 reveals that there is both *sexual* complementarity and *gender* complementarity embedded in God's good creation. To understand the difference between these two, we must understand the conventional distinction between sex and gender. Sex refers to one's biological organization for

---

[23] So David J. A. Clines, "What Does Eve Do to Help? and Other Irredeemably Androcentric Orientations in Genesis 1–3," chap. 1 in *What Does Eve Do to Help? and Other Readerly Questions to the Old Testament*, JSOTSup 94 (Sheffield: JSOT Press, 1990), 37–40. Clines writes, "The name of the woman by the man, on both occasions, I conclude, signifies his authority over her" (Clines, 39).

[24] Douglas Moo, "What Does It Mean Not to Teach or Have Authority Over Men?," in *Recovering Biblical Manhood & Womanhood: A Response to Evangelical Feminism*, ed. John Piper and Wayne Grudem (Wheaton, IL: Crossway, 1991), 190.

[25] Bobby Jamieson, "Book Review: *On the Meaning of Sex*, by J. Budziszewski," 9Marks, July 30, 2018, https://www.9marks.org/review/book-review-on-the-meaning-of-sex-by-j-budziszewksi/#_ftnref1.

reproduction. Gender refers to the social manifestation of one's biological sex.[26] Sex is a physical, bodily reality. Gender is a socio-cultural reality. The spirit of the age says that the relationship between gender and sex is purely conventional and in no way essential. It claims that gender is a social construct—that is, a set of customs and behaviors that one learns but which has no essential, intrinsic relation to biological sex. And that is why, they argue, that it is possible for someone's gender identity to mismatch their bodily identity.

The spirit of the age, therefore, involves a direct conflict with Scripture on this point. In a variety of ways, Scripture reveals that God has so made the world that there is a normative, holy connection between biological sex and gender. Notice that the social roles of the first man and woman in Genesis 2 are inextricably connected to their biological sex, and later scriptural revelation reaffirms that connection. Later scriptural revelation cites these roles not merely as descriptive of the first marriage but as normative for every subsequent marriage (1 Cor 11:3; Eph 5:21–33). Moreover, the social order of the first family forms the foundation for leadership norms within the Christian church (1 Cor 11:3–16; 1 Tim 2:12–13). All of this presumes a normative connection between biological sex and social roles designed for that sex.[27] It also presumes that a man understands himself to be a man and that a woman understands herself to be a woman.

When someone adopts a gender identity at odds with their bodily identity, they are tearing asunder something that God has joined together—that a male body should coincide with a male self-concept and that a female body should coincide with a female self-concept. That is how God designed the first man and the first woman, and that is how he designed all of us. And even though in a fallen world, some people feel that connection to be broken, we know that God aims to restore that connection in the new creation.

The binary reality of gender and sex is what existed before the fall in Adam and Eve, and it will be a part of the restoration of creation in the age to come. In his 1990 book *Everything You Ever Wanted to Know about Heaven*, Peter Kreeft asks the question "Is there sex in Heaven?" He answered the question with a yes. Why? Because the new creation defines what we will be, not the fallenness that we observe now. The new creation restores what was normative in Eden before any sin entered into the world. On the assumption that our persons are a psychosomatic unity, Kreeft writes, "If sexuality is part of our inner essence, then it follows that there is sexuality in Heaven, whether or not we 'have sex' and whether or not we have sexually distinct social roles in Heaven."[28]

---

[26] Anderson, *When Harry Became Sally*, 2.

[27] I have developed the foregoing more fully in *What Is the Meaning of Sex?*, 162–67.

[28] Peter Kreeft, *Everything You Ever Wanted to Know about Heaven—But Never Dreamed of Asking* (San Francisco: Ignatius, 1990), 120.

Quoting Thomas Aquinas, Kreeft writes, "If sexual differences are natural, they are preserved in Heaven, for 'grace does not destroy nature but perfects it.'"[29]

There will be no transgender identities in the new creation. Men will know themselves as men, and women will know themselves as women. Even though there is no marriage in the age to come (Mark 12:25; Luke 20:35), there will be male and female bodies in the resurrection, and our self-understanding will reflect that distinction.

## THE DISTINCTION BETWEEN MALE AND FEMALE IS GOOD

Perhaps this final point is the one that is most contested today. Certain voices even within the evangelical tradition question the male-female binary and its necessity for human good and flourishing. In her book *Sex Difference in Christian Theology*, Megan DeFranza argues that the existence of intersex persons calls into question the male-female binary of Genesis 1–2. She suggests that Adam and Eve are "progenitors" of human difference but not *paradigms* of such difference.[30] Adam and Eve may manifest a sexual binary, but those two sexes must not be construed as the only two options. Indeed, she argues that in the new creation there will be male, female, and others who are "more than females or males."[31] Her approach calls into question not only the existence of the male-female binary. It also calls into question whether the binary is good.

Is this perspective consistent with Scripture? I argue that it is not. The apostle Paul writes: "For everything created by God is good, and nothing is to be rejected, if it is received with gratitude; for it is sanctified by means of the word of God and prayer" (1 Tim 4:1–5). Where does Paul get the idea that everything created by God is good? When Paul says that God's creation is good, he is simply taking his cues from the creation narratives in Genesis where it says that throughout the six days of creation, God looked at what he had made and said that it was "good" (Gen 1:4, 10, 12, 18, 21, 25). When God made the first male and female bodies, he said it is "very good" (Gen 1:31). In 1 Tim 4:4, therefore, Paul affirms that what was true about male and female design before the fall is still true after the fall. This means that even though God's good design in creation may be *marred* by the fall and by sin, God's good design is not *erased* by the fall and by sin. Adam and Eve are indeed paradigms of difference even after the fall, and those complementary differences have been pronounced "good" by God.

---

[29] Kreeft, 121.
[30] DeFranza, *Sex Difference in Christian Theology*, 238.
[31] DeFranza, 184.

If this is true, then our appraisal of male and female distinction in this fallen world must be the same as God's appraisal of male and female distinction. If God says it is good, we must not say that it is otherwise.

As mentioned above, "Brain-Sex Theory" says that our brains "script" us toward male or female behaviors and dispositions.[32] It also allows that sometimes our brain's gender doesn't match up with that of our biological sex. When that is the case, many clinicians think that what a person *thinks* about him- or herself should trump what God has *revealed* through biological sex. In other words, what a person perceives about their gender identity trumps what God's word reveals about the normative connection that God establishes between biological sex and gender identity—a connection rooted in God's good creation. The severing of this connection is what makes transgender identities plausible to some. It's also what makes people think they should resolve their gender identity conflict in a way that reshapes their body to conform to their thinking rather than reshaping their thinking to conform to their body. But we have to ask the obvious question: Is this the right way to think about things?

I am concerned that many people have failed to think through the implications of believing that one's psychological identity should trump one's biological identity when the two seem to be out of sync. In 2009, Fox News conducted an anonymous interview with a person named "John" who had been consumed with feelings of dissatisfaction with his body for as long as he could remember.[33] Ever since he was a child, John says that he felt like a one-legged man trapped inside a two-legged man's body. He suffered psychological angst his entire life because of his two legs. Even as an adult after forty-seven years of marriage, he still hoped to have one of his legs amputated. He says, "When I see an amputee—when I imagine the amputee—there is this inner pull that says 'Why can't I be like that?'" He never wanted to reveal his desire to amputate his leg to anyone and only shared his secret with his wife after being married for forty-two years. John says, "As you can understand, my wife was not exactly pleased with finding out that I wanted to get a leg lopped off. . . . She asked me and said, 'You know, you're a rational man, you should be able to deal with this.' . . . And what I answered is that most of the things we hold deep within us—are not rational."

John has a perception about himself that is at odds with the biological reality that he has two healthy legs. The primary ethical question is whether a man in John's position would be right to amputate an otherwise healthy limb. Would it be right for a doctor to remove his leg so that John can feel whole?

---

[32] Yarhouse, *Gender Dysphoria*, 67.

[33] Jessica Mulvihill and Karlie Pouliot, "Determined to Amputate: One Man's Struggle with Body Integrity Identity Disorder," Fox News, May 20, 2009, http://www.foxnews.com/story/2009/05/20/determined-to-amputate-one-man-struggle-with-body-integrity-identity-disorder.

If John *feels* himself to be a one-legged man inside a two-legged man's body, why not encourage him to have his leg amputated? At a gut level, most people recoil at the suggestion. Nevertheless, this is the implication of the view that psychological identity trumps bodily identity.

Psychiatrists have classified John's condition as "Body Integrity Identity Disorder." According to a 2012 study, the only known treatment that provides psychological relief is amputation.[34] Nevertheless, doctors have by and large resisted this "treatment" as a violation of the Hippocratic Oath. For this reason, people suffering from this disorder typically cannot find doctors willing to do the surgery unless they injure themselves first and force the issue. I have seen the testimonies of two men who did just that. One froze his own leg in dry ice until it was irreparably damaged, and another shot himself in the leg with a shotgun.[35] They now have the amputations that they long desired.

Most people read the story above about John and conclude that his mind is at odds with reality and that it is immoral and wrong to destroy healthy body parts to accommodate John's misperception about himself.[36] We should not deny that John had a real desire to amputate his leg or that he was experiencing real distress. We should, however, recognize that the best way to remedy that distress is not by destroying his leg but by restoring his mind. We want to resolve his distress in a way that doesn't harm his body through destructive "medical" interventions.

If we accept the goodness of the body's design when it comes to legs and other organs, why would we treat the design of sexual organs any differently? And yet, that is exactly what the medical professionals are doing when it comes to treating people with gender dysphoria. The prevailing view in "the mental health field is to address gender dysphoria through cross-gender identification and expression," which may lead to hormone treatments and gender reassignment surgery.[37] In other words, the prevailing view in the mental health field is that psychological identity—one's own self-perception—should trump one's bodily identity. Yet that position is directly at odds with what Scripture teaches. It disputes with God about what is "good." It disputes with God about what he intends for us as male and female created in his image.

And that is why a Christian response must always seek to encourage people experiencing these conflicts to resolve those conflicts in keeping with their biological sex. But this is precisely the point that has come into dispute. In his

---

[34] Rianne M. Blom, Raoul C. Hennekam, and Damiaan Denys, "Body Integrity Identity Disorder," *PLoS ONE* 7, no. 4 (April 2012), https://doi.org/10.1371/journal.pone.0034702.

[35] Carl Elliott, "Costing an Arm and a Leg," *Slate*, July 10, 2003, http://www.slate.com/articles/health_and_science/medical_examiner/2003/07/costing_an_arm_and_a_leg.html. See also the excerpt from the film *Whole* at "Whole Excerpt," YouTube video, 0:59, posted June 29, 2009, https://youtu.be/r46Y2DbYRts.

[36] Much of the following is adapted from Burk, "Transgender Test," 96–98.

[37] Yarhouse, *Gender Dysphoria*, 156.

book, Mark Yarhouse says that while he prefers the "least invasive" approaches to managing gender identity conflicts, he does not rule out other approaches:

> Hormonal treatment and sex reassignment would be the most invasive. This is not to say a Christian would not consider the most invasive procedures; I know many who have. But they would not begin there, nor would they take such a decision lightly.[38]

> I see the value in encouraging individuals who experience gender dysphoria to resolve dysphoria in keeping with their birth sex. Where those strategies have been unsuccessful, *there is potential value in managing dysphoria through the least invasive expression* (recognizing surgery as the most invasive step toward expression of one's internal sense of identity).[39]

Notice that Yarhouse does not rule out gender reassignment surgery, but he leaves that possibility on the table even for Christians. He positively affirms "least invasive" measures which include cross-dressing and assuming the gender role of the opposite sex. And by the way, these least invasive methods are also recommended for children with gender identity problems. But this is precisely where a Christian pastor or counselor cannot go. To even present these as possibilities is to tell people that God's creation is not "good" for them. And Christian pastors and counselors are not loving them well or serving them well if we lead them away from what God says is "good" for them. As Vaughn Roberts has written:

> Accepting our bodies as gifts from God certainly doesn't mean that it's wrong to try and correct what's wrong with them and seek to bring healing. But as we do so, we should follow the 'art restoration principle'. The aim is to restore the Creator's intention; but we are not to try to change it.[40]

Should a person ever be encouraged to amputate otherwise healthy limbs? Is the trouble here with limbs or with the mind? As Robertson McQuilkin and Paul Copan have asked, "Does the body need adjusting, or does the thinking?"[41] I daresay most people would answer that in this case the mind needs to be changed, not the body.

That is precisely why we need to be critical about the claims of the transgender movement. Yes, we need to be compassionate towards those who experience deep conflict between their psychological identity and their body. The

---

[38] Yarhouse, 124.
[39] Yarhouse, 137 (emphasis mine).
[40] Vaughan Roberts, *Transgender*, Talking Points (UK: The Good Book Company, 2016), 40.
[41] Robertson McQuilkin, *An Introduction to Biblical Ethics*, 2nd ed. (Wheaton, IL: Tyndale House, 1995), 271.

church would do well to come alongside them to support them and love them. But that kind of care will involve persuading them to change their minds before surgically and permanently altering their bodies. If we wish to affirm what is good for them, we have to affirm what God's Word says is good for them.

## CONCLUSION

Complementarians have long been making the case that while God has created man and woman equally in his image, he has also designed them with distinct, complementary differences. They have physical differences related to the body's organization for reproduction. They also experience social differences related to the body's organization for reproduction. God declares all of those differences to be good. At the end of the day, what God declares to be good is what *is* indeed good, even if fallen minds don't perceive it to be so. That means that male-female difference can only be ignored to our own hurt. It also means that the claims of transgender proponents are on a collision course not only with human flourishing but also with God's blessing.

As we face questions about transgenderism, we are not talking about how many angels can dance on the head of a pin. We are not spinning our wheels about *adiaphora* or some issue of moral indifference. We are declaring what it means to be a male or female image-bearer. To get these questions wrong is to walk away from Jesus, not to him. There is no more central concern than that.

*Chapter 16*

# The Great Commission Story

*by Brian Vickers*

## INTRODUCTION: GRATITUDE AND THANKS

I came to Southern Seminary originally for one reason: to study with Tom Schreiner. When I heard that Tom was heading to SBTS, my wife and I dropped all our plans and headed for Louisville, KY. The first thing I did on the first day of the semester was find Tom's office. I knocked, he opened the door, and before he could say anything I said, "I'm Brian Vickers; I came here for the sole reason of doing a PhD under you. I have to finish an MDiv first, but I hope that's going to work out." It did. That was twenty years ago. Not only was Tom my supervisor, we served as elders together for several years, and I count him as one of my closest friends. My thanks and gratitude to Tom are boundless. If I listed all the things I admire about Tom it would take up this entire chapter, so I'll comment on three.

Soon after I met Tom, he left on an overseas, short-term trip to teach students and pastors. Here was a well-known biblical, particularly Pauline, scholar who had already published several books and multiple articles, was firmly established in evangelical scholarship, going to another country to help Christians who do not have the privileges that many of us take for granted every day. I soon learned that such trips were common for Tom. In time, thanks to his influence, I too began travelling overseas to teach, do discipleship among believers, and share the gospel in cross-cultural settings.

In addition to Tom's personal example there is, of course, the vast influence of his godly scholarship. His ability to work at the highest scholarly level yet write, teach, and apply that scholarship to Christians at all levels and from all backgrounds (including me!) is, I believe, unparalleled. Through Tom, I developed not only exegetical skills, but a vision of how the entire Bible witnesses to God's glorious salvation in Christ. Put the two things together and you have an exemplary Pauline model—a biblical theologian who views missions (both home and abroad) as part and parcel of the message of the Bible and the responsibility of all those who name Christ Jesus as their Savior and Lord.

The third, and perhaps most important, way Tom has and continues to influence me is through his relentless adherence and submission to the authority of Scripture. "What does the *text say?*" I cannot count the number of times I've heard Tom ask that question (mostly directed to me). Our exegesis, interpretation, and biblical theology must always stand under the scrutiny of the Bible. The text of Scripture alone has authority, and our interpretations must ever bow to it. We must not allow our biblical-theological conclusions to become our reference point for either exegesis or theology, and it is on that note that I offer the following before exploring the "story" of missions in the Bible.

## BIG PICTURES AND STORIES: A WARNING

What follows in this chapter is essentially a simple framework of a major story line in the Bible, or rather the building blocks upon which readers may construct a more substantial framework for placing the Great Commission in the context of the larger story of Scripture. Before going further, however, a word of warning about taking such an approach to the Bible is in order, I would even say long overdue. With all the emphasis these days, for better and worse, on the "big picture" of Scripture, it is hardly groundbreaking to speak of the Bible as story. Putting emphasis on how the Bible hangs together coherently through the Old and New Testaments makes a positive and lasting impact on Christians around the world. When I teach overseas, or in the classroom, or at conferences, and have limited time there is one thing I do—teach the big picture of Scripture. There are many ministry and teaching contexts in which presenting the big picture of Scripture is appropriate and beneficial to people at all stages of the Christian faith—and, just as importantly, to those outside the faith (though that application is often missed).

One thing about big-picture perspectives on the Bible that does not receive nearly enough emphasis, however, is the potentially serious danger inherent to all attempts at presenting *the story* of the Bible, including the one in this chapter. The Bible is not raw material waiting for us to give it proper form and coherence wrapped up nice and neat in a story. The Bible is, and always will be, more than any reconstructed story of salvation can contain. It is easy practically to forget that every big-picture presentation of the Bible is always an abstraction rather than exactly the way the Bible itself reveals God and his salvation in

Christ. Our big pictures of the Bible can only ever approximate the thing itself, and therein lies the most serious danger. Teachers, preachers, and scholars can get so lost in a big picture of their own making, or that they found in any of the numerous books on the history of salvation, that the reconstructed story of Scripture becomes the main reference point rather than the Bible. Exegesis and exposition can be replaced with simply making connections to the grand narrative; connections that do not always have solid textual warrant. Even the word "story" presents something of a problem since the Bible so clearly is not all story, not all narrative. If God had willed to reveal himself to us simply in a story he could have done so. That he did not do so should be all that's needed to keep our salvation-history stories in check. So, while I am a proponent of big-picture-of-the-Bible approaches, I believe such presentations of Scripture must be undertaken with thoughtfulness for the revealed text and seen as one tool among many for teaching and preaching. Potential danger is not a reason to refrain from speaking of the big picture or story of the Bible but a reason to proceed with caution.

## MISSIONS AND LIFE

As Christians we tend to think of "missions" as one of the things we do, or at least one of the things that God calls some Christians—specifically those who take the gospel overseas—to do. Of course, missions is an activity; it is something we "do," but if we only think of it as one of many Christian activities, then we haven't understood fully what the Bible has to say about it. We might also think of missions as a command we have from Jesus, and it certainly is that. But like thinking of missions as simply one Christian activity, thinking of it only as a command doesn't do justice to the witness of Scripture. The Bible has a much larger view of missions and what it means for us. If we can see and grasp that view, then the way we conceive of the mission and our own personal roles in it—not to mention how we perceive our lives and the way we view ourselves in the world—may well be transformed.

## MISSIONS AND THE STORY

Just about everyone loves a good story. We love reading, hearing, and retelling stories of all kinds. Each of us also has our own personal story. That is, each of us has a story to tell, an autobiography including all the people, places, and events that make up our lives. We like to talk about them too. We even have different versions depending on who we are talking to, how much time we have, and what kind of mood we're in when we tell them. One of the reasons a good testimony ("good" means engaging, not necessarily dramatic) can be such an effective tool for evangelism is because stories connect with people. For

Christians, though each has a different personal version, our personal story is part of a much larger story—one that goes beyond our personal salvation story and family background. A Christian's story is, by its very nature, set within the largest story of all. That larger story is, of course, the Bible. As Christians, our stories, both corporate and individual, are inseparable from the story of the Bible. The key is to look at the story within the Bible not simply as events that took place a long time ago among ancient people, nor as only the historical account of what God did in and through Jesus of Nazareth, but as a story in which God calls us and in which he places us. To put it another way, the Bible contains a story within which we are called to live out our own stories. Richard Bauckham, in his book, *Bible and Mission,* says this:

> We all instinctively understand the world by telling stories about it. If the Bible offers a metanarrative, a story of all stories, then we should be able to place our own stories within that grand narrative and find our own perception and experience of the world transformed by that connection.[1]

At the heart of that "story of all stories" is the Bible story of God's revelation of himself and his own "mission."[2] God's mission and subsequently our mission in the world come together in the biblical story of the Great Commission.

## THE GREAT COMMISSION PROMISE

If you ask Christians where we get our idea of missions, most would say, "from the Bible." But how would we answer if asked a follow up question: "Where in the Bible?" My guess is that most of us would quote or mention one text above all others—what we usually call "the Great Commission" in Matt 28:18–20:

> Then Jesus came to them and said, "All authority in heaven and on earth has been given to me. Therefore go and make disciples of all nations, baptizing them in the name of the Father and of the Son and of the Holy Spirit, and teaching them to obey everything I have commanded you. And surely I am with you always, to the very end of the age." (NIV)[3]

The Great Commission is usually thought to be *the* missions text in the Bible, but in truth this text is really the tip of the iceberg when it comes to

---

[1] Richard Bauckham, *Bible and Mission: Christian Witness in a Postmodern World,* (Grand Rapids: Baker, 2003), 12.

[2] My understanding of the Bible as a story about missions is substantially shaped by reading Christopher J.H. Wright, *The Mission of God: Unlocking the Bible's Grand Narrative* (Downers Grove, IL: InterVarsity Press, 2006). Readers of that book will easily notice the pervasive influence here.

[3] THE HOLY BIBLE, NEW INTERNATIONAL VERSION®, NIV® Copyright © 1973, 1978, 1984, 2011 by Biblica, Inc.® Used by permission. All rights reserved worldwide.

missions in the Bible. In fact, a stronger and broader case for biblical missions that includes everyone (not just "missionaries") is built not on amassing "missionary" texts but in biblical, redemptive history. The Great Commission is Jesus's command and invitation to take part in an ancient promise about the blessing of the nations.[4]

### Hope in Hopelessness

The beginning of the Great Commission came at a bleak time in the history of the world.[5] From the fall of Adam and Eve in the garden of Eden the human race went from bad to worse. Even after God saved Noah and his family from judgment in the flood it is immediately clear that people are not going to improve on their own. Then in Genesis chapter 11, we find a genealogy through which God will work to bring about the accomplishment of his gracious plan to redeem his people. This genealogy, however, doesn't hold out much hope:

> This is the account of Terah. Terah became the father of Abram, Nahor and Haran. And Haran became the father of Lot. While his father Terah was still alive, Haran died in Ur of the Chaldeans, in the land of his birth. Abram and Nahor both married. The name of Abram's wife was Sarai. . . . Now Sarai was barren; she had no children. (Gen 11:27–30)[6]

Who's Abram? What's special about him? Nothing in particular, except that he is a descendent of Noah's son Shem who is singled out for blessing in Genesis (9:26–27). What sets Abram apart is that God chooses him. But at this point in the Bible there is no future for Abram until God comes on the scene:

> The LORD had said to Abram, "Leave your country, your people and your father's household and go to the land I will show you. "I will make you into a great nation and I will bless you; I will make your name great, and you will be a blessing. I will bless those who bless you, and whoever curses you I will curse; and all peoples on earth will be blessed through you. (Gen 12:1–3)

---

[4]  As Wright puts it: "Fundamentally, our mission (if it is biblically informed and validated) means our committed participation as God's people, at God's invitation and command, in God's own mission within the history of God's world for the redemption of God's creation. . . . Our mission flows from and participates in the mission of God." *Mission of God*, 23.

[5]  Without doubt, the full story must be traced back to Adam, just as Paul does in Rom 5:12–21. The goal of this chapter, however, is to trace the Great Commission beginning with Abraham. I am not, obviously, trying to build a full picture of salvation history or biblical theology. In fact, I don't consider this a work of biblical theology. I am simply following a rudimentary thread of cues from Scripture regarding God's promise of blessing to the nations and its fulfillment.

[6]  Unless otherwise noted, biblical translations are the author's own.

This is one of the pivotal moments in Scripture, and it's even more astonishing if we begin reading before chapter 12. After all, what do you need to become a great nation? You need children. How can Abraham become a great nation if his wife can't have children? With a background of a hopeless future, the stage is set for God to act.

It takes many years for Abram (who will be renamed Abraham, which means "exalted father" [Gen 17:5]), to receive the fulfillment of the promise, but over the years God repeats his promise: Abram's descendants will be greater than stars in the sky (Gen 15:5). Finally, Isaac is born to Abraham and Sarah (Genesis 21) and the great promise of God starts to unfold.

### From One to Many

If we fast forward in Scripture, we find a nation trapped in slavery, and that nation springs from Abraham. When God meets Moses in the burning bush—he comes naming himself as the "God of your fathers, the God of Abraham, Isaac, and Jacob" (Exod 3:15). Then he says he's heard their suffering and he's going to act on their behalf—remember this is God keeping his promise to Abraham. And so in the narrative of Scripture we have moved from the single man Abraham, to the people of Israel.

This nation began with a man in the desert, then a son, then his grandson Jacob and his twelve sons and they end up out among the nations enslaved in Egypt. And what does God do? He takes them out of there and establishes them in their own land. Before they get to that land, they have grown into quite a nation. The book of Numbers begins with a section we might be tempted to skip or skim over quickly. In chapters 1 and 2 the tribes of Israel are spelled out in detail as they are given their places in order around the tabernacle. One of the most significant things here is the testimony to God keeping his word: the nation that began with one man and his barren wife now number more than 600,000.[7] Israel is already a great nation.

### A Nation of Promise and a Light to the Nations

When Israel finally gets to the promised land—their journey filled with rebellion and tragedy—they are to be a light, a sign post if you will, that points the surrounding nations to their God. They are God's nation among the nations. Did Israel, however, have a "mission" in the way we use the word? In a word, no.[8] There is no OT version of the "Great Commission." Missions in the Bible

---

[7] Stephen G. Dempster, *Dominion and Dynasty: A Theology of the Hebrew Bible*, New Studies in Biblical Theology (Downers Grove, IL: InterVarsity Press 2003), 110.

[8] Wright, *Mission of God*, 24. His convincing treatment of this topic takes up a substantial part of *The Mission of God* and interested readers should consult it. Rather than cite it continually, I fully acknowledge

await a specific message. In the meantime, Israel is to live in their land, faithfully worship God and keep his law, and stand as a testimony to their God in the midst of the surrounding nations, but they don't have a mandate to go out and make disciples:

> See, I have taught you decrees and laws as the LORD my God commanded me, so that you may follow them in the land you are entering to take possession of it. Observe them carefully, for this will show your wisdom and understanding to the nations. (Deut 4:5–6)

So there is a sense in which we could say Israel had a "mission" in a general way—but not in the way we speak of "missions." Israel's mission was more to "be" but not "go." They certainly did, or were meant to, bear witness to their covenant God, but there was no grand command for them to go make Israelites of the nations.[9] Exceptions like Jonah notwithstanding, the only time Israel went to the nations was in punishment for being faithless and disobedient to God and for giving God a bad name among the nations (Ezek 36:19–21).

Nevertheless, there are hints here and there about the promise to the nations through Israel. There is Tamar the Canaanite involved in the incident with her father-in-law Judah, the third son of Jacob, in Genesis 38. Jacob, on his deathbed, prophesies that "The scepter shall not depart from Judah, nor the ruler's staff from between his feet, until tribute comes to him; and to him shall be the obedience of the peoples" (Gen 49:10 ESV). From the line of Judah, through Perez the illegitimate son born of Tamar, comes Salmon who married Rahab the prostitute in Jericho—who helped Israel (Josh 6:25; Matt 1:5). She was the mother of Boaz, the husband of Ruth the Moabite (Ruth 4:13). Ruth was the mother of Obed, the father of Jesse, who was the father of David, who is the ancestor of Jesus (Ruth 4:21–22; Matt 1:5, 16). God's promise to bless the nations unfolds through the bloodline of the baby who will be born to Mary and Joseph centuries later.

Particular individuals from the nations receive special attention at times as well. There is Namaan the Syrian, whom Elisha directs to cleanse himself in the river for the healing of his leprosy (2 Kings 5; See also Luke 4:27). Elisha also visits the Shunammite woman in 2 Kings 4 and tells her that she will have a son in spite of her husband's advanced age, then he later restores her son's life (2 Kgs 4:8–26). There is the tragic figure of Uriah the Hittite, wife of Bathsheba, whom David sent to the front lines to be killed in battle (2 Sam 11:17; [Bathsheba, by the way, is in the same genealogy that contains Tamar

---

my dependence on Wright's work.

[9] There are examples of proselytizing in Israel's history, but that hardly equals missions in the New Testament sense.

and Ruth in Matt 1]). There are others I could name, but there's a good reason why I can name them—because they stand out as exceptions in the narrative. The point is that even during the Mosaic covenant, when the nations were by and large enemies of Israel, God was at work among them.

Besides David's line and the handful of prominent Gentiles in the Old Testament there are also texts that remember and look forward to God's promise to the nations. Here are just four examples[10]:

**Psalm 86:9:** All the nations you have made will come and worship before you, O Lord; they will bring glory to your name.

**Isaiah 12:4:** In that day you will say: "Give thanks to the LORD, call on his name; make known among the nations what he has done, and proclaim that his name is exalted.

**Isaiah 66:19:** I will set a sign among them, and I will send some of those who survive to the nations—to Tarshish, to the Libyans and Lydians (famous as archers), to Tubal and Greece, and to the distant islands that have not heard of my fame or seen my glory. They will proclaim my glory among the nations.

**Habakkuk 2:14:** For the earth will be filled with the knowledge of the glory of the LORD, as the waters cover the sea.

One of the things these texts have in common is that they look forward to a time when God's promise to the nations will be fulfilled, but the fulfillment awaits the message of good news—it awaits the gospel. From a New Testament perspective, texts like these echo with both "through you all the nations on the earth will be blessed," and "go . . . make disciples of all nations."

## FULFILLMENT OF THE PROMISE TO THE NATIONS

Space does not allow us to consider all the ways the Gospel writers begin their narratives with words of fulfillment of God's promise in Jesus Christ, but one text in Luke will help tie the Old Testament expectation to the goal in the New Testament. Early in Luke's Gospel, Mary and Joseph bring their baby to the temple in observance to the Law. There in the temple is an old man who spent his life watching and waiting for God to act and fulfill his promise. The nation of Israel is back from exile, at least physically, but they've suffered centuries of occupation and war since returning from Babylon and now Rome rules the land. The old man, named Simeon, sets his eyes on the baby, takes him in his hands, and says the most remarkable thing (try to imagine being the parents):

---

[10] Unless otherwise noted, biblical translations are the author's own.

"For my eyes have seen your salvation, which you have prepared in the sight of all people, a light for revelation to the Gentiles and for glory to your people Israel." The child's father and mother marveled at what was said about him (Luke 2:29–32 NIV)

This is what the OT strained toward. The time of blessing to Israel and the fulfillment of the promise to bless the nations is revealed in the Christ child held in Simeon's hands. With the incarnation of Christ, and his death, burial, and resurrection, there is now good news to proclaim among the nations. Jesus is the fulfillment of the promise to Abraham, as Paul says in Gal 3:16: "Now the promises were spoken to Abraham and to his seed. He does not say, 'And to seeds,' as referring to many, but rather to one, 'And to your seed,' that is, Christ."

All this—Old Testament background and New Testament fulfillment—helps us to see the Great Commission as more than a proof text to motivate us for missions. The Great Commission is Jesus's directive to go out and proclaim that God has kept his promise.[11]

## IMPLICATIONS FOR TODAY

The goal of this chapter is to provide readers with a basic framework for the biblical story of missions. My hope is that pastors, students, evangelists, and missionaries will find it a useful building block for developing a fuller biblical understanding of missions. More importantly, I hope that readers will sense that this story calls for personal involvement—taking our own place in God's mission to the nations. Too often we read the Bible as a story of people who lived a long time ago in lands far, far away and miss making a personal connection to the story revealed in the Bible. We think of it as objective, historical information that explains salvation—and it is that—but it is more than a divinely revealed account of God's redemptive history. The Bible reveals a living story, one that encapsulates our lives, gives us purpose, and in which we find fulfillment. The story of the Great Commission is our story—God has made us part of that story and calls us to take part in it. Doing missions isn't just one of the things we "do" as Christians, but it is part and parcel of what we are if we claim to believe in the One in whom all the promises are fulfilled. At the same

---

[11] In the new covenant the OT texts that speak of the nations coming to Israel (e.g., Psalm 86) are fulfilled by Jesus sending his disciples to the nations. Reflecting on such texts, Goheen says, "Yet it now seems that this is not a pilgrimage of the nations to the center but a sending of 'Israel' to the periphery (John 20:21). . . . The change from a centripetal to a centrifugal movement, indeed the transformation of the very form of God's people, can be explained only on the basis of the words of Jesus. He gathers his little flock and sends it to the nations, charging it to continue the gathering process that he has begun." Michael W. Goheen, *A Light to the Nations: The Missional Church and the Biblical Story*" (Grand Rapids: Baker, 2011), 115.

time, missions is not something done only in particular areas, by particular people who travel overseas to remote places that lack gospel witness. Where are the nations? We live in them. And what's more, for those of us living in America the "nations" (people/language groups) have quite literally come to us. This doesn't mean that we can't speak or think of career missions, or that overseas missions is a thing of the past—God forbid, as Paul might say—but we must also start to see our lost family members, neighbors, and others with whom God connects us as being part of the nations that need to hear the gospel. The "nations" are right outside, sometimes inside, our doors. If you believe in Jesus, that means God kept his promise to Abraham and included you in it. You were among the number God was talking about when he told Abraham to try to count the stars. It means that the big story of God's mission in the Bible is your story, and that's what Jesus calls you and me to go share with people, to go make disciples of all nations. When you share the gospel, you are standing firmly in a story that tells about the world the way it really is, the origins of the world and everyone in it, and God's answer in Christ to the ravages of sin and death. All God calls you to do is live it and share it. Put your own story in line with God's ancient promise to a man from Ur of the Chaldees. God calls you to own that story for the sake of his glory in Christ among the nations waiting for the day when the Great Commission promise reaches its ultimate fulfillment:

> After this I looked and there before me was a great multitude that no one could count, from every nation, tribe, people and language, standing before the throne and in front of the Lamb. They were wearing white robes and were holding palm branches in their hands. And they cried out in a loud voice: "Salvation belongs to our God, who sits on the throne, and to the Lamb." (Revelation 7:9–10 NIV)

*Chapter 17*

# The Pastoral Theologian

*by Jason Meyer and John Kimbell*

## INTRODUCTION: THE PASTORAL
## THEOLOGIAN IN RECENT LITERATURE

Pastoral ministry today suffers from an identity crisis. People can have *the title* of "pastor" without understanding or embracing *the calling* of a pastor. Gerald Hiestand and Todd Wilson correctly assert that pastors "don't know who they are or what they are supposed to be."[1] This identity crisis is tragic because it means that the church has lost the once dominant and compelling vision of the pastor as a theologian. Our day has witnessed a subtle shift from the pastor as a producer of theology to a consumer of theology. Pastors are secondhand streams, not firsthand fountains. Theology in the pulpit is not fresh like farm to plate. It is theology that was packaged, frozen, thawed, and reheated. It is not a firsthand discovery; it is secondhand regurgitation.

Hiestand and Wilson agree with this assessment. People no longer see the pastorate as an "intellectual" calling.[2] Pastors now function more as "intellectual middle management, passive conveyors of insights from theologians to laity."[3] What happened? Pastors Wilson and Hiestand argue that the identity crisis in pastoral ministry came from separating the roles of pastor and

---

[1] Gerald Hiestand and Todd Wilson, *The Pastor Theologian: Resurrecting an Ancient Vision* (Grand Rapids: Zondervan, 2015), 15. Hiestand and Wilson also quote Princeton Seminary president Craig Barnes in support of this assertion. This crisis is characterized by "confusion about what it means to be the pastor." See M. Craig Barnes, *The Pastor as Minor Poet: Text and Subtexts in the Ministerial Life* (Grand Rapids: Eerdmans, 2009), 4.

[2] Hiestand and Wilson, *Pastor Theologian,* 11.

[3] Hiestand and Wilson, 11.

theologian.[4] John MacArthur likewise asserts that "pastors have outsourced doctrine to the academy."[5]

Therefore, recent literature offers a clarion call to resurrect the pastoral theologian. John MacArthur passionately pleads for the pastor to take up the calling of "theologian, biblical scholar, and guardian of sound doctrine."[6] Hiestand and Wilson make the case that "some pastors must take up the mantel of theologian by providing solid thought leadership to the church and its theologians even as they tend the garden of their own congregations."[7]

Hiestand and Wilson helpfully provide a threefold taxonomy for the pastoral theologian: (1) local theologian, (2) popular theologian, and (3) ecclesial theologian. A local theologian is "a pastor theologian who constructs theology for the laity of his local congregation."[8] A popular theologian is "a pastor theologian who provides theological leadership to Christian laity beyond his own congregation."[9] The ecclesial theologian is "a pastor theologian who constructs theology for other Christian theologians and pastors."[10]

These descriptions define a pastoral theologian according to intended audience: (1) local laity, (2) wider laity, and (3) other pastors and theologians. This seems to be the same approach taken by Kevin Vanhoozer and Owen Strachan in their book.[11]

There is a sense in which the Lord determines which of the three audiences each pastor will shepherd. The Bible is clear that a "person cannot receive even one thing unless it is given him from heaven" (John 3:27 ESV). The Lord has given Thomas R. Schreiner a ministry that serves all three audiences (local laity, wider laity, and pastors and theologians). Rather than document Schreiner's influence over all three spheres, we will focus in this essay on the exemplary way that Thomas R. Schreiner has fulfilled his calling as a local theologian. This approach has the benefit of addressing every pastor because not all pastors are called to be influential popular or ecclesial theologians. Every pastor, however, receives the charge from Christ to be a local theologian.

---

[4] Hiestand and Wilson, *Pastor Theologian*, 15. See also *Becoming a Pastor Theologian: New Possibilities for Church Leadership*, ed. Todd Wilson and Gerald Hiestand (Downers Grove, IL: InterVarsity Press, 2016), 2.

[5] John MacArthur, *The Shepherd as Theologian: Accurately Interpreting and Applying God's Word* (Eugene, OR: Harvest House, 2017), 6.

[6] MacArthur, 6.

[7] Hiestand and Wilson, *Pastor Theologian*, 15.

[8] Hiestand and Wilson, 80.

[9] Hiestand and Wilson, 80.

[10] Hiestand and Wilson, 80. Hiestand and Wilson issue a call for ecclesial pastors who construct theology for the church that will shape other Christian theologians and pastors. We completely agree that this is a crucial calling.

[11] Kevin Vanhoozer and Owen Strachan, *The Pastor as Public Theologian: Reclaiming a Lost Vision* (Grand Rapids: Brazos, 2015).

## THE PROFILE OF A LOCAL THEOLOGIAN.

Hiestand and Wilson provide an overarching description of a local theologian.

> In this model, the pastor theologian is a theologically astute pastor who ably services the theological needs of a local church. This theological leadership is most immediately accomplished through a theologically rich preaching ministry but also through theologically thick pastoral care, counseling, and organizational leadership. A local theologian has a solid working knowledge of the primary Christian doctrines and is able to draw connections between biblical truth and lived experience.[12]

This basic description has much to commend it. A pastoral theologian must be theologically astute, and his ministry should service the theological needs of a local church through "theologically rich" preaching and "theologically thick" pastoral care and organizational leadership.

This description is a good thumbnail sketch, but it fails to fire the imagination. Pastoral ministry is an awe-inspiring calling and responsibility. Charles H. Spurgeon once said that pastors should not stoop to be kings. Boiling down being a pastoral theologian to servicing "the theological needs of a church" sounds too pedestrian. It lacks the biblical aroma of awe that has come face-to-face with a full view of the splendor of God's holiness. We need a bigger, bolder biblical vision that will awaken pastors to the breathtaking privilege and responsibility of pastoral ministry.

*Thesis*: A pastoral theologian takes the exalted vision of God, breathed out in the Scriptures, and labors with all his might to see it fleshed out in the shared life of a people. A pastoral theologian is driven by an all-consuming question: What would this glorious vision of God I savor look like in the life of the people I shepherd?

This perspective on a pastoral theologian is close to what Kevin Vanhoozer has laid out in *The Drama of Doctrine*. Vanhoozer argues that theology must be performed, not merely believed. Doctrine is "a condensed form of Christian wisdom, rooted in the Scriptures and accumulated over the centuries, about how rightly to participate in the drama of redemption."[13] Therefore, canonical doctrines are like stage directions for a church's performance of the gospel.

> The Father is the playwright and the producer of the action; the Son the climax and summation of the action. The Spirit, as the one who unites us to Christ, is the dresser who clothes us with Christ's righteousness, the prompter who helps

---

[12] Hiestand and Wilson, *Pastor Theologian*, 81.
[13] Kevin Vanhoozer, *The Drama of Doctrine: A Canonical-Linguistic Approach to Christian Theology* (Louisville: Westminster John Knox, 2005), 448.

us remember our biblical lines, and the prop master who gives gifts (accessories) to each church member, equipping us to play our parts. While the Holy Spirit is the primary director who oversees the global production, *it is the pastor who bears the primary responsibility for overseeing local performances.*[14]

Vanhoozer writes elsewhere:

The pastor is a social geographer, one who wants to "write" the gospel onto the minds and hearts of a people gathered in a particular place. The pastor of a local church is a place-maker whose mission is to make a congregation into a fit dwelling place for the Spirit of Christ, a place in which certain activities will enact corporate heavenly citizenship under historical earthly conditions. The pastor wants to help each member of the flock to find his or her place in the world, to know how to follow Christ here and now as his disciple.[15]

This pastoral labor is a work of discipleship. "Pastors lead their flocks into maturity in Christ. It's a matter of learning to live *into* Christ in order to live Christ *out.*"[16] Being a pastor theologian is a "theological building project—the formation of a people set apart to love God and their neighbors as themselves. Pastors are public theologians because they work with people to do lived theology. This is hard work; it's harder to work with people than ideas. If you want a real challenge, don't go into academic theology; go into the pastorate. But God's people—local churches—are public places where the life of Christ is remembered, celebrated, explored, and exhibited. Stated simply, the pastor's task is to help congregations become what they are in Christ."[17]

This is the "Great Pastoral Commission: to make disciples who come to share the heart, mind and hands of Jesus Christ."[18] One could take individual doctrines and show how the "Great Pastoral Commission" would be fleshed out in each one, but this essay is a broader brush stroke focusing on a big, satisfying, sweepingly glorious vision of God himself. John Piper's assessment still holds true today: "people are starved for the greatness of God." Therefore, what would a people look like who are satisfied with the greatness of God?

Pastors must minister out of the overflow of being satisfied by the all-sufficiency of Christ. Pastors are called to do their work with overflowing joy or else it is no benefit to the people. The pastoral theologian knows that people need a vision *of* God, not just a vision *from* God. The pastoral theologian must

---

[14] Kevin Vanhoozer, *Drama of Doctrine*, 448.
[15] Kevin Vanhoozer, "The Pastor Theologian as Public Theologian," in Wilson and Hiestand, *Becoming a Pastor Theologian*, 39.
[16] Vanhoozer, 39.
[17] Vanhoozer, 41.
[18] Vanhoozer, 43.

first see and savor this vision of God before seeking to shepherd people to be transformed by that theological vision.

Therefore, a pastoral theologian is not merely someone who has two separate passions: theology and people. A pastoral theologian blends both of those passions together into a unified vocational mission: shepherding his people into a shared vision of God that will impact every aspect of their lives. A pastoral theologian wants to shepherd the people of God to be a God-besotted people.

Let us look at the two parts of this phrase "pastoral theologian" separately and then fuse them together into a unified vocation. A pastoral *theologian* is a theologian because he is captivated by a glorious vision of God. A *pastoral* theologian is a pastor because he is captivated by a calling to shepherd a specific flock. Therefore, a *pastoral theologian* is driven by an all-consuming question: "what would this glorious vision of God look like in the life of a people?" What if my people were to savor this vision of God such that they would cast down their idols? How would this vision of God impact their parenting? How would it shine through in their marriage? How would it transform how they work and how they interact with others in the workplace?

Therefore, a pastoral theologian wants the glorious vision of God he savors to become a shared vision with the people he pastors. He wants to see what it would look like to get fleshed out experientially and practically. In other words, a pastoral theologian is not someone who has two separate loves (theology and people). A theologian may love a vision of God. A pastor may love a flock. A pastoral theologian makes it his mission to see those two precious realities come together in God-glorifying, Christ-exalting, Spirit-empowered ways.

## PART 2: PERSONAL REFLECTIONS ON THOMAS R. SCHREINER AS A PASTORAL THEOLOGIAN

My (John's) first Sunday visiting Clifton Baptist Church in Louisville, KY, was the first Sunday of a church merger. The year was 2001. Trinity Baptist, a young church plant just moving out of infancy, had merged together with Clifton Baptist, a historic Louisville church established in 1893. Tom Schreiner had been preaching regularly at the young, growing church plant for three years, and the mostly aged, declining Clifton congregation had just called Tom to be their pastor. This decision included welcoming the entire membership of Trinity into their midst.

Their first Sunday together felt a bit awkward and clunky, as these two church families began their journey of becoming one new, blended family. Based on that initial visit and even a surface-level knowledge of what was happening, it was evident that a variety of pastoral challenges lay ahead. My wife and I quickly decided to visit other churches in the area.

However, in God's kind providence, we soon returned to Clifton and became members before my first semester of seminary had ended. Presently, I am writing from the perspective of one who has observed and experienced the fruit of Tom's ministry as a pastoral theologian at Clifton Baptist Church over the past seventeen years. It is a ministry God has used to shape a congregation that is today united around the gospel and growing in the grace of Christ.

In considering the distinguishing marks of a pastoral theologian, the question may arise how these characteristics might play out concretely in a particular man and a particular ministry. The helpful portrait set forth above can take on a variety of distinct hues and tones depending on a man's gifting and personality. Certainly, this has been true of Tom and his ministry. Nevertheless, there are some essential features that shine through and are worthy of emulation by all who aspire to this great work. Here are a few that I commend for your consideration from the ministry of Tom Schreiner.

### A Prioritization of the Gospel

In seeking to make the glory of God known and experienced by his local congregation in a transforming way, Tom has tirelessly held up the priority of the gospel of Jesus Christ. He has delivered hundreds of sermons and preached through numerous books of the Bible from beginning to end. Whether it was a text from Proverbs or Romans or Revelation, in *every* case he would seek to make clear "the light of the knowledge of the glory of God in the face of Jesus Christ" (2 Cor 4:6 ESV). This has not come in the form of a "canned" gospel presentation, detached from that week's text or artificially tacked on at the end of a sermon. Rather, he has proclaimed Christ and his saving grace toward sinners from all of Scripture in a way that meaningfully rises up from the particulars of each text.[19]

Those who have directly experienced Tom's pastoral labors would quickly testify that this prioritization has not simply stemmed from a theological perspective, but from his personal experience of the grace of God through Jesus Christ. It is this personal experience of grace that feeds and flows into all the rest of the marks of Tom's ministry. He is a sinner saved by grace, who continues to delight in and depend on that grace, and who therefore is eager to proclaim that same grace to others from the Scriptures.

---

[19] In addition to his sermons, Tom has modeled this prioritization of the gospel and approach to the Scriptures in numerous writings. See especially *The King in His Beauty: A Biblical Theology of the Old and New Testaments* (Grand Rapids: Baker Academic, 2013).

## *A Childlike Dependence on God's Word*

For all of Tom's intellectual gifting and academic accomplishments, his service as a pastoral theologian is profoundly marked by a childlike dependence on God's Word. This dependence is rooted in the theological conviction that it is not fundamentally the creativity or ingenuity of the pastor that brings lasting growth and change to a congregation. Rather, God Himself brings about change through the faithful, Spirit-empowered proclamation of his own Word.

Tom's trusting dependence in this regard is shown in part by his simple and direct style of preaching. Indeed, some who hear Tom initially are not overly impressed by his homiletics. Truth be told, when I first began attending Clifton as a new seminary student, neither was I. And yet, after sitting under his preaching for a couple years, I began to realize that the Lord was bringing about significant spiritual growth in my family through the clear and simple proclamation of truth from God's Word week after week. Having the opportunity to look back after almost two decades, I now see how God has used such preaching to shape and grow an entire congregation into greater conformity to Christ. In addition to strengthening his own congregation, God has used the model of Tom's preaching to grant courage to scores of men sent out from Clifton to enter preaching ministries of their own with confidence in the power of God's Word.[20]

This dependence on the power of God's Word has also been shown by Tom's confidence that *every* text of Scripture, when rightly understood, will bring benefit to God's people. Practically, this has meant a consistent practice of preaching verse by verse through entire books of the Bible rather than selecting favorite or favored texts according to his own discernment. Indeed, such uninhibited confidence once led Tom to preach to us on the harlot of Babylon from Revelation 17 on Mother's Day. On another occasion, when celebrating the tenth anniversary of the merger between Trinity and Clifton, he preached from 2 Kgs 10:15–17, which recounts King Jehu's slaughter of all those remaining loyal to Ahab. We may debate the wisdom of preaching a particular text on a particular occasion, but no one can question Tom's belief that the Word of God is powerful down to every last verse of Scripture!

## *A Commitment to Biblical Clarity*

Tom has modeled service as a pastoral theologian through his commitment to biblical clarity in all facets of his ministry. I have represented Tom's preaching as simple and clear, and I affirm the value of this as a reproducible quality of his

---

[20] I include myself in this group of men. Certainly, God gives as gifts to the church some preachers who stand apart in their creativity and homiletical gifts. These are to be received with thanksgiving. But one of the values of Tom's approach to preaching is that it is eminently imitable.

ministry. At the same time, I have also come to appreciate that achieving theological clarity and simple (not simplistic!) preaching, while broadly imitable, is not necessarily "easy" or broadly *achieved* among pastors or theologians. John C. Ryle once wrote, "To make hard things seem hard . . . is within reach of all, but to make hard things seem easy and intelligible is a height attained by very few speakers."[21] C. H. Spurgeon also commended clarity as an essential part of a minister's Christlike humility and love.

> Some would impress us by their depth of thought, when it is merely a love of big words. To hide plain things in dark sentences, is sport rather than service for God. If you love men better, you will love phrases less. How used your mother to talk to you when you were a child? There! Do not tell me. Don't print it. It would never do for the public ear. The things that she used to say to you were childish, and earlier still, babyish. Why did she thus speak, for she was a very sensible woman? Because she loved you. There is a sort of *tutoyage*, as the French call it, in which love delights.[22]

This is perhaps one of Tom's greatest gifts that God has used to serve so many in his own congregation and beyond. There have been numerous Sunday mornings when Tom has preached on a text that initially seemed difficult to understand or apply, and yet our congregation left the sermon deeply convicted and encouraged by the clear meaning and application of God's Word. What is particularly telling is that we have not left thinking, "How was he able to pull that truth from that particular text?" Rather, we have left thinking, "Now that he has explained it, I see the truth so clearly in the text!" As a result, the Word of God has been set free through Tom's ministry to work powerfully in the lives of his congregation.

### A Life of Disciplined Study

Often, people think an individual's passion is displayed by his public persona. In reality, our passions are more clearly measured by the way we prioritize our time over the course of years when no one is watching. In this regard, Tom Schreiner has demonstrated a passion to see the glory of God made known to his congregation and lived out through the gospel by devoting himself to the consistent and disciplined personal study of the Scriptures over a lifetime.

Tom recently commented to me how much he enjoys studying and writing when he has large blocks of time to do so. He is able to sustain this for hours on end. I have also attended conferences with him where I see him making the

---

[21] J. C. Ryle, *Simplicity in Preaching* (Carlisle, PA: Banner of Truth, 2010), 5.

[22] C. H. Spurgeon, *An All-Round Ministry: Addresses to Ministers and Students* (London: Passmore & Alabaster, 1900), 353.

most of even brief moments of free time to read or study. I am struck by how much he hungers to know more of God through his Word even at this later stage of his life and ministry. In the midst of being a full-time seminary professor and writing numerous articles, commentaries, and works of theology, Tom carved out time to consistently preach and teach at Clifton Baptist Church for seventeen years. This type of productive teaching, writing, and preaching is only made possible through a remarkably disciplined life of studying God's Word. And such a life is the fruit of a genuine passion to know God personally through his Word and to make him known to others.

### Humility and Approachability

Most people know of Tom Schreiner through his extensive published works. Those who do probably think of him first and foremost as an accomplished scholar and theologian. However, if you ask the members of his church who know him personally what stands out to them about Tom Schreiner, many would speak *first* of his humility and approachability. How can such an accomplished scholar be so down-to-earth and approachable? The answer is gospel-generated humility.

Tom is not impressed with himself. He is impressed with God. As one who is captivated by the glory of God, he has been freed from the pursuit of his own glory in ministry. Specifically, Tom's joy is grounded in his experience of the glorious mercy of God in Christ given to him personally. Therefore, for all of the ways he has distinguished himself as a scholar, he sees far more common ground with fellow sinners around him than any distinction in himself. This flows out into a relational ease among all types of people, an approachability that welcomes any who would desire to interact with him, and a humble patience with others. This model of humility and approachability over years of ministry has powerfully influenced the culture of leadership at our church as well as the entire culture of our congregation.

### The Value of Shared Leadership

Finally, Tom's ministry as a pastoral theologian in the local church has been characterized by the value of shared leadership. This stems from a formal theological conviction regarding the New Testament model of a plurality of elders in the local church.[23] And yet this theological conviction can only be joyfully embraced and effectively practiced through the gospel humility and personal faith of one who joyfully submits to Christ as the Chief Shepherd.

---

[23] For a concise defense of this view, see Benjamin L. Merkle, *40 Questions about Elders and Deacons* (Grand Rapids, MI: Kregel, 2008), 161–65.

As the primary preaching pastor of Clifton for years, Tom has certainly exercised a unique leadership and influence through his pulpit ministry to our congregation. However, this leadership has been marked throughout by a glad partnership with multiple men, whom Tom has received as gifts to the church to lead alongside him in ministry. Rather than suppressing the rise of leaders around him out of a fear of competition, Tom has encouraged and raised up fellow elders to join him in the work. In particular, this included a significant span of years in which he shared the pulpit ministry almost equally with me, giving me time to grow and mature in preaching alongside him in ministry.

### *Radically Ordinary*

When one steps back to survey the distinctives of Tom Schreiner's ministry as a pastoral theologian, the list may come across as rather ordinary. Indeed, one of the ways I have heard Tom describe himself is "remarkably ordinary." I would submit, however, that such "ordinary" distinctives, sustained over the life and ministry of a pastoral theologian, is profoundly radical and rare. Only the supernatural grace of God, working in a man personally captured by the glory of God and delighted in the mercy of Christ will ever lead to such a life and ministry. And as we see in the life of Tom Schreiner, such is a life and ministry that bears profound spiritual fruit in the lives of those he shepherds to the glory of God.

# Chapter 18

# For the Glory of God through Theological Education: The Academic Ministries of Thomas R. Schreiner (1954–) and Andrew of Caesarea (563–637)

*by Robert L. Plummer*

## INTRODUCTION

About a half mile from Tom Schreiner's office at The Southern Baptist Theological Seminary is the Louisville Presbyterian Theological Seminary (LPTS). A plaque inside the entrance of the LPTS chapel proclaims that the school exists "For the Glory of God through Theological Education." Within sight of this plaque is the newly renovated "Gender Neutral Bathroom" (formerly a ladies' restroom). LPTS has capitulated to worldly and political agendas, and the plaque certainly does not reflect its current mission. Tom Schreiner's life, on the other hand, is fittingly described by the phrase, "for the glory of God through theological education." Here is a man whose life has been lived for the glory of God—as a husband, as a father, as a pastor, and perhaps most publicly, through the academic ministry of theological education as a scholar and teacher.

My assigned topic in this chapter is to reflect practically on ministry in the field of academia. In the first half of this chapter, I will begin by offering some personal memories and reflections on the life of Tom Schreiner. In the second half, I make observations on the academic ministry of Andrew of Caesarea (563–637), as illustrated through his commentary on the Book of Revelation. I first read Andrew's commentary in the fall of 2016—the same time I was reading Schreiner's new commentary on the same book (Crossway, forthcoming). I was struck by the similar humility and competence in the lives of two Christian scholars separated by nearly 1500 years.

## PERSONAL REFLECTIONS ON THE ACADEMIC MINISTRY OF TOM SCHREINER

Tom Schreiner would be the first to admit that he is a sinner. He believes and proclaims the gospel! Yet, in many ways, he has lived a model life as an academic minister. To honor Tom and edify readers, I will begin by briefly reflecting on some of his exemplary qualities. Oftentimes when I read biographical reflections on a scholar's life, it is the illustrative anecdotes that stay with me the most. Thus, I will not hesitate to include personal memories and testimonials about Tom.

1. *Competency*—Schreiner knows his material, reads widely, and communicates his knowledge with clarity and accuracy. Recently, in discussing an issue in the New Testament doctoral colloquium, Tom was able to recall obscure details he had read years ago. One would be hard-pressed to find a more competent evangelical New Testament scholar. In Tom's life, we find the fruit of both natural gifting and many decades of diligently tending that fruit through research, writing, dialogue, and reflection.

2. *Humility*—Schreiner is well known for changing his opinions, and he is not shy to publicly disagree with views he formerly espoused in one of his many published books. Such shifting views are not evidence of an erratic mind, but a humility that continually returns to the biblical text and bows before the Word of God. I personally recall an incident that sealed in my mind the gracious nature of Tom Schreiner. Quite a few years ago, at an annual meeting of the Evangelical Theological Society, a "theologically progressive" presenter got into a shouting match with a prominent traditional scholar in the room. I do not recall the presenter's exact words, but he pointed to Tom Schreiner and said something to the effect of: "Tom Schreiner disagrees with me, but does so in Christian love—and without twisting my views . . . unlike you!" Let the reader take note. Within evangelicalism, there are scholars who speak the truth, and then scholars who "speak the truth in love " (Eph 4:15). Tom has modeled the latter approach.

3. *Church-Based Application*—If you know Tom Schreiner, you know he is a man who loves the church. For much of the last fifteen years, he has served as the main preaching pastor of Clifton Baptist Church in Louisville, KY.

Though I am an elder at another church in Louisville, our family has listened to Tom's sermons for the spiritual nourishment we receive from his clear and faithful biblical teaching. Tom is not an ivory tower theologian. He's in the trenches, doing ministry, teaching the Bible, and loving people.

4. *Collegiality*—Tom is the consummate team player. An administrator once confided in me that he didn't want Tom to give the introductory endorsement of a colleague being considered for promotion at a meeting. Tom's introduction, he explained, would not make as marked an impression, because "Tom is for everyone." What a loving disparagement! Even in Christian churches and institutions, to be known as "for everyone" (i.e., on the side of everyone) is a rare and beautiful quality.

5. *Christian Love*—Tom is a man who loves his students in word and deed. In light of how much the man writes, I'm always shocked to see his unhurried and caring conversations with students around campus. He is also a model of Christian love in interacting with students who disagree with him or who need correction. Roughly seventeen years ago, Tom was scheduled to give an open lecture on "Women in Ministry," including reasons why he believes the New Testament forbids women from being pastors. My wife and I were both students at the time and she decided to prank call him. Disguising her voice, she left him a voicemail indicating that she was coming to his lecture as a representative of the Women's Student Preacher Organization (a fictitious entity). "I am going to have some questions for you!" she threatened. Later, after Tom's lecture, we found he thought the voicemail was from a real female preacher (not a prank), and he was prepared to interact lovingly with a hostile questioner. Similarly, I heard a story about Tom—that at his former place of employment (Bethel Seminary), even a local female pastor invited him to fill the pulpit in her absence. Though she knew Tom's views on women in ministry, she trusted his faithfulness to the Scripture and love for God's people.

## ANDREW OF CAESAREA (563–637) AS A MODEL FOR ACADEMIC MINISTRY

As mentioned above, the academic ministries of Tom Schreiner and Andrew of Caesarea intertwined for me in the fall of 2016. I was concurrently reading the draft of Tom's forthcoming commentary on the Book of Revelation alongside one of the earliest extant Greek commentaries on Revelation by Andrew of Caesarea. At this time I also became acutely aware of some shrill evangelical interactions in social media. In particular, one famous evangelical scholar publicly shamed another, claiming that he had "laughed out loud" (in disdain) when he had read the other scholar's recent work. Oh how my heart pined for more "Tom Schreiners" and more "Andrews of Caesarea" in the evangelical guild!

It has become trendy, of late, for scholars to revisit the church fathers. Thomas Oden, for example, has looked to the "consensual Christianity" of the Fathers as a means of both renewing mainline American churches and providing an orthodox basis for worldwide ecumenism.[1] I applaud Oden's legacy, while contending that more discernment is needed as to the value of a church father's particular insights. Nevertheless, if we are looking for a church father from whom we can learn much regarding both exegesis and academic ministry, Andrew of Caesarea provides such a model. Andrew, Archbishop of Caesarea, Cappadocia, composed his Greek commentary on Revelation around the year 611, a work that was subsequently translated into Armenian, Slavic, and Georgian.[2] Below I will briefly survey five features of Andrew's commentary that give evidence of his skill and wisdom in academic ministry—characteristics that are still much needed in the evangelical academy today.

1. *Concern for Church-Based Practical Application*—While granting that the genre of ancient biblical commentary and modern biblical commentary are quite different, Andrew exhibits a consistent concern for how a proper understanding of the Book of Revelation will affect ordinary Christians. For example, let us consider Andrew's comments on Revelation 22:17 ("Both the Spirit and the bride say, 'Come!' Let anyone who hears say, 'Come!' Let the one who is thirsty come. Let the one who desires take the water of life freely."[3]). He writes:

> Crying out in our hearts "Abba, Father," [here we see] the church and the Spirit in her call for the coming of the only-begotten Son of God. Indeed, every faithful person who hears prays to God the Father as he has been taught, "Your kingdom come!"

> To make secure the possession of that which is received, it is necessary to thirst for the drinking of life. This is especially so since such a gift is offered not to those who are hardly wearied at all but to those who bring

---

[1] Read the fascinating story of Thomas C. Oden's mission in his own words in *A Change of Heart: A Personal and Theological Memoir* (Downers Grove, IL: InterVarsity Press, 2014).
[2] Eugenia Scarvelis Constantinou, "Andrew of Caesarea and the Apocalypse in the Ancient Church of the East" (Ph.D. thesis, Laval University, 2008).
[3] All English Bible translations come from the Christian Standard Bible (2017).

nothing worthy of the magnificence of the gift, such as gold or silver or bodily labors, but bring only a genuine and ardent mind.[4]

2. *Preserving the Link between History and Theology*—In our current herme-neutical environment of "interpretive communities" and the Theological Interpretation of Scripture movement, it's not uncommon for one to feel that theology is being severed from history. Although Andrew is concerned for doctrine and application, his observations frequently remind his readers that he believes in a historical author, John the Apostle, who, though writing a work in the apocalyptic genre, refers to real historical events and persons. For example, in commenting on Rev 1:9, Andrew clearly understands "Patmos" as a real island on which John was genuinely exiled, and on which he had visionary experiences. Andrew, in fact, is such a literalist when it comes to the events reported in the text that he interprets the thorny grammar of Rev 11:1 as indicating that the measuring rod *spoke* to the apostle John.[5] We might call this Andrew's "Disney exe-gesis" (cf. Lumière or Cogsworth from *Beauty and the Beast*). He writes:

> Through the measuring rod it is revealed that everything that appears in heaven and that is inanimate among us are intellectual, including the altar and the throne and the other things. How else did the measuring rod given to him say, 'Rise and measure the temple of God'?[6]

It appears Andrew is the original literal interpreter, applying a grammatical-historical exegetical method, but unfortunately in this case, without attention to the solecisms of Revelation (cf. Rev 1:17).

3. *Humility and Grace when Interacting with Other Views*—Only one other Greek commentary on Revelation that predates Andrew's work has sur-vived. This commentary is reportedly by Oecumenius of Isauria (c. sixth century) and is frequently quoted by Andrew. Interestingly, when Andrew

---

[4] Andrew of Caesarea, *Commentary on the Apocalypse*, trans. William C. Weinrich, ed. Thomas C. Oden, in *Greek Commentaries on Revelation: Oecumenius and Andrew of Caesarea*, Ancient Christian Texts (Downers Grove, IL: InterVarsityPress, 2011), 206.

[5] The Greek text of Rev 11:1 reads: Καὶ ἐδόθη μοι κάλαμος ὅμοιος ῥάβδῳ, λέγων· ἔγειρε καὶ μέτρησον τὸν ναὸν τοῦ θεοῦ καὶ τὸ θυσιαστήριον καὶ τοὺς προσκυνοῦντας ἐν αὐτῷ. David Mathewson rightly explains the participle λέγων accordingly: "While adverbial participles generally take the same subject as the verb they modify, here the subject of the participle is not the subject κάλαμος, but the implied agent of ἐδόθη, probably an angelic being who now speaks to John. This is probably the reason for the addition of καὶ εἱστήκει ὁ ἄγγελος in some manuscripts. *Revelation: A Handbook on the Greek Text* (Waco: Baylor University Press, 2016), 139–40.

[6] Andrew of Caesarea, *Apocalypse,* 151.

disagrees with Oecumenius (which he often does), he never cites him by name. Far from shaming his predecessor, Andrew is concerned to correct erroneous interpretations without personally disparaging the holders of those views. For example, in explaining the vision of the temple of God in Rev 11:1, Andrew first cites the view of Oecumneius: "We should know that some understand the temple of God to represent the old covenant and the court outside the new covenant . . . "[7] After clearly and charitably explaining Oecumenius's position, Andrew adds, "But *we think* the church is called 'the temple of the living God,' for in it we offer spiritual sacrifices to God. And *I think* that the court outside is the assembly of the unbelieving Gentiles and Jews, and so by virtue of their impiety they are unworthy to be measured by the angel" (emphasis added).[8]

4. *Eagerness to Praise and Credit Others*—Several plagiarism scandals have recently rocked the world of evangelical scholars and preachers. In contrast, even though lacking modern standards of citing other works, Andrew is fastidious in giving credit to those from whom he has learned. For example, in discussing Rev 6:2, Andrew twice cites Methodius, Bishop of Olympus (d. 311). Andrew writes, "But we have read Methodius and note how he spoke concerning the text. . . . In this passage Methodius is expounding the fall of the red dragon as though he were already subdued."[9] Such explicit appeals to his forebearers are frequent in Andrew's writing.

5. *Appropriate Tentativeness*—Revelation is a difficult book to interpret. In the opening of his commentary on Revelation, Schreiner approvingly cites the quip of Gilbert K. Chesterton, "And though St. John the Evangelist saw many strange monsters in his vision, he saw no creature so wild as one of his own commentators."[10] Any careful interpreter of Revelation will, at certain points, graciously cite multiple options and express appropriate tentativeness about his conclusions. One such example in Andrew's commentary is when he discusses the symbolic meaning of Jesus's feet being described as "like fine bronze as it is refined in a furnace." Note the four possible interpretations that Andrew lists:

> *The divine Gregory interpreted* the feet to refer to the economy according to the flesh. For the feet, having been added to Christ's deity, effected our salvation. And the feet are also the foundations of the church. And they

---

[7] Andrew of Caesarea, *Apocalypse*, 151
[8] Andrew of Caesarea, 151.
[9] Andrew of Caesarea, 133
[10] Gilbert K. Chesterton, *Orthodoxy* (New York: John Lane, 1909), 29, as cited by Tom Schreiner in the draft manuscript of his commentary on the Book of Revelation.

are 'like bronze incense,' which the medical people say, possesses a good smell when burned and which is called by them masculine incense. *There is another interpretation*: since the bronze refers to the human nature and the incense refers to the divine nature, through these is indicated the sweet odor of the faith and the unconfusedness of the unity. *Or another interpretation*: the bronze shows the euphony of the proclamation, while the incense shows the conversion of the nations, from which the bride is commanded to come. *The feet of Christ are also the apostles* who have been purified in the furnace of temptations according to the imitation of their teacher (emphasis added).

## CONCLUSION

I am honored to contribute this short essay in celebration of Tom Schreiner's sixty-fifth birthday and in recognition of his exemplary academic ministry. In sharing reflections and anecdotes about Tom's life, I hope to challenge readers to "follow Tom," as Tom follows Christ (see 1 Cor 11:1). In this chapter, I also hope to introduce modern readers to a faithful academic minister from 1,500 years ago, Andrew of Caesarea. The gracious scholarship and careful study of both Tom Schreiner and Andrew of Caesarea challenge us to Christian faithfulness in both life and doctrine (1 Tim 4:16).

# Chapter 19

# The Kingdom of God and the Public Square

*by Russell D. Moore*

From the moment that I met Tom Schreiner, I viewed him as though he were a kind of Sasquatch, a fleeting image of a reputedly mythical being one can see and record, but probably cannot verify the existence of to anyone who wasn't there themselves. I was a doctoral student, just arrived on the campus from Mississippi, and met the renowned new biblical scholar on the faculty, one of the wave of "northern evangelicals" brought in to reclaim orthodoxy as part of the vision of seminary president Albert Mohler. I had just read a book review by Schreiner in an academic journal, a review in which Schreiner articulated a particular view on the "third-wave" charismatic approach to spiritual gifts. I gathered up the nerve to ask the professor about his view and was stunned by his response. "That's a very flawed book review," he said. "I was wrong in my view, and have learned a great deal since I wrote it. I have another article coming out, actually taking almost the opposite view." He went on to say that after writing the review, a colleague had marshaled biblical arguments he hadn't considered, showing him where he was wrong. The debate wasn't unusual. What was unusual was that Schreiner considered the evidence and changed his mind. That almost never happens in academic circles of any sort. As a matter of fact, far more often such a critique leads to professional feuds that sometimes go on for decades, instead of a scholar concluding, "I was wrong on that one."

As the years went by, I ended up provost and dean at Southern Seminary, serving with Tom Schreiner as my associate dean and, as providence turns out, as my next-door neighbor. My initial sense of wonder at this humble, brilliant scholar never subsided. Many times I would say to seminary president Mohler,

"Tom Schreiner could be the silver-backed gorilla of this place, dominating everyone else, but he never does so. It's almost as though he doesn't even realize how big of a deal he is." Tom Schreiner was, after all, the most respected biblical scholar in Baptist life, arguably since Archibald T. Robertson roamed the same wing of Norton Hall. He published more than a committee of faculty members could, with shelves heaving with commentaries, biblical theologies, and articles in peer-reviewed journals. Someone with that much cache in an academic institution could easily wield some power. If nothing else, such a faculty member could demand to teach almost nothing, to devote himself to further research. Such a faculty member could make demands for pay, for recognition, for the best office, for the prime teaching hours. And such a faculty member could, if not granted such, just threaten to leave. I will admit now that had Tom Schreiner made such demands, I would have given him virtually anything he wanted that would have been allowed by the penal code or the seminary's doctrinal statement. He was the most important scholar we had, and I would not have ever wanted to lose him. But, if he knew that reality, he never once took advantage of it. He seemed, if not oblivious to his "power" in that setting, then at the very least uninterested and unimpressed with it.

In the evenings, my wife and I could look out our kitchen window and watch Tom and his wife, Diane, tending to the irises in their yard, transplanted from his family's flower nursery in Oregon. As we watched the couple in conversation, we would know that, whatever else they may be talking about, we could be sure of what they were not talking about—nursing some grudge at an academic rival. Instead, here there was kindness, gentleness, patience, self-control, humility—and a first-rate intellect, all at once.

"Academic power struggles are so vicious because the stakes are so small." I wish I could footnote this sentence, but I cannot, because there's hardly any consensus on who said it, or at least on who said some version of it first. Some variation on that quotation has been attributed to everyone from Samuel Johnson to political scientist Wallace Sayre to former Secretary of State Henry Kissinger. Perhaps that's an appropriate little irony that a statement about small-stakes academic wrangling is made in a quote academics could argue about endlessly as to who should get credit for crafting it. Nonetheless, the statement is quoted so often because almost anyone who has been in more than one faculty meeting can see at least some truth in it, whether that faculty meeting is at Springdale Consolidated Elementary School or at King's College, Oxford. Academic life is thought to be almost abstracted from human nature, the "ivory tower" of intellectuals aspiring to the purity of thought. And yet, few things can be as petty, and as incendiary, as academics at war with one another, using procedural syllabus votes and tenure reviews and disciplinary journal book reviews as weaponry.

In reality, though, the old saw is unfair to academics. The "red in tooth and claw" reality described here can be seen in virtually any human endeavor. In a question-and-answer session with high school students a year or so ago, one of them asked me how I managed the "stress" of appearing on television and dealing with the "hostile secular media." I shrugged and said that dealing with media is probably the least stressful thing I do. The church is where the Darwinian, power politics can be seen, and the sooner they get to know that, the better they will be at combatting cynicism. A Christian who had served in secular political life told me once how disoriented he was to serve on the board of his denomination, and to find carnal power struggles everywhere. "I would much rather be in the secular world where someone will scream profanities at me than with someone who will smile and say, 'So good to see you, sweet brother,' while they are plotting behind my back. At least with the first I know where I stand. The second seems sacrilegious." Human nature is fallen, and there is no arena of life that can serve as a holding area exempt from original sin. Nor is it fair of the old cliché about academic politics to imply that there's anything unique about the small-stakes of petty campus rivalries. The stakes are small all over, and that's nowhere more evident than in the so-called "political" divisiveness we see in American life.

When I say the stakes are small, I don't mean the issues aren't of importance—ultimately, of course, issues of statecraft could end up with a planet dead and irradiated by nuclear weaponry. I mean instead that the stakes are often not really the stakes. Many of the most contentious "battles" conducted in the American public square—whether on the floor of the United States Senate or on cable television talk shows or, perhaps most intensely, on social media platforms of people heatedly debating the issues of the day or the personalities behind those issues. For many years, we assumed that what kept America divided were ideologies—conservative versus progressive, that we were split apart by a culture war. If so, though, how do we explain the fact that central tenets of these ideologies can be thrown overboard, instantly, by partisans—not as the result of new data or a change of heart but simply on the basis of what "our side" (whatever the side is) now believes? This is because the issues weren't the basis of the division. They were just the tools of the warfare. At root, often, something else is afoot—namely the attempt to find something transcendent to believe, and some community to which to belong, something that can promise us significance, community, and power. In the contemporary American milieu, politics is the vehicle for all of that. That's one reason why American public life is so often mean, trivial, and devoid of character, integrity, or decency. Few really expect to *do* anything. They just want to "own" the other side, whether through a winning election or through a humiliating retort in cyberspace. The American public square has turned into one big faculty meeting, at some sort of shady, for-profit degree mill, where all the professors must scream and jump up and down in order to be noticed enough to gain tenure. After long enough, this starts to feel "normal." And, in one sense, it is.

Commentator Jonah Goldberg argues that Western civilization is on the verge of suicide, largely because we assume that civilization is itself the status quo. The status quo for humanity for most of our existence, Goldberg counters, is barbarism. The sort of civic life that is resolved through institutions devoted to stability and the common good is a relatively recent invention, and is a "miracle" in a human story largely defined by violence and misery.[1] Goldberg is certainly right about the threat of the present moment—with democratic norms and institutions globally imperiled by a rising tribalism of various forms of ethno-nationalism and authoritarianism of both the Left and the Right emerging in places thought to be long-ago made secure for constitutional order and freedom, even if he is wrong in his sometimes bleak Darwinian naturalism on the way to his conclusions. Goldberg fears that world order could easily slip back into animalistic survival-of-the-fittest tribe against tribe, and such would be awful. "It was inevitable when we stopped looking up to God for meaning and started looking down into ourselves that we would look to find fulfillment, belonging, and meaning in tribes and crowds," Goldberg asserts, and yet civilization requires quite the reverse from the hive-mind. "It takes moral leadership to keep a crowd from becoming a mob and losing its way," he concludes. "And moral leadership can come only from conversation, from reminding the crowds that their unity is a means, not an end."[2]

What Goldberg sees at this point should be starkly visible for Christians whose revelation warns us of the danger of an animalized humanity. Our story does indeed tell us what happens when a humanity created to image God starts to act like a "beast of the field" instead. Jewish philosopher Leon Kass, contemplating Genesis 3, notes that serpents "are often used as images both of voracity and of hyper-rationality. For the serpent is a mobile digestive tract that swallows its prey whole; in this sense the serpent stands for pure appetite."[3] Indeed, the New Testament applies this "pure appetite" to the motives of the spirit-behind-the-serpent. Satan is, the Apostle Peter warns, "a lion seeking whom he may devour" (1 Pet 5:8). This view of a bestialized, satanized humanity in which the appetites lead inevitably to violence is pictured repeatedly in Scripture, from the grasping Nebuchadnezzar who ends up irrational, eating grass like a beast in the field (Dan 4:33), to the panoramic view of the Apocalypse in which humanity, in asserting its own godhood, becomes

---

[1] Jonah Goldberg, *The Suicide of the West: How the Rebirth of Tribalism, Populism, Nationalism, and Identity Politics Is Destroying American Democracy* (New York: Crown Forum, 2018).

[2] Goldberg, 340–41.

[3] Leon R. Kass, *The Beginning of Wisdom: Reading Genesis* (Chicago: University of Chicago Press, 2003), 81.

a murderous "Beast" (Revelation 13). This is what Paul warns against when he confronts the Galatian church about the self-interested, appetite-driven "works of the flesh"—"For the whole law is fulfilled in one word: 'You shall love your neighbor as yourself.' But if you bite and devour one another, watch out that you are not consumed by one another" (Gal 5:14–15).

The world seems, at the moment, exhausted by the norms of liberal democracy that served to check and balance these fallen drives of humanity. Even in an American system where rakes and demagogues once felt the need to appeal to the idealisms of the founding era's Declaration of Independence, increasingly raw power is seen as its own justification. One need not "win" in order to carry out certain ideas. One needs instead to speak about ideas in order to "win," and to discard them, sometimes more or less immediately, when other ideas will "win" easier. It is no surprise then that we live in a moment in which many evangelicals are driven to near despair, some to crises of faith, over the American civic arena. In one sense, it seems ridiculous to think of the need to encourage evangelical Christians to "engage" in the public arena. After all, evangelicals seem to be not just engaged but obsessed with public life at the moment. When one looks beneath the surface, though, one realizes that those most identified as "evangelicals" in the secular political space are most often those who are not theologically robust, rooted in some intellectual or liturgical tradition but instead those who are the most entrepreneurial in the arenas of direct-mail fundraising or political mobilization. Within the so-called "evangelical movement," those who deny essential matters about the definition of the gospel—such as teachers of the heresy of the prosperity gospel—are received as "evangelicals" provided they are aligned on politics and "values." Meanwhile, the most politicized aspects of evangelicalism rarely articulate a vision of, say, justification by faith, but define themselves often with rigid boundaries around shared cultural memes or political personalities. It is no surprise then that the most theologically minded Christians of the coming generation are the most likely to want to walk away from the public square entirely. This has implications for the state as well as for the church because theologically defined evangelicalism is the only kind of evangelicalism reproducing itself in a secularizing American culture. The Left need not pretend to embrace a "Christian century" (as they once did), when identity politics and a Hegelian sense of history's onward march is all that's needed. And, increasingly, the intellectual energy on the Right that's heeded by the emerging generation is grounded in Darwinian biology, Jungian psychology, and its own kind of "blood-and-soil" identity politics. In such circles, "Christianity" is defined not in terms of the historical claim to a crucified-and-resurrected Messiah, or the gospel he has unveiled, but in terms of European "Christian" civilization—that is, an identification not with a church or with a Christ but with a culture.

For gospel Christians, in a time like this, there are no easy answers. What is clear, though, is that American Christianity faces a crisis of its own. American Christianity is old, sick, tired, and exhausted—and does not seem to recognize its state. American Christianity could, faced with undeniable currents of secularization, continue to deny the demographic realities in front of it, and collapse when the baby boomer generation of cultural Christianity is finally gone. American Christianity could also face the current moment by seeking to emulate the power struggles of the world around us. We could seek to join ourselves—as a remora to the underside of a shark—to some political leader or movement, of the Left or of the Right, promising us protection, power, and significance. Or, we could do something quite different. We could see the shaking of the old structures and idolatries around us as a sign to look for something we should have been seeking first all along—the kingdom of God.

The kingdom of God is the persistent problem of evangelical identity in the public square. Whatever the "shaking" going on in the world's political systems today, it can hardly be more shocking than the fall of the "eternal city" of Rome, signaling the collapse of the world order in the fifth century. Augustine of Hippo, though, pointed beyond the political catastrophe to a discourse on the distinction between the "City of Man" and the "City of God." What he was distinguishing, of course, were the kingdoms of this age from the kingdom of God. In much more recent times, American evangelicalism has sought to define itself in terms of the relation between the kingdom of God and the kingdoms of the world. As the contemporary American evangelical movement mobilized in the years after World War II, the kingdom of God was seen as a key obstacle. Evangelicals needed to avoid the pitfalls of the previous generation of conservative Protestants, who had splintered over secondary and tertiary matters. One could not, after all, form a National Association of Evangelicals to talk about "united action" rooted in the gospel if that association were consumed with debates over the proper mode of baptism or the meaning of the millennium in Revelation 20. It made sense to avoid doctrinal questions that were contentious between Bible-believing Christians. Many of the intramural debates of the time were related to the meaning of the kingdom of God.

Dispensationalists—a key part of the fundamentalist coalition against the modernists—saw the kingdom as an almost wholly future reality—a millennial reign centered around ethnically defined Israel, while those holding to various degrees of covenant theology emphasized the "present reality" of the kingdom—as those united to the presently reigning Christ were anointed with his Spirit. These battles over the kingdom—from Walter Rauschenbusch on the one side to Lewis Sperry Chafer on the other—were largely fought in an academic context, but that hardly meant they were "ivory tower" concerns. After all, these academic arguments filtered down to the popular level—a Christian man or woman who could hardly understand any of these debates might have Rauschenbusch's theology on his or her nightstand in the narrative of Charles Sheldon's popular novel *In His Steps*, or he or she might have the kingdom counterpoint on his or her kitchen table in the dispensationalist Scofield Study Bible.

Evangelical theologian Carl F. H. Henry saw this, rightly, as a problem. The lack of consensus about the kingdom of God meant that evangelicals were unable to provide an alternative to a liberal social gospel that downplayed personal sin, personal atonement, and personal regeneration, on the one hand, and a world-denying fundamentalism, on the other hand, that saw Christianity merely in terms of individual redemption while seeking to paper over an "uneasy conscience" on matters such as slavery, lynching, and racial bigotry.[4] Henry, and his compatriots, knew that an evangelicalism that avoided the subject of the kingdom for fear of fracturing alliances would have to avoid the topic of most of the Bible itself. Without a reflection on the kingdom of God, an evangelicalism would have to unhinge itself from the content of the *evangel*. Jesus, after all, said, "I must preach the good news of the kingdom of God to the other towns as well, for I was sent for this purpose" (Luke 4:43). Henry thus contrasted evangelical reticence about speaking too much of the kingdom of God with the witness of the New Testament: "There does not seem much apostolic apprehension over kingdom preaching."[5] Indeed, he argued, Jesus "proclaimed kingdom truth with a constant exuberant joy. It appears as the central theme of his preaching. To delete his kingdom references, parabolic and non-parabolic, would be to excise most of his words."[6]

Since the post war era, a startling consensus has emerged in evangelical scholarship on the kingdom, both in terms of the centrality of the kingdom as the integrating theme of the canon and in terms of the nature of the kingdom as both presently inaugurated and yet-to-be consummated.[7] Few must argue in the present milieu, as did Henry's contemporary George Eldon Ladd, that the kingdom of God has both an "already" and a "not yet" aspect.[8] Instead, most contemporary evangelical scholarship assumes an inaugurated eschatology, with the differences coming in terms of emphasis on the present or the

---

[4] Carl F. H. Henry, *The Uneasy Conscience of Modern Fundamentalism* (Grand Rapids: Eerdmans, 1947).
[5] Henry, 53.
[6] Henry, 52.
[7] I have traced this developing consensus out in *The Kingdom of Christ: The New Evangelical Perspective* (Wheaton, IL: Crossway, 2004).
[8] See, for instance, George Eldon Ladd, *Crucial Questions About the Kingdom of God* (Grand Rapids: Eerdmans, 1952); *The Gospel of the Kingdom: Scriptural Studies in the Kingdom of God* (Grand Rapids: Eerdmans, 1959); *New Testament Theology* (Grand Rapids: Eerdmans, 1974); *The Presence of the Future: The Eschatology of Biblical Realism* (Grand Rapids: Eerdmans, 1974).

future, much like the differences Mennonite scholar John Howard Yoder described, in a debate with Reformed theologian Richard Mouw, of the dueling emphases of Reformed and Anabaptist views of creation: "*created* but fallen" versus "created but *fallen*."[9] The scholarly debates now within the evangelical community on the kingdom are not "already" versus "not yet," but instead "*already* but not yet" versus "already but *not yet*."

Tom Schreiner's work in canonical, and especially, New Testament scholarship has been an important part of this development. His magnum opus *New Testament Theology*, for instance, starts with the crucial nature of the "already/ not yet" fulfillment of the kingdom in the person of Jesus of Nazareth, both in the Gospels and in the epistles.[10] The difficulties in distinguishing between the present reality and the future expectation of the kingdom are, Schreiner shows, by no means a recent development. He can thus show a key problem in the Corinthian church is an over realized eschatology. "The Corinthians may believe that they reign now, but Paul emphasizes that the kingdom will be consummated in the future," he writes. "Unfortunately, the Corinthians have forgotten the 'not yet' element relative to the kingdom of God."[11] Moreover, most of the work Schreiner has done on questions of, say, the relation between law and gospel and the relation between faith and works in perseverance are questions about inaugurated eschatology, about the kingdom of God. New Testament questions about the relevance of the Mosaic law are, after all, questions about how Jesus fulfills the purposes of Israel. Issues of Sabbath or of the Israelite civil code are not, then, just about how to interpret passages in Leviticus or Deuteronomy, but, more to the point, about how to read the whole Bible as centering on the glory of God in Jesus Christ.[12] How is the kingdom fulfilled in Jesus? Moreover, questions about the "warning passages" in the book of Hebrews are not simply about determining who is right in the Arminian/Calvinist debates over "eternal security." The question is what does it mean to enter the kingdom of God? This is especially relevant in a time when perhaps the most dangerous doctrinal error in Baptist life turned out to be not the old Arminian error countered in almost all of our doctrinal statements of the possibility of "falling away from grace" (though that is certainly an error), but the far more deadly error, which defines faith that is reduced to a one-time cognitive assent, divorced from ongoing repentance and following of Christ. To make such a claim, one must not only ignore much of what the

---

[9]  Richard J. Mouw, *Abraham Kuyper: A Short and Personal Introduction* (Grand Rapids: Eerdmans, 2011), 70.

[10]  Thomas R. Schreiner, *New Testament Theology: Magnifying God in Christ* (Grand Rapids: Baker, 2008), 41–118.

[11]  Thomas R. Schreiner, *Paul, Apostle of God's Glory in Christ: A Pauline Theology* (Downers Grove, IL: InterVarsity Press, 2001), 92.

[12]  Thomas R. Schreiner, *The Law and Its Fulfillment: A Pauline Theology of Law* (Grand Rapids: Baker, 1993).

New Testament (not just James, but Jesus and Paul as well) teaches on the "living" nature of faith, but one must also redefine what it means to inherit the kingdom of God, in light of, for instance 1 Cor 6:9–10. The kingdom, in such constructions, must be reduced to—in contradiction to two millennia of church teaching—the millennial era, so that repentant Christians gain the "rewards" of entrance to the kingdom while unrepentant Christians who reject the lordship of Christ are said to receive eternal life but will "inherit" one thousand years of glory. Schreiner's treatment of the "warning" passages in Hebrews and elsewhere takes seriously both the present and future aspects of the kingdom, and anchors, as does the canon, the kingdom to Christ himself. One cannot have the one without the other. To those religious leaders who sought the kingdom but did not want Jesus, Jesus announced, "The kingdom of God is in the midst of you" (Luke 17:21). Likewise, those who would want Jesus (or heaven through Jesus) without kingdom (voluntary submission to the reign of Jesus Christ) likewise will find that what God has joined together, they cannot tear asunder.

For Schreiner, the warnings and promises of God are the means God uses to spur believers onward in their pilgrimage into the eternal future. These warnings and promises are efficacious for those indwelled by the Holy Spirit. The sheep hear the voice of their Shepherd and, with many interventions from rod and staff, ultimately they follow him. That is a matter of exegetical interpretation, yes, and of practical moral application, yes, but it is, behind all of that, an explanation of the kingdom of God—what does it mean for Jesus to rule, now, and how are we being prepared, now, to rule with him. "Much of the theological wrangling that has taken place between Calvinists and Arminians, between defenders of so-called lordship-salvation and the self-designated advocates of free grace, has been due to a failure to take seriously and consistently the biblical evidence for the already-but-not-yet elements that fill the pages of the New Testament," Schreiner and his co-author Ardel Caneday write.[13] In this, we should be reminded how confusion about the kingdom of God can lead not just to intramural fractures, but, at the most extreme, to an obscuring of the gospel itself.

The scholarly division within evangelicalism over the kingdom of God may have grown toward consensus, but the grassroots confusion over the kingdom might be as deep and wide as ever. This has less to do with elaborate dispensationalist theories (which are if not extinct then certainly endangered species) and more to do with a popular biblical illiteracy, in which the Bible is more a mine for memes than a "strange new world" of narrative the reader

---

[13] Thomas R. Schreiner and Ardel B. Caneday, *The Race Set before Us: A Biblical Theology of Perseverance and Assurance* (Downers Grove, IL: InterVarsity Press, 2001), 44.

enters. Many can quote Jeremiah: "For I know the plans I have for you, declares the Lord, plans for welfare and not for evil, to give you a future and a hope" (Jer 29:11). And yet few of those so doing know anything about the exile Jeremiah foresaw, of the new covenant he foretold, of where this promise fits with the rest of the prophecy of Jeremiah, much less the rest of the canon. Without this, though, we end up with no knowledge of who the "you" are to whom God promised a "future," no sense of what this "hope" would actually look like. Few are now arguing that the Lord's Prayer or the Beatitudes are irrelevant to the church, applying only to the "kingdom people" of some future Israelite state. And yet, this does not mean the prayer of the kingdom or the announcement of the way of the kingdom seem any less distant from us. As Walker Percy put it a generation ago, about the Christ-haunted Bible Belt American South: "And how curiously foreign to the South sound the Decalogue, the Beatitudes, the doctrine of the Mystical Body."[14]

Evangelical misfires in the public square—whether in attempts at a shrugging dismissal of concern for the social and civil aspects of maintaining justice for neighbor or in an idolatrous political identity for the people of God—are more than just symptoms of a flawed mode of public engagement (though they are certainly that).[15] They are, like the various antinomianisms and legalisms that war against a gospel understanding of personal discipleship, a sign that something has gone awry in our view of the kingdom of God. This should concern us as Christians, whatever our concerns or interests as citizens. After all, the kingdom is not some abstract concept but the reigning authority and presence of Jesus himself. Without the kingdom, there is no gospel. Jesus is, after all, the "Christ," that is, the Spirit-anointed king of the seed of Abraham, of the tribe of Judah, of the house of David. An evangelical Christianity centered on Christ is then, by necessity, to be centered on the kingdom of God. And, since Jesus told Nicodemus, that "Truly, truly I say unto you, unless one is born again he cannot see the kingdom of God" (John 3:3), a born-again Christian must, by necessity, be defined around the kingdom of God. Otherwise, the question is, born again into what? As Schreiner rightly underscores, even the most basic evangelistic aspect of the "Romans Road" to personal conversion—the confession of Jesus as Lord and belief in the heart that God has raised him from the dead—is a conviction about the kingdom of God. "The Old Testament teaches that Israel's rule over the world will be theirs at the resurrection (Isa 26:19; Ezek 37:1–14; Dan 12:1–3; Hos 5:15–6:3; cf. 2 Macc 7), and the resurrection is the inauguration of the new age," Schreiner writes. "Paul argues that the

---

[14] Walker Percy, *Signposts in a Strange Land* (New York: Farrar, Straus, Giroux, 1991), 84.
[15] For a compelling case for the failure of evangelical attempts at political engagement, see James Davison Hunter, *To Change the World: The Irony, Tragedy, and Possibility of Christianity in the Late Modern World* (New York: Oxford University Press, 2010).

promised resurrection has begun in the resurrection of Jesus (Rom 1:4), and thus the new age has arrived and Jesus is Lord."[16]

A deep eschatology is necessary for evangelical public engagement, furthermore, because the concept of the kingdom—as understood canonically and covenantally—is what prevents such public engagement from veering off into utopianism or dystopianism, both of which lead ultimately to disillusioned cynicism. Against a cultural and political moment defined by illusions of permanent victory or permanent defeat, an evangelical view of the kingdom of God sees the present age as a spiritual battle-zone, in which the kingdom marches forward invisibly in the midst of, in every era, opposition and spiritual darkness. That darkness is not defined exclusively by one set of ideologies or another but by "the flesh," the creaturely attempt to set humanity up as its own god. There are false messiahs everywhere, including in each of our own hearts, left to ourselves. Without a strong sense of the already and the not yet, we can easily find ourselves seeking to fight social Darwinism with social Darwinism, Nietzschean power worship with our own Nietzschean power worship. And in so doing, we can repeat the errors of our Israelite ancestors as outlined in the book of Isaiah (as well as over and over again in the other major and minor prophets). As Schreiner points out, "Yahweh pledged that he would rescue his people from Sennacherib, but they wanted something more practical and concrete to cling to. They formed an alliance with Egypt to gain security from the Egyptian threat."[17]

Such is hardly an abstract threat, and is not a threat susceptible to only by the people of God, to substitute another totalizing kingdom for the kingdom of God. See, for instance, the work of the atheist "transhumanist" Ray Kurzweil, who advocates downloading human consciousness into hard drives, thus ensuring immortality, and the construction of artificial intelligences that can transcend humanity. As philosopher John Gray notes, Kurzweil's book *The Singularity Is Near* is a clear allusion to, of all people, John the Baptist, in his proclamation "the kingdom of heaven is near" (Matt 3:2).[18] There will always be human beings seeking to substitute other kingdoms—whether political, cultural, or technological—to fill their inchoate longings for peace, order, power, glory, significance, and escape from the void of death. Christians must be those who can remind them, and ourselves, that all kingdoms are but dust,

---

[16] Thomas R. Schreiner, *Paul,* 165; see also Schreiner, *Romans,* Baker Exegetical Commentary on the New Testament (Grand Rapids: Baker, 1998), 37–45.

[17] Thomas R. Schreiner, *The King in His Beauty: A Biblical Theology of the Old and New Testaments* (Grand Rapids: Baker, 2013), 328.

[18] John Gray, *Seven Types of Atheism* (London: Allen Lane, 2018), 66–67; Ray Kurzweil, *The Singularity Is Near: When Humans Transcend Biology* (New York: Penguin, 2006).

save the kingdom of the house of David summed up in the God-man Jesus of Nazareth, reigning right now from heaven.

A focus on the kingdom of God defines then for the church what matters, and who matters. When Jesus unveiled his kingdom in his inaugural sermon in his hometown synagogue, he spoke of the fulfillment of the Year of Jubilee— good news for the poor, for the blind, for the prisoners (Luke 4:18–19). He pointedly demonstrated that this future kingdom—where those often ignored in the present are set free—has present implications, tearing down the idolatries of tribal senses of superiority, which are, themselves, merely expressions of idolatry (Luke 4:25–27). In a fallen world, decisions in the public square are made often in terms of what constituency is the most powerful—economically or socially or politically. The kingdom reframes such expectations. "Listen, my beloved brothers," James writes, "Has not God chosen those who are poor in the world to be rich in faith and heirs of the kingdom, which he has promised to those who love him" (Jas 2:5). Again, that future kingdom vision has present implications, James contends: "But you have dishonored the poor man" (Jas 2:6). These priorities do not translate into a comprehensive public policy, but they do shape and form the consciences of the church to ask who is kept invisible by the principalities and powers around us, and to ask why.

A wise friend once told me that a surefire way to see where one's deepest affections lie is to see what most easily inflames one's emotions. It is here that we see the massive gap between our own cultural and subcultural foment and the emotional life of Jesus. Jesus cared about Caesar's coin questions (Matt 22:21). Yet, those questions did not dominate his emotional energy. He felt more than free to denounce Herod as a "fox"—in context, a withering repudiation—but he kept right on walking toward Golgotha (Luke 13:32). Caesar never prompted Jesus to rejoice (Luke 10:21), and he never prompted him to sweat blood. Why? Jesus saw the transcendence of the kingdom of God—a kingdom rooted in the bloody cross of substitutionary atonement, a kingdom that would, by God's sovereign purpose, triumph over all rivals. Jesus was tranquil before the state, and passionate about the church.

When a religion reflects a different set of priorities, that religion is following something or someone other than Jesus. Indeed, much of what emotionally mobilizes the twenty-first century North American church is not related to Christian life and doctrine and mission at all, but to "Christianity" defined as a set of cultural values under siege by the dominant culture.

Indeed, it is hard to keep up with a politically defined religion. After all, the values one would need to affirm to be "in the tribe" in one year might well be those that don't matter in the next. The cultural degradations one would denounce loudly, right along with the rest of one's politically or culturally or ethnically defined herd, in one year would become acceptable in the next, just depending on the pet sins and injustices of one's "side" and its reigning personalities of the moment. What would be characterized as watching at the wall of righteousness in one year might well be deemed pharisaical self-righteousness in another, not because of some exegetical development but because what was at stake all along was never the Bible but the interests of the "side." Such is inevitable whenever Christianity is identified with a cultural or political system rather than with the transcendent theological claim of the multinational, multiethnic, multigenerational kingdom of God, which joins heaven to earth in the person of Jesus Christ (Eph 1:9–22). A church freed to seek first the kingdom would not sideline social ethics. The Bible defines what justice is, and calls us to pursue it. But a church that follows the kingdom of God, not any substitute, will be defined by the Bible, and not adjust what we speak to and what we keep silent about on the basis of what's counted important or useful by some ideology or movement.

That's what I've learned the most from the life and scholarship of Tom Schreiner, though I don't recall ever having a single conversation with him or reading a single word he's written on the so-called "public square." Instead, though, I saw him model a kingdom-first mentality, by pursuing academic excellence without idolizing academic success, of pouring himself into his life as a professor without finding his identity there, of holding strong convictions but never at the expense of Spirit-driven kindness. Instead, I saw someone who held every temporal thing lightly. Rather than grasping and clawing for his place at the table—whatever table—he shrugged off both accolades and criticisms, as he looked toward another kingdom, a different glory. If more of us did the same, we might see the evangelical witness in the public square transformed, and in the private square as well. We might grow to be known for our peace, love, gentleness, and patience, and all because we know that there is so much, and so little, at stake.

# Afterword: A Personal Reflection

*by Patrick Schreiner*

I f you have read portions of this book, then your wheels probably turn on biblical scholarship. You love a good argument, biblical history, and precise grammatical analysis with a theological backbone.

But if you think my father is defined by these things then you would be mistaken.

Most people only saw pieces of his life—the books, lectures, sermons, and conference presentations. But I want you to know the man behind the books, behind the lectern, behind the pulpit. I want to focus on the things you might not know.

These things don't get written in commentaries, or biblical theologies, or Pauline theologies, yet these things make men stand tall.

Three things are worth overviewing that might otherwise get neglected. They include (1) a history of his life, (2) reflection on our family dynamics, and (3) a few ministry notes.

My aim is to honor my father, showing you that his personal life was a tapestry of double love for God and others. As Augustine said, "So anyone who thinks that he has understood the divine scriptures or any part of them, but cannot by his understanding build up this double love of God and neighbor, has not yet succeeded in understanding them."[1]

From my perspective, he succeeded in understanding the divine Scriptures because he lived them.

---

[1] Saint Augustine, *On Christian Teaching,* trans. R. P. H. Green (Oxford: Oxford University Press, 1997), 76.

## HISTORY

Tom Schreiner was born in 1954 in Salem, Oregon. He and his family lived on land just off Interstate 5 and Quinaby Road. His early memories were of being outdoors, working on the farm, and getting into trouble with his younger brother Patrick. He has never really lost the relaxed West Coast air, although he now resides in Southern panache. For example, last summer he got really excited about finding sweatpants that look just like jeans.

He was the son of a nurseryman, and the brother of seven siblings. His father, Gus, was a jolly man, who had a loud booming voice, smoked three packs of cigarettes a day, struck fear in the hearts of his children, but could also make them laugh the loudest. His mother, Patricia, was gentle but forthright. The family was Catholic and he grew up going to mass. Even today, when they get together as a family, the decibel level rises to inordinate heights with all the laughter and talking, something our family happily inherited.

He became a Christian in high school through the ministry of Diane Pike, his future wife. He remembers being shocked and impressed with the personal nature of her relationship with God. God was not something just done on Sunday, but someone who defined the word "life." His ministry, in many ways, cannot be spoken of in completeness without speaking of his wife.

Diane Pike and Tom Schreiner were married on June 20, 1975. They spent their youthful days ministering in the local church together, a ministry he would never leave on the curb in pursuit of scholarship. He began to hunger for more confidence and knowledge in interpreting God's Word and therefore enrolled at Western Seminary in Portland for his MDiv and his ThM (Old Testament). Later, he studied under Donald Hagner at Fuller Seminary and earned his doctor of philosophy in New Testament. He was a Bible man through and through, knowing Hebrew and Greek and learning tracing from Hagner.

His first teaching job was at Azusa Pacific in Southern California in 1984. Shortly afterward, Bethel Seminary in St. Paul, Minnesota, called him to teach. He spent eleven years at Bethel teaching and ministering to students preparing for ministry. He was also an elder at Bethlehem Baptist Church during his time in Minnesota. I remember him telling me one time that when the family moved to Minnesota he was almost at the point of giving up on the church because of the lackluster theological feebleness and exegetical woes he was hearing from the pulpit. That changed when he heard John Piper, a preacher who combined strong theological convictions, the gift of communication, and hyphenated words.

In 1997, the family moved to Louisville, KY, for him to be a part of the faculty at The Southern Baptist Theological Seminary. He has told me that he has never felt so at home as he does at Southern, and he never stops speaking about how thankful he is to have a theologian leading the school as president. He has been teaching there ever since and has spent most of his time pastoring at Clifton Baptist Church. In 2015, he stepped down as preaching pastor to pass the baton to the next generation, although he still remains an elder.

## FAMILY DYNAMIC

I could tell many stories about my family life. Some would be endearing, and others would make you laugh. I have told some of these other stories publicly so I will focus on one recent situation that revealed his character.

I am currently sitting in my office at Western Seminary surrounded by books my dad gave me. Three years ago to the day, my mom was in a bicycle accident where she was on the verge of losing her life. Our family is not what you would call the affectionate type. This does not mean that I failed to see my mom and dad loving each other, but I didn't see it in an overtly physical or affectionate way.

But when my mom had her accident something clicked in my dad. It was as if a light had turned on that he could lose his wife. Throughout the time in the hospital, he rarely left her side. He clung to her at the beginning, begging her to live. He cried over her, sang over her, read Scripture over her, and prayed for her. He was like Velcro, clinging to her with all his might.

After many weeks, when she began to regain consciousness, there was a new appreciation in his eyes for her. It was not that they had a bad relationship before this, because their love was always vibrant and strong. But now the relationship had changed. He held her hand more; he looked at her differently.

I wanted to tell this story because in some circles my dad might be known for his complementarian position. I have seen snarky Facebook comments from people who don't know him. I have read pieces attempting to slash through his arguments, but they have not really bothered me. I just laugh each time, because I watched my mom and dad's relationship.

Now this is anecdotal evidence that does not prove his arguments on this position. There are many people on both sides of this debate who have admirable family relationships. My point is simply that he lived his convictions. Or as a more reputable source (Augustine) said, "Faith will start tottering if the authority of scripture is undermined; then with faith tottering, charity itself also begins to sicken."[2]

---

[2] Augustine, *Teaching Christianity* (*De Doctrina Christiana*), ed. John E. Rotelle; trans. Edmund Hill (New York: New City Press, 1996), 124.

My dad held to his convictions and his love for my mom did not sicken. Theology and praxis united in his life. He hasn't merely written about family and church dynamics—he lived them.

## MINISTRY NOTES

You might think those who write books spend most of their time in isolation. It is true; isolation is necessary to write a book. But what I remember growing up was that our house was always swarming with guests. His life was a relational symphony. Missionaries, students, church members, old friends, new friends, and neighbors would come to visit.

Although overwhelming at times, points to a few realities. My parents were people who desired to know and be known by people. They wanted people in the living rooms of their lives. They formed friendships quickly, and these friendships rarely petered out. All sorts of people were friends with them. This was probably a result of natural friendliness, an unassuming nature, but also a deep love for people. There were the old, the young, the working class, the rich, the racially diverse, countryfolk, and the guests who stayed way too long. Once the kids were out of the house, it basically became a regular bed and breakfast for friends from ages past.

He was not one to shun personal interaction because he wanted to write the next book. Writing and interaction were both interconnected like a diamond on a ring. The pages of his theology had faces written over and under them.

As I already mentioned, you can't really speak about my dad without speaking about my mom. Although mom's name is not printed on the bottom of the books, her ministry is woven through every line. They are true partners in ministry.

Their ministry also extended beyond their local house with their financial generosity. The way they have been able to do this is by living annoyingly simple lives (I say annoying because I had to live with it!).

Their microwave is over twenty years old and takes forever to heat up things. When the oven went out in the house, my mom went out and tried to find one exactly like it. A student once commented that their economical rental place had the same oven. When you walk into their closet you can count on one hand the clothes they have bought in the last five years. The fridge at the house is regularly empty; I still have no idea what my parents eat. Their bathrooms and kitchens are long overdue for an update. The never-dying, never-changing microwave is an allegory for their life.

Because of all of this, they have more money to give to others—missionaries, the church, and individuals. I know very few people who live with such simplicity and also live so generously.

## CONCLUSION

I have given three brief snapshots of my dad because knowing the Scriptures is about knowing the one who is the Word. My dad knows the Scriptures intellectually, but he also knows that knowledge is nothing unless it builds up. All knowledge is vain without sound ethics. My dad loves people, he loves his family, he loves God, he loves the Scriptures, he loves teaching, he loves his wife.

His most important work has been the life he has written, into me and the others around him, and he is still writing it.

You can read his books, you can listen to his lectures, but I have read and listened to his life. Whether it was at home, in the pulpit, behind the lectern, or in his La-Z-Boy chair writing his books, he sought to please the Messiah in all he did.

To God be the glory.

# Bibliography of the Writings
# of Thomas R. Schreiner

*Compiled by Joshua M. Greever*

## BOOKS

### Single-author

*1, 2 Peter, Jude.* New American Commentary. Nashville, TN: B&H, 2003.

*1 Corinthians: An Introduction and Commentary.* Tyndale New Testament Commentary. Downers Grove, IL: InterVarsity Press, 2018.

*40 Questions About Christians and Biblical Law.* Grand Rapids, MI: Kregel, 2010.

*Commentary on Hebrews.* Biblical Theology for Christian Proclamation. Nashville, TN: B&H, 2015.

*Covenant and God's Purpose for the World.* Short Studies in Biblical Theology. Wheaton, IL: Crossway, 2017.

*Faith Alone: The Doctrine of Justification: What the Reformers Taught . . . and Why It Still Matters.* The Five Solas. Grand Rapids, MI: Zondervan, 2015.

*Galatians.* Zondervan Exegetical Commentary on the New Testament. Grand Rapids, MI: Zondervan, 2010.

*Interpreting the Pauline Epistles.* Grand Rapids, MI: Baker, 1990; 2nd ed., 2011.

*The King in His Beauty: A Biblical Theology of the Old and New Testaments.* Grand Rapids, MI: Baker, 2013.

*The Law and Its Fulfillment: A Pauline Theology of Law.* Grand Rapids, MI: Baker, 1993.

*Magnifying God in Christ: A Summary of New Testament Theology*. Grand Rapids, MI: Baker, 2010.

*New Testament Theology: Magnifying God in Christ*. Grand Rapids, MI: Baker, 2008.

*Paul, Apostle of God's Glory in Christ: A Pauline Theology*. Downers Grove, IL: InterVarsity Press 2001.

*Romans*. Baker Exegetical Commentary on the New Testament. Grand Rapids, MI: Baker, 1998; 2nd ed., 2018.

*Run to Win the Prize: Perseverance in the New Testament*. Wheaton, IL: Crossway, 2010.

### Co-author

Schreiner, Thomas R., and Ardel B. Caneday. *The Race Set before Us: A Biblical Theology of Perseverance and Assurance*. Downers Grove, IL: InterVarsity Press 2001.

### Edited

Alexander, T. Desmond, Andreas J. Köstenberger, and Thomas R. Schreiner, eds. *Biblical Theology for Christian Proclamation Commentary*. Nashville, TN: B&H, 2015–present.

Crawford, Matthew R., and Thomas R. Schreiner, eds. *The Lord's Supper: Remembering and Proclaiming Christ Until He Comes*. NAC Studies in Bible and Theology 10. Nashville, TN: B&H, 2010.

Grudem, Wayne, C. John Collins, and Thomas R. Schreiner, eds. *Understanding the Big Picture of the Bible: A Guide to Reading the Bible Well*. Wheaton, IL: Crossway, 2012.

Grudem, Wayne, C. John Collins, and Thomas R. Schreiner, eds. *Understanding Scripture: An Overview of the Bible's Origins, Reliability, and Meaning*. Wheaton, IL: Crossway, 2012.

Köstenberger, Andreas J., Thomas R. Schreiner, and H. Scott Baldwin, eds. *Women in the Church: A Fresh Analysis of 1 Timothy 2:9–15*. Grand Rapids, MI: Baker, 1995; 2nd ed.: *Women in the Church: An Analysis and Application of 1 Timothy 2:9–15*, 2005; 3rd ed.: *Women in the Church: An Interpretation and Application of 1 Timothy 2:9–15*, Wheaton, IL: Crossway, 2016.

Merkle, Benjamin L., and Thomas R. Schreiner, eds. *Shepherding God's Flock: Biblical Leadership in the New Testament and Beyond*. Grand Rapids, MI: Kregel, 2014.

Schreiner, Thomas R., and Bruce A. Ware, eds. *The Grace of God, the Bondage of the Will*. 2 vols. Grand Rapids, MI: Baker, 1995. Repr., *Still Sovereign: Contemporary Perspectives on Election, Foreknowledge, and Grace*. Grand Rapids, MI: Baker, 2000.

Schreiner, Thomas R., and Shawn D. Wright, eds. *Believer's Baptism: Sign of the New Covenant in Christ*. NAC Studies in Bible and Theology 2. Nashville, TN: B&H, 2006.

## CHAPTERS IN BOOKS

"Baptism in the Epistles: An Initiation Rite for Believers." Pages 67–96 in *Believer's Baptism: Sign of the New Covenant in Christ*. Edited by Thomas R. Schreiner and Shawn D. Wright. NAC Studies in Bible and Theology 2. Nashville, TN: B&H, 2006.

"A Biblical Theology of the Glory of God." Pages 215–34 in *For the Fame of God's Name: Essays in Honor of John Piper*. Edited by Sam Storms and Justin Taylor. Wheaton, IL: Crossway, 2010.

"Does Romans 9 Teach Individual Election unto Salvation?" Pages 89–106 in vol. 1 of *The Grace of God, the Bondage of the Will*. Edited by Thomas R. Schreiner and Bruce A. Ware. Grand Rapids, MI: Baker, 1995. Repr., pages 89–106 in *Still Sovereign: Contemporary Perspectives on Election, Foreknowledge, and Grace*. Grand Rapids, MI: Baker, 2000.

"Does Scripture Teach Prevenient Grace in the Wesleyan Sense?" Pages 365–82 in vol. 2 of *The Grace of God, the Bondage of the Will*. Edited by Thomas R. Schreiner and Bruce A. Ware. Grand Rapids, MI: Baker, 1995. Repr., pages 229–46 in *Still Sovereign: Contemporary Perspectives on Election, Foreknowledge, and Grace*. Grand Rapids, MI: Baker, 2000.

"Good-bye and Hello: The Sabbath Command for New Covenant Believers." Pages 159–88 in *Progressive Covenantalism: Charting a Course between Dispensational and Covenant Theologies*. Nashville, TN: B&H, 2016.

"Head Coverings, Prophecies, and the Trinity: 1 Corinthians 11:2–16." Pages 124–39 in *Recovering Biblical Manhood and Womanhood: A Response to Evangelical Feminism*. Edited by Wayne C. Grudem and John Piper. Wheaton, IL: Crossway, 2006.

"In My Place Condemned He Stood." Pages 43–46 in *Risking the Truth: Interviews on Handling Truth and Error in the Church*. Edited by Martin Downes. Fearn, Ross-shire, Scotland: Christian Focus, 2009.

"An Interpretation of 1 Timothy 2:9–15: A Dialogue with Scholarship." Pages 163–226 in *Women in the Church: An Interpretation and Application of 1 Timothy 2:9–15*. 3rd ed. Edited by Andreas J. Köstenberger and Thomas R. Schreiner. Wheaton, IL: Crossway, 2016.

"Interpreting the Pauline Epistles." Pages 412–32 in *Interpreting the New Testament: Essays on Methods and Issues*. Edited by David Alan Black and David S. Dockery. Nashville, TN: B&H, 2001.

"Justification apart from and by Works: At the Final Judgment Works Will Confirm Justification." Pages 71–98 in *Four Views on the Role of Works at the*

*Final Judgment.* Edited by Alan P. Stanley. Counterpoints. Grand Rapids, MI: Zondervan, 2013.

"New Dimensions in New Testament Theology." Pages 46–68 in *New Dimensions in Evangelical Thought: Essays in Honor of Millard J. Erickson.* Edited by David S. Dockery. Downers Grove, IL: InterVarsity Press 1998.

"Original Sin and Original Death: Romans 5:12–19." Pages 271–88 in *Adam, the Fall, and Original Sin: Theological, Biblical, and Scientific Perspectives.* Edited by Hans Madueme and Michael Reeves. Grand Rapids, MI: Baker, 2014.

"Overseeing and Serving the Church in the Pastoral and General Epistles." Pages 89–117 in *Shepherding God's Flock: Biblical Leadership in the New Testament and Beyond.* Edited by Benjamin L. Merkle and Thomas R. Schreiner. Grand Rapids, MI: Kregel, 2014.

"Paul: A Reformed Reading." Pages 19–47 in *Four Views on the Apostle Paul.* Edited by Michael F. Bird. Counterpoints. Grand Rapids, MI: Zondervan, 2012.

"Penal Substitution View." Pages 67–98 in *The Nature of the Atonement: Four Views.* Edited by James K. Beilby and Paul R. Eddy. Downers Grove, IL: InterVarsity Press 2006.

"Reading the Epistles." Pages 128–34 in *Understanding the Big Picture of the Bible: A Guide to Reading the Bible Well.* Edited by Wayne C. Grudem, John Collins, and Thomas R. Schreiner. Wheaton, IL: Crossway, 2012.

"The Theology of the New Testament." Pages 109–17 in *Understanding the Big Picture of the Bible: A Guide to Reading the Bible Well.* Edited by Wayne C. Grudem, John Collins, and Thomas R. Schreiner. Wheaton, IL: Crossway, 2012.

"Understanding Truth according to Paul." Pages 259–73 in *Studies in the Pauline Epistles: Essays in Honor of Douglas J. Moo.* Edited by Matthew S. Harmon and Jay E. Smith. Grand Rapids, MI: Zondervan, 2014.

"The Valuable Ministries of Women in the Context of Male Leadership: A Survey of Old and New Testament Examples and Teaching." Pages 209–24 in *Recovering Biblical Manhood and Womanhood: A Response to Evangelical Feminism.* Edited by Wayne C. Grudem and John Piper. Wheaton, IL: Crossway, 2006.

"Women in Ministry." Pages 177–235 in *Two Views on Women in Ministry.* Edited by James R. Beck and Craig L. Blomberg. Counterpoints. Grand Rapids, MI: Zondervan, 2001.

## DISSERTATION

"Circumcision: An Entrée into 'Newness' in Pauline Thought." PhD diss., Fuller Theological Seminary, 1983.

## JOURNAL ARTICLES

"The Abolition and Fulfillment of the Law in Paul." *Journal for the Study of the New Testament* 35 (1989): 47–74.

"Another Look at the New Perspective." *The Southern Baptist Journal of Theology* 14.3 (2010): 4–18.

"A Biblical Theologian Reviews Gerald Bray's *Systematic Theology*." *Themelios* 39.1 (2014): 9–16.

"A Building from God—2 Corinthians 5:1–10." *The Southern Baptist Journal of Theology* 19.3 (2015): 121–29.

"The Centrality of God in New Testament Theology." *The Southern Baptist Journal of Theology* 16.1 (2012): 4–17.

"The Church as the New Israel and the Future of Ethnic Israel in Paul." *Studia Biblica et Theologica* 13 (1983): 17–38.

"Corporate and Individual Election in Romans 9: A Response to Brian Abasciano." *The Journal of the Evangelical Theological Society* 49 (2006): 373–86.

"Did Paul Believe in Justification by Works? Another Look at Romans 2." *Bulletin for Biblical Research* 3 (1993): 131–58.

"Does Romans 9 Teach Individual Election unto Salvation? Some Exegetical and Theological Reflections." *The Journal of the Evangelical Theological Society* 36 (1993): 25–40.

"From Adam to Christ: The Grace That Conquers All Our Sin (Romans 5:12–19)." *The Southern Baptist Journal of Theology* 15.1 (2011): 80–90.

"Interpreting the Pauline Epistles." *The Southern Baptist Journal of Theology* 3.3 (1999): 4–21.

"Is Perfect Obedience to the Law Possible? A Re-examination of Galatians 3:10." *The Journal of the Evangelical Theological Society* 27 (1984): 151–60.

"Israel's Failure to Attain Righteousness in Romans 9:30–10:3." *Trinity Journal* 12 (1991): 209–20.

"Justification by Works and *Sola Fide*." *The Southern Baptist Journal of Theology* 19.4 (2015): 39–58.

"Justification: The Saving Righteousness of God in Christ." *The Journal of the Evangelical Theological Society* 54 (2011): 19–34.

"Loving One Another Fulfills the Law: Romans 13:8–10." *The Southern Baptist Journal of Theology* 11.3 (2007): 104–09.

"An Old Perspective on the New Perspective." *Concordia Journal* 35 (2009): 140–55.

"A New Testament Perspective on Homosexuality." *Themelios* 31.3 (2006): 62–75.

"*Paul and Gender*: A Review Article." *Themelios* 43.2 (2018): 178–92.

"*Paul and the Gift*: A Review Article." *Themelios* 41.1 (2016): 52–58.

"Paul and Perfect Obedience to the Law: An Evaluation of the View of E. P. Sanders." *Westminster Theological Journal* 47 (1985): 245–78.

"Paul's Place in the Story: N. T. Wright's Vision of Paul." *Journal for the Study of Paul and His Letters* 4 (2014): 1–26.

"Paul's View of the Law in Romans 10:4–5." *Westminster Theological Journal* 55 (1993): 113–35.

"Perseverance and Assurance: A Survey and a Proposal." *The Southern Baptist Journal of Theology* 2.1 (1998): 32–62.

"Preaching and Biblical Theology." *The Southern Baptist Journal of Theology* 10.2 (2006): 20–29.

"*Reading Romans Theologically*: A Review Article." *The Journal of the Evangelical Theological Society* 41 (1998): 641–50.

"Response to Gerald Bray." *Themelios* 39.1 (2014): 26–28.

"Some Reflections on *Sola Fide*." *The Journal of the Evangelical Theological Society* 58 (2015): 5–14.

"William J. Webb's *Slaves, Women, and Homosexuals*: A Review Article." *The Southern Baptist Journal of Theology* 6.1 (2002): 46–64.

"'Works of Law' in Paul." *Novum Testamentum* 33 (1991): 217–244.

## DICTIONARY ARTICLES

"Circumcision." Pages 137–39 in *Dictionary of Paul and His Letters: A Compendium of Contemporary Biblical Scholarship*. Edited by Gerald F. Hawthorne, Ralph P. Martin, and Daniel G. Reid. Downers Grove, IL: InterVarsity Press 1996.

"Commandments." Pages 238–41 in *Dictionary of the Later New Testament and Its Developments: A Compendium of Contemporary Biblical Scholarship*. Edited by Ralph P. Martin and Peter H. Davids. Downers Grove, IL: InterVarsity Press 1997.

"Law." Pages 644–49 in *Dictionary of the Later New Testament and Its Developments: A Compendium of Contemporary Biblical Scholarship*. Edited by Ralph P. Martin and Peter H. Davids. Downers Grove, IL: InterVarsity Press, 1997.

"Law of Christ." Pages 542–44 in *Dictionary of Paul and His Letters: A Compendium of Contemporary Biblical Scholarship*. Edited by Gerald F. Hawthorne, Ralph P. Martin, and Daniel G. Reid. Downers Grove, IL: InterVarsity Press, 1993.

"Obedience and Lawlessness." Pages 821–23 in *Dictionary of the Later New Testament and Its Developments: A Compendium of Contemporary Biblical Scholarship*. Edited by Ralph P. Martin and Peter H. Davids. Downers Grove, IL: InterVarsity Press 1997.

"Works of the Law." Pages 975–79 in *Dictionary of Paul and His Letters: A Compendium of Contemporary Biblical Scholarship*. Edited by Gerald F. Hawthorne, Ralph P. Martin, and Daniel G. Reid. Downers Grove, IL: InterVarsity Press 1993.

## BOOK REVIEWS

Review of A. Andrew Das, *Paul and the Jews*. *The Southern Baptist Journal of Theology* 8.3 (2004): 114–15.

Review of A. Andrew Das, *Paul, the Law, and the Covenant*. *The Southern Baptist Journal of Theology* 6.3 (2002): 110–12.

Review of A. Andrew Das and Frank J. Matera, eds., *The Forgotten God: Perspectives in Biblical Theology*. *The Southern Baptist Journal of Theology* 7.3 (2003): 81–83.

Review of Abraham J. Malherbe, *Paul and the Popular Philosophers*. *Themelios* 17.1 (1991): 29–30.

Review of Alan J. Thompson, *The Acts of the Risen Lord Jesus: Luke's Account of God's Unfolding Plan*. *Themelios* 36.3 (2011): 517–19.

Review of Andreas J. Köstenberger, L. Scott Kellum, and Charles L. Quarles, *The Cradle, the Cross, and the Crown: An Introduction to the New Testament*. *Themelios* 35.1 (2010): 87–88.

Review of Arland J. Hultgren, *The Parables of Jesus: A Commentary*. *The Southern Baptist Journal of Theology* 7.3 (2003): 89–90.

Review of Brian J. Abasciano, *Paul's Use of the Old Testament in Romans 9:10–18: An Intertextual and Theological Exegesis*. *Themelios* 38.3 (2013): 450–53.

Review of Bruce D. Chilton, *Rabbi Paul: An Intellectual Biography*. *Bulletin for Biblical Research* 18 (2008): 339–41.

Review of Bruce W. Winter, *Philo and Paul among the Sophists*. *Trinity Journal* 19 (1998): 246–49.

Review of Charles H. H. Scobie, *The Ways of Our God: An Approach to Biblical Theology*. *The Southern Baptist Journal of Theology* 8.1 (2004): 112–13.

Review of Christoph Heil, *Die Ablehnung der Speisegebote durch Paulus: Zur Frage nach der Stellung des Apostels zum Gesetz*. *Critical Review of Books in Religion* 9 (1996): 227–29.

Review of Clinton E. Arnold, *The Colossian Syncretism: The Interface between Christianity and Folk Belief at Colossae*. *Trinity Journal* 20 (1999): 100–05.

Review of Colin Brown, *Jesus in European Protestant Thought: 1778–1860*. *The Journal of the Evangelical Theological Society* 29 (1986): 367–68.

Review of Colin G. Kruse, *Paul's Letter to the Romans*. *Themelios* 38.3 (2013): 470–71.

Review of Colin G. Kruse, *Paul, the Law, and Justification*. *The Journal of the Evangelical Theological Society* 42 (1999): 511–13.

Review of D. A. Carson, *Exegetical Fallacies. The Journal of the Evangelical Theological Society* 29 (1986): 100–2.

Review of D. A. Carson, Peter T. O'Brien, and Mark A. Seifrid, eds., *The Complexities of Second Temple Judaism*. Vol. 1 of *Justification and Variegated Nomism. The Southern Baptist Journal of Theology* 6.2 (2002): 81–83.

Review of Dan Phillips, *The World-Tilting Gospel: Embracing a Biblical Worldview and Hanging on Tight. Themelios* 37.1 (2012): 148–49.

Review of Darrell Bock, *Blasphemy and Exaltation in Judaism and the Final Examination of Jesus: A Philological-Historical Study of the Key Jewish Themes Impacting Mark 14:61–64. The Southern Baptist Journal of Theology* 4.4 (2000): 104–6.

Review of Don Garlington, *Faith, Obedience and Perseverance: Aspects of Paul's Letter to the Romans. The Journal of the Evangelical Theological Society* 40 (1997): 474–75, and 41 (1998): 654–56.

Review of Douglas A. Campbell, *The Deliverance of God: An Apocalyptic Rereading of Justification in Paul. Bulletin for Biblical Research* 20 (2010): 289–90.

Review of Edward William Fudge and Robert A. Peterson, *Two Views of Hell: A Biblical and Theological Dialogue. The Southern Baptist Journal of Theology* 7.3 (2003): 87–88.

Review of Frank Thielman, *Paul and the Law: A Contextual Approach. Trinity Journal* 6 (1995): 101–4.

Review of Gilbert Bilezikian, *Beyond Sex Roles: A Guide for the Study of Female Roles in the Bible. The Journal of the Evangelical Theological Society* 30 (1987): 99–100.

Review of Gordon D. Fee, *1 and 2 Timothy, Titus. The Journal of the Evangelical Theological Society* 34 (1991): 531–33.

Review of Gordon D. Fee, "Praying and Prophesying in the Assemblies: 1 Corinthians 11:2–16." Pages 142–60 in *Discovering Biblical Equality*. Edited by Ronald W. Pierce and Rebecca Merrill Groothuis. *The Journal for Biblical Manhood and Womanhood* 10.1 (2005): 17–21.

Review of Günter Wagner, ed., *An Exegetical Bibliography of the New Testament: Romans and Galatians. Ashland Theological Journal* 32 (2000): 114–15.

Review of Hans Conzelmann and Andreas Lindemann, *Interpreting the New Testament: An Introduction to the Principles and Methods of New Testament Exegesis. The Journal of the Evangelical Theological Society* 34 (1991): 417.

Review of Jack Deere, *Surprised by the Power of the Spirit: A Former Dallas Seminary Professor Discovers That God Speaks and Heals Today. The Journal of the Evangelical Theological Society* 39 (1996): 151–52.

Review of Jacob Neusner and William Scott Green, eds., *Dictionary of Judaism in the Biblical Period: 450 B.C.E. to 600 C.E. The Southern Baptist Journal of Theology* 4.4 (2000): 106–7.

Review of James D. G. Dunn, *The Theology of Paul the Apostle. Trinity Journal* 20 (1999): 95–100.

Review of James D. G. Dunn, ed., *Paul and the Mosaic Law: The Third Durham-Tübingen Research Symposium on Earliest Christianity and Judaism. The Journal of the Evangelical Theological Society* 42 (1999): 158–60.

Review of James R. Beck and Craig L. Blomberg, eds., *Two Views on Women in Ministry. The Journal for Biblical Manhood and Womanhood* 6.2 (2001): 24–30.

Review of Jan Botha, *Subject to Whose Authority? Multiple Readings of Romans 13. The Journal of the Evangelical Theological Society* 40 (1997): 476–77.

Review of Jeremy R. Treat, *The Crucified King: Atonement and Kingdom in Biblical and Systematic Theology. Themelios* 39.3 (2014): 560–62.

Review of Kent L. Yinger, *Paul, Judaism, and Judgment according to Deeds. The Journal of the Evangelical Theological Society* 43 (2000): 137–39.

Review of Kurt Niederwimmer, *The Didache: A Commentary. The Southern Baptist Journal of Theology* 7.3 (2003): 95–96.

Review of Larry W. Hurtado, *Lord Jesus Christ: Devotion to Jesus in Earliest Christianity. The Southern Baptist Journal of Theology* 9.1 (2005): 100–1.

Review of Markus Bockmuehl, *Jewish Law in Gentile Churches: Halakhah and the Beginning of Christian Public Ethics. The Southern Baptist Journal of Theology* 8.1 (2004): 105–7.

Review of Matthew C. Hoskinson, *Assurance of Salvation: Implications of a New Testament Theology of Hope. Themelios* 35.2 (2010): 306–7.

Review of Michael Winger, *By What Law? The Meaning of Νόμος in the Letters of Paul. The Journal of Biblical Literature* 112 (1993): 724–26.

Review of N. T. Wright, *Paul and the Faithfulness of God: Christian Origins and the Question of God. The Southern Baptist Journal of Theology* 18.2 (2014): 131–35.

Review of Paul N. Anderson, *The Christology of the Fourth Gospel: Its Unity and Disunity in the Light of John 6. The Southern Baptist Journal of Theology* 5.2 (2001): 110–12.

Review of Philip B. Payne, *Man and Woman, One in Christ: An Exegetical and Theological Study of Paul's Letters. Themelios* 35.1 (2010): 88–90.

Review of Rebecca Merrill Groothuis, *Good News for Women: A Biblical Picture of Gender Equality. Themelios* 23.1 (1997): 89–90.

Review of Richard J. Goodrich and Albert L. Lukaszewski, *A Reader's Greek New Testament. The Southern Baptist Journal of Theology* 9.2 (2005): 82.

Review of Robert Jewett, *Romans: A Commentary*. Bulletin for Biblical Research 19 (2009): 446–48.

Review of Rodrigo J. Morales, *The Spirit and the Restoration of Israel: New Exodus and New Creation: Motifs in Galatians*. Themelios 36.1 (2011): 103–5.

Review of Sang-Won (Aaron) Son, *Corporate Elements in Pauline Anthropology: A Study of Selected Terms, Idioms, and Concepts in the Light of Paul's Usage and Background*. Trinity Journal (2003): 137–39.

Review of Scot McKnight, *The Blue Parakeet: Rethinking How You Read the Bible*. The Journal for Biblical Manhood and Womanhood 14.1 (2009): 60–67.

Review of Scott J. Hafemann, ed., *Biblical Theology: Retrospect and Prospect*. Bulletin for Biblical Research 14 (2004): 286–88.

Review of Scott J. Hafemann, *Paul, Moses, and the History of Israel: The Letter/Spirit Contrast and the Argument from Scripture in 2 Corinthians 3*. The Journal of the Evangelical Theological Society 41 (1998): 493–96.

Review of Scott J. Hafemann, *Paul's Message and Ministry in Covenant Perspective: Selected Essays*. Bulletin for Biblical Research 26.3 (2016): 434–35.

Review of Simon J. Gathercole, *Where Is Boasting? Early Jewish Soteriology and Paul's Response in Romans 1–5*. The Southern Baptist Journal of Theology 8.2 (2004): 92–95.

Review of Stanley E. Porter, *The Letter to the Romans: A Linguistic and Literary Commentary*. Themelios 41.1 (2016): 123–24.

Review of Stanley G. Grenz with Denise Muir Kjesbo, *Women in the Church: A Biblical Theology of Women in Ministry*. Trinity Journal 17 (1996): 114–24.

Review of Stephen H. Travis, *Christ and the Judgement of God: The Limits of Divine Retribution in New Testament Thought*. Themelios 34.3 (2009): 385–87.

Review of Stephen Westerholm, *Israel's Law and the Church's Faith: Paul and His Recent Interpreters*. Trinity Journal 9 (1988): 123–25.

Review of Thomas R. Edgar, *Satisfied by the Promise of the Spirit: Affirming the Fullness of God's Provision for Spiritual Living*. The Journal of the Evangelical Theological Society 41 (1998): 652–54.

Review of Tom Wells and Fred Zaspel, *New Covenant Theology: Description, Definition, Defense*. The Southern Baptist Journal of Theology 7.3 (2003): 94–96.

Review of Victor Paul Furnish, *II Corinthians*. The Journal of the Evangelical Theological Society 28 (1985): 348–50.

Review of Wesley Hill, *Paul and the Trinity: Persons, Relations, and the Pauline Letters*. Themelios 41.1 (2016): 118–20.

Review of William A. Dyrnes, *Let the Earth Rejoice: A Biblical Theology of Holistic Mission*. The Journal of the Evangelical Theological Society 27 (1984): 335–36.

## EDITORIALS

"Evangelism and God's Power." *The Southern Baptist Journal of Theology* 5.1 (2001): 2–3.

"The Foolishness of the Cross." *The Southern Baptist Journal of Theology* 6.3 (2002): 2–3.

"Foundations for Faith." *The Southern Baptist Journal of Theology* 5.3 (2001): 2–3.

"History Matters." *The Southern Baptist Journal of Theology* 3.4 (1999): 2–3.

"The Hope of the Gospel." *The Southern Baptist Journal of Theology* 3.3 (1999): 2–3.

"The Impact of Francis Schaeffer: Faith, Hope, and Love." *The Southern Baptist Journal of Theology* 6.2 (2002): 2–3.

"The Importance of Ethics." *The Southern Baptist Journal of Theology* 4.1 (2000): 2–3.

"Loving Discipline." *The Southern Baptist Journal of Theology* 4.4 (2000): 2–3.

"Marriage and the Family." *The Southern Baptist Journal of Theology* 6.1 (2002): 2–3.

"Mentors in the Faith." *The Southern Baptist Journal of Theology* 6.4 (2002): 2–3.

"The Perils of Ignoring Postmodernism." *The Southern Baptist Journal of Theology* 5.2 (2001): 2–3.

"A Plea for Biblical Preaching." *The Southern Baptist Journal of Theology* 3.2 (1999): 2–3.

"Practical Christianity." *The Southern Baptist Journal of Theology* 4.3 (2000): 2–3.

"Sovereignty, Suffering, and Open Theism." *The Southern Baptist Journal of Theology* 4.2 (2000): 2–4.

"Standing for Life." *The Southern Baptist Journal of Theology* 7.2 (2003): 2–3.

"Understanding the Controversy." *The Southern Baptist Journal of Theology* 7.1 (2003): 2–3.

"A Unity Based on Truth." *The Southern Baptist Journal of Theology* 5.4 (2001): 2–3.

## BIBLE TRANSLATIONS

Co-chair, CSB Translation Oversight Committee. *Christian Standard Bible.* Nashville, TN: Holman Bible, 2017.

Editor. *The ESV Study Bible.* Wheaton, IL: Crossway Bibles, 2008.

Review Scholar. *English Standard Version.* Wheaton, IL: Crossway Bibles, 2001.

# Editors and Contributors

### *Editors:*

*Denny Burk,* professor of biblical studies, director, The Center for Gospel and Culture, Boyce College, and associate pastor, Kenwood Baptist Church, Louisville, KY

*James M. Hamilton Jr.,* professor of biblical theology, The Southern Baptist Theological Seminary, and pastor of preaching, Kenwood Baptist Church, Louisville, KY

*Brian Vickers,* professor of New Testament interpretation and biblical theology, The Southern Baptist Theological Seminary

### *Contributors:*

*Clinton E. Arnold,* dean, Talbot School of Theology, and professor of New Testament language and literature, Biola University

*Ardel Caneday,* professor of New Testament studies and Greek, University of Northwestern Saint Paul

*D. A. Carson,* emeritus professor of New Testament, Trinity Evangelical Divinity School

*Simon Gathercole,* reader in New Testament studies, director of studies in theology, Fitzwilliam College, University of Cambridge

*Joshua M. Greever,* professor of New Testament, Grand Canyon University

*Donald A. Hagner,* George Eldon Ladd Professor Emeritus of New Testament, senior professor of New Testament, Fuller Theological Seminary

*Barry Joslin,* professor of Christian Theology, Boyce College, and worship pastor, Ninth and O Baptist Church, Louisville, KY

*John Kimbell,* pastor of preaching and discipleship, Clifton Baptist Church, Louisville, KY

*Jason Meyer,* associate professor of preaching, Bethlehem College and Seminary, and pastor for preaching and vision, Bethlehem Baptist Church, Minneapolis, MN

*R. Albert Mohler Jr.,* president, The Southern Baptist Theological Seminary

*Russell D. Moore,* president, Ethics and Religious Liberty Commission of the Southern Baptist Convention

*Ray Van Neste,* professor of biblical studies, director, R. C. Ryan Center for Biblical Studies, Union University

*John Piper,* founder and teacher, desiringGod.com and chancellor, Bethlehem College and Seminary

*Robert L. Plummer,* professor of New Testament Interpretation, The Southern Baptist Theological Seminary

*Patrick Schreiner,* assistant professor of New Testament language and literature, Western Seminary

*Mark A. Seifrid,* professor of exegetical theology, Concordia Seminary

*Bruce A. Ware,* T. Rupert and Lucille Coleman Professor of Theology, The Southern Baptist Theological Seminary

*Jarvis J. Williams,* associate professor of New Testament interpretation, The Southern Baptist Theological Seminary

*Shawn D. Wright,* professor of church history, The Southern Baptist Theological Seminary

*Robert W. Yarbrough,* professor of New Testament, Covenant Theological Seminary

# Name Index

# Scripture Index